COMMERCIAL BANKS IN INDIA
X-Efficiency and Total Factor Productivity Growth

COMMERCIAL BANKS IN INDIA

X-Efficiency and Total Factor Productivity Growth

DR. JYOTI SURI

REGAL PUBLICATIONS

New Delhi - 110 027

COMMERCIAL BANKS IN INDIA
X-Efficiency and Total Factor Productivity Growth

ISBN 978-81-8484-099-5

Typeset by
RAHUL COMPOSERS
358, Pocket-B, Phase-2, Sector-16 B, Dwarka, New Delhi - 110 075

Printed in India at
MAYUR ENTERPRISES
WZ Plot No. 3, Gujjar Market, Tihar Village, New Delhi - 110 018

Published by
REGAL PUBLICATIONS
F-159, Rajouri Garden, New Delhi - 110 027 • Phone : 45546396
E-mail : regalbookspub@yahoo.com

Dedicated to

My

Great Master

Contents

Preface

Banking sector, considered as the prime driver of economic growth, has brought tectonic swings in the economic landscape of the nation, which in turn depends upon diversity of socio-economic factors. Among economic factors, efficiency and productivity growth, reflected by the degree of technological progress and the use of these technologies have been recognized as the kingpin for stimulating the growth of banking institutions. This book is a comprehensive attempt to explain the notion of efficiency and productivity growth in an organized manner. However, the attempt towards the completion of this task was not so easy. So, I take the opportunity to express my gratitude to the persons who helped me a lot during the course of my study.

In the first place, I express my profound gratitude to 'Great Master', the spiritual pillar in this life and the next one, with whose grace and warm blessings, I have been able to complete another chapter of my life. I am also indebted to University Grants Commission, New Delhi, for providing me the funds under Research Fellowship Scheme for pursuing my Ph.D. work at Guru Nanak Dev University, Amritsar.

I extend special thanks to my esteemed supervisor Dr. (Mrs.) Gian Kaur, Professor, Punjab School of Economics, Guru Nanak Dev University, Amritsar for her invaluable inspiring guidance, keen interest, untiring and ever willing help, constructive criticism and helpful suggestions throughout the course of my study. Among the faculty members, my gratitude goes to Dr. Sunil Kumar, Reader, Punjab School of Economics, Guru Nanak Dev University, Amritsar for discussion on various issues with regard to my study. I also express my humble thanks to the faculty members of Government College, Gurdaspur for their incessant inspiration and endless encouragement to me.

My sincere thanks are due to all staff members of Ratan Tata Library, New Delhi; J.N.U. Library, New Delhi; Science Library, New Delhi; ICSSR Library, New Delhi; Institute of Economic Growth, New Delhi; NCAER Library, New Delhi; Punjab National Bank Library, New Delhi; Punjab School of Economics Library, Amritsar and Bhai Gurdas Library, Amritsar for a help in procuring extensive literature and data.

I convey my deep sense of appreciation to my father Sh. Baldev Raj Suri and mother Smt. Satya Suri, because, without their patience, moral support, endless encouragement and understanding, this undertaking would not have been possible. The words do not come up to the mark to qualify the feeling in my heart for my dear sister Neetu, brothers Sanjeev and Rakesh and uncle Sh. Hakikat Rai for providing the required stimulus, encouragement and moral support during the tenure of this work. My heartless thanks are also due to all the people who assisted me in one way or the other in completing the work.

DR. JYOTI SURI

List of Abbreviations

AE	—	Allocative Efficiency
AIE	—	Allocative Inefficiency
ARF	—	Asset Reconstruction Fund
BCC	—	Banker, Charnes and Cooper
CBs	—	Commercial Banks
CCR	—	Charnes, Cooper and Rhodes
CMIE	—	Center for Monitoring Indian Economy
CPI	—	Consumer Price Index
CRR	—	Cash Reserve Ratio
CRS	—	Constant Returns to Scale
DEA	—	Data Envelopment Analysis
DMU	—	Decision-making Units
DRTS	—	Diminishing Returns to Scale
EFFCH	—	Efficiency Change
FIs	—	Financial Institutions
GDP	—	Gross Domestic Product
GOI	—	Government of India
IA	—	Intermediation Approach
IBA	—	Indian Banks' Association
IRTS	—	Increasing Returns to Scale
IT	—	Information Technology
MPI	—	Malmquist Productivity Index

NBs — Nationalized Banks
NCR — Narasimham Committee Report
NIM — Net-Interest Margin
NIRS — Non-Increasing Returns to Scale
NPA — Non-Performing Assets
OBC — Oriental Bank of Commerce
PA — Production Approach
PEFFCH — Pure Efficiency Change
PLR — Prime Lending Rate
PSBs — Public Sector Banks
PTE — Pure Technical Efficiency
PTIE — Pure Technical Inefficiency
RBI — Reserve Bank of India
ROA — Return on Asset
RRBs — Regional Rural Banks
RTS — Returns to Scale
SD — Standard Deviation
SBI — State Bank of India
SCBs — Scheduled Commercial Banks
SE — Scale Efficiency
SFA — Stochastic Frontier Approach
SIE — Scale Inefficiency
SLR — Statutory Liquidity Ratio
TCH — Technological Change
TE — Technical Efficiency
TFP — Total Factor Productivity
TIE — Technical Inefficiency
UCA — User Cost Approach
UCO — United Commercial Bank
VRS — Variable Returns to Scale
VRS — Voluntary Retirement Scheme
XE — X-Efficiency
XIE — X-Inefficiency

1

Introduction

Banking sector, considered as the prime driver of economic growth, has brought tectonic swings in the economic landscape of the nation. It has transformed Indian economy to be more opened, liberalized and one of the fastest growing economies of the world. The growth of the banking sector is considered as a proxy for the economy as a whole, due to banks' wide spectrum of exposure across industries. Thus, we cannot expect any nation to be prosperous in which sound banking system does not exist. Moreover, when the world economy has entered in the phase of globalization, sound banking remains very high on the agenda of the policy-makers particularly in developing economies like India.

Indian banking industry has witnessed phenomenal growth in response to a series of fundamental developments aimed at enhancing the efficiency, productivity and international competitiveness. This is directly due to the structural changes in business environment, financial markets, increased competition, technological advancements, mandatory disclosures, customer's awareness and expectations. This has taken Indian banking sector from the doorsteps of traditional class banking to modern mass banking and has been the moving spirit behind the dissemination of financial information at global level.

The globalization of the financial markets has enhanced the economic links between different nation's markets and accelerated the demand of international banking products and services. Thus, governments of various nations are under pressure to relax economic controls in order to improve the working of domestic banks. Moreover, banks are more inclined to provide quality products and services at the lowest market rate to the customers both in domestic and international markets. Consequently, the institutional and systematic structure of the financial sector in general and banking sector in particular has drastically changed.

The development of banking sector has well acknowledged as the life support system for accelerating the economic development of a nation. Banking and economic development are synonyms to each other. In fact, banking affects economic development both as the cause and effect of the latter. The banks perform the process of financial intermediation through the institutionalization of savings and investments and as such, foster economic growth. The gains of real sector economy also depend on how efficiently the financial sector performs the function of intermediation to influence economic activity. Therefore, even though a country has enough resources to generate adequate capital accumulation, its growth potential can be hindered if the domestic financial intermediation mechanism fails to allocate these savings to available investment opportunities efficiently (Stulz, 2001). An efficient financial intermediation mechanism increases the expected returns to the investment, which can promote innovation resulting in further positive implications for economic growth (Collins, 2002). Moreover, banks do not simply collect funds but also serve as a guide to customers regarding the investment of funds, which subsequently lead to the worldwide dispersal of credit.

In the ongoing knowledge-based economy, the customer continues to be the centre-point of bank's business strategy. Thus, banks try to attract and retain the customers by introducing innovative products, enhancing the quality of customer services and marketing a variety of products through diverse channels, which in turn enhances the economic prosperity of the nation.

Banks have been playing a crucial role in enriching the economic and social life of the nation. In the modern economy, bankers are not merely considered as the dealers in money, but are more realistically the leaders in development. Banks are not just the storehouse of the country's wealth but are the reservoirs of resources necessary for economic development. Schumpeter (1934) stressed the role of banking sector as a financier of productive investments and thus an accelerator of economic growth.

Banking system is also regarded as the core determinant of economic system of a country. A sound banking system is quintessential for a sound and dynamic economic system. Banking sector provides the strength to monetary and credit mechanism, through it, monetary authority regulates the entire mechanism in confronting to the requirements of economic system. Therefore, both the soundness and dynamism of the economic system and banking system are interdependent; each sustains the other and is sustained by the other.

Banks play a pivotal role in the upliftment of various sectors of an economy. To equip the agriculture sector with new technological impediments is indispensable to facilitate dynamic shift from agriculture to industrial sector and subsequent to service sector. The banking sector provides all the requisite facilities to these sectors in order to run their operations in a harmonious manner. Secondly, the banks promote innovational activities in order to eliminate the techno-eco backwardness prevalent in various sectors of an economy. Thirdly, in under-developed economies, the entrepreneurs generally hesitate to invest the funds in new and risky ventures due to the shortage of funds. The banks offer them the loans on reasonable terms and encourage them to take risky ventures. In addition, banks also impart dramatic and drastic effect on the overall growth of an economy especially in times of adverse agricultural shocks and industrial slowdowns.

Banks also influence economic activity by raising human capital formation through various development programmes. The sharpening of intellectual as well as special skills in diverse business activities enables them to attract and retain the customers in such a dynamic economic environment. Moreover, the qualified and highly skilled manpower resources assist banks to capture high market share in the domestic as well as international market.

On the whole, the development of banking sector entails a synergic influence on the economic development of the nation.

COMPOSITION OF BANKING SYSTEM IN INDIA

Banking sector in India has a wide mix, comprises of joint sector (scheduled and non-scheduled banks), nationalized sector (Reserve Bank of India, State Bank of India, other nationalized commercial banks and post office savings bank), co-operative sector (co-operative banks and land development banks) and foreign sector (foreign commercial banks and exchange banks).

Indian banking industry consists of 288 scheduled commercial banks (SCBs) out of which RRBs constitute a large number of 133 banks on March 2006 (as shown in Figure 1.1). Regional Rural Banks (RRBs) play a pivotal role in the all around development of privileged sections of the society. These banks have been set-up to meet the credit requirements of rural affluent agricultural laborers, small and marginal farmers and small entrepreneurs, etc. Apart from RRBs, other commercial banks are 84 in number, comprise of 28 PSBs, 27 private sector banks and 29 foreign banks as on March 2006. Public sector banks' category includes 20 nationalized banks and State Bank of India (SBI) and its seven subsidiaries. In the financial set-up of our country, PSBs as a group holds a major share of 72.3 percent in the total assets of SCBs. Despite some of the operational constraints, PSBs are still in the possession of certain core strengths like wide branch network, large customer base and geographical coverage. A major change occurred in the institutional set-up of the country when RBI, the central bank of India, freed the entry of private sector banks to function side by side with PSBs in Indian banking market. Foreign banks were also allowed to continue in the new milieu, but their expansion was stringently regulated

(Hanson and Kathuria, 1999). The entry of private, new private and foreign banks inculcated the elements of competition in Indian banking sector, which in turn led to the paradigm shifts in the market scenario. The commercial banks irrespective of any category transact all types of commercial banking business. As on March 2006, private sector banks (20 old private and 7 new private banks) accounts for nearly 19.4 percent while foreign banks constitutes just 7.2 percent share in the total assets of SCBs.

In addition to it, the scheduled co-operative banks also form the part of SCBs in India, are 71 in number. Out of 71 scheduled co-operative banks, 55 banks are scheduled urban co-operative and 16 banks are scheduled state co-operative banks as on March 2006. These banks have been set-up on unit banking principle are mainly rural-based, nevertheless, there are some banks in urban areas too. The co-operative banks and land development banks have a wide network at tehsil level, district level and state level. These banks provide funds to agriculture sector channeled through state co-operative and central co-operative banks.

FIG. 1.1

Scheduled Banking Structure in India#
(As on March, 2006)

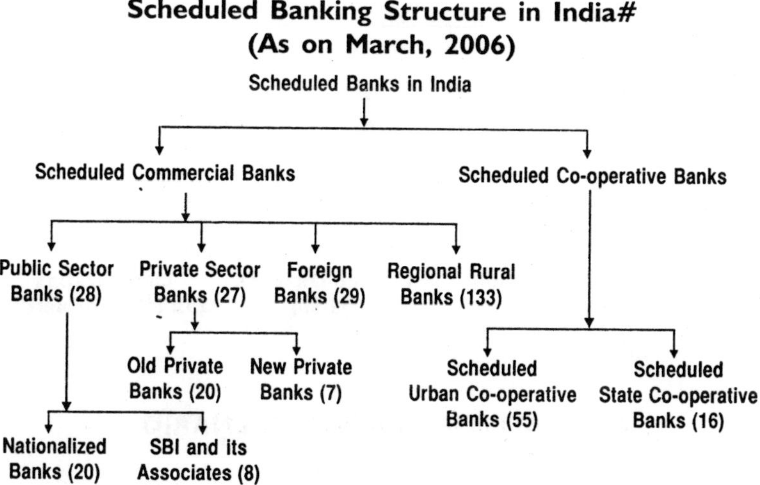

As indicated in the second schedule of the Reserve Bank of India Act, 1934.
**Note* : Figures in brackets indicate number of banks in each group.

EVOLUTION OF THE STRUCTURE OF INDIAN BANKING INDUSTRY

Over the past three decades, Indian banking industry has witnessed momentous and radical changes in macro-economic developments. The monetary and banking policies as well as internal and external environment have marked a significant impact on the evolution of Indian banking sector in different ways. Thus, if we see through the hindsight of an economist, the evolution of Indian banking sector can be analyzed through distinct phases (as depicted in Figure 1.2). The first phase comprises the period from (1949-68), known as *'Foundation Phase'*, the second phase relates to the period (1969-90), named as *'Expansion Phase'*. The third phase, popularly recognized as *'Reforms Phase'* covers the period from 1991 onwards. This phase is the current phase of Indian banking sector.

FIG. 1.2

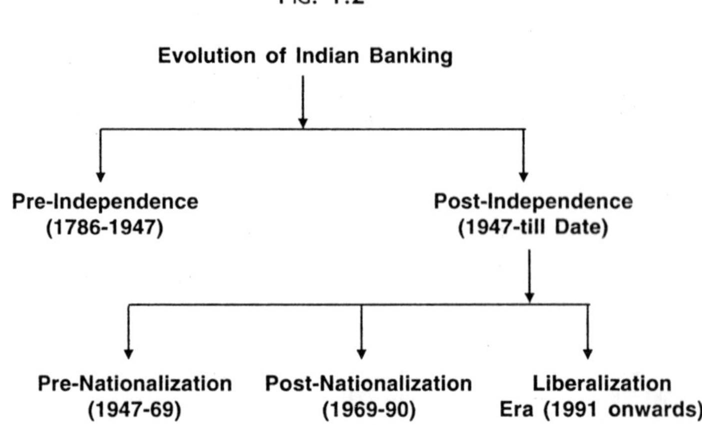

Source : RBI Bulletin, 2004.

PRE-NATIONALIZATION SCENARIO

Indian banking system inherited in ancient times of pre-nationalization period was patterned on indigenous banking system. The Indian banking system was predominantly owned and controlled by money lenders who carried on their functions for centuries. With the entry of East India Company in Indian market, private entrepreneurs organized as joint stock companies started to handle all the banking operations. The banking system inherited at that time was supposed to be biased in terms of big industrial houses and against the poor section of the society (Joshi and Little, 1996). The companies' activities were highly concentrated on financing foreign trade while the domestic trade was handled by money lenders. Moreover, the banking industry at the time of independence was primarily caused by poor and unsound method of operation and inadequate capital structure. The banking activities were highly confined to urban affluent customers and thus, out of the reach of rural section of the society. A big chunk of the population was remained exploited by private entrepreneurs and the most leading and sensitive sector of Indian economy was not supported by banking sector in any form. To even out these discrepancies, Banking Regulation Act 1949 was enacted by Government of India (GOI) in consultation with Reserve Bank of India (RBI) in which a wide array of guidelines was issued to operate the banking system in an efficient manner.

In response to these guidelines, although, Indian banking sector registered considerable progress in terms of geographical coverage and its functions but there were still many rural and urban areas that were not served by the banks. The small scale industries and agriculture sector did not receive the attention they deserved; however, a major part of the credit was enjoyed by big industrialists.

The systematic form of Indian banking was started in 1951, when First Five Year Plan was launched. The first step in this direction was the nationalization of Imperial Bank of India in 1955 to create State Bank of India. In the 1960s, more regulatory and control measures were taken to shape the banking system as an instrument of economic development. Government of India (GOI) imposed 'social control' over the banks in December 1967 to ensure efficient distribution of bank resources and to cater better the needs of deserving sector in conformity with the changing requirements of the economy. However, the commission did not have much time to accomplish the task as it was undertaken. In light of this, Government of India took initiative of the nationalization of banks in two waves starting in 1969 and 1980. On July 19, 1969, Government of India nationalized fourteen major scheduled commercial banks in India and six more banks were nationalized on April 15, 1980 so as to extend the area of public control over the Indian banking system. The period of regulated growth from 1950 till 1969 witnessed a number of far-reaching changes in the banking system. Branches expanded by an annual growth of 1.6 percent during 1950s (i.e., 1950-60), with deposits and credit growth of 6.9 percent and 8.2 percent respectively. Further, during 1960s (i.e., 1960-70), the annual growth of the expansion of branches, deposits and credit grew significantly higher than that of 1950s. In contrast, net profits of the banks recorded decline from Rs. 14.09 crore to Rs. 13.80 crore during 1960-70. The population served per office was as high as 65,000 at the end of this phase.

NATIONALIZATION SCENARIO

The nationalization of banks was a turning point in the history of Indian banking. The major objectives of nationalization were growth; increased flow of assistance to hitherto neglected and deserving sectors of an economy; to give a professional bent to bank management with a view to remove control by few; to fill the credit gaps in agriculture and small scale industries and to serve better the growth-oriented needs of Indian economy in conformity with plan priorities. The two significant aspects of nationalization were branch expansion and deployment of resources on priority basis.

In response to mass nationalization, Indian banking system witnessed remarkable achievements in terms of expansion of banking network and its penetration to rural sector, manifold increase in credit to different sectors of an economy, introduction of new technology and diversification of business operations. A number of innovations were also made in the field of social banking and large volumes of credit were lent under the programmes like 'Integrated Rural Development Progmamme' (IRDP) and '20 point Economic Programme', etc.

Besides this, several self-employment schemes or poverty alleviation programmes were also assisted by the banks. Moreover, on account of mass-nationalization, public sector banks (PSBs) became the dominant player with more than 90 percent of banking business in India.

During 1969-92, there was commendable progress in extending its geographical coverage and functional reach. The number of bank branches registered an increase from 8,262 to 60,570, deposits accelerated to Rs. 4,646 crore to Rs. 2,37,566 crore and advances from Rs. 3,599 crore to Rs. 1,31,520 crore, reflecting a rapid growth of Indian banking. The share of priority sector lending in the total banks' lending also grew. In 1969, 14 percent of the bank credit was apportioned to priority sector but this share went up to 43 percent by the year 1990. India's domestic savings increased to 24.20 percent in 1991 as against 15.7 percent in 1970. Although, the banks catered the credit needs of rural sector of Indian economy but the amount of credit to weaker sections was not satisfactory. Therefore, Narasimham Committee recommended the establishment of Regional Rural Banks (RRBs) under the 'Regional Rural Banks Act, 1975' especially to meet the credit requirements of rural artisans, marginal farmers, small farmers and small scale industrialists.

The growth of Indian banking sector over the two decades prior to reforms gave rise to several problems, which became visible from the mid-80s. Substantial and increasing amount of credit was channeled to the government at below-market rates through high and increasing cash reserve requirements (CRR) and statutory liquidity requirements (SLR) in order to fund a large and increasing government deficit at relatively low cost (Sen and Vaidya, 1997). Bank deposit rates and lending rates were highly administered and the directed investments in the form of SLR and CRR hindered operational flexibility and income earning potentials. The dominance of PSBs and excessive focus on quantitative achievements started to generate monopolistic tendencies and killed the competition among banks. It further eroded the level of profitability and efficiency and raised the level of non-performing assets. In addition, the rate of returns worked out to be lower by international standards, the portfolio quality suffered due to political and administrative interference and the banks were characterized by technological backwardness. Therefore, nationalization of commercial banks was a mixed blessing. The branch expansion programme especially in rural areas led to increase in the amount of savings and investments but the credit controls put negative impact on the efficiency, productivity and profitability of banks. In addition, bank nationalization also created the problems of bureaucratization, red-tapism and oppositions among trade unions in regard to the apportionment of credit. On the whole, all the signs of 'financial repression' were found to be existed in Indian banking system. In recognition of these growing ills and the growing need to catch up the international standards, the Government of India decided to overhaul the 'financial repression' in Indian banking industry. The roadmap for the first phase of banking sector reforms was prepared in 1992 on the basis of path breaking recommendations of Narasimham Committee Report I (NCR 1). The main rationale of this phase was to create a sound and efficient banking system in a competitive environment.

Liberalization Phase: The third phase, the regime of reforms started with radical departure of the banking system from highly regulated and administered environment to more liberal and deregulated one. Although a series of reforms was initiated from 1985 onwards but first phase of reforms was undertaken comprehensively in June 1992. The Government of India constituted a high power committee under the chairmanship of Sh. M. Narasimham in 1991 to critically examine all the aspects related to banking. The recommendations of Narasimham Committee (1991) provided the blueprint for the first phase reforms of financial system. These recommendations are recognized as a landmark in the evolution of banking in India. The salient features of Narasimham Committee Report I are outlined as:

Recommendations of Narasimham Committee Report I

Phased Reduction of Statutory Pre-emption: The committee has proposed the view that investment in liquid assets to comply SLR and holding of cash balances with RBI to satisfy CRR affected the profitability of the banks as the rates of return on this property is lower than market-related interest rates. So, it has been recommended that SLR should be reasonably reduced to 25 percent over a period of five years starting with some reduction in the current year itself. On the other hand, CRR should not be used as a tool to contain credit and expansion and should be brought at a reasonable level of around 10 percent.

Interest Rates Deregulation: The committee is of the view that the present structure of administered interest rates is highly complex and rigid, therefore, proposes that the interest rates on bank deposits, loans and government borrowings should be gradually deregulated to bring it in line with market determined rates. However, the interest rates on bank deposits may continue to be regulated. The structure of interest rates should bear a broad relationship to the bank rate, which should be used as a anchor to signal the RBI's monetary policy stance. The spreads between the bank rate, the bank deposit rate and the Government borrowing rate and prime rate may be determined by RBI broadly in accordance with the criterion laid down by Chakarabarty Committee.

Capital Adequacy Norms: Indian banking system is primarily infected by resource constraints. Thus, Narasimham Committee suggested that banks and financial institutions should achieve a minimum of 4 percent CAR in relation to risk weighted assets by March 1993, of which Tier 1 capital should not be less than 2 percent. The BIS standard of 9 percent should be achieved by March 2006 to keep in line with internationally accepted capital adequacy standards prescribed by Base committee.

Income Recognition: In regard to income recognition, the committee recommends that the banks and financial institutions, which are following the accrual system of accounting, no income should be recognized in the accounts in respect of non-performing assets. An asset would be considered non-performing if interest on such assets remains past due for a period exceeding 180 days at the balance sheet date. The committee further recommends that banks and financial institutions be given a period of three years to move towards the above norms in a phased manner beginning with the current year.

Asset Classification and Provisioning: The committee has proposed that the proper and uniform asset classification based on the realizable value of loans and investments should be made by banks and DFIs. Banks and DFIs should follow uniform accounting practice with regard to income recognition and provision against doubtful debts. The assets should be classified into four heads viz., standard, sub–standard, doubtful and loan assets in line with the then present health code system of classification. In regard to standard assets, no provision has been made. As for sub-standard assets, a general provision should be created equal to 10 percent of the total outstanding under this category. In respect of doubtful assets, provision should be created to the extent of 100 percent of the security shortfall. In respect to secured portion of doubtful assets, further provision should be created, ranging from 20 percent to 50 percent, depending on the period for which such assets remains in the doubtful category. Loss assets should either be fully written off or provision should be created to the extent of 100 percent.

Liberal Policy towards Banking Expansion: The committee has recommended that branch licensing should be abolished and the matter of opening and closing of banks should be left on the discretion of banks. Furthermore, there should be no ban on the entry of new banks in private sector provided they confirm to the essential requirements in regard to capital and other prudential norms prescribed by RBI. In addition, RBI policy should be more liberal in respect of allowing the foreign banks to open branches of subsidiaries. Foreign banks, when permitted to operate in India should be subjected to same requirements as applicable to domestic banks.

Setting Up Tribunals to Speed Up the Process of Recovery: Since the banks experience a lot of difficulties in the recovery of loans. Therefore, the committee has recommended that Government of India should set-up special recovery tribunals to ensure quick and timely recovery of bank loans as suggested by Tiwari Committee.

Phasing out of Directed Credit Programmes: The committee has recommended that the directed credit programmes like priority sector lending should be phased out. It has therefore proposed that priority sector should be redefined to comprise small and marginal farmers, tiny sector of industry, small business, transport operators, rural artisans and other weaker sections. The credit target should be fixed at 10 percent of aggregate credit for this redefined priority sector. Moreover, a review of directed credit programme should be undertaken after a period of three years to assess the need to continue or terminate such programmes.

Supervision of Banks: Since, Indian banking system is at present over regulated and over administered. Thus, the committee has recommended that supervision should be based on evolving prudential norms and regulations, which should be adhered to rather than excessive control over administrative and other aspects of bank organization and functioning. The inspection by supervisory authorities should be based essentially on the internal audit and inspection reports.

Establishment of Asset Reconstruction Fund: The committee has recommended the setting up of asset reconstruction fund (ARF), which would take over a portion of bad and doubtful assets from banks and developmental financial institutions at discount, suggested by independent auditors on the basis of stipulated guidelines. This process would enable the banks to recycle the funds realized into more productive assets. The ARF should be provided with special powers of recovery and the capital of ARF should be subscribed by PSBs and financial institutions.

Transparency: The committee has recommended that balance sheets of banks and financial institutions should be made more transparent and full disclosures made in the balance sheets as recommended by the International Accounting Standard Committee. This should be done in a phased manner commencing with the current year.

Restructuring the Banks: With a view to restructure the banks, the committee has proposed the below said system:

1. Three or four large banks including State Bank of India could become international in character;
2. Eight to ten national banks with a network of branches throughout the country engaged in universal banking;

3. Local banks whose operations would be confined to a specific region;
4. Rural banks including (RRBs) whose operations would be confined to rural areas and whose business would be predominantly engaged in financing agriculture allied activities.

RBI as a sole regulatory authority: Committee has recommended the abolition of duality of control over the banking system by RBI and Ministry of Finance. RBI should be the primary and sole agency for the regulation of banking system.

The first phase of reforms did not register remarkable progress quantitatively but qualitative performance was there. Moreover, the progress was slow and steady. Therefore, a need was crept to initiate second-generation reforms in consistent with the objectives highlighted in Narasimham Committee Report I to a greater extent. Therefore, Narasimham Committee was again constituted in 1997 and it submitted its report on April 22, 1998. The main emphasis of this phase was on:

a. Substantial dilution of government stakes in nationalized banks;
b. Mergers and closures of banks;
c. Structural changes; and
d. Streamlining procedures, upgrading technology and human resource development in order to align the Indian standards with international best practices.

To keep in view these broad-based objectives, the chief features that emerge from the recommendations of the Narasimham Committee Report II (NCR-II) have been outlined as:

Recommendations of Narasimham Committee Report II

1. The committee on banking sector reforms has favoured merger of strong banks and closure of potentially weaker banks in case their rehabilitation

was not possible. Thus, it favoured merger of strong banks, as this would have a 'multiplier effect' on industry. At the same time, it has been argued that strong banks should not be merged with weak banks, as it will have adverse affect upon the asset quality of the stronger banks.

2. The committee has recommended that for potentially viable weak banks, corrective actions such as recapitalization be undertaken. But for those banks, where early and complete correction was not possible, alternative approaches including closure be carefully examined. Weak banks, which are not capable of revival over a period of three years, should be referred to the commission.
3. PSBs should be encouraged to go in the market to enhance and raise their capital base. PSBs should be given more flexibility to determine managerial remuneration levels taking into account market trends.
4. The committee suggested that, as asset will be classified as doubtful if it is in the sub-standard category for 18 months in first instance and eventually for 12 months and lost if it has been identified but not written-off.
5. In order to improve the financial health of banking sector, capital adequacy ratio should be raised to 10 percent by the year 2002. Capital adequacy ratio should take into account market risks in addition to credit risks.
6. The committee proposed that all loan assets in the doubtful and loss categories should be identified along with their realizable value. Further, these funds should be transferred to 'Asset Reconstruction Fund', which would issue NPA swap bond to the banks, representing the realizable value of the assets transferred provided stamp duties are not very much excessive.
7. Banks are required to pay more attention to asset and liability management and risk management practices.

8. A general provision of 1 percent on standard assets should be introduced.
9. Dedicated and effective machinery should be established in order to ensure timely and quick recovery of loans for banks and financial institutions.
10. The committee has recommended that more transparency in bank accounts should be ensured so as to judge the soundness of a particular bank in the market.
11. Wrong reporting and inaccurate disclosures be subject to punitive penalty.

In order to identify weak PSBs, Narasimham Committee report II reported the criterion that accumulated losses and net NPAs exceed the net worth of the bank or operating profits less income from recapitalization bonds are negative for three consecutive years. Indian bank, United Bank of India and United Commercial Bank were identified as weak banks on the basis of proposed criterion.

Further, the Reserve Bank of India set-up a working group in February 1999 under the Chairmanship of Shri M.S. Verma to suggest measures for the revival of weak public sector banks in India. The major findings of the Working Group are listed below:

Seven parameters covering three areas have been identified; these are :

1. Solvency (capital adequacy ratio and coverage ratio)
2. Earning Capacity (return on assets and net interest margin).
3. Profitability (ratio of operating profit to average working funds, ratio of cost to income and ratio of staff cost to net interest income + all other income).
    - The seven parameters can be used to evolve benchmarks for competitive level of performance by public sector banks. On the basis of these criteria, Indian Bank, United Commercial Bank and United Bank of India have been identified as weak banks.

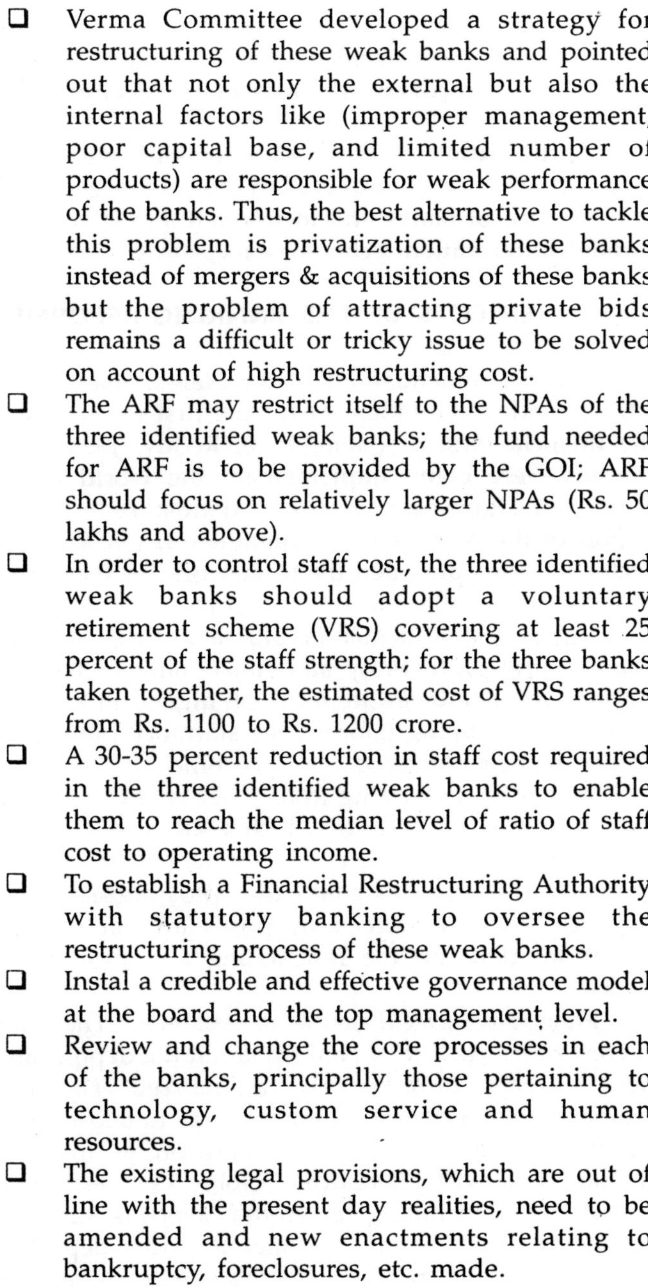

- Verma Committee developed a strategy for restructuring of these weak banks and pointed out that not only the external but also the internal factors like (improper management, poor capital base, and limited number of products) are responsible for weak performance of the banks. Thus, the best alternative to tackle this problem is privatization of these banks instead of mergers & acquisitions of these banks but the problem of attracting private bids remains a difficult or tricky issue to be solved on account of high restructuring cost.
- The ARF may restrict itself to the NPAs of the three identified weak banks; the fund needed for ARF is to be provided by the GOI; ARF should focus on relatively larger NPAs (Rs. 50 lakhs and above).
- In order to control staff cost, the three identified weak banks should adopt a voluntary retirement scheme (VRS) covering at least 25 percent of the staff strength; for the three banks taken together, the estimated cost of VRS ranges from Rs. 1100 to Rs. 1200 crore.
- A 30-35 percent reduction in staff cost required in the three identified weak banks to enable them to reach the median level of ratio of staff cost to operating income.
- To establish a Financial Restructuring Authority with statutory banking to oversee the restructuring process of these weak banks.
- Instal a credible and effective governance model at the board and the top management level.
- Review and change the core processes in each of the banks, principally those pertaining to technology, custom service and human resources.
- The existing legal provisions, which are out of line with the present day realities, need to be amended and new enactments relating to bankruptcy, foreclosures, etc. made.

- For speeding up the recovery process, a mechanism should be worked out to make debt recovery tribunals more effective.

As the result of these path-breaking measures, concrete steps have been undertaken to even out the dismal performance of banks and to upgrade the standards of banks through information technology measures.

EFFECTS OF THE BANKING REFORMS

The recommendations of the Narasimham Committee in 1991 provided the blueprint for the first generation reform of the financial system (Jalan, 2000; Reddy, 1999). While these reforms were being implemented, the world economy also witnessed significant changes. Against such backdrop, the Report of the Narasimham Committee II (NCR-II) on Banking Sector Reforms provided the framework for the current reform process. The visible impact of reforms is evident from:

Progressive reduction in SLR and CRR: A major factor affecting the profitability and functioning of banks was pre-emption of resources in form of higher SLR and CRR. In response to banking reforms, the statutory pre-emptions have gradually been lowered. The combined pre-emptions under CRR and SLR, amounting to 63.5 per cent of net demand and time liabilities in 1991 (of which CRR was 25 percent) have been reduced to 32.5 per cent (of which, the SLR is 25 per cent). This has enabled banks to deploy a greater quantum of resources for commercial purposes and in turn marked a significant dent on the functioning and profitability of the banks.

Progressive deregulation of interest rates: The administered interest rate structure of banks both on the deposit and lending side has been progressively rationalized. The main thrust behind the deregulation of interest was to allow banks greater flexibility and encourage competition in Indian banking system. Thus, with effect from October 1997, interest rate of all time deposits including fifteen-day deposits have been freed. On deposit side, banks can offer any rate depending on its assets and liability position; only saving rates are mandated by

Reserve Bank of India. Scheduled commercial banks have now the freedom to set interest rates on their deposits subject to minimum floor rate (4.5 percent) and maximum ceiling rate (11 percent). Currently, the only administered interest rate is on saving deposit (presently fixed at 4 percent), which is used by individuals as current account. Banks can also charge differential rates on deposits of similar maturity. In addition, banks can charge any rate on lending operations depending on risk perception. On the lending side, it is essential to announce prime lending rate (PLR), which is determined by board of individual banks rather than Reserve Bank of India. The loans to prime borrowers can be extended at sub-PLR at the bank's discretion. In order to ensure transparency, the maximum spread (not exceeding 4 percent on the PLR) is required to be announced. The first step in deregulating interest rate was taken on October 1994. With regard to interest rate on the smaller loan (i.e., up to Rs. 2 lakh), banks cannot charge above PLR.

Enhancement in Competition: Steps have been initiated to strengthen PSBs and inject competition into the banking system through the establishment of new banks in private sector and liberal entry of foreign banks. Towards strengthening PSBs, the Government of India initiated steps to improve their autonomy and increase their capital base. The legislative measure adopted by GOI in this direction gradually reduced the government shareholding in PSBs and enable them to raise resources directly from the market through public shareholding. The private shareholding in four PSBs has been noted to be up to 10 percent and up to 49 percent in case of 11 PSBs as on March 2006. In addition to it, measures have undertaken to broaden the ownership base of PSBs. On the other hand, steps have been initiated to introduce foreign direct investment in private sector banks in conformity with the guidelines issued by RBI time to time. The foreign investment limit from all sources in private banks was raised from a maximum of 49 percent to 74 percent in March 2004.

Micro-Prudential Norms: A set of micro-prudential measures have been stipulated, aimed at imparting strength to banking system as well as ensuring safety and soundness on a prospective basis. With regard to prudential requirements, norms for income recognition and asset classification (IRAC), introduced in 1992, have been consolidated over the years in line with international best practices. A strategy to introduce the attainment of CRAR of 8 percent in a phased manner was put in place. Banks were required to raise their CRAR from 4 percent in the initial year (i.e., 1992-93) to 8 percent over a period of three years (i.e., by end-March 1996), to 9 percent over a period of four years (i.e., by end-March 2000). Banks with international presence were required to attain the prescribed CRAR of 8 percent by 1993-94. At the end of March 2006, 78 out of 90 banks maintained CRAR at or above 10 percent as against 42 out of 92 banks at the end of March 1996 and 84 out of 101 banks at the end of March 2000.

Transparency: In consequent to reform measures, the banking system has attained greater transparency. This applies with regard to prudential norms (disclosure of capital adequacy ratios-tier I and tier II separately, net non-performing assets (NPAs) ratios, provisions and contingencies and more recently, the maturity profile of loans and advances, investments, movements in NPAs and lending to sensitive sectors such as capital market, real estate and commodities) as well as securities portfolio. Public sector banks (PSBs) would be attaching the balance sheet of the subsidiaries to their balance sheets beginning from 2000-01 in order to bring greater transparency in operations and move towards consolidated supervision.

Asset-Liability Management and Risk Management Practices: The introduction of asset-liability management and risk management practices since April 1999, covering broadly the areas of credit, market and operational risks have enabled the banks to have a more clear idea of asset-liabilities mismatches and undertake the preventive steps.

Cost Control Measures: The steps have been initiated in the direction of downsizing manpower resources through voluntary retirement scheme. This practice has not only cut down the future staff costs but also increased the performance levels of staff in long-run.

Profitability and other Measures: On the verge of reform measures, there was a significant improvement in the performance of the banking system as depicted in Tables 1.1

TABLE 1.1

Operating Profit of Commercial Banks in India—1991-92 to 2005-06

(Amount in Rs. billion)

Year	*SBI Group*	*NBs Group*	*PSBs*	*Private Banks*	*Foreign Banks*	*SCBs*
1991-92	31	24	55	3	13	71
1992-93	23	9	32	3	6	39
1993-94	21	17	38	4	13	54
1994-95	25	30	55	7	15	78
1995-96	39	36	75	10	15	102
1996-97	45	44	89	14	20	123
1997-98	47	56	103	18	25	147
1998-99	47	59	106	15	19	140
1999-00	59	72	131	26	27	185
2000-01	57	81	138	29	31	197
2001-02	87	130	297	46	35	298
2002-03	112	185	217	71	37	406
2003-04	143	251	394	82	49	527
2004-05	153	235	388	77	46	510
2005-06	151	230	381	98	67	544

Source : Computed from Statistical Tables Relating to Banks in India.

and 1.2. The profitability of SCBs reported a marked improvement, measured in terms of operating profits (from Rs. 39 billion in 1992-93 to Rs. 185 billion in 1999-00 and to Rs. 544 billion in 2005-06) as well as in terms of net profits (from Rs. -41 billion in 1992-93 to Rs. 74 billion in 1999-00 and Rs. 246 billion in 2005-06). As for various forms of banks, PSBs showed a distinct improvement in terms of operating profits (i.e., from Rs. 32 billion in 1992-93 to Rs. 131 billion in 1999-00 and to Rs. 381 billion in 2005-06) as well as in terms of net profits (from Rs. -33 billion in 1992-93 to Rs. 51 billion in 1999-00 and Rs. 166 billion in 2005-06). The operating profits of private banks also witnessed a substantial increase (from Rs. 3 billion in 1992-93 to Rs. 26 billion in 1999-00 and to Rs. 98

TABLE 1.2
Net Profit of Commercial Banks in India —1991-92 to 2005-06

(Amount in Rs. billion)

Year	*SBI Group*	*NBs Group*	*PSBs*	*Private Banks*	*Foreign Banks*	*SCBs*
1991-92	2	6	8	1	4	13
1992-93	3	-36	-33	1	-8	-41
1993-94	4	-47	-43	1	6	-36
1994-95	8	3	11	4	7	22
1995-96	8	-12	-4	5	7	9
1996-97	17	14	31	7	7	45
1997-98	24	26	50	8	6	65
1998-99	15	18	33	7	7	47
1999-00	27	24	51	12	10	74
2000-01	22	21	43	12	10	65
2001-02	34	49	123	18	15	116
2002-03	45	78	83	29	18	170
2003-04	56	109	165	35	22	223
2004-05	57	98	155	35	20	209
2005-06	60	106	166	50	31	246

Source : Computed from Statistical Tables Relating to Banks in India.

billion in 2005-06) as well as in terms of net profits (from Rs. 1 billion in 1992-93 to Rs. 12 billion in 1999-00 and Rs. 50 billion in 2005-06). The operating profits of foreign banks raised (from Rs. 6 billion in 1992-93 to Rs. 27 billion in 1999-00 and to Rs. 67 billion in 2005-06) and net profits (from Rs. -8 billion in 1992-93 to Rs. 10 billion in 1999-00 and Rs. 31 billion in 2005-06). Thus, the favourable impact of reforms is clearly discernable on the profitability level of banks in India.

Table 1.3 depicts the trend of return on assets ratio (ROA) of CBs in India. On account of banking reforms, SCBs registered considerable increase in ROA ratio from -1.06 percent in 1992-93 to 0.67 percent in 1999-00 and further to 0.88 percent in 2005-06. PSBs also recorded substantial increase

TABLE 1.3
Return on Assets of Commercial Banks in India—1991-92 to 2005-06

(*Per cent*)

Year	*SBI Group*	*NBs Group*	*PSBs*	*Private Banks*	*Foreign Banks*	*SCBs*
1991-92	0.17	0.32	0.26	0.70	1.59	0.38
1992-93	0.24	-1.70	-0.98	0.56	-2.52	-1.06
1993-94	0.28	-1.98	-1.14	0.44	1.80	-0.83
1994-95	0.51	0.11	0.25	1.04	1.85	0.43
1995-96	0.43	-0.38	-0.08	1.10	1.47	0.15
1996-97	0.83	0.40	0.56	1.16	1.25	0.67
1997-98	1.03	0.62	0.77	0.99	0.92	0.82
1998-99	0.52	0.37	0.43	0.68	0.91	0.49
1999-00	0.80	0.43	0.57	0.88	1.21	0.67
2000-01	0.55	0.33	0.42	0.73	0.98	0.50
2001-02	0.76	0.69	0.96	0.67	1.34	0.76
2002-03	0.91	0.99	0.72	0.98	1.55	1.00
2003-04	1.02	1.18	1.12	0.95	1.61	1.13
2004-05	0.91	0.85	0.87	0.82	1.30	0.89
2005-06	0.87	0.80	0.82	0.87	1.55	0.88

Source : Computed from Statistical Tables Relating to Banks in India.

in ROA ratio from -0.98 percent in 1992-93 to 0.57 percent in 1999-00 and further to 0.82 percent in 2005-06. The increase in ROA ratio among PSBs may be attributed to the fall in the amount of NPAs. The ROA ratio of private banks increased from 0.56 percent in 1992-93 to 0.88 percent in 1999-00 but it marginally declined to 0.87 percent as on March 2006. Besides this, the ROA ratio of foreign banks is found to be quite high at 1.55 percent as on March 2006 in contrast to 1.21 percent in 1999-00 and -2.52 percent in 1992-93. This sharp increase in ROA ratio may be attributed to the contribution of income from off-balance sheet activities to the profits.

Non-interest income or exposure of off balance sheet items to total income ratio reflects the diversification of business operations of the banks. Non-interest income is traditionally lower in PSBs than its counterpart groups due to the lack of diversification in their business activities. Lower the ratio, the lesser efficient is the banking system. Table 1.4 delineates that non-interest income to total income ratio of SCBs accelerated to 16.03 percent as on March 2006 in contrast to 13.78 percent in 1999-00 and 10.71 percent in 1992-93. The non-interest income to total income ratio of PSBs has been noted to be lowest among all the bank groups as on March 2006 but at individual level, they registered an increase in non-interest income to 13.70 percent as on March 2006 in contrast to 12.54 percent in 1999-00 and 11.08 percent in 1992-93.

TABLE 1.4

Non-Interest Income to Total Income of Commercial Banks in India —1991-92 to 2005-06

(*Per cent*)

Year	*SBI Group*	*NBs Group*	*PSBs*	*Private Banks*	*Foreign Banks*	*SCBs*
1991-92	12.59	9.52	10.72	6.67	21.62	11.81
1992-93	12.86	9.95	11.08	10.53	7.50	10.71
1993-94	14.39	11.97	12.87	12.50	17.50	13.27
1994-95	13.13	11.11	11.86	14.71	19.57	12.75
1995-96	16.99	10.88	13.22	15.09	18.03	13.69
1996-97	14.59	10.53	12.07	13.51	18.42	12.73
1997-98	14.86	11.66	12.83	16.84	21.84	14.10
1998-99	14.33	10.51	11.93	13.04	19.39	12.70
1999-00	14.12	11.60	12.54	16.20	21.15	13.78
2000-01	13.71	11.21	12.16	12.65	20.83	12.94
2001-02	13.42	14.48	16.58	20.67	25.38	15.95
2002-03	16.36	16.71	14.08	22.78	25.62	18.36
2003-04	21.00	20.07	20.42	22.96	30.77	21.61
2004-05	17.72	16.15	16.74	19.57	29.77	18.09
2005-06	16.16	12.28	13.70	18.71	30.51	16.03

Source : Computed from Statistical Tables Relating to Banks in India.

On the other hand, non-interest income to total income ratio of private banks recorded increase from 10.53 percent in 1992-93 to 16.20 percent in 1999-00 and to 18.71 percent in 2005-06. Foreign banks are noted to be outperformers as compared to its counterparts with non-interest income to total income ratio of 30.51 percent as on March 2006 as against 21.15 percent in 1999-00 and 7.50 percent in 1992-93. This clearly reflects that foreign banks are highly involved in modern banking activities and earning substantial amount of income in form of fees, exchange and brokerage, etc.

Net-interest margin (measured as the difference between interest earned and interest expended) to the total assets ratio indicates the ability of the banks to commit their funds to generate income from credits and investment operations. Lower the ratio; the more efficient is the banking system. Table 1.5 highlights that net-interest margin (NIM) to total

TABLE 1.5

Net-Interest Margin to Total Assets of Commercial Banks in India —1991-92 to 2005-06

(*Per cent*)

Year	*SBI Group*	*NBs Group*	*PSBs*	*Private Banks*	*Foreign Banks*	*SCBs*
1991-92	3.81	2.89	3.25	4.20	3.97	3.31
1992-93	3.05	1.98	2.38	2.81	3.47	2.51
1993-94	2.70	2.19	2.38	3.07	4.19	2.55
1994-95	3.26	2.73	2.92	2.61	4.23	3.01
1995-96	3.32	2.95	3.08	3.07	3.77	3.14
1996-97	3.47	2.98	3.16	2.97	4.11	3.21
1997-98	3.14	2.79	2.91	2.47	3.98	2.94
1998-99	2.83	2.77	2.79	2.12	3.52	2.78
1999-00	2.77	2.67	2.71	2.12	3.86	2.72
2000-01	2.76	2.90	2.85	2.33	3.63	2.84
2001-02	2.69	2.75	2.73	1.57	3.21	2.57
2002-03	2.77	3.00	2.91	1.97	3.35	2.77
2003-04	2.84	3.05	2.97	2.18	3.45	2.86
2004-05	3.08	2.83	2.91	2.34	3.39	2.83
2005-06	3.08	2.73	2.85	2.40	3.61	2.81

Source : Computed from Statistical Tables Relating to Banks in India.

assets ratio of SCBs increased from 2.51 percent in 1992-93 to 2.72 percent in 1999-00 and further accelerated to 2.81 percent as on March 2006. Furthermore, net-interest margin to total assets ratio of PSBs increased to 2.85 percent as on March 2006 in contrast to 2.71 percent in 1999-00 and 2.38 percent in 1992-93. On the other hand, NIM to total assets ratio of private banks recorded fall from 2.81 percent in 1992-93 to 2.12 percent in 1999-00 but it increased to 2.40 percent in 2005-06. Foreign banks are emerged to be outliers as compared to its counterparts and registered increase in NIM to total assets ratio from 3.47 percent in 1992-93 to 3.86 percent in 1999-00 but declined to 3.61 percent as on March 2006.

The operating cost to total assets ratio indicates the expenditures incurred by a bank in handling the business operations. Larger the ratio, lower is the efficiency of a bank. This ratio has been used to reflect the intermediation cost of the banks by some researchers. As depicted in Table 1.6, SCBs

TABLE 1.6

Operating Cost to Total Assets of Commercial Banks in India —1991-92 to 2005-06

(*Per cent*)

Year	*SBI Group*	*NBs Group*	*PSBs*	*Private Banks*	*Foreign Banks*	*SCBs*
1991-92	2.51	2.68	2.62	2.80	2.38	2.61
1992-93	2.65	2.65	2.65	2.81	2.84	2.64
1993-94	2.70	2.65	2.67	2.63	2.69	2.64
1994-95	2.94	2.76	2.83	2.09	2.65	2.76
1995-96	3.10	2.95	3.00	2.41	2.73	2.94
1996-97	2.94	2.84	2.88	2.31	3.04	2.84
1997-98	2.66	2.64	2.65	2.10	2.91	2.63
1998-99	2.69	2.62	2.65	2.03	3.39	2.65
1999-00	2.47	2.56	2.53	1.83	3.14	2.49
2000-01	2.66	2.76	2.72	1.90	3.05	2.64
2001-02	2.11	2.39	2.25	1.46	3.03	2.19
2002-03	2.11	2.34	2.28	2.00	2.84	2.24
2003-04	2.20	2.19	2.20	2.01	2.79	2.20
2004-05	2.14	2.06	2.09	2.03	2.86	2.13
2005-06	2.28	1.93	2.05	2.10	2.96	2.12

Source : Computed from Statistical Tables Relating to Banks in India.

registered a substantial decline in operating cost, stood at 2.12 percent as on March 2006 contrary to 2.49 percent in 1999-00 and 2.64 percent in 1992-93. As for various categories of banks, PSBs recorded a notable decline in operating cost at 2.05 percent as on March 2006 as compared to 2.53 percent in 1999-00 and 2.65 percent in 1992-93. The sharp decline in the operating cost to total asset ratio of PSBs has been observed on account of rationalization of the workforce through voluntary retirement scheme. On the other hand, operating cost of private banks declined from 2.81 percent in 1992-93 to 1.83 percent in 1999-00 but further increased to 2.10 percent in 2005-06. This reflects that private banks are incurring huge expenditures on technological upgradation measures. Further, the operating cost to total assets ratio is found to be highest in foreign banks as compared to its counterpart groups, stood at 2.96 percent as on March, 2006 as against 3.14 percent in 1999-00 and 2.84 percent in 1992-93. This shows that foreign banks are more likely to make huge expenditures on their workforce and offer them attractive salary and other perks.

The most significant improvement has been witnessed in terms of reduction in NPAs as shown in Table 1.7. As

TABLE 1.7

Non-Performing Assets to Total Advances of Commercial Banks in India

(Per cent)

Year	*PSBs*		*Private Banks*		*Foreign Banks*	
	Gross NPAs	*Net NPAs*	*Gross NPAs*	*Net NPAs*	*Gross NPAs*	*Net NPAs*
1997-98	16	8.2	8.7	5.3	6.4	2.2
1999-00	14	7.4	8.2	5.4	7.0	2.4
2000-01	12.4	6.7	8.4	5.4	6.8	1.8
2001-02	11.1	5.8	9.6	5.7	5.4	1.9
2002-03	9.4	4.5	8.1	5.0	5.3	1.8
2003-04	7.8	3.0	5.8	2.8	4.6	1.5
2004-05	5.4	2.1	3.9	2.2	2.9	0.9
2005-06	3.7	1.3	3.34	1.36	1.9	0.8

Source : Computed from Statistical Tables Relating to Banks in India.

proportion of total advances, gross NPAs of PSBs declined from 14.0 percent in 1999-00 and to 3.7 percent as on March 2006; net NPAs declined from 7.4 percent in March 2000 to 1.3 percent in March 2006. The private sector banks also registered decline in gross NPAs from 8.2 percent in 1999-00 to 3.34 percent in 2005-06 while net NPAs decelerated from 5.4 percent in 1999-00 to 1.36 percent in 2005-06. On the other hand, foreign banks witnessed decline in gross NPAs from 7.0 percent in 1999-00 to 1.9 percent in 2005-06 and net NPAs from 2.4 percent in 1999-00 to 0.8 percent in 2005-06.

The classification of loan assets of scheduled commercial banks (as shown in Table 1.8) has also undergone a transformation with over 96.7 percent in the 'standard' category and less than 1 percent in the 'loss' category as on March 2006 contrary to 87.2 percent in the 'standard' category and 1.6 percent in the 'loss' category as on March 2000. As for various categories of banks, the loan assets in 'standard' category worked out to be 96.2 percent for PSBs, 95.6 percent for old private banks and 98 percent for foreign banks as on March 2006 as against 86 percent for PSBs, 88.8 percent for old private banks and 93 percent for foreign banks as on March 2000.

Furthermore, the assets in 'loss' category have been noted to be 0.5 percent for PSBs, 0.6 percent for old private banks and 0.5 percent for foreign banks on March 2006 as against 1.7 percent for PSBs, 1.0 percent for old private banks and 1.9 percent for foreign banks as on March 2000.

The assets of SCBs under 'sub-standard' and 'doubtful' heads have also illustrated perceptible reduction from 4.1 percent to 1 percent and from 7.1 percent to 2 percent respectively from March 2000 to March 2006. The sub-standard assets of PSBs recorded considerable decline from 4.3 percent to 1 percent, old private banks from 4.5 percent to 0.8 percent and foreign banks from 2.9 percent to 1.0 percent. On the other hand, the doubtful assets of PSBs registered sharp decline from 8.0 percent to 2.2 percent, old private banks from 5.8 percent to 3.0 percent and foreign banks from 2.1 percent to 0.7 percent.

Besides this, the capital adequacy ratio for PSBs also increased significantly at the end March 2006, all PSBs had

TABLE 1.8

Classification of Loan Assets of Commercial Banks as the Percentage of Total Advances

(Per cent)

Bank Group/Loan Assets	*Years 1999-00*					*2005-06*				
	Standard	*Sub-Standard*	*Doubtful*	*Loan Assets*	*Total NPAs*	*Standard*	*Sub-Standard*	*Doubtful*	*Loan Assets*	*Total NPAs*
(1)	*(2)*	*(3)*	*(4)*	*(5)*	*(6)*	*(7)*	*(8)*	*(9)*	*(10)*	*(11)*
SCBs	87.2	4.1	7.1	1.6	12.8	96.7	1.0	2.0	0.4	3.3
PSBs	86.0	4.3	8.0	1.7	14.0	96.2	1.0	2.2	0.5	3.7
Old Private Banks	88.8	4.5	5.8	1.0	11.3	95.6	0.8	3.0	0.6	4.4
New Private Banks	95.9	2.5	1.3	0.4	4.2	98.3	0.7	0.8	0.2	1.8
Foreign Banks	93.0	2.9	2.1	1.9	7.0	98.0	1.0	0.7	0.5	2.0

capital levels exceeding 10 percent of risk weighted assets; 23 out of 27 private banks and 27 out of 29 foreign banks had capital levels exceeding 10 percent of risk weighted assets.

To sum up, the analysis of these accounting ratios highlights a remarkable impact of reforms on the performance level of banks in India, though; the degree of tangible benefits has noticed to be varied across the ownership groups. It is worth mentioning that PSBs have responded well to the liberalization and enhanced competition especially after the banking sector reforms came into force (since 1999-00). The PSBs have registered notable achievements in terms of cutting down the operating cost and fall in the amount of NPAs. The significant increase in profitability and income levels on account of increase in the exposure to off-balance sheet activities has moved Indian banking industry closer to the global levels.

Challenges Ahead

(i) *Improving profitability*: The deregulated environment inculcates the spirit of intense competition, compresses the interest margins and in turn affects the profitability of the banks. The key challenge for banks is how to manage higher provisioning requirements for the settlement of NPAs with thinning margins and low profitability levels. This is particularly important because with dilution in banks' equity, shareholders now closely track their performance. Thus, with falling spreads, rising provision for NPAs and falling interest rates, greater attention will need to be paid to reduce transaction costs. Moreover, the greater thrust should be on the diversification of business operations to raise the level of non-interest income and profitability.

(ii) *Reinforcing technology*: Indian banking industry is going to be information technology driven. The networking of banks, Tele banking, ATM facilities, Any Time and Any Where banking etc., has become integral part of modern banking. This enables the banks to offer qualitative products and services at a competitive cost with better risk management practices. Thus, banking institutions are under pressure to undertake extensive computerization in order to have an edge over others. Moreover, in the recent knowledge-based economy, customers have become more demanding and thus, banks have to deliver customized products through multiple channels.

(iii) *Risk-based Market Segmentation:* The increasing deregulation, rising global competition, introduction of innovative products and delivery channels have pushed risk management to the forefront of today's challenges, which brings in its wake the risk-based market segmentation. As for the low risk areas, the banks will have to develop technology-based risk management tools. As for high-risk areas, better techniques, skills and external advice from experts are indispensable. Moreover, banks will have to set-up their own R&D unit to have independent advice. Risk management functions will be fully centralized and independent from the business profit centers. Overall, banks will have to upgrade their credit assessment, risk management skills, developing a cell of specialists and introducing technology driven management information systems.

(iv) *Sharpening skills*: To meet the challenges of fast growing economy, fundamental swing in the human resources development is highly required in banking. Therefore, large investments will have to be made in information technology and human resources development programmes for imparting knowledge and special skills in retail banking, treasury, risk management, foreign exchange and development banking, etc. On the whole, twin pillars of the banking sector i.e., human resources development and information technology will have to be strengthened.

(v) *Greater customer orientation*: Indian banking industry is at the forefront of highly dynamic and intensified competitive era. Thus, banks will have to attract and retain the customers by introducing innovative products, enhancing the quality of customer service and marketing a variety of products through diverse channels targeted at specific customer groups.

(vi) *Corporate governance*: Corporate governance in banking will require a new orientation on account of dilution of Government stakeholding and for creating shareholder value. As the board of banks will become suppress in all the matters relating to banking, therefore, it is essential to bring greater professionalism in the quality of top management. Further, as the ownership of banks gets broad-based on account of financial liberalization, the importance of institutional and individual shareholders will increase. In the above backdrop, banks will need to put in a place a code for corporate governance for benefiting all stakeholders of a corporate entity.

(vii) *International standards*: In an increasingly globalize environment, the banks will have to follow universally accepted standards and codes for strengthening the domestic financial set-up. This includes best practices in the area of corporate governance and full transparency in disclosures. The focus on these standards will help the domestic banks to enhance the economic links with world financial markets.

In summation, banking sector reforms has provided the platform for the banking sector to grow on the basis of operational flexibility, competition, functional autonomy, and thereby enhancing the efficiency, productivity and profitability. The future would be of those banks that would able to avail the productive opportunities offered to them in terms of various relaxations and removal of the barriers to the performance.

OBJECTIVES OF THE STUDY

The main objective of the present study is to analyze scale economies, x-efficiency and total factor productivity growth of commercial banks in India during pre-reforms and post-reforms periods. Specifically, the following are the key objectives of the study:

1. To examine x-efficiency and its sources among commercial banks in India;
2. To measure scale economies and pure technical efficiency of commercial banks in India;
3. To pinpoint the sources of inefficiency among commercial banks in India;
4. To rank the efficient banks on the basis of their performance;
5. To examine total factor productivity growth and its sources among commercial banks in India;
6. To analyze the impact of ownership and banking reforms on the efficiency and total factor productivity growth of commercial banks in India;
7. To study the impact of environmental factors affecting x-inefficiency of commercial banks in India; and
8. To test the phenomenon of convergence/divergence in the performance level of banks in India.

The present book has been organized into seven chapters.

Chapter I : Introduction

Chapter 1 is introductory in nature concentrating on the importance of banking, role of banks in economic development, its evolution and detailed analysis of banking sector reforms in India. It further outlines objectives, rationale of the study and plan of the study.

Chapter 2 : Review of Study Made

This chapter reviews the literature focusing on the key issues viz., scale economies, x-efficiency and total factor productivity growth of banks. This chapter includes the studies both of the national and international character.

Chapter 3 : Methodology for Analysis

This chapter illustrates database, various issues related to the measurement of variables in banking sector and the selection of variables for present study. It also discusses methodological framework of the applied techniques to examine efficiency and productivity growth of commercial banks in India.

Chapter 4 : Scale Economies and X-Efficiency of Commercial Banks in India

This chapter elaborates empirical findings on scale economies and x-efficiency of commercial banks in India for the period 1985 to 2005-06. The entire study period has been classified into three distinct sub-periods: (i) Pre-liberalization period, (ii) Initial post-liberalization period, and (iii) Post-liberalization period. The empirical findings present inter-temporal, ownership-wise and inter-bank analysis of x-efficiency and its decompositions among commercial banks in India with the use of Data Envelopment Analysis (DEA) approach. In addition, it sheds light on the relationship of bank size and scale economies among commercial banks in India. Besides this, this chapter focuses on identifying the super efficient banks and ranking them by the level of influence.

Chapter 5 : Total Factor Productivity Growth of Commercial Banks in India

This chapter illustrates empirical results on total factor productivity growth and its components among commercial banks in India for the period 1985 to 2005-06. The entire study period has been classified into three distinct sub-periods: (i) Pre-liberalization period, (ii) Initial post-liberalization period, and (iii) Post-liberalization period. The empirical findings present inter-temporal, ownership-wise and inter-bank analysis of TFP growth and its related indices among commercial banks in India using DEA-based Malmquist Productivity index approach. Besides this, the relationship of bank size and TFP change along with its indices has been explored among commercial banks in India. Moreover, an attempt has been made to discriminate the banks on the basis of TFP growth, technology change and efficiency change.

Chapter 6 : Determinants of X-Efficiency and Convergence/ Divergence among Commercial Banks in India

Chapter sixth has been divided into two sections. First part of the chapter focuses on the theoretical framework of the determinants of efficiency, review of the existing studies, methodological framework of the applied model, determinants of banks' x-inefficiency in India and the empirical findings pertaining to the impact of environmental factors on the x-inefficiency of commercial banks in India. The second part of the chapter discusses theoretical framework of the concept of convergence, methodological framework of the adopted model and empirical results relating to the process of catching up or convergence in the efficiency/productivity growth of commercial banks in India.

Chapter 7 : Summary and Conclusions

This chapter presents the brief summary of the study and concludes with the suggestions and scope for further study.

Review of Studies Made

In this chapter, an attempt has been made to review the empirical studies related to scale economies, x-efficiency and total factor productivity growth of banks. The chapter has been divided into two broad sections. Section I provides the review of studies on scale economies and x-efficiency of banks at national and international level. Section II reviews the empirical studies on efficiency and total factor productivity growth of banks related to India and rest of the world. The final section presents some concluding remarks.

SECTION I

Glass and Mckillop (1991) fitted Translog function to measure efficiency of Irish banking sector for the period 1972-90. They considered advances and investments as output and labor, capital and deposits as input variables. The empirical findings provided the evidence of diseconomies of scale for most of the sub-periods considered in the study. The banks reported 0.024 level of overall scale efficiency, 0.169 level of product specific scale economies with reference to securities held while 0.018 to advances outstanding during the study period. Irish banking industry did not seem to enjoy cost benefits in producing advances and securities jointly. The contribution of technology was estimated to be quite high at the rate of 6.1 percent per annum to total factor productivity growth. The average value of non-neutral technical change turned out to be (-0.11) for the entire study period, which may be attributed to the inefficient adoption of labor saving technology. Finally, the results led to conclude that new employment packages should be introduced to reduce the labor costs from 63-64 percent to 52 percent.

Gropper (1991) fitted Translog functional form to investigate the changes in scale economies of commercial banks in America for the period 1979-86. Besides total cost, he defined outputs in terms of investments, total loans and trust accounts and inputs in terms of labor, capital and funds. The findings indicated significant scale economies for small-sized banks (less than $100 million in total assets) but significant diseconomies of scale for large-sized banks in earlier sample years. The branch banks, having less than 100 $ million total assets, reported significant economies of scale. The similar but somewhat less strong pattern of scale economies was observed in unit banking states. This may be due to the difference in the size of unit banking and branch banking states. He also found that the level of scale economies has increased over the study period. Further, the empirical findings reported that large banks might get cost advantage over that, which existed in previous years due to recent regulatory and technological changes.

Yue (1992) employed data envelopment analysis (DEA) approach to measure efficiency of 60 Missouri banks for the period 1984 to 1990. Banks' outputs have been proxied in terms of interest income, non-interest income and total loans and inputs in terms of interest expenses, non-interest expenses and transaction and non-transaction deposits. He applied two models viz., CCR model and additive model to estimate the efficiency of Missouri banks. It has been observed that five of Missouri banks are technologically efficient; however, these banks did not find to be operating at the most efficient scale of operation. The efficiency scores estimated from both of the models did not indicate scale inefficiency as the major source of overall technical inefficiency. Nevertheless, managerial incapabilities emerged to be the responsible factor of technical inefficiency.

Fukuyama (1993) employed DEA approach to measure the extent of technical efficiency and scale efficiency of 143 banks in Japan. The banks have been categorized into three ownership groups viz., city banks, regional banks and former Sogo banks. To view this objective, he incorporated labor, capital and funds from customers as input variables and loans and revenue from business activities as output variables for the year 1990. Japanese banks experienced average technical efficiency to the tune of (0.8645), which in turn highlighted about (14 percent) level of inefficiency in the utilization of critical inputs to produce outputs. The average scale efficiency estimate (0.9844) of banks indicated negligible that is, less than (2 percent) level of scale inefficiency. Thus, a considerable amount of technical inefficiency has occurred due to the managerial inefficiency rather than scale-related problems. As for returns to scale, about 81 percent sample banks were found to be operating at increasing returns to scale (IRS) and 12 percent at diminishing returns to scale (DRS). City banks appeared to be best performers on each dimension. Regional banks performed better than former Sogo banks for pure technical efficiency and overall technical efficiency, but ranking was noted to be reversed in scale efficiency estimates. Moreover, scale efficiency estimates were found to be weakly associated with bank size. On the other hand, the relationship of PTE and overall TE with bank size has not been clearly indicated.

Ray and Sanyal (1994-95) analyzed the cost behavior of commercial banks in India for the year 1990. They fitted Translog cost function on the cross sectional data set of 16 banks having assets size ranging from Re 3.40-Re 80.50 trillion. To view this objective, they considered input prices of labor, capital and deposits and outputs viz., total deposits, loans and investments. The overall scale expansion of sample banks was estimated to be highly cost efficient. The sample banks were observed to get substantial scale economies over the study period. However, economies of scale were noticed to be inversely associated with size of banks. The expansion of output with existing branches was observed to be more cost effective rather than expansion of output with new branches for a moderate scale of operation. Branch expansion was found to be cost inefficient measure due to the heavy burden on cost structure of banks but observed to be desirable for cost efficiency in case of substantial growth programme. The results also indicated upward revision of wages as cost-neutral in the sense that it leaves the marginal cost of output unaffected.

Favero and Papi (1995) constructed DEA model to measure technical and scale efficiency on a cross -ection of 174 Italian banks in 1991. They adopted both the asset approach and intermediation approach to accomplish the objective. As per asset approach, outputs are defined in terms of loans, investments and non-interest income and inputs in terms of labor, capital, loanable funds and financial capital. The second definition differed from the first one in that the status of current accounts and saving deposits (constituents of loanable funds) has been shifted from inputs to outputs. The CRS efficiency score worked out to be 0.878 as per intermediation approach and 0.794 as per asset approach while the VRS efficiency came out to be 0.909 for intermediation approach and 0.839 for asset approach. The results did not report much sensitivity to the definition of inputs and outputs. The results also provided the evidence of small deviations in the efficiency scores obtained under CCR and BCC model. Thus, Italian banks did not register considerable amount of scale inefficiency during the study period.

Żaim (1995) employed DEA model to study the impact of liberalization on the economic efficiency of commercial banks in Turkey. He incorporated total of demand deposits, time deposits, short-term loans and long-term loans as output variables and total number of employees, interest expenses, depreciation expenses and expenses on materials as input variables for the period 1981 to 1990. The results reported on an average 10 percent increase in the level of technical efficiency; however, decline in average technical efficiency differences of the banks from the period 1981 to 1990. The proportion of banks that operated at optimal scale increased from 59 percent in 1981 to 68 percent in 1990 through considerable scale adjustments. The findings indicated pure technical component (i.e., 0.833 in 1981 and 0.936 in 1990) as the major determinant of technical inefficiency of commercial banks in Turkey relative to the scale component (0.972 in 1981 and 0.976 in 1990). The rate of change of technical efficiency turned out to be greater in private sector banks as compared to state and foreign banks. As for cost efficiency, the empirical findings illustrated that Turkish banks have registered substantial fall in costs that is, from 75 percent in 1981 to 38 percent in 1990. The effect of technical inefficiency and allocative inefficiency on cost increases was found to be different for private banks and state banks. A considerable portion of cost inefficiency was noted to be due to allocative inefficiency for state banks. However, technical inefficiency was found to be the responsible for cost inefficiency among private banks. Finally, the results led to conclude that deregulation has succeeded in stimulating Turkish banks to enhance the level of economic efficiency.

Bhattacharya, Lovell and Sahay (1997) conducted a study to measure the productive efficiency of 70 Indian commercial banks for the period 1986-91. They employed DEA using interest and operating expenses as input variables and advances, investments and deposits as output variables. They also applied SFA to measure the variation in efficiency to a set of temporal, ownership and random noise components. Public banks turned out to be the best performers while foreign banks the least efficient banks in the utilization of critical resources. The average efficiency of PSBs was estimated to be highest (87 percent) followed by private banks (75.88 percent) and foreign banks (75.37 percent) during the study period. Domestic banks showed less variation in their efficiency scores while the opposite was true for foreign banks. Most of the banks were observed to operate at diminishing returns to scale. Furthermore, the results recorded (5.7 percent) portion of variation in efficiency, that is, unexplained by temporal and ownership form effects. The empirical findings also provided the evidence of temporal improvement in the average efficiency of foreign banks, almost negligible improvement of (0.07 percent) in private banks and a temporal decline of (2.69 percent) in the performance of PSBs during the study period.

Chatterjee (1997) made an attempt to identify the scale economy aspect of commercial banks in India for the year 1994-95. He considered two measures of scale economy viz., ray scale economy (under constant output mix) and expansion path scale economy (under changing output mix). To view this objective, he fitted Tranlog function on total cost, factor prices of labor, capital and purchased funds and two outputs viz., total advances and total investments. The empirical findings provided the evidence of substantial scale economies among sample banks. The results also illustrated that it would be more cost effective to expand the business with existing branches keeping output mix unaltered. In addition, only the small-sized and medium-sized private sector banks would enjoy cost efficiency by opening up new branches to handle the business under constant output mix. The scope for increased cost efficiency was estimated to be narrow in case of changing output mix with new branches. The empirical findings reported that private banks of all sizes and small PSBs would get benefits from the output expansion with existing branches. However, the banks of any size-group did not provide the evidence of scale economies on the inclusion of branches with output variables. Finally, the study recommended mergers and regrouping of the banks to realize maximum benefits of scale economies.

De Young (1997) employed distribution free approach to estimate x-efficiency of 618 U.S. commercial banks for the period 1984 through 1994. He also applied diagnostic test to reveal the point at which adding an additional year of data no longer improves the resultant estimates of x-efficiency. He considered labor, physical capital and borrowed funds as input and total loans, transaction deposits and fee-based income as output variables. The diagnostic test indicated that data of six years is adequate for distribution free approach, where x-efficiency estimates contain small amount of random error. However, the use of data for more than 8 years violated the assumption of constant bank level efficiency and introduced bias in the efficiency estimates over the time. The results reported average x-efficiency within the range of 77 to 79 percent from $t = 1$ to $t = 4$ settled at 80 percent efficiency (approx) for $t > 5$.

Altanbus and Chakravarty (1998) conducted a study to detect inefficiency estimates of 13603 banks in Europe. To view this objective, they fitted fourier flexible form over the period 1988-95. The empirical findings reported that mean inefficiency score of European banking sector has turned out to be (0.24893) with dispersion measure of (0.04403). Commercial banks reported higher level of dispersion in inefficiency estimates (0.05590), followed by saving banks (0.01754). Saving banks were found to be homogenous, which reflect most probably the sale of narrower range of products. The results provided the evidence of country differences in the level of x-efficiency, which may be attributed to the difference in the structure of banking system and removal of cross border restrictions. Finally, the authors argued that comparison of banks efficiency across national frontier entails an examination of the difference between countries' institutional structure of the banking system.

Fat and Hua (1998) investigated the impact of x-efficiency on the share prices of banks in Singapore. They applied non-parametric, DEA technique on three input and two output variables for the period 1992-96. The efficiency scores have been further modified and ranked according to Andersen and Petersen's Model. The empirical findings reported that banks have experienced remarkable level of x-efficiency (95.3 percent) with standard deviation measure of (0.953) during the study period. The average profit efficiency of six Singapore listed banks was estimated to be (82.6 percent) for the period 1992-96. The results further reported average scale p-efficiency in tune of (95 percent), scale x-efficiency (97 percent) and pure technical profit efficiency (87 percent) among banks in Singapore. Thus, the inefficient production of profits rather than wrong scale of operations was found to be responsible for profit inefficiency. Besides this, larger banks appeared to be more profit and cost efficient than smaller ones. Finally, the results led to conclude that change in share prices or market tends to over-react to year-on-year changes in profit efficiency rather than cost efficiency.

Das (1999-00) employed DEA approach to measure the performance of PSBs in India for the year 1998. To view this, he used deposits, borrowings and number of employees as input variables and margin and other income as output variables. The overall average efficiency of PSBs turned out to be 57.18 percent for the year 1998. A considerable amount of efficiency was estimated to be due to technical component (81.44 percent) than allocative component (70.08 percent). Alternatively, PSBs indicated the scope of producing 1.23 times as much output from the same level of inputs. State Bank of India group appeared to be excellent performer in each of DEA efficiency estimates. SBI group performed well with efficiency measure of (96.5 percent) followed by NBs group (75.1 percent). SBI group registered less variation in each of the DEA efficiency estimates relative to NBs. Corporation Bank and Oriental Bank of Commerce emerged to be best performers. However, Indian Bank, United Commercial Bank and United Bank of India proved to be worst performers, which may be attributed to the shift in accounting practices and high level of non-performing assets. Finally, the empirical findings suggest PSBs to concentrate on business with existing level of non-profit liabilities and branches.

Aslan (2002) applied stochastic frontier approach (SFA) to study the impact of deregulation and financial crisis on the productive efficiency of 35 private and 6 foreign Turkish banks for the period 1992-98. A production function technology of three outputs viz., total loans, securities, commission and fee income and three inputs viz., labor, capital and deposits has been conceptualized. He put greater reliance upon management efficiency, which accounts for a higher proportion of costs. The overall mean efficiency turned out to be 73 percent and equivalently the wastage of 27 percent of costs relative to best practice one. The efficiency score of Turkish banks was found to be lower than U.S. and South Korean banks, which may be attributed to Asian ,financial crisis. The subsequent regression estimates reported financial and currency crisis as the major determinant of overall efficiency. The unstable economic environment was held responsible for a remarkable change in efficiency scores. Finally, the empirical findings suggested Turkish banks to understand the determinants of inefficiency and adopt appropriate policies to even out cost inefficiencies.

Grigorian and Manole (2002) employed data envelopment analysis to explore efficiency estimates of banks from 17 transition countries for the period 1995-98. They incorporated labor, fixed assets and interest expenses as input and revenues, deposits with net loans and liquid assets as output variables. The results reported more disadvantageous position of the banks in Commonwealth of Independent States (CIS) on the basis of service-based index. Although, the banks in CE (Central Europe) and SEE (Southern and Eastern Europe) did not experience significant lag in terms of revenue generating capacity but the banks in central Europe were found to be efficient in both the terms of revenue generating capacity and ability to provide services to their clients except in the year 1997. The banks in CIS countries have been observed to grow on average (30 percent) followed by SEE countries (16 percent) and CE countries (11 percent) on the basis of service-based index.

Kumar and Verma (2002-03) applied DEA to measure the extent of technical inefficiency, benchmarks and targets of PSBs in India. They proxied bank inputs in terms of labor, physical capital and loanable funds and outputs in terms of spread and non-interest income for the year 2001. The overall level of technical inefficiency turned out to be 17 percent, indicating the scope of producing 1.21 times more output from the same level of inputs. SBI group outperformed NBs in terms of operating efficiency. State Bank of India, Corporation Bank and Oriental Bank of Commerce were found to be highly efficient whereas United Bank of India was found to be poor performer as per benchmarking exercise. From the target setting exercise, it has been observed that the inefficient banks will have to reduce physical capital, staff and loanable funds by 52 percent, 22 percent and 21 percent, respectively to attain the level of best practice ones. The relationship of bank size and technical efficiency highlighted that large-sized banks are more effective in utilizing critical inputs in the production process as compared to small-sized and medium-sized banks. The relationship of efficiency and profitability noted that about 63 percent of PSBs have the potential of increase in the profitability level through efficiency improvement. The Corporation Bank, Oriental Bank of Commerce, State Bank of

Patiala, State Bank of Indore, State Bank of Bikaner and Jaipur and State Bank of Hyderabad were found to be the banks with high efficiency and high profitability. In addition, Corporation Bank emerged to be an ideal benchmark on both the efficiency and profitability dimension of performance.

Pastor (2002) conducted a study to examine credit risk and efficiency in European banking system for the period 1988-94. He applied a new three stage sequential technique based on DEA model and on the decomposition of risk into its internal and external factors to obtain efficiency measures adjusted for risk and environment. To view this objective, he considered the sample of 1144 French, 387 Italian, 524 Spanish and 543 German commercial banks. A production function technology of three outputs, two inputs and environment variables has been conceptualized. The results were found to be consistent with all the methods except for single stage method. The efficiency in risk management improved in Spanish banking system, deteriorated in France and remained stable in Italy and Germany. The estimate of average portion of risk management due to internal factors was found within the range of 13 percent to 26 percent. The results also provided that Italian banking industry has recorded higher proportion of bad loans (87 percent) due to internal factors as compared to Spain and Germany (73 percent) each. The measurement of efficiency without adjusted for risk was estimated to be considerably different from 'adjusted for risk efficiency' especially in case of 'Efficient in Risk Management' countries such as Spain and Germany. The efficiency adjusted for risk and environment favorably affected the position of those countries having unfavorable environment effect such as Italy and to lesser extent Spain (with an environment effect of 0.83 and 0.96 respectively) whereas it unfavorably affected German banking sector (with an environment effect of 1.02). The average efficiency of French banking sector did not seem to suffer from any alteration (with an environment effect of 0.99).

Ray and Sanyal (2002) fitted Translog cost function to measure x-efficiency of 27 PSBs in India. They used loans and other earning assets as output and labor, capital and physical capital as input variables for the period 1990-91 to 1995-96. The findings reported an improvement in x-efficiency only in case of 13 banks while 14 banks showed deterioration from their respective positions. The trend of improvement was observed to be significant at more than 95 percent level for three banks (State Bank of India, Central Bank of India and Bank of India). However, the trend of deterioration was found to be significant at 95 percent level of significance for UCO Bank. Overall x-efficiency clustered in a narrow range of 25-40 percent for 17 banks and 40-50 percent for 9 sample banks. The variant part of x-efficiency turned out to be statistically significant than invariant part. The empirical findings reported that PSBs have experienced invariant TE to the tune of (75 percent), which may be attributed to short time lag in the diffusion of new technology. Bank of Maharashtra emerged to be the most efficient bank with efficiency measure of 55 percent. In contrast, Syndicate Bank emerged to be the least efficient bank with efficiency measure of 29 percent. The relationship between size and x-efficiency revealed that x-efficiency is unrelated to the size of banks. The upper limit of average x-efficiency worked out to be 86 percent for small-sized, 89 percent for large-sized and 92-95 percent for medium-sized banks. Furthermore, they observed that lower limit falls with an enlargement of bank size while irregularity persists over its upper limit for variant part of x-efficiency.

Altanbus, Carbo and Molyneux (2003) conducted a study to measure efficiency of European and U.S banks for the period 1990-00. This study covered the sample set of 10274 commercial, 8042 saving and 7425 cooperative banks in view of this objective. They fitted Translog function in which total cost and total profit regressed on the input prices, outputs and time trend. The findings reported that saving banks are more cost efficient than their private sector counterparts in all sample countries (apart from Finland, Netherlands and Portugal). The empirical findings provided the little evidence that private commercial banks are more cost efficient than the mutual sector banks. The commercial banks were found to be more profit efficient than their mutual sector competitors (apart from Finland, Netherlands and Portugal). The greater profit efficiency of CBs might be due to some kind of market power and revenue generating factors. On the other hand, lower level of cost efficiency of CBs over the mutual saving and cooperative banks might be attributed to high quality services, risk management procedures and greater brand. Large banks, of each ownership type, emerged to be more profit efficient but less cost efficient as compared to small banks from the same ownership category.

Hasan and Marton (2003) made an attempt to measure the efficiency of Hungarian banking sector for the period 1993 to 1997. To view this, they fitted Translog function with total cost, total profit, input prices of labor and borrowed funds and outputs viz., total loans, investments, fee related income and total interest bearing borrowed funds. The sample banks reported (28.76 percent) level of cost inefficiency and (34.50 percent) profit inefficiency for the entire study period. The banks, having no foreign involvement, reported higher cost inefficiency (33.84 percent) and profit inefficiency (38.02 percent) than cost inefficiency (26.07 percent) and profit inefficiency (31.84 percent) of foreign counterparts. Banks, with at least 75 percent foreign involvement, appeared to be the most efficient group, with cost inefficiency score of (24.73 percent) and profit inefficiency score of (30.03 percent). The banks with 25 percent foreign involvement were found to be relatively less efficient among foreign-based groups with cost inefficiency score of (28.30 percent) and profit inefficiency score of (35.13 percent). These scores were noted to be still lower than the inefficiency score of Hungarian–owned domestic bank group. Therefore, the empirical findings provided that the extent of foreign involvement variable is significantly associated with lower inefficiency. The higher level of efficiency experienced by foreign banks in Hungary can be attributed to better local market conditions to exploit comparative advantages in terms of lower costs. The merged institutions revealed negative association with inefficiency estimates and got substantial benefits in new banking environment. Despite much development of the banking sector in various dimensions, the empirical findings indicated underdevelopment of Hungarian banking system in terms of provision of credit to enterprises.

Isik and Hasan (2003) conducted a study to measure efficiency for various ownership forms of banks in Turkey. They employed DEA using three input and four output variables for three years viz., 1988, 1992 and 1996. The empirical findings highlighted that Turkish banks have experienced average cost efficiency in order of about (72 percent), allocative efficiency (87 percent), technical efficiency (82 percent), pure technical efficiency (92 percent) and scale efficiency (88 percent). Thus, technical inefficiency is found to be the major responsible factor of cost inefficiency, driven mainly by scale related problems. As for ownership analysis, public sector banks and foreign banks emerged to be better performers in terms of cost efficiency and technical efficiency as compared to private sector banks. Public sector banks were also noted to be allocatively efficient banks on account of lower factor prices than that of its counterpart group.

Li, Hung and Chiu (2003) derived a theoretical framework to predict ranking in the TE of 4 public, 15 mixed and 24 private banks in Taiwan after deregulation. Translog distance function has been fitted to estimate technical efficiency (TE) and to study the relationship among TE and government shareholding for the period 1997-99. To view this objective, they incorporated bank staff, fixed assets and total deposits as input and loans, investments and non-interest income as output variables. The mixed banks experienced highest level of TE to the tune of (0.958) followed by PSBs (0.953) and private banks (0.926) in both the years of 1997 and 1999. The mixed banks reported average technical efficiency at the level of (0.941) followed by private banks (0.932) and PSBs (0.930) in the year 1998. Commercial banks in Taiwan on an average, showed worse performance after Asian financial crisis in the year 1997. The results suggested that public banks in Taiwan could improvè their TE by mixed ownership at diminishing rate (where government shareholding ranges between 0.1 percent to 99.9 percent). Finally, the study recommended that loan quality could be incorporated to make the estimation more accurate.

Sathye (2003) employed non-parametric DEA technique to measure the productive efficiency of 27 PSBs, 33 private sector and 34 foreign banks in India. He constructed two DEA models to show how efficiency scores vary with the use of alternative set of input and output variables. Model A considered interest expenses and non-interest expenses as inputs and interest income and non-interest income as outputs while Model B used deposits and staff as inputs to produce net loans and non-interest income for the year 1998. Indian banking industry, on an average, achieved (83 percent) level of TE as per Model A and (62 percent) as per Model B. PSBs recorded highest level of average technical efficiency (0.89), followed by foreign banks (0.84) and private sector banks (0.78) as per Model A. But the ranking reversed in Model B, where foreign banks observed to be most efficient with efficiency measure of (0.80) followed by PSBs (0.60) and private banks (0.45). Thus, the results provided that efficiency scores are highly sensitive to the alternative set of input and output variables. Moreover, the empirical findings provided the evidence of higher efficiency scores with the use of interest income and non-interest income as output variables. Thus, the study recommended bringing down the existing level of non-performing assets and curtailing establishment expenses through voluntary retirement scheme (VRS) for bank staff over a period of time so as to enhance the income levels and subsequently to achieve world best practice.

Bos and Kool (2004) estimated stochastic profit and cost frontiers for a balanced panel data set of 401 banks in Netherlands to measure efficiency. A production function technology of five input and four output variables has been specified for the year 1998-99. The empirical findings registered average profit efficiency to the tune of (0.945) and cost efficiency (0.913) with bank specific input prices. The results suggested that banks could, on an average, increase their profit efficiency by (5.5 percent) and cost efficiency by (8.7 percent) per annum. It has also been observed that least profit efficient banks can increase their profit efficiency by (26.8 percent) and the worst performing banks can improve by (39.3 percent) on its current cost efficiency. The total profit efficiency did not alter much under the influence of market specific output prices. However, average cost efficiency increased by 6.1 percent with market specific input prices. The large majority of sample banks were found to operate very closely to the frontier when using bank specific input prices. This empirical finding provided the signal that input prices does have direct impact on costs rather than profits.

De, Prithwis Kumar (2004) empirically examined the relationship between ownership, reforms and efficiency for three categories of public, private and foreign banks in India. He applied SFA model to measure both the time-variant and time-invariant measure of TE for the period 1985 to 1995-96. He defined labor, physical capital and purchased funds as inputs and gross income (Y_1) and total earning assets (Y_2) as output variables. On time-variant efficiency measures, out of 18 banks, only 14 banks improved their efficiency scores in the post-liberalization period. Bank of Tokyo gained the most in TE; however, Vijaya bank attained the least in post-reforms era. State Bank of India, the largest public sector bank, improved its technical efficiency from 47 percent in pre-reforms period to 50 percent in post-reforms period. The average time-variant TE score worked out to be (58.21 percent) for output measure (Y_1) and (79.43 percent) for output measure (Y_2) during the study period. The empirical findings reported that foreign banks have achieved the highest average efficiency compared to privately owned and publically owned banks. However, the variations in efficiency scores were estimated to be highest for foreign banks and lowest for PSBs for both the output measures, which may be due to the fact that PSBs are more familiar to the regulatory system. Further, the disaggregated analysis highlighted highest level of efficiency in case of Bank of Nova Scotia whereas lowest level of efficiency in case of Central Bank of India for output measure (Y_1). Moreover, it has been observed that only 23 banks out of 65 banks have reported an improvement in efficiency scores in post-reforms periods in comparison of pre-reforms period. The average time-invariant technical efficiency for the banking industry as a whole worked out to be (64.32 percent and 82.90 percent) for output measures (Y_1) and (Y_2) respectively. The average time-invariant technical efficiency for the banking industry as a whole has estimated to be higher than that of time-variant technical efficiency scores. As for ownership-wise analysis, foreign banks emerged to be top performers irrespective of output measure. PSBs as a group recorded lowest efficiency at the level of 55 percent for output measure (Y_1) whereas private banks reported the lowest efficiency at the level of 79 percent for output measure (Y_2). Besides this, foreign banks captured top positions in ranking on both the time-variant and time-invariant efficiency measures. Overall, the findings did not provide the evidence of an improvement in the efficiency of Indian banking industry after the liberalization in 1991-92.

Haunar (2004) employed DEA to detect the extent of cost efficiency differences among German and Austrian banks. He incorporated labor and aggregate funds as input and loans and securities as output variables for the period 1995-99. The average cost efficiency of all the sample banks was estimated to be 0.63 for the sample period. Therefore, the results imply cost inefficiency of about (27 percent) which may be attributed more to the use of wrong mix of inputs at the given prices rather than the wastage of resources. German banks achieved significantly higher level of cost efficiency (66 percent) followed by Austrian banks (42 percent). Austrian smaller and German larger banks emerged to be more efficient than other ones. Medium-sized banks on average appeared to be more scale efficient than small-sized and large-sized banks. Besides this, the findings provided no evidence of an improvement in average productivity growth in response to deregulation and merger wave of 90s over the study period. Neither cost efficiency nor scale efficiency and technology inhibited significant changes in TFP growth of banks over the period of time. Finally, the findings recommended the rationale for mergers and acquisitions among banks with similar product portfolios due to increasing economies of scale and decreasing economies of scope in German and Austrian banking sector.

Matousek (2004) conducted a study to measure cost efficiency and scale economies of 1174 banks in eight accession countries namely Czech Republic, Poland, Hungary, Slovenia, Slovakia, Latvia, Estonia and Lithonia. To view this objective, full distribution approach has been applied on unbalanced panel data set for the period 1994-01. Total cost has been taken as dependent variable and regressed on the input prices of labor and physical capital. The empirical findings provided the evidence of decline in scale economies with bank size. Economies of scale was estimated to be exhausted at the level above US $1000 thousands. The findings indicated the dominance of increasing returns to scale (IRS) among small-sized banks having total assets in the range of US $100-300 thousand. On the other hand, gradual decreasing returns to scale (DRS) started to set in when total assets of the banks reach to the threshold limit of US $1000 thousands). The magnitude of x-inefficiency was estimated to be lowest in foreign banking segment than its counterparts. Small banks as well as foreign banks recorded higher efficiency than large banks in all the sample countries. The study led to conclude that further mergers among large CBs can harm the efficiency of banking system as optimal size of the banks seems to be not more than US $1000 thousands.

Shanmugam and Das (2004) fitted SFA to measure technical efficiency of various ownership categories of commercial banks in India for the period 1992-99. They incorporated labor, capital, deposits and borrowings as inputs to produce loans, investments, interest-margin and non-interest income as per intermediation approach. The results provided the evidence of larger gaps between the actual and potential performance of banks due to technical inefficiency. The efficiency of raising interest margin was estimated to be time-invariant while efficiencies of raising other outputs like non-interest income, investments and credits were noticed to be time-variant. Indian banking industry displayed considerable progress in terms of efficiency of raising non-interest income, investments and credits but failed to raise interest margin since 1992. SBI group and foreign banks were observed to be more efficient as compared to their counterparts. The reform period indicated a relatively high efficient period for augmenting investments especially in private sector.

Das, Nag and Ray (2005) employed data envelopment analysis to examine efficiency of commercial banks in India for the period 1997-03. A production function technology of four inputs viz., borrowed funds, number of employees, fixed assets and equity and three outputs viz., investments, performing loan assets and non-interest fee-based incomes has been specified. The results reported that gradual liberalization in 1990s has strengthened and improved the level of operational efficiency of the financial system. Indian banks were not found to be much differentiated in terms of input-oriented or output-oriented technical efficiency and cost efficiency, which may be due to the fact that the input and output prices are yet to be determined by the free play of market forces of demand and supply. In contrast, banks were observed to be sharply differentiated in terms of revenue efficiency and profit efficiency. Bank size, ownership and the fact of being listed on stock exchange were some of the factors, which had a positive impact on average profit efficiency and to some extent on revenue efficiency scores after 1999-00. Finally, the study reported that median efficiency scores of Indian banks in general and of bigger banks in particular has improved considerably during the post-reform period. Thus, it can be concluded that liberalization has imparted positive impact on the performance of Indian banking sector.

Fries and Taci (2005) adopted SFA to examine cost efficiency of 289 banks in 15 East European countries for the period 1994-01. They incorporated labor and capital as inputs variables to produce loans and deposits. An average-sized bank in the sample was found to be operated at a point that is close to constant returns to scale (CRS). Small banks were observed to be operated with significant unrealized economies of scale. This suggested that consolidation of small banks would enhance the level of cost efficiency in banking. The cost efficiency scores recorded substantial increase in initial stage of reforms, which started to decline in advanced stage of reforms. The non-linear relationship among cost efficiency estimates and reforms reflected the transition from defensive restructuring to deeper restructuring (i.e. from cost cutting to innovations), which increases the quality and value added of the banking services. Private sector banks performed better with average cost efficiency measure of (75 percent) than that of state owned banks (53 percent). However, significant variations have been noticed among the average efficiency scores of private sector banks. Privatized banks with majority of foreign ownership were found to be more cost efficient, followed by newly established domestic as well as foreign owned private banks. Privatized banks with majority of domestic ownership were observed to be least cost efficient but still better than state owned banks.

Singh and Kumar (2005) employed data envelopment analysis to efficiency of various categories of banks in India for the year 2002-03. They considered deposits and operating costs as input and loans, investments and other income as output variables. They also estimated stochastic coefficient production approach by taking spread as the function of deposits, borrowings and labor as input variables. The empirical findings reported deposits as the major determinant of spread with input value of (0.59214) followed by borrowing (0.14982) and labor (0.10951). The mean TE measure worked out to be (99.65 percent) for deposits, (87.48 percent) for borrowings and (68.45 percent) for staff. Therefore, all the banks have been observed with efficient use of deposits but not the borrowings and staff as for input use efficiency. SBI and its associates were found to be relatively more efficient with regard to borrowing and staff use followed by nationalized banks and foreign banks. The average input use efficiency of borrowings and staff worked out to be lowest in private banks. As per DEA efficiency estimates, foreign banks emerged to be most economically efficient banks as compared to its counterparts. The average efficiency of PSBs (0.63) has noticed to be much higher than private sector banks (0.40) but lower than foreign banks (0.71). The same observation has been also noted to be true in technical efficiency and allocative efficiency estimates. Finally, the results suggested that banks should go for a system-wide analysis to performance evaluation of banking in general and efficiency evaluation in particular, which can provide long-term sustainable solutions and policy implications.

Sanjeev, Gunjan M. (2006) adopted DEA to evaluate the technical efficiency of public, private and foreign banks operating in India for the period 1997-01. The inputs used in the study are interest expenses and non-interest expenses while interest income and non-interest income have been taken as outputs. The empirical findings indicated that the efficiency of CBs has improved during the study period. Foreign banks appeared to be top most performers with average technical efficiency measure of (64 percent). On the other hand, public sector banks were found to be least efficient banks with technical efficiency measure of (31 percent). The decline in the dispersion of TE scores indicated that banks have become more competitive in response to liberalization and deregulation. The highest level of standard deviations in technical efficiency scores has been observed by foreign banks (0.22) however, the lowest by private banks (0.05). The empirical findings further provided the evidence of negative relationship between non-performing assets (NPAs) and technical efficiency scores in Indian banking industry. Thus, the results suggested loan managers to sharpen their skills in order to improve loan quality. Finally, the study concludes that the banks have responded positively to the reform measures.

SECTION II

Hunter and Timme (1991) fitted Translog function to study the impact of technological change on the size of firm, efficient scale of output and product mix of large U.S commercial banks for the period 1980-86. They used total loans and produced deposits as output and labor, capital and funds as input variables. Overall, the sample banks experienced significant technological change over the study period. The sample banks experienced (–0.96) percent level of TE change and indicated reduction in costs by approximately (1 percent) per year due to innovation. Larger banks experienced more technical change and rapid proportionate reduction in real costs than smaller banks. The banks within the assets range of (0.75$ billion to 5$ billion) reported significant scale of output to become cost efficient. Contrarily, the banks within the assets range of (10$ billion to 25$ billion) provided the evidence of slight diseconomies of scale. Technical change was found to be responsible factor for efficient scale size. The empirical findings violated the Galbraith–Schumpeter hypothesis (GSSB) as larger banks could not innovate at a faster rate than the smaller banks. Therefore, the empirical findings suggested that these banks couldn't use innovation alone to outpace smaller banks in the long-run. Further, technological change was observed to be biased with regard to scale and product mix. Finally, the empirical findings suggested somewhat more concentrate banking structure for significantly lower costs.

Berg, Forsund and Jansen (1992) studied the impact of deregulation on the productivity growth of Norwegian banks for the period 1980-89. They employed Malmquist Index by incorporating labor and materials as input and short-term loans, long-term loans and produced deposits as output variables. The results displayed considerable variations among average and best practice productivity growth rates. Overall, the empirical findings reported little productivity growth at the frontier. However, there was substantial improvement in the relative efficiency of banks during the study period. The results also reported that productivity level of banks has become more equal which indicates that deregulation may have created a more competitive industry. The productivity growth was noted to be rapid in largest banks, which may be attributed to the utilization of excess capacity to some extent, increased domestic competition resulting from deregulation and their effort to become competitive internationally. The regress in total productivity prior to deregulation period may be ascribed to the building up of idle capacity in the advent of deregulation. The productivity growth registered slight decline on the inclusion of loan loss variable in output list. This decrease in total growth has been observed due to the negative frontier growth and poor catching up effect. Overall, the findings reported striking impact of deregulation on the productivity growth of Norwegian banks.

Bhattacharyya, Bhattacharyya and Kumbhkar (1997) fitted Translog model to examine productivity growth on panel data set of PSBs in India for the period 1970 to 1992. They incorporated labor and physical capital as inputs; loans, branches and deposits as outputs and the sum of paid up capital and reserve capital as quasi-fixed factor. They estimated two intermediate models, one with only autocorrelation correction Model A and other with heteroskedasticity correction Model B. The average annual TFP growth rate of PSBs was estimated to be 1.81 percent as per Model A and 2.05 percent as per Model B. Model B not only exhibited higher rate of TFP growth, but also significantly lower rate of scale-related growth as compared to Model A. As per Model B, productivity growth was observed to be declined in initial years of nationalization and it was until 1975 that the overall productivity index showed an upward trend. The system regained its base 1970 level of productivity only after 1977. In addition, the effect of technological change was observed to be unfavorable during the first few years. This downward trend reversed after 1973, technology attained its base 1970 level only after 1975. The results suggest that it took the CBs a few years to absorb the shock of nationalization. But after getting over this initial shock, technology started improving at a constant pace more or less. A positive estimate of scale efficiency index provided the evidence of TFP growth augmented by output expansion. Finally, the study concluded that deregulation or economic liberalization is likely to boost the level of productivity growth and technological progress.

Grifell-Tatze and Lovell (1997) studied the impact of deregulation on productivity change of saving and commercial banks in Spain for the period 1986-93. DEA-based Malmquist index has been applied on two input and three output variables to accomplish the objective. The results provided the evidence of productivity growth rates in excess of 2 percent per year within each sector. The sample banks experienced productivity growth due to the improvement in the performance of best practice ones in each sector and decline in the dispersion of productivity measures of remaining saving banks. The dispersion in managerial inefficiency was found to be more serious in commercial banks as compared to saving banks sector. The empirical findings reported that scale economies have made a minor contribution to the productivity growth. However, it affected the productivity growth of very large and small banks of each type (both saving banks and commercial banks). The superior productivity performance of saving banks sector over the CBs sector may be attributed to the expansion of several large CBs operating in the region of diminishing returns to scale (DRS). The results reported highest rate of productivity growth in case of those saving banks and CBs that succeeded in reducing their operating expenses, whether or not they shed labor. Banks, which increased their operating expenses, experienced no productivity growth. The isolation of managerial inefficiency from the existed institutional efficiency reported saving banks as the more efficient form of organizational structure.

However, the elimination of managerial inefficiency narrowed down the level of institutional efficiency differentials during the study period. The results reported, on an average, less than (1 percent) per annum rate of potential productivity growth. The potential productivity growth (out of managerial efficiency) was noted to be much slower than actual productivity growth. Therefore, most of the measured productivity growth was found to be associated with managerial efficiency component of generalized Malmquist productivity indices.

Altanbus Goddard and Molyneux (1999) conducted a study to analyze the impact of technical change on the costs of 15 national banking markets in Europe. They applied stochastic cost function based on fourier flexible functional form, in which total costs depend upon the input prices of labor, loanable funds and physical capital. The outputs they considered are loans, securities and off balance sheet business. To view this, they considered sample set of 3779 observations for the period 1989-96. The empirical findings provided the evidence of reduction in total costs on account of technological progress, which accelerated to 3.6 percent by the year 1996 contrary to 2.8 percent in the year 1989. The pure and scale augmenting components of technological change emerged to be the dominant components for the reduction in costs. Besides this, smaller banks were found to be highly engaged in off balance sheet business during early to mid 1990s, which was predominantly undertaken by largest banks at the start of the study period. Thus, the results reported reduction in the efficient scale of operation for off balance sheet business. As for input cost shares, the results indicated fall in its coefficient due to the downward trend of European national interest rates during early 1990s. The fall in the interest cost share coefficient matched with a corresponding increase in the share of labor cost. Thus, labor cost savings failed to make a major contribution to the overall cost savings. Large banks were found to get more benefits from cost savings in lieu of effective adoption of new technology as compared to smaller counterparts.

Mendas and Rebelo (1999) conducted a study to examine efficiency, technological change and productivity of Portuguese banks for the period 1990-95. Translog variable cost function and a stochastic frontier model have been applied using deposits and loans as output and deposit, labor and other materials as input variables. The average inefficiency of Portuguese banks worked out to be 0.057 for the study period. This suggested that banks could save 5.7 percent of variable costs to capture the position on best practice frontier. Despite intense competition, the sample banks did not reveal better performance over the last few years. Larger banks (having net assets more than 1000 million cantos) were found to be more efficient relative to average sized banks (more than 100 million and less than 300 million cantos). Cost efficiency and scale economies did not seem to be correlated with size. The optimal size of banks was noticed to be somewhere in the asset range of 50-100 million cantos. As for technological progress, the empirical findings provided the evidence of technological regress among sample banks over the study period. The average annual real growth rate of costs was estimated to be (6 percent) due to technological recess. Moreover, technological progress/regress did not seem to be related with the size of banks. Further, the investment in new technology and diversification of products did not register positive influence on cost reductions.

Drake (2001) applied non-parametric, DEA technique on panel data set of nine U.K. banks for the period 1984-95 to estimate relative efficiencies and productivity change. He adopted two DEA models and considered inputs viz., fixed assets, labor and deposits and outputs viz., loans, other income, liquid assets+investments as per Model A. As per Model B, he considered fixed assets and number of employees as input and loans, other income, deposits and liquid assets + investments as output variables. The results provided the evidence of increasing returns to scale for smaller banks but strong evidence of diminishing returns to scale for big four UK banks during the study period. The alternative use of input and output specification produced somewhat different results of scale efficiency estimates. The minimum efficient scale of operation in UK banking was most probably estimated to be in real asset range of 18.5 dollar billion to 25 dollar billion. It has been also observed that scale inefficiencies are more severe problems in UK banking than x-inefficiencies (pure technical inefficiency). Besides this, large banks were found to be more pure technical efficient than their smaller counterparts especially in later years of study period. The DEA based MPI suggests that UK banking as a whole experienced productivity growth over the study period driven exclusively by positive frontier shifts rather than negative catch up effect. The productivity estimates obtained as per Model 2 (PA) were noted to be considerably higher than those based upon Model 1(IA). Further, most of the sample banks realized productivity gains on account of negative catch up effect but positive frontier effect. Much of the frontier shifts may be attributed to various efforts undertaken in the elimination of excess capacity in the face of intensified competition in UK financial services.

Kumbhakar, Vivas, Lovell and Hasan (2001) examined the impact of deregulation on the performance of Spanish saving banks for deregulatory period (1986-90) and post-deregulatory period (1991-95). They employed flexible variable profit function on three inputs, two outputs and two quasi input variables towards this objective. The time varying output technical inefficiency models reported deterioration in technical efficiency over the study period. The overall mean technical inefficiency and profit technical inefficiency was estimated to be varying from 19.79 to 20.76 percent and from 25.28 to 30.91 percent respectively over the study period. All the models provided the evidence of technological progress. The overall mean technical progress was noticed to be within the range of 4.31 percent to 5.86 percent during these periods. The positive productivity growth of Spanish saving banks occurred more due to technical change and profit technical efficiency change. The period-wise analysis substantiated that Spanish saving banks have experienced slightly higher productivity growth at the rate of (1.90 percent) per annum in post-deregulation period than deregulation period (1.15 percent) per annum. Finally, the results led to conclude that competition and deregulation have prompted the banking institutions into a more competitive industry.

Das (2002) conducted a study to explore the relationship among risk, capital and productivity growth of PSBs in India for the period 1995-96 to 2000-01. A production function technology of four inputs viz., deposits, borrowings, fixed assets and contingencies and provisions and two outputs viz., bank credit and investment has been specified. The results provided that higher productivity leads to decrease in credit risk and it has positive impact on bank capitalization. This supported the fact that poor performers are more prone to risk taking than better-performing banking institutions. The results also highlighted positive effect of productivity on capital, which can be attributed to regulatory pressure, especially for the banks, which fall short of the prescribed minimum capital adequacy standards. Further, it has been observed that higher capital leads to a rise in productivity of medium-sized banks. For the large and small banks in particular, higher loan growth translated into lower productivity levels. Small-sized banks experienced improvement in productivity growth on account of investment in risk free bonds, less priority sector lending and increased government shareholding. The empirical findings suggested larger banks to have limited government shareholding to improve productivity levels.

Dogan and Fausten (2002) constructed DEA-based Malmquist index to measure productivity growth and technical change of Malaysian banking sector. The sample period, they considered, is 1989-98, divided into two sub-periods of 1989-93 and 1994-98. To view this objective, interest expenses and personnel expenses have been used as inputs to produce investments, loans and deposits as outputs. The results revealed considerable variability in average efficiency and relative performance of least efficient banks for the entire study period. However, no sustained and stable year-to-year trend is discernable during the entire study period, but the point observations for the initial year and terminal years of the study period reported long-term improvement in average efficiency. All the sample banks experienced decline in mean productivity by (3.3 percent) due to technical change (-4.4 percent), change in pure technical efficiency (0.9 percent) and change in scale efficiency (0.3 percent) during first sub-period. The decline in mean productivity due to the technological regress was moderated later due to improvement in technical efficiency and scale efficiency. The empirical findings reported an erosion in mean productivity by (5.6 percent) on account of technological change (-6.0 percent) somewhat counterbalanced by pure technical efficiency increases (0.3 percent) in second sub-period. Scale efficiency did not seem to contribute anything to the changes in mean productivity during this sub-period.

Carbo, Gardner and Williams (2003) used fourier flexible cost function approach to estimate technical change for a large sample of European saving banks between 1989 and 1997. A production function technology of three inputs viz., labor, funds and physical capital and three outputs viz., loans, investments and off balance sheet activities has been conceptualized. The results reported that on an average, technical progress has reduced the total cost of European banks by (3.4 percent) per annum while pure TE change reduced the total cost at a diminishing rate from 2.04 percent in 1989 to 1.52 percent in 1997. Therefore, technical progress played a key role in reducing the total cost of large saving banks due to its greater influence on input prices. However, technological arrangements did not uniformly reduce total cost of all the sample banks. Large saving banks showed more efficiency in altering their input mix in response to change in technology. Thus, large banks emerged to be market leader however, small banks to be market borrowers. Finally, the study concluded that large banks have gained more from technological progress, which may be a dominant factor for promoting consolidation in European banking system.

Kumbhakar and Sarkar (2003) analyzed the relationship between deregulation and total factor productivity (TFP) growth of PSBs in India over the period 1985-96. They defined bank inputs in terms of labor, capital and equity and outputs in terms of loans, deposits and branches. They used generalized shadow cost function and tested whether regulation has led to distortions in input uses of Indian banking and whether such distortions have declined overtime. The results indicated the presence of significant distortion in input uses of PSBs under the impact of regulation. Further, it resulted in over employment of labor relative to capital throughout the study period. The results noted that magnitude of distortion has declined at marginal rate over the sample years. Thus, the empirical findings provided the evidence of lower productivity levels in PSBs as compared to private banks. The results also reported that private sector banks have improved their performance over the PSBs due to the freedom to expand output while public sector banks did not seem to respond well to deregulation measures. Overall, the results indicated the presence of weak ownership effect on the performance of Indian banking sector.

Galagedra and Edirisuriya (2004) employed DEA-based Malmquist productivity index to investigate efficiency and total factor productivity growth of commercial banks in India over the period 1995-02. Using total deposits and operating expenses as input variables and other earning assets as output variables, no significant growth in productivity (0.6 percent) has been registered. The rate of increase in productivity growth though small was due to technical efficiency, which may be further attributed to scale efficiency (1.6 percent) than that of managerial efficiency (0.1 percent). They also found that there has been no growth in productivity of private sector banks whereas public sector banks witnessed a modest positive productivity change through the study period 1995-02. The results also highlighted that Indian banking industry is progressing towards the competitive industry as compared to pre-deregulation period. However, the pace of progress did not seem to be satisfactory. The study also illustrated that changes in the national and international market environments and the introduction of new technologies have forced authorities to relax controls over the Indian banking industry to make it more competitive and efficient. Finally, the study suggested that deregulation and more competition should be allowed within the banking sector to make it more efficient and productive.

Margano (2004) conducted a study to estimate cost efficiency, scale economies, technological progress and productivity growth of banks in Indonesia. He considered the sample set of 28 state and local government banks, 28 joint venture/foreign banks and 78 private national banks. To view this, he applied flexible fourier form of cost function for three inputs viz., labor, funds and capital and two outputs viz., aggregate loans and securities. The average efficiency of Indonesian banking sector worked out to be 79.68 percent for pre-Asian crisis period (1993-97) and it declined to 53.4 percent in post-Asian crisis period (1998-00). The empirical findings reported an increase in cost efficiency only by 1.26 percent per annum from 1998 to 2000 as compared to 6.33 percent from 1993 to 1997. The ownership-wise analysis reported that joint venture/foreign banks and private banks are more cost efficient than PSBs in both the periods. The level of average scale economies increased to 0.90574 in post-crisis period contrary to 0.83535 in pre-crisis period. The empirical findings provided the evidence of scale economies in public and private banks but diseconomies of scale in joint venture/foreign banks. Besides this, small banks having assets less than 500 billion rupiah provided the evidence of scale economies in both the pre-crisis and post-crisis period. The empirical findings also reported that on average, Indonesian banks have benefited from technological progress and reduced the average cost by 2.98 percent in pre-crisis period. However, technological progress raised the average cost by 6.4 percent in post Asian-crisis period. The empirical findings reported the existence of technical progress for all sized class banks in pre-crisis period but the converse was found to be true in post-crisis period. Further, the results reported that average TFP growth of banks has declined by 1.5 percent in pre-Asian crisis period and by 6.4 percent in post-crisis period. The worse position of Indonesian banking sector in post Asian-crisis period was observed due to the poor performance of joint venture/foreign banks. This may be attributed to the fact that joint venture/foreign banks have less information on the quality of borrowers. Besides this, smaller banks displayed better performance in terms of productivity growth than that of largest banks. Overall, sample banks were found to be less productive in post-crisis period except in case of those banks having assets more than 999.9 billion rupiah.

Mohan and Ray (2004) conducted a study to measure and compare the productivity growth of PSBs relative to old private and foreign banks in India for the period 1992-00. They applied Tornquist and DEA based malmquist productivity index using interest and operating costs as input and loans, investments and non-interest income as output variables as per Model A. Tornquist TFP growth has been computed using deposit and operating cost as input variables with same set of output variables that of Model A. According to the empirical findings, foreign banks performed well with technical efficiency measure of (0.9403), followed by PSBs (0.8787) and private sector banks (0.6473). The productivity estimates delineated that foreign banks tend to operate at (-3.07 percent) average growth rate relative to PSBs (0.77 percent) and private banks (0.49 percent) as per Tornquist index applied on Model A. As per Model B, private banks experienced productivity growth at the rate of (0.72 percent) followed by foreign banks (-0.11 percent) and PSBs (-0.58 percent). Total factor productivity growth turned out to be low with the use of loans and investments as output variables. As per Malmquist index, foreign banks recorded total factor productivity growth at the rate of (9.22 percent) per annum followed by PSBs (0.80 percent) and private banks (-1.76 percent) per annum. Further, the results provided that TE change has imparted most favorable influence on foreign banks i.e. at the rate of (0.331 percent), marginal decline in case of PSBs (-0.075 percent) and significant decline in private banks (-3.416 percent). Overall, PSBs experienced highest total factor productivity growth as per Tornquist index but lowest growth as per Malmquist index approach as compared to its counterparts. Finally, the study justified the privatization of PSBs on account of considerable performance gaps among various categories of banks.

Zhao, Casu and Ferrari (2007) employed DEA-based Malmquist productivity index to study the impact of deregulation on the total factor productivity growth of commercial banks in India. The study is based upon the panel data set of 27 PSBs, 20 domestic private and 18 foreign banks for the period 1992-04. They proxied inputs in terms of total operating costs and outputs in terms of performing loans, other earning assets and fee-based income as per Model A. In Model B, same set of input and output variables has been incorporated that of Model A, except the variable total loans has been replaced with performing loans to investigate the risk taking behavior of market participants. The average overall efficiency of Indian banking industry worked out to be (78 percent) for the entire study period, which suggested that banks can go for average reduction in input usages by (22 percent) through best practices to become fully efficient. The magnitude of input waste was estimated to be significantly lower in second sub-period (1998-04) as compared to first sub-period (1992-97). Foreign banks displayed excellent performance with overall efficiency measure of (81 percent) followed by PSBs (78 percent) and private banks (75 percent) for the entire study period. The period-wise analysis highlighted that foreign banks have achieved highest level of TE (82 percent), followed by PSBs (71 percent) and private banks (71 percent) during the first sub-period. The same observation did not find to be true in second sub-period where PSBs emerged to be top most performers with technical efficiency measure of (84 percent) followed by foreign banks (80 percent) and private banks (78 percent). The substantial amount of technical inefficiency in Indian banking industry has been observed due to scale-related problems rather than pure technical inefficiency. PSBs and private banks showed more serious scale-related problems as compared to foreign banks. As far as productivity is concerned, Indian banking industry registered an average annual TFP growth rate of 5.1 percent over the entire study period, attributed more to technological progress (4.3 percent) rather than an improvement in technical efficiency (0.8 percent). All sample banks witnessed substantial increase in the TFP growth rate of (8.7 percent) in second sub-period as against (0.2 percent) in first sub-period. The TFP growth and growth of its indices reported positive upshot of reforms especially in second sub-period. The findings also provided that various ownership groups have experienced productivity gain either due to positive catching up effect or positive frontier effect. Furthermore, most of the foreign banks emerged to technological innovators, which highlight their important role in the introduction of new technology in Indian banking industry. Finally, the empirical findings suggested an urgent need of professional risk management under the new operational environment.

Rezvanian, Rao and Mehdian (2008) employed DEA-based MPI to estimate efficiency change, technological change and productivity growth of 20 PSBs, 19 private banks and 16 foreign banks operating in India. In view of this, they considered advances, securities and other earning assets as output variables and borrowed funds, labor and fixed assets as input variables for the period 1998-03. A substantial amount of overall efficiency has been observed due to allocative efficiency rather than technical efficiency. Foreign banks reported highest level of overall efficiency to the tune of (65 percent), followed by private banks (39 percent) and PSBs (36 percent). The estimated inefficiencies of private sector banks (61 percent) and PSBs (64 percent) have been observed both due to input over utilization and input mix sub-optimization. The analysis of sources of overall efficiency demonstrated that foreign banks have achieved highest level of TE (80.9 percent), followed by PSBs (58.6 percent) and private sector banks (55 percent). On the other hand, average allocative efficiency has noted to be (80.6 percent) for foreign banks, followed by private banks (73.6 percent) and PSBs (64.3 percent). Thus, the results highlighted technical inefficiency as the main cause of overall inefficiency among both the PSBs and private sector banks. Further, scale related problems were found to the major source of technical inefficiency existing among PSBs and foreign banks than managerial incapabilities. However, the opposite was noted to be true for private sector banks. As for returns to scale, most of the sample banks were found to be operating below their optimal level. The results suggested that these banks can improve their cost efficiency by expanding their size of operation. Besides this, all the sample banks experienced an improvement in productivity growth. However, an improvement in productivity growth of foreign banks was estimated to be significantly higher than those of private banks and public banks. Foreign banks experienced total factor productivity growth on account of an improvement in TE as well as technological progress. Contrarily, PSBs and private banks observed productivity growth exclusively due to technological progress rather than improvement in technical efficiency. Finally, the results suggested that Indian Government should encourage Indian banking industry to enhance its performance and efficiency by setting out the policies to support entry and presence of foreign banks and to encourage mergers and acquisitions among the banks in India.

Concluding Remarks: A review of the studies on the efficiency and productivity growth of banking sector demonstrates that the results of efficiency and productivity growth may differ due to the difference in choice of techniques, different set of input and output variables, measurement of those variables, types of data and number of other factors about the applied techniques. As far as techniques of measurement are concerned, parametric and non-parametric approaches have been widely applied in literature. It has been observed that the results may differ significantly between parametric and non-parametric approach mainly due to the intrinsic features of these models. The application of non-parametric approach (DEA methodology) will lead to results that are more effective over the parametric approach (SFA methodology) due to the advantages of DEA as the performance evaluation criteria compared to parametric approach.

3

Methodology for Analysis

In this chapter, some very essential and important theoretical underpinnings of efficiency and productivity growth have been discussed, upon which the empirical findings of the study depend. To present the discussion in a systematic manner, this chapter has been divided into five distinct sections. Section I explains the composition of sample data and specifications of input and output variables used in banks to measure efficiency and productivity growth. Section II briefly discusses the techniques impaired for the measurement of efficiency and justifies the methodology selected for the present study. Section III elaborates the theoretical exposition and methodological framework of different models applied to analyze various measures of efficiency among commercial banks (CBs) in India. Section IV concentrates on the theoretical framework of TFP growth with a brief discussion on the techniques adopted for measuring productivity change in general. Section V sheds light on the development of Malmquist productivity index (MPI) employed to measure total factor productivity growth of commercial banks in India in the present study.

SECTION I

3.1.1 Data Base

The study has considered the sample period spanning form 1985 to 2005-06 to ascertain efficiency and productivity growth of commercial banks in India. The entire study period has been divided into three distinct sub-periods: (i) Pre-liberalization period (1985 to 1991-92), (ii) Initial post-liberalization period (1992-93 to 1998-99), and (iii) Post-liberalization period (1999-00 to 2005-06). The analysis of pre-liberalization and post-liberalization period is justifiable on the ground that it assists us to ascertain the impact of liberalization on the efficiency and productivity growth of banks. To keep in lines with Howcroft and Attaullah (2006) and Zhao *et. al.* (2008), post-liberalization period has been bifurcated into initial post-liberalization period or first-generation reforms and post-liberalization period or second-generation reforms period. This attempt helps us to analyze the changes in the behavior of productivity growth of banks with the change in the degree of deregulation.

The data for 1985, 1986 and 1987 covers the period from January 1 through December 31, according to calendar year basis. The data for the year 1988-89 consists of 15 months from the period January 1, 1988 through March 31, 1989 due to the change in fiscal year. Thus, following Bhattacharyya *et. al.* (1997), data for the year 1988-89 has been divided by 1.25 to convert it on 12 months basis. The data for rest of the sample years covers data on financial year basis, i.e., starting from 1st April of current year to 31st March of next (successive) year. The sample period selected is constrained to the availability of data on input and output variables considered in the present study.

The present study is based upon secondary data and requisite data have been culled out from following sources:

Indian Banks Association's Publications

- IBA Bulletins;

- Performance Highlights of Banks, and
- Financial Analysis of Banks (Volume I and II)

Reserve Bank of India's Publications

- Statistical Tables Relating to Banks in India;
- Annual Accounts of Banks;
- Report on Trend and Progress in Banking;
- Profile of Banks;
- RBI Bulletins; and
- Report on Currency and Finance.

These reports provide us the information regarding the assets and liabilities and earnings and expenses of banks on individual as well as group basis. Basically, Balance Sheet and Profit and Loss account compiled by Indian Banks Association constitute the main source of data for the present study. Moreover, National Income Statistics published by Center for Monitoring Indian Economy (CMIE) has been used for calculating GDP price deflator. Consumer Price Index (CPI) for Urban Non-Manual Employees has been taken from 'Brochure on Group and Sub-Group CPI Number', published by Central Statistical Organization, Ministry of Statistics and Programme Implementation, Government of India, New Delhi.

3.1.2 Sample Banks

There are more than 217 commercial banks operating in India including RRBs. Not all the commercial banks can be included for analytical purpose due to the lack of comparable data in published form. Thus, this study has considered balanced panel data set of 19 nationalised banks (NBs), State Bank of India (SBI) and its 7 subsidiaries and 18 old private sector banks to make a homogenous group of banks. Only those banks have been considered in the present study, which have been continuously operating since 1985 to 2005-06.

New private sector banks (came into operation in 1995-96) have been dropped from the analysis because inclusion of these banks results to have unbalanced data set. As far as foreign banks are concerned, before executing the study, it was suspected that most of these banks might be outliers. As per Avkiran's (2006) rule of thumb, if any DMU yields super efficiency score greater than two, considered to be clear outlier. To detect whether the banks are outliers or not, Andersen and Petersen's DEA super efficiency model (1993) was employed, which provided efficiency score greater than two for most of the foreign banks. These banks emerged to be clear outliers, on account of which, foreign banking segment has been excluded from the empirical analysis. Therefore, this study is confined only to PSBs and old private sector banks in India.

3.1.3 Input and Output Specification

> *"The concept of an economic activity as an input and output process is perhaps the most basic concept of economics. Nevertheless, it is vague and curious difficulties emerge when an effort is made to specify the inputs and outputs involved, and to define the nature of transformation implied (Boulding, 1961)".*

The specification of input and output variables is an important and crucial issue to be resolved in banking. Despite substantial literature on this issue, still, there has been a controversy regarding the input-output status of the variables in banking. The disagreement over the appropriate definition of bank output can be attributed essentially to the multi-product nature of banks. According to Sealey and Lindley (1977), the failure to carefully analyze the technical and economic aspects of production at financial institutions generates the lack of agreement concerning the appropriate measures of outputs and inputs for the financial firm.

Fixler and Zieschang (1991) attributed the controversial nature of the discussion on measuring bank output to long held differences in how interest is viewed. Some prefer to view interest as transfer payment from borrower to lender for foregone consumption, while other views interest a payment to depositor (payment on deposits, record-keeping and safe-keeping) and to the borrower (funding and credit rating).

The controversial nature of the discussion on measuring bank output and input status of variables may be attributed to two different types of bank revenues: net interest (the difference between interest calculated on loans and interest payments made to deposits) and explicit service charges. Net interest consists of the revenue from implicit service charges but is insufficient to cover non-interest costs of operations (wages, rent, etc.). This means that some of services provided by banks are paid for by interest income rather than explicit service charges. On this view, it is easier to accept that banks use net interest income partly to pay for services that are not explicitly charged to customers.

Long lasting debate also surrounds around the input and output status of deposits. Berg *et. al.* (1991) argued to consider deposit as output because they act as a resource consuming activity but Berger *et. al.* (1993) considered deposits as input that take interest paid on purchased funds into consideration. Extending this argument further, it has been proposed that classification of deposits should be relied upon the structure and characteristics of banks in the representative sample.

Thus, in banking literature, measurement of inputs and outputs remains a prominent and controversial issue. Although, a variety of approaches has been followed. Mester (1987) highlighted two approaches (production and intermediation), which are most commonly used in banking literature. First, the production approach views banks as the producer of deposits and loans with the use of labor and physical capital. The deposits and various categories of assets are defined in terms of number of accounts. This approach takes into account only the operating cost; however, interest cost does not form the part of total cost. Sherman and Gold (1985) viewed financial institutions as producer of loan and deposit accounts and defining outputs as number of such accounts and transactions. Benston (1965) incorporated number of accounts of loans and securities instead of dollar value of these accounts; he argued that bank operations, and hence costs, is closely related to the number of accounts, they possess.

Although, production approach has been widely used in various studies related to banks' performance (Berger *et. al.*

1987 and Berger and Humphrey, 1997 etc.) but this approach is not free from some limitations. Firstly, the major problem associated with this approach is that it fails to capture key role of financial intermediation played by banks. Secondly, this approach ignores interest cost from the total costs, which generally accounts for a major proportion of one half to two-third of the total cost.

Intermediation Approach (IA) originally developed by Sealey and Lindley (1977) stems from the activity of direct intermediation between two parties that mobilize financial assets from surplus to deficit units. Banks are considered as the intermediators of financial services rather than the producers of loan and deposit accounts. Sealey and Lindley (1977) considers loans and other assets as bank output, as they generate bulk of the direct revenue that bank earn; deposit and other liabilities as inputs to the intermediation process because they provide the raw material of investible funds. Hence, under this approach, dollar value of loans, investment and other earning assets are proxied in terms of outputs and labor, capital and deposits are proxied in terms of inputs. Under IA, both the interest cost and production (operating) cost form the part of total cost. This approach has been found to be more appropriate for financial institutions as it includes interest expenses, which often accounts for one half to two-third of the total cost. Most of the researchers have followed this approach in their studies related to banks' performance such as Barr *et. al.*, (1994); Sathye, (2001) and Kumar and Verma, (2002-03) etc.

Although IA has been extensively used in studies related to banking, the major downside of this approach is that banks provide substantial services to depositors, which are not treated as output in this approach. Another criticism of this approach is that its grouping of inputs and outputs is arbitrary—the choices made by some researchers are disputed by others, and the approach admits no mechanisms for resolving such debates (Triplett: Comments on Berger and Humphrey (1992)). Thus, disagreement among researchers remains over the measurement of output of a bank.

A variant of the intermediation approach is so called asset approach, which focuses on recent developments in the theory of intermediation. This approach uses labor, capital, deposits and other liabilities as inputs. Outputs are strictly defined by assets and mainly by the production of loans. Elyasiani and Mehdian (1990) and English *et. al.* (1993) used asset approach for defining input and output variables in banking.

The user cost approach (UCA) considers net revenue generated by a financial asset to determine whether the financial product is an input and output. If the financial return of an asset exceeds the opportunity cost of the funds, the instrument is considered to be output and if the opposite is true, then instrument is recognized as input. But the downside of the approach is that returns depend upon pricing and market conditions for that financial product. This would imply that during an economic upturn and downturn, an instrument might turn into input in next period which was considered as output in existing period and *vice versa*. This approach is less frequently used on account of less reliability of prices and available revenues.

Under value added approach, the items in the balance sheet with a substantial share of value added are treated as outputs while the others are treated as either inputs or intermediated products. This approach considers both the deposits and loans as output variables. This approach takes into account operating costs implicitly rather than determining the costs explicitly. This approach has been widely used by Berger *et. al.* (1987) and Berger and Humphrey (1997), etc.

There are different opinions among the authors regarding the choice of input and output status of variables used in banking. Despite voluminous literature on this specific issue, no coherent definitional and empirical aspect of this issue has been explored. There is long lasting debate on this controversial issue, which is going on.

3.1.4 Specification of Variables for Present Study

3.1.4.1 Measurement of Inputs

Berger and Humphrey (1997) suggest that the intermediation approach is best suited for analyzing bank level efficiency, whereas the production approach is well suited for measuring branch level efficiency. This is because, at the bank level, management will aim to reduce total costs and not just the non-interest expenses, while at the branch level, a large number of customer service processing take place and bank funding and investment decisions àre mostly not under the control of branches. Therefore, following Berger and Humphrey (1997), the most commonly used IA has been selected for the present study.

Following intermediation approach, the input parameters are defined in terms of Labor (X_1) and Loanable Fund (X_2) to keep in lines with Das (1997), Hasan and Marton (2003) and Sathye (2003), etc. The number of full time personnel has been considered as a measure of labor input. The other input parameter loanable fund (purchased fund) includes the rupee value of both the deposits and borrowings at the end of the financial year.

3.1.4.2 Measurement of Outputs

For the present study, two measures of output have been considered, which are particularly applicable in Indian banking industry. After the financial liberalization, the banks are paying key attention to raise the level of non-interest income. As noted by Rogers (1998) some measures of non-traditional activities of banks must be included in assessing efficiency as his findings show that banks' efficiency measures differ significantly when estimated by using models with or without non-traditional outputs. Therefore, the output variable has been defined in terms of non-interest income (measured as the difference between total income and interest income) for a given period. It reflects the income received by banks from commission, exchange, fees and brokerage plus other receipts. This measure also shows output for the recent services provided by the banks to customers. The other output variable is defined in terms of spread (measured as the difference between interest earned and interest expanded) for a given period. This variable accounts for net income received by the banks from their traditional activities—advancement of loans and investment in government and other approved securities. This measure reflects output for the key role of financial intermediation, performed by the banks. Both the outputs have been measured in terms of rupee crores. Most of the studies in Indian banking industry viz., Das (1997), Das (2000) and Kumar and Verma (2002-03) have followed this measure of output. The choice of output variables is consistent to the objective of economic growth being pursued by Indian banking industry. The detailed specification of input and output variables has been shown in Table 3.1.

In present study context, GDP price deflator (Banking and Insurance) has been used to deflate two outputs viz., spread and other income and loanable fund input. In addition, the expenditure incurred on employees has been deflated by Consumer Price Index for Urban Non-Manual Employees. All the nominal data has been converted into real prices (base 1999-00 = 100) to mitigate the impact of rise in price level. Further, the real values of input and output variables except staff have been divided by number of branches to reduce the effects of random noise due to the measurement error in inputs and outputs.

3.1.4.3 Measurement of Input Prices for X-Efficiency

In order to derive x-efficiency estimates, it is essential to have information on input prices. Table 3.2 highlights the method of calculating the input prices for computing cost x-efficiency scores in the existing empirical literature. To keep in lines with Gautam Chatterjee (1997), Ray and Sanyal (2002), Estrada and Osorio (2004) and Rudersensarma (2005), the price of labour has been calculated as:

$$\text{Price of Labour} = \frac{\text{Establishment Expenses}}{\text{Number of Employees}}$$

On the other hand, price of loanable fund has been calculated to keep in lines with Gautam Chatterjee (1997) and Isik and Hasan (2003), which is as follows:

$$\text{Price of Loanable Fund} = \frac{\text{Total Interst Expenses on Loanable Fund}}{\text{Total Loanable Fund}}$$

SECTION II

3.2 APPROACHES FOR EFFICIENCY MEASUREMENT

A vast majority of studies have been conducted on the efficiency measurement of financial institutions in last few decades. According to the existing literature, ratio analysis was the most popularly adopted technique to ascertain the performance of financial institutions. Although, these financial ratios mostly used in extant literature are simpler to conceptualize and easier to calculate but ignore the multi-dimensional aspect of bank performance. This analysis just provides a restricted and incomplete picture of the process. Yeh (1996) noted that the major demerit of this approach is its reliance on benchmark ratios. These benchmarks could be arbitrary and may mislead an analyst.

The main weakness of financial ratio analysis adopted by Verma Committee (1999) is that the choice of a few or a single ratio does not provide enough information about various dimensions of performance. As a result, a bank that is poorly managed on certain dimensions may appear to be performing well as long as it compensates in other dimensions. Furthermore, it is a short-run analysis that may be inappropriate for describing actual efficiency of the banks in long-run, since it fails to consider the value of management actions and investment decisions that will affect future performance. Another problem that may arise is the choice of a benchmark against which to compare a univariate and multivariate score from ratio analysis. Also, commonly used performance ratios fail to consider multiple outputs (services and/or transactions) provided with multiple inputs.

Apart from ratio analysis, now there is a trend towards measuring bank performance using one of the frontier analysis methods. A frontier function represents a best practice technology against which the efficiency of the firms within the industry can be measured (Coelli, 1995). If a firm belongs to the frontier, it is efficient. If a firm is beneath the efficiency frontier, then it is inefficient and further analysis identifies the sources and extent of the inefficiency. In frontier analysis, the institutions that perform well relative to a particular standard

TABLE 3.1

Specification of Input and Output Variables

Variables	*Definition*
Total Assets	The rupee value of fixed assets (premises, fixed assets under construction and other fixed assets) and other assets like interest accrued, tax paid, stationery and stamps, inter-office adjustments and others.
Interest Earned	The income received as the interest on advances/bills, investments, balances with RBI and other inter-bank funds.
Interest Expended	The amounts paid on interest on deposits, RBI/inter bank borrowings and others.
Non-Interest Income	The income generated from sources other than banking activities such as commission, exchange, brokerage, net income from the sale of investments, revaluation of investments, on the sale of land, building and other assets, on exchange transaction and miscellaneous income.
Total Income	The income generated from both the banking and non-banking activities.
Loans	The rupee value of total loans provided in terms of bills purchased and discounted, cash credit, overdrafts & loans and term loans.
Investment	The rupee value of total investments made in government securities, other approved securities, shares, debentures & bonds and subsidiaries & joint ventures in India + total investments made in government securities, subsidiaries & joint ventures outside India
Deposits	Total funds collected on deposit mobilization like demand deposits, saving bank deposits, term deposits and deposits of branches in India as well as outside India.
Borrowings	Total funds collected through borrowings from different sources like RBI, other banks, other institutions and agencies in India and Total funds collected through borrowings outside India.
Purchased Funds	It includes the amount of deposits and borrowings.
Spread	It is equivalent to interest earned minus interest expended.
Total Earning Assets	It is equal to the sum of loans and investments.
Establishment Expenses	The expenditures incurred on bank staff such as wages etc.
Labor	Total number of full-time workers.
Profit/Loss	The excess of total income over the total expenditures is profit/loss.

TABLE 3.2

Method of the Calculation of Input Prices in Existing Studies

Author's Name	*Price of Labor*	*Price of Physical Capital*	*Price of Purchased Funds*
(1)	*(2)*	*(3)*	*(4)*
Barbara Casu	Personnel Expenses / Total Assets	Total Capital Expenses / Total Fixed Assets	Interest Expenses / Customer and Short - Term Funding
Dr. Kheswar Jankee	Staff Expenses / Number of Employees	Book value of premises and fixed assets the net of depriciation / Operating expenses other than staff expenses	—
Estrada and Osoria	Personnel Expenses / Total Assets	Administration Fees / Fixed Assets	Interest Expenses / Total Funds
Gautam Chatterjee	Establishment Expenses / Number of Employees	Sum of expenses on rent, repairs and depriciation / Total value of Assets	Total Interest Expenses / Deposits + Borrowings

Hadiye Aslan	$\frac{\text{Establishment Expenses}}{\text{Number of Employees}}$	$\frac{\text{Total Expenses of Premises and Fixed Assets}}{\text{Fixed Assets}}$	$\frac{\text{Total Interest Expenses}}{\text{Total Funds}}$
Hasan and Marton	$\frac{\text{Non-Interest Expenses}}{\text{Number of Employees}}$	—	$\frac{\text{Total Interest Expenses}}{\text{Total Interest bearing Borrowed Funds}}$
Isik and Hasan	$\frac{\text{Total Expenses on Employees}}{\text{Number of Employees}}$	$\frac{\text{Total expenses of premises and fixed assets}}{\text{Book value of premises and fixed assets}}$	$\frac{\text{Total Interest Expenses on Loanable Funds}}{\text{Total Loanable Funds}}$
Ray and Sanyal	$\frac{\text{Staff Expenses}}{\text{Number of Employees}}$	$\frac{\text{Paid up Capital}}{\text{Total Fixed Assets}}$	$\frac{\text{Total Interest}}{\text{Interest bearing Liabilities}}$
Rudar Sensarma	$\frac{\text{Establishment Expenses}}{\text{Number of Employees}}$	$\frac{\text{Capital Expenses}}{\text{Fixed Assets}}$	—

are separated from those that perform poorly. Such separation can be done either by applying non-parametric or parametric frontier approach to firms within the financial service industry.

The parametric frontier specification of the production function is usually performed by applying stochastic frontier analysis (SFA). The essential idea behind SFA is that it specifies a particular functional form, which characterizes the relevant economic production function and cost function. Hence, the resultant efficiency score partially depends upon how well the chosen functional form represents the production relationship (i.e., the relationship between inputs/resources and outputs). Further, the deviation from the frontier could be partly out of the control of analyzed firm and thus leaves a room for random noise. The stochastic frontier approach adds the problem of decomposition of the error term into inefficiency and noise.

Contrary to parametric approach, non-parametric does not assume a specific functional form to represent the relevant production and cost function. All banks face the same frontier and the magnitude of inefficiency of a specific bank is measured through its deviation from the estimated frontier. The non-parametric specification of the production function is most commonly performed by Data Envelopment Analysis (DEA) approach. The main idea behind this approach is that DEA calculates the efficiency of a bank within a group relative to the best-practice one. It does not take into account possible statistical noise and attribute all deviations from the best-practice frontier to inefficiency. In other words, it does not decompose error term into inefficiency and random noise like parametric approach.

Both the parametric and non-parametric approaches have certain strengths and some inherent weaknesses. There is no specific set of criterion to select the most relevant approach for constructing the frontier. Tortosa-Ausina (2002a) pointed out that the choice of technique, either non-parametric or parametric, is somewhat arbitrary, depending on the aims pursued. However, the researchers can apply any of the production frontier approach. Nevertheless, application of parametric approach allows analyst to test their hypothesis, which may and may not provide robust estimation of the relative efficiency of DMUs. In view of this, researchers prefer DEA, non-parametric, frontier approach to measure efficiency of any business undertaking. In the present study too, DEA, non-parametric frontier approach has been applied to examine the performance measures of banks in India. The selection of the DEA approach in the present study is justifiable due to its distinct advantages, which have been outlined as:

Strengths of DEA Technique

The wide acceptance of DEA as a measurement tool for measuring efficiency of the financial institutions may be attributed to some inherent features. First, it does not require a pre-specified functional form to represent the relevant production and cost function. Second, DEA can easily handle disaggregated and multiple inputs and outputs to derive the relative results. The latter property is especially desirable in DEA approach. Third, the different measurement units of variables do not affect the calculation of efficiency scores. Fourth, in addition to measure efficiency, it identifies reference units, which can help to find out causes and remedies for inefficiencies and therefore, it has gained more advantage in managerial applications. Fifth, it can also adjust exogenous variables and can incorporate categorical (dummy) variables. It can also accommodate judgment when desired. Sixth, DEA is capable of identifying any perceived slack in input used or output produced and provides insight on possibilities for increasing output or conserving input for an inefficient DMU to become efficient.

Weaknesses of DEA Technique

Inspite of these powerful features, DEA approach is not free from some limitations, which encourage researchers to prefer parametric methods over the non-parametric methods. Some of these weaknesses have been outlined as: First, DEA is very sensitive to variable selection, model specification, and data errors. The DEA results generally differ with the use of alternative set of input and output variables. Second, DEA gives us relative not absolute efficiency scores, which further signify that best performing unit is deemed to be 100 percent efficient and rest of the DMUs will be benchmarked against this one. Third, DEA may suffer from substantial finite sample error, especially if the number of input and output variable is high relative to number of observations. Fourth, another problem that might occur with the use of DEA models refers to the dimensionality of the input/output space relative to the number of observations. The dimensionality problem arises when the number of observations is relatively small compared with the number of inputs and outputs used (Suhariyanto, 2000). Fifth, however, being non-stochastic, the DEA approach does not distinguish data noise and inefficiency (Lovell, (1993) and Coelli, (1995)). Sixth, DEA is a non-parametric technique, which makes hypothesis testing difficult.

Restrictions on Number of Inputs and Outputs

The ratio between the number of observations and number of inputs and outputs is another point, which is very essential to keep in mind. So, some discussion on sample size is warranted. There are various rules of thumb for specifying sample size relative to inputs and outputs. Charnes and Cooper (1990) stated that ratio should equal at least three, while Fernandez-Cornejo (1994) argued that it should exceed five. Smith (1997), after conducting a simulation study, found that even in cases when number of observations exceeded the number of factors by more than thirteen times, DEA still can overestimate true efficiency by 27 percent. In this context, Cooper *et. al.* (2000) stated that number of observations should be at least three times the sum of input and output variables. Higher the number of DMUs, better is the discrimination power. Thus, to keep in view the aforementioned rules of thumb, the present study has incorporated two input and two output variables and sample size of 45 banks is quite reasonable and feasible to have better discrimination power.

While using DEA, it is either to use an input-oriented or output-oriented approach. Hence, the choice of approach depends upon the objective of the firm. Generally, input-oriented models measure cost-efficiency (input efficiency) aimed at cost minimization while output-oriented models measure profit efficiency (output efficiency) aimed at revenue maximization. As the present study aims to measure cost x-efficiency and productivity growth of banks, therefore, input-orientation approach has been selected to view the objective. This approach also reflects banks' tendency to focus on costs to challenge competition from new market entrants. The input-orientation approach has been also selected on the ground that outputs of the banks may be driven by market factors, which are beyond the control of management but banks may have a better control over the inputs.

SECTION III

3.3.1 Technical and Scale Efficiency: Conceptual Framework

As mentioned earlier, linear programming based Data Envelopment Analysis technique has been applied to measure the efficiency of commercial banks, where production function technology has been characterized by multiple inputs and outputs. DEA computes technical efficiency on the basis of estimated piece-wise linear frontier made up by a set of efficient DMUs. The DMUs that lie on the frontier are termed as best practice ones and retain efficiency score equals to one. Further, this frontier helps to ascertain the performance of all other DMUs that do not capture the position on the frontier. These DMUs are considered as relatively inefficient and their efficiency score lie in the range between zero and one. These banks can conserve their inputs and still can produce the same level of outputs as well as augment their outputs with the same level of resources.

A graphical conceptualization of technical efficiency in input-oriented framework has been represented in Figure 3.1, where the efficient frontier drawn refers to an elementary case with two inputs (X_1 and X_2) and one output (Y) under the assumption of constant returns-to-scale (CRS). The DMUs say A, B, C, D and E are most efficient ones, thus, located on the boundary of best-practice frontier. DMU F has been observed to be relatively inefficient in that it produces same level of outputs using more of atleast one of the inputs. DMU F uses OH amount of input (X_1) and OM amount of input (X_2) to produce a given level of output Y. DMU F will have to proportionally reduce the level of input (X_1) from OH to OG and input (X_2) from OM to ON to become technically efficient as firm C. In other words, the distance CF represents the amount of technical inefficiency of DMU F by which the use of inputs can proportionally be reduced without any reduction in output level. The score of technical efficiency is just the ratio of OF to OC, as shown in Figure 3.1.

The above representation of technical efficiency is based upon the assumption of constant returns to scale (CRS). The efficiency score corresponding to CRS frontier is referred as overall technical efficiency (OTE), which indicates the combined effect of pure technical efficiency and scale efficiency. PTE measure reflects the capability of the management to convert the resources into outputs and thus, can be treated as an index of managerial quality. On the other hand, scale efficiency is used to determine how close a firm is to the most productive scale size (Forsund and Hjalmarsson, 1979 and Banker and Thrall, 1992). A firm may be scale inefficient if it exceeds the most productive scale size (therefore experiencing diminishing returns to scale) or if it is smaller than the most productive scale size (therefore failing to take full advantage of increasing returns to scale).

FIG. 3.1
Input-Oriented Technical Efficiency

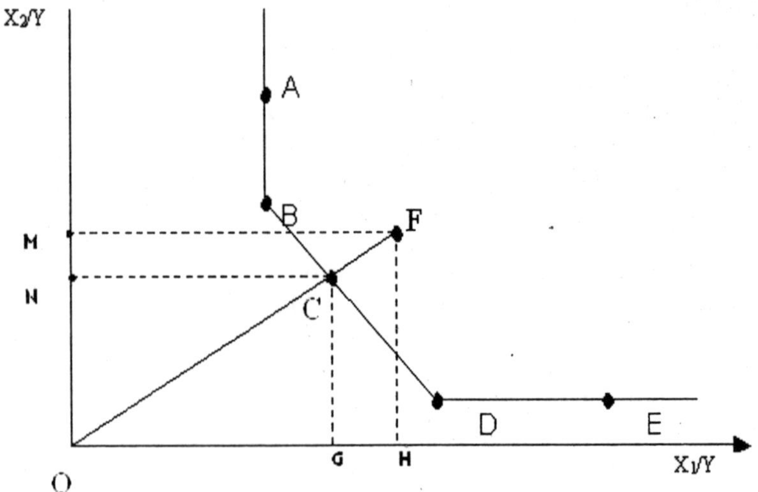

Figure 3.2 illustrates diagrammatic decomposition of OTE into PTE and SE in envelopment surface in single-input and single-output space. As shown, the envelopment surfaces may be either linear as in constant returns to scale case, or convex as in case with variable returns to scale. The CRS surface is shown by the straight line OBD and the convex possibility set of VRS surface is just right to the linear surface of CRS and bounded by solid line ZZ'. The input-oriented TE of the firm operating at the point P would be $\frac{AB}{AP}$ under CRS and $\frac{AC}{AP}$ under VRS, and scale efficiency would be $\frac{AB}{AC}$ (TE_{CRS}/TE_{VRS}).

Once the scale efficiencies are determined, further the analysis can reveal whether a particular DMU is operating in the region of increasing returns to scale (IRTS) (scale economies) and diminishing returns to scale (DRTS) (scale diseconomies). To view this, non-increasing returns to scale (NIRS) DEA frontier has been plotted in Figure 3.2. If the efficiency score for a particular DMU under VRS equals to

FIG. 3.2
Input-Oriented Decomposition of Technical Efficiency

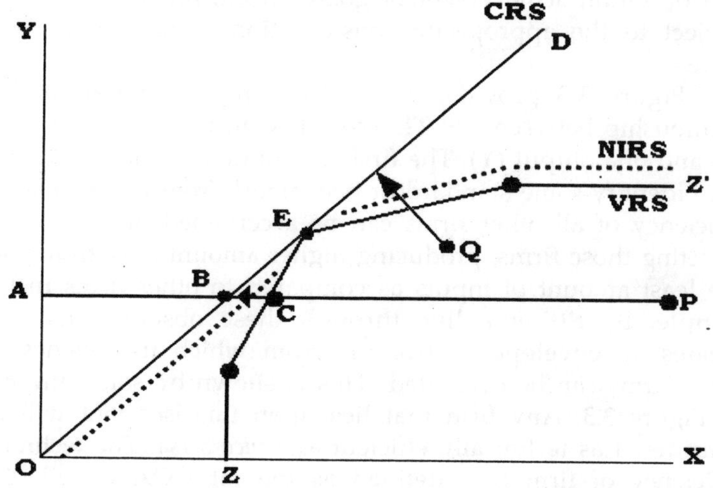

[Adapted from Tim Coelli (1996)].

NIRS TE score, then that DMU must be operating under DRTS. If otherwise, then it implies that a DMU is operating under IRTS. The NIRS TE score and VRS TE score are unequal at point P in Figure 3.2, IRTS is said to exist for that DMU. The NIRS TE score is equal to VRS TE score (as shown at point Q in Figure 3.2); it means that a DMU is operating under DRTS. Following, Singh, S.K. (2002), it is noteworthy that the concept of return to scale (RTS) and economies of scale have been used interchangeably in the present study.

3.3.2 X-Efficiency

The productive (global or overall, economic, x or cost) efficiency is the firm's ability to produce the given level of an output using the appropriate mix of given inputs at minimum possible cost.

Lovell (1993) relates the efficiency of the firm to a comparison between observed and optimal values of its outputs and inputs. If the optimum is defined in terms of production possibilities, the resulting comparison measures technical efficiency. If the optimum is defined in terms of behavioral goals of the firm (e.g., profit or revenue maximization and cost minimization), then efficiency is economic and is measured by comparing a firms' observed and optimum achievement of goals (profit, revenue and cost) subject to the appropriate consideration of technology and prices.

Figure 3.3 provides a graphical representation of the relationship between XE, TE and AE with two inputs (X_1 and X_2) and one output (Y). The first step in determining efficiency is to identify some standard or benchmark from which relative efficiency of all other firms can be ascertained. It is done by selecting those firms, producing higher amount of output from the least amount of inputs as compared to other firms in the sample. By fitting a line through these observations, one creates an envelope or frontier, from which inefficiency of other firms can be evaluated. This is shown by solid line BB' in Figure 3.3. Any firm that lies upon this isoquant will be considered as technically efficient and *vice versa*. The technical efficiency of firm P is defined as the ratio OA to OP. The technical inefficiency of firm P can be represented by the

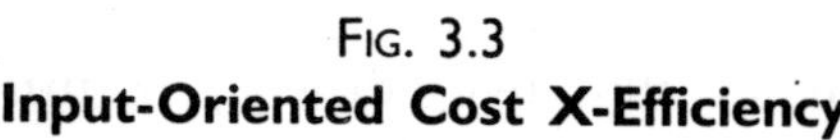

FIG. 3.3

Input-Oriented Cost X-Efficiency

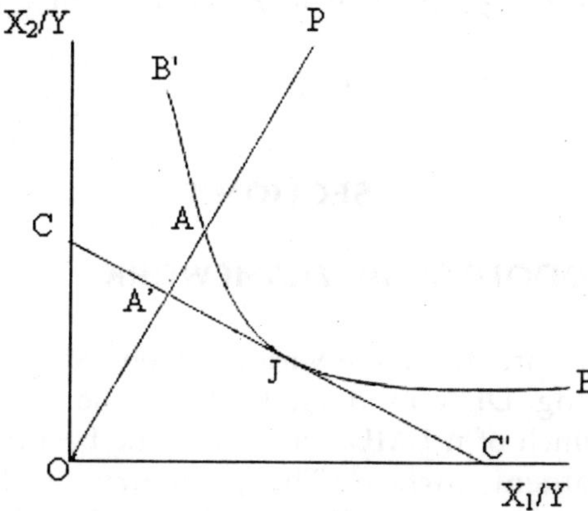

distance AP, which is the amount by which all the inputs can proportionally be reduced without any reduction in outputs. Thus, A depicts technically efficient point for firm P.

Assuming input prices are known, isocost line CC′ describes the rate at which two inputs can be traded off in the market (i.e., their relative costs) or it represents different input combinations that can be purchased from a fixed budget. The cost efficiency of firm P can be defined as the ratio of OA′ to OP. And, cost inefficiency of firm P can be depicted through the distance A′P, which firm P can proportionally reduce by reducing the use of atleast one of the inputs (X_1). The problem with point A′ is that any firm locating on this point is cost efficient but not technically efficient. It is the point J that shows both the technical efficiency and cost efficiency, which firm P can capture by reducing the amount of input (X_2). The allocative efficiency of firm P is just equal to the ratio of OA′ to OA, hence the distance AA′ denotes the amount of allocative inefficiency for firm P. This indicates that firm P can lower down the level of allocative inefficiency by reducing the use of costly input (X_2) and increasing the use of cheaper input (X_1).

The ratio $\frac{OA}{OP}$ represents technical efficiency; hence the ratio $\frac{OA'}{OA}$ denotes allocative efficiency of firm P. Economic efficiency is the product of technical efficiency and allocative efficiency, since the ratio turns out to be $\frac{OA'}{OP}$.

SECTION IV

3.4 METHODOLOGICAL FRAMEWORK

In literature, there are various extended versions of linear programming DEA models. Each of the models seeks to establish which of n DMUs determine the best practice frontier or envelopment surface. The geometry of this surface is prescribed by the specific DEA model employed. In the present study, CCR model named after Charnes Cooper and Rhodes (1978) and BCC model named after Banker, Charnes and Cooper (1984) have been applied to estimate efficiency under CRS and VRS assumptions, respectively.

3.4.1 CCR and BCC Model

To illustrate CCR input-oriented DEA model, consider a set of decision making units (DMUs) j = 1, 2...n utilizing quantities, we can denote x_{ij} the amount of ith input used by j^{th} DMU and y_{rj}, the amount of rth output produced by j^{th} DMU. They developed DEA model under the assumption of constant returns to scale (CRS), strong disposability of inputs and outputs and convexity of the production possibility set.

CCR Efficiency Measure

$$\text{Max } G_0 = \frac{\sum_{r=1}^{s} u_r y_{rjo}}{\sum_{i=1}^{m} v_i x_{ijo}}$$

subject to :

$$\frac{\sum_{r=1}^{s} u_r y_{rj}}{\sum_{i=1}^{m} v_i x_{ij}} \leq 1 \tag{1}$$

u_r, v_i $\geq \in$ j =1, 2... n, r =1, 2... s, i =1, 2... m

u_r = the weights given to output r,

v_i = the weights given to input i,

x_{ij} = the quantity of input i used by unit j,

y_{rj} = the quantity of output r achieved by unit j,

n = the number of decision-making units (DMUs),

s = the number of outputs,

m = the number of inputs, and

$\in$ = a non-Archimedean (infinitesimal) constant.

In the above model, the objective function defined by G_o aims to maximize the ratio of weighted outputs to weighted inputs of DMU under evaluation (j_o). It measures the efficiency of DMU (j_o) relative to the efficiency score of other DMUs in the sample. The weighted outputs and inputs ratio is maximized subject to the constraints that: first, the efficiency ratios of all DMUs cannot exceed one and second, the weights are positive and known. The justification of ε is two-fold: first, to ensure that denominator is never zero and second to ensure that each input and output variable is considered. The above fractional programming problem can be transformed into a linear programming model (CCR) as shown in Equation 3.

CCR Efficiency Measure (Linear Form)

$$\text{Max } G_0 = \sum_{r=1}^{s} u_r y_{rjo}$$

subject to:

$$\sum_{r=1}^{s} u_r y_{rj} - \sum_{i=1}^{m} v_i x_{ij} \leq 0$$

$$\sum_{i=1}^{m} v_i x_{ijo} = 1 \qquad (2)$$

$u_r \geq \in, \ v_i \geq \in \ j = 1, 2... n, \ r = 1, 2... s, \ i = 1, 2... m$

The above linear programming model aims to maximize the sum of weighted outputs of DMU (j_o) subject to the virtual inputs of DMU (j_o) while maintaining the condition that the virtual outputs cannot be exceeded by virtual inputs of any DMUs. One possible solution to the linear programming model is to formulate a dual companion. The dual form of the problem can be formalized by denoting input weights of DMU (j_o) by (θ_{jo}) and input and output weights of other DMUs in the sample by λ_j.

CCR Input-Oriented Measure

$$\text{Mini} \quad \theta_{jo} - \varepsilon\left(\sum_{r=1}^{s} S_r^{+} + \sum_{i=1}^{m} S_i^{-}\right)$$

subject to

$$\sum_{j=1}^{n} \lambda_j x_{ij} + S_i^{-} = \theta_{jo} x_{ijo}$$

$$\sum_{j=1}^{n} \lambda_j y_{rj} - S_r^{+} = y_{rjo} \qquad (3)$$

$$\lambda_j \geq 0$$

$$S_r^{+}, \ S_i^{-} \geq 0$$

$$0 \leq \in \leq 1 \quad j = 1, 2... n, \ r = 1, 2... s, \ i = 1, 2... m$$

The primal problem has n + s + m + 1 constraints while dual form has m+s constraints. The number of DMUs should be considered larger than the number of inputs and outputs variables (s+m) in order to provide a fair degree of discrimination of results. Thus, dual model (Model 3) is easier and simpler to solve as it has n+1 fewer constraints than the primal form (Model 2). It is important to note that both the primal (popularly known as Multiplier form) and dual form (known as Envelopment form) have the same solution.

The presence of ε in the objective function of Model 3 effectively allows minimization over θ_{jo} to preempt the optimization involving the slacks S_i^+ and S_r^+. In the present study, Model 3 has been solved in order to obtain the efficiency scores of CBs in India.

3.4.2 The Variable Returns to Scale (VRS) Model and Economies of Scale

Underlying the CCR method is based upon the assumption of CRS, which is only appropriate when all DMUs are operating at optimal scale. Nevertheless, imperfect competition and financial constraints does not allow a DMU to operate at optimal scale. Therefore, Banker, Charnes and Cooper (1984) modified CRS model to account for VRS situation. This is performed simply by adding an additional convexity constraint $\left(\sum_{\lambda=1}^{n} \lambda_j = 1\right)$ in the formulation of Model 3. By adding this constraint to the basic Model 3, they defined the type of envelopment surface against which relative efficiency of each DMU would be evaluated. The use of VRS specification will permit the calculation of TE devoid of scale efficiency (SE) effects whereas the use of CRS specification provides only the measure of TE, which is confounded by scale efficiencies.

The BCC input-oriented model has been presented as follows:

BCC Input-Oriented Model

$$\text{Mini } \theta_{jo} - \varepsilon\left(\sum_{r=1}^{s} S_r^+ + \sum_{i=1}^{m} S_i^-\right)$$

$$\text{S.T.} \quad \sum_{j=1}^{n} \lambda_j x_{ij} + S_i^- = \theta_{jo} x_{ijo} \tag{4}$$

$$\sum_{j=1}^{n} \lambda_j y_{rj} - S_r^+ = y_{rjo}$$

$$\sum_{j=1}^{n} \lambda_j = 1$$

$$\lambda_j,\ S_r^+,\ S_i^- \geq 0 \quad j = 1, 2 \ldots n,\ r = 1, 2 \ldots s,\ i = 1, 2 \ldots m$$

The BCC model provides the performance measures of OTE, PTE and SE. Pure technical inefficiency (PTIE) directly results from managerial sub-performance, i.e., the inability of the management to convert inputs into outputs. The inefficiency reflected from scale efficiency score arises due to the choice of either sub-optimal scale size (i.e., increasing returns-to-scale) (IRS)) and supra-optimal scale size ((i.e., decreasing returns-to-scale) DRS). As far as nature of scale inefficiencies is concerned, it can be ascertained by adding an additional convexity constraint of $\sum \lambda_j \leq 1$ in Model 3 with the assumption of non-increasing returns to scale (NIRS). If (NIRS) TE score of VRS TE score, increasing returns to scale is said to prevail (economies of scale) and If (NIRS) TE score = VRS TE score, decreasing returns to scale is said to exist (diseconomies of scale).

3.4.3 Constant Returns to Scale (CRS) and X-Efficiency

In measuring input-oriented technical efficiency, all the inputs are treated equally and the objective is to reduce all the inputs by same proportion to the maximum possible extent. Thus, if the reduction of any input becomes restricted for the production process, then no further input reduction is made. If one has price information, then more costly input attains priority to be reduced than cheaper one. In this case, efficiency lies in producing the target output bundle at the minimum cost. Therefore, if a firm wants to consider a behavioral objective such as cost minimization and revenue maximization, then it will have to measure both the technical efficiency and allocative efficiency. CCR input-oriented DEA model is run (as shown in earlier part) to get the measure of technical efficiency under the assumption of CRS. Furthermore, cost minimization DEA program is run to get the measures of cost x-efficiency and allocative efficiency. The cost-minimization DEA model can be outlined in following manner:

X-Efficiency Measure

Mini $w_i x_i^*$

subject to

$$\sum \lambda_j y_{rj} - y_{rjo} \geq 0 \quad (5)$$

$$x_{ijo}^* - \sum \lambda_j x_{ij} \geq 0$$

$$\lambda \geq 0$$

where w_i is a vector of input prices for the ith DMU and x_i is the cost minimizing vector of input quantities for the ith DMU given the input prices w_i and the output level y. The total cost efficiency or economic efficiency of ith DMU will be calculated as CE (XE) = $\frac{w_i x_i^*}{w_i x_i}$, that is the ratio of minimum cost to observed cost. On the other hand, allocative efficiency is the ratio of cost-x efficiency to technical efficiency, thus AE = $\frac{CE}{TE}$.

3.4.4 Andersen and Petersen's Super-Efficiency Model

As stated earlier, CCR model assigns efficiency score equals to unity to all the efficient DMUs whereas less than unity to all the inefficient ones. Resultantly, we can discriminate and rank the inefficient DMUs by the means of their efficiency scores but not the efficient DMUs using classical CCR model. The Super-Efficiency DEA model developed by Andersen and Petersen overcomes this limitation of standard CCR model. This model assigns efficiency score greater than unity to efficient DMUs and strictly discriminates and ranks the efficient DMUs. Under constant returns to scale, Andersen and Petersen's model is similar to CCR model (1975), except that the unit under evaluation is not included in the reference set. As in CCR model, the main objective is to proportionally reduce the inputs use and still to produce the prescribed level of output, whereas for efficient units (the efficiency score is equal to one or greater than one), the optimal solution may be interpreted as the maximum possible proportional increase in inputs while keeping the same level of efficiency. In this way, a complete ranking of efficient units is possible. Andersen and Petersen's Super-Efficiency DEA model can be outlined as:

$$\text{Mini } \theta_{jo}^{super} - \varepsilon\left(\sum_{r=1}^{s} S_r^{+} + \sum_{i=1}^{m} S_i^{-}\right)$$

$$\text{S.t:} \quad \sum_{j=1}^{n} \lambda_j x_{ij} + S_i^{-} = \theta_{jo}^{super} x_{ijo} \qquad (6)$$

$$\sum_{j=1}^{n} \lambda_j y_{rj} - S_r^{+} = y_{rjo}$$

$$\theta_{jo}^{super}, \text{ free}$$

$$\lambda_j \geq 0$$

$$S_r^{+}, S_i^{-} \geq 0$$

$0 \leq \epsilon \leq 1$, j = 1, 2... n, r = 1, 2... s, i = 1, 2... m

SECTION V

3.5.1 Conceptual Framework of Total Factor Productivity Growth

Besides measuring efficiency, it is important to assess the extent of TFP growth on technical efficiency and technological grounds over time. Productivity is defined as the ratio of output produced per unit of input used, measured as a partial measure and a total factor productivity measure. Partial productivity indices refer to the ratio of output to each categories of inputs for which separate data exists. In the empirical economic literature, the most commonly used partial productivity indices are labor and capital productivity which are defined as output per unit of labor and output per unit of capital, respectively.

$$\text{Labor Productivity} = \frac{Q}{L}$$

$$\text{Capital Productivity} = \frac{Q}{K}$$

where Q, L, K denote the aggregate level of output, labor and capital, respectively.

However, this measure takes into consideration only one measure of inputs and ignores all the other inputs, which tend to overestimate the level of productivity. However, productive efficiency of a firm is affected by the changes in the compositions of inputs, therefore, partial measure provides a distorted view of the productive efficiency.

The concept of TFP gained more popularity especially in case when production function technology is characterized by multiple inputs and multiple outputs. Total factor productivity (TFP) is an overall indicator of how well an organization uses all of its resources to create its products and services. TFP can be thought as a comprehensive measure of technical change, which sums up the partial productivities of all inputs in a production process, so that the efficiency with which all inputs are utilized and combined can be captured jointly. Moreover, TFP is a broader measure of economic and technical efficiency reflecting a diversity of factors including managerial efficiency, economies of scale, research and development, market structure and human capital utilization (Denison, 1967), etc.

Total factor productivity growth is a composite measure of technological change and changes in efficiency with which known technology is applied to production (Ahluwalia, 1991). Therefore, it is important to distinguish between technological progress and improvement in technical efficiency. The technological change may be the outcome of technological upgradation, shocks (financial crisis), changes in market structure (high concentration due to M&As) and regulatory policies (financial deregulation), etc. that leads to the shift in the frontier. On the other hand, technical efficiency change may be attributed to improved management practices, better industrial relationships and diffusion of new technological knowledge.

3.5.2 Approaches to the Measurement of Total Factor Productivity Growth

The researchers have propounded several theories and methods to total factor productivity measurement over the last past three decades. The literature spells out two basic approaches to measure total factor productivity growth. (1) The parametric estimation of production, cost and other functions, and (2) The construction of index number with the help of non-parametric techniques. The empirical evidence suggests the most common use of Index number approach and the most frequently accepted indices are Tornquist index (Tornquist, 1936), Fisher Ideal index (1922) and Malmquist index (Malmquist, 1953). The popularity of Tornquist and Fisher approach can be stemmed due to two reasons. First, both can be calculated directly from price and quantity data. Secondly, it does not require the specification of a particular functional form for the relevant function (e.g., production function, cost function, revenue function, distance functions or other functions) like parametric approach.

But, Malmquist index has some distinct advantages over Tornquist index and Fisher index, which have been outlined as: (1) It does not require information on prices, therefore this approach is suitable even when price data is not available or price data is distorted. (2) It uses panel data and decomposition of productivity growth into two components viz., technical efficiency change and technological change. Thus, these components lend themselves in a natural way to the identification of catching up and innovation, respectively. (3) No assumption is required to be made regarding the market structure or economic behavior (such as, cost minimization and revenue maximization) in the construction of Malmquist indices.

In light of this, DEA-based MPI index approach has been adopted to ascertain the total factor productivity growth of commercial banks in India.

3.6 MALMQUIST PRODUCTIVITY INDEX

Caves, Christensen and Diewert (CCD) initially introduced the DEA-based MPI approach in 1982 and empirically applied by Fare, Grosskopf, Lindgren and Roos (FGLR) in 1992 and Fare, Grosskopf, Norris and Zhing (FGNZ) in 1994. Fare *et. al.* (1989) developed techniques, which allowed decomposition of productivity growth into two mutually exclusive and exhaustive components: changes in technical efficiency over time and shifts in technology over time. Later on, Fare (1994a) proposed an alternative decomposition of TFP change that measures technical efficiency change relative to VRS technology and an alternative method for computing scale efficiency change.

The Malmquist productivity index measures the change in TFP between two points of time say (t and t+1), based on the geometric means of the ratios of distance functions. Distance functions allow one to describe a multi-input and/or multi-output production technology without the need to specify a behavioral objective (such as cost minimization and revenue maximization) (Coelli *et. al.* 1998). Malmquist indexes of total factor productivity, which can be defined as the ratio of distance functions (Fare, *et. al.* 1989), provides information on both the degree of production changes and its components.

Caves *et. al.* (1982) argued, "There are two natural approaches to the measurement of productivity differences. One approach treats productivity differences as differences in maximum output conditional on a given level of inputs. This approach leads to *output-based productivity indexes*. The alternative approach treats productivity differences as differences in minimum input requirements conditional on a given level of outputs. This view leads to *input-based productivity index*. The Malmquist approach is most commonly used in banking for input comparisons. Therefore, an input-oriented approach has been specified in the present study. The following outlines this process, using the Farrell (1957) definition of micro level efficiency and the Malmquist index approach to efficiency measurement of Fare *et. al.* (1994).

In order to specify input-oriented Malmquist productivity index, let S′ be the production technology available at period t = 1, 2 ...T such that S_t = (x_t, y_t): x can produce y at time t), describes all feasible set of input/output factors.
where $x \in R^n$ is a vector of inputs used to produce vector of output $y \in R^m$. The input distance function D_i is defined for S technology in period t as:

$$D_i^t\left(x_t, y_t\right) = \min\left\{\theta : \left(y_t, \theta x_t\right) \in S_t\right\} \quad 2.1$$

Similarly, an input distance function D_i at time t+1 is defined as

$$D_i^{t+1}\left(x_{t+1}, y_{t+1}\right) = \min\left\{\theta : \left(y_{t+1}, \theta x_{t+1}\right) \in S_{t+1}\right\} \quad 2.2$$

It is important to note that $D_i^t\left(x_t, y_t\right) \leq 1$ 1 if and only if $\left(x_t, y_t\right) \in S_t$ and $D_i^t\left(x_t, y_t\right) = 1$ if and only if $\left(x_t, y_t\right)$ is on the technology frontier.

In addition to this, mixed-period distance functions can be defined as:

$$D_0^t\left(x_{t+1}, y_{t+1}\right) = \min\left\{\theta : \left(y_{t+1}, \theta x_{t+1}\right) \in S_t\right\} \quad 2.3$$

and

$$D_o^{t+1}\left(x_t, y_t\right) = \min\left\{\theta : \left(y_t, \theta x_t\right) \in S_{t+1}\right\} \quad 2.4$$

It is important to note that $D_i^{t+1}\left(x_t, y_t\right) \leq 1$ if and only if $\left(y_t, \theta x_t\right) \varepsilon\ S_{t+1}$ and $D_i^t\left(x_{t+1}, y_{t+1}\right) \leq 1$ 1 if and only if $\left(y_{t+1}, \theta x_{t+1}\right) \varepsilon\ S_t$. In mixed period instances, the distance function $D_i^t(x_{t+1}, y_{t+1})$ measures maximum proportional reduction of inputs in period t+1 relative to period t technology. Similarly, the distance function $D_i^{t+1}\left(x_t, y_t\right)$ measures the maximum proportional reduction of inputs in period t relative to period t+1 technology. In mixed period instances, the value of distance function may exceed one if observation being evaluated is not feasible in other period. This is more likely to occur due to technological progress or shift in production frontier between-period t and t+1. Following Fare *et. al.* (1994), the input oriented MPI can be expressed using input distance functions with respect to two periods as follows:

$$M_i(x_t, y_t, x_{t+1}, y_{t+1}) = \left[\left(\frac{D_i^t\left(x_{t+1}, y_{t+1}\right)}{D_i^t\left(x_t, y_t\right)}\right)\left(\frac{D_i^{t+1}\left(x_{t+1}, y_{t+1}\right)}{D_i^{t+1}\left(x_t, y_t\right)}\right)\right]^{\frac{1}{2}} \quad 2.5$$

A graphical illustration of MPI based DEA technique in input-oriented framework is represented in Figure 3.4 in terms of simple one input (X) and one output (Y) model. The production frontier exhibits constant returns to scale (CRS) and two different frontiers for current period (t) and for successive period (t+1) are labeled as F_t (CRS) and F_{t+1} (CRS), respectively. Firm A is producing at point A (x_t, y_t) in period t and point H (x_{t+1}, y_{t+1}) in period t+1. In each period, firm A is operating below the production frontier.

We can now represent the input distance functions that constitute relevant co-ordinates.

(i) Distance Functions with CRS Assumption

TE in period t relative to frontier t = $D_i^t(x_t, y_t) = \dfrac{MB}{MA}$

TE in period t+1 relative to frontier

t + 1 = $D_i^{t+1}(x_{t+1}, y_{t+1}) = \dfrac{NE}{NH}$

TE in period t relative to frontier

t + 1 = $D_i^{t+1}(x_t, y_t) = \dfrac{MC}{MA}$

TE in period t+1 relative to frontier

t = $D_i^t(x_{t+1}, y_{t+1}) = \dfrac{NF}{NH}$

(ii) TFP Growth and Its Indices

The Δ in TE can be expressed geometrically as:

$$\Delta E = \frac{D_i^{t+1}\left(x_{t+1}, y_{t+1}\right)}{D_i^t\left(x_t, y_t\right)}$$

$$\Delta E = \frac{NE}{NH} \times \frac{MA}{MB}$$

(iii) Change in Technology

$$\Delta T = \left[\left(\frac{D_i^t\left(x_{t+1}, y_{t+1}\right)}{D_i^{t+1}\left(x_{t+1}, y_{t+1}\right)}\right)\left(\frac{D_i^t\left(x_t, y_t\right)}{D_i^{t+1}\left(x_t, y_t\right)}\right)\right]^{\frac{1}{2}}$$

$$\Delta T = \left[\left(\frac{NF}{NH} \times \frac{NH}{NE}\right) \times \left(\frac{MB}{MA} \times \frac{MA}{MC}\right)\right]^{\frac{1}{2}} = \left[\frac{NF}{NE} . \frac{MB}{MC}\right]^{\frac{1}{2}}$$

As eluded earlier, TFP growth is the product of technical efficiency and technological change.

Therefore, TFP Growth (M) = ΔE * ΔT

$$\Delta \text{ TFP} = \frac{D_i^{t+1}\left(x_{t+1}, y_{t+1}\right)}{D_i^t\left(x_t, y_t\right)}\left[\left(\frac{D_i^t\left(x_{t+1}, y_{t+1}\right)}{D_i^{t+1}\left(x_{t+1}, y_{t+1}\right)}\right)\left(\frac{D_i^t\left(x_t, y_t\right)}{D_i^{t+1}\left(x_t, y_t\right)}\right)\right]^{\frac{1}{2}}$$

$$\Delta \text{ TFP} = \frac{NE}{NH} \times \frac{MA}{MB}\left[\frac{NF}{NE} . \frac{MB}{MC}\right]^{\frac{1}{2}}$$

The Malmquist productivity index having value greater than one signals productivity gain and value less than one indicates productivity loss. Same interpretation also applies to the numerical values obtained through technical efficiency and technological change indices. Formally, there is no presumption that both the indices move in same direction. For instance, an improvement in productivity is entirely compatible with the opposite movements in technical efficiency and technology, provided an improvement in one of the components is greater than deterioration in other component. So, Higher efficiency change from one period to another period does not necessarily mean an improvement in productivity rather technology may differ and same is true in

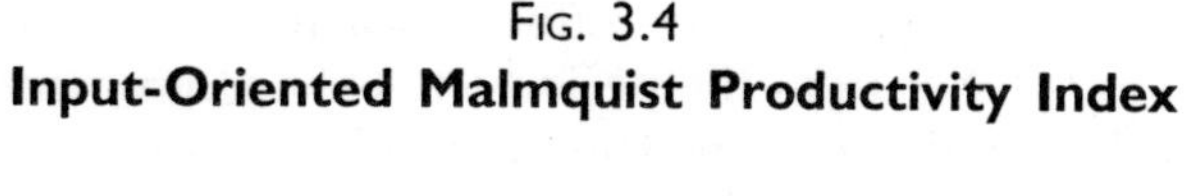

FIG. 3.4

Input-Oriented Malmquist Productivity Index

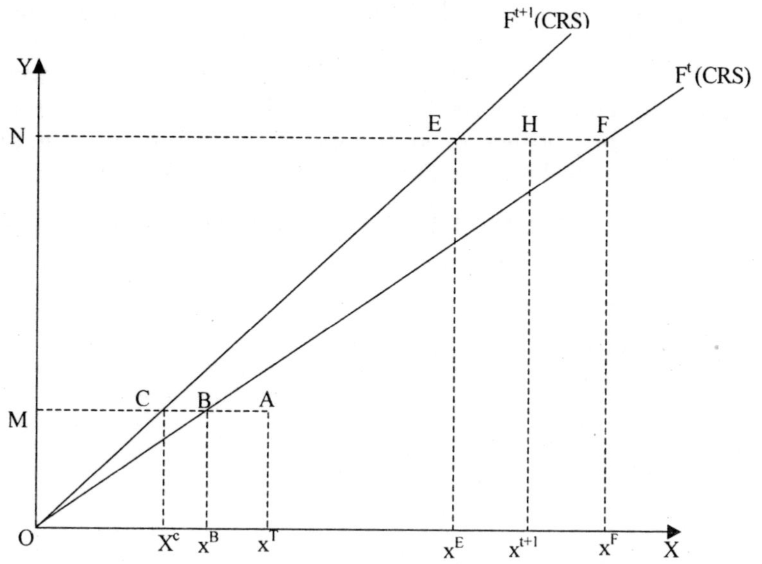

case of higher technological levels but at the same time deterioration in technical efficiency. For instance, $M_0 = 1.5$ (which indicates productivity gain) could result from catching up effect (ΔE) of less than 1 say 0.6 indicates a deterioration in technical efficiency and frontier effect (ΔT) is greater than 1, say 2.5.

$$\text{TFP Growth} = \Delta E \times \Delta T$$
$$= 0.6 * 2.5 = 1.5$$

TFP Growth

= Technical Efficiency Change × Technological Change
(Catching up Effect) (Frontier Effect)

The TE change or catching up effect determines, to what extent, a DMU is moving closer to or farther away from the frontier between the period t to t + 1. The value of TE change greater than one, equals to one and less than one in turn exhibits the relative performance of an individual observation i.e., improving, unchanging and declining, respectively. The technological change (frontier effect) measures the shift in the production frontier from the period t to t+1 with regards to the rate of technology adoption. The Malmquist productivity index is the product of technical efficiency change (catching up) and technological change (frontier effect).

In literature, there were several extended versions of MPI approach. Here, we have followed Fare *et. al.* (1994) to calculate the values of distance functions using linear programming techniques. For a given panel of k observations using inputs and outputs $\left(x_n^{k,t}, y_m^{k,t}\right)$ the frontier technology in period t can be constructed as:

$$S^t = (x_t, y_t) : y_m^t \leq \sum_{k=1}^{k} \lambda^{k,t} Y_m^{k,t}$$

$$\theta x_n^t \geq \sum_{k=1}^{k} \lambda^{k,t} X_n^{k,t}$$

$$\sum_{k=1}^{k} \lambda^{k,t} \leq 1; \lambda^{k,t} \geq 0 \qquad 2.6$$

(m =1, 2, ——, M, n = 1, 2, ——, N, k = 1, 2, ——, K)

where $\lambda^{k,t}$ is an intensity variable, which serves to form the convex combinations of observed inputs and outputs, thus form the technology or reference set.

We have to calculate four distance functions to obtain the Malmquist productivity index. These distance functions are

$$D_i^t(x_t, y_t), D_i^{t+1}(x_t, y_t), D_i^t(x_{t+1}, y_{t+1}) \text{ and } D_i^{t+1}(x_{t+1}, y_{t+1})$$

Let us consider the linear program to find $D_i^t(x_t, y_t)$ and to minimize clutter, omit the number of observations k, output M and inputs N in the following expression. Hence, the distance functions are reciprocal to traditional Farrell input-oriented measure, thus, this problem can be written as:

I $\left[D_i^t(x_t, y_t)\right]^{-1} = \min_{\varphi\lambda} \theta$

S.T $\varphi x_{kt} - x_t\lambda \geq 0$

$-y_{kt} + y_t\lambda \geq 0$

$\lambda \geq 0$

II $\left[D_i^{t+1}(x_{t+1}, y_{t+1})\right]^{-1} = \min_{\varphi\lambda} \theta$

S.T $\varphi x_{k,t+1} - x_{t+1}\lambda \geq 0$

$-y_{k,t+1} + y_{t+1}\lambda \geq 0$

$\lambda \geq 0$

III $\left[D_i^t(x_{t+1}, y_{t+1})\right]^{-1} = \min_{\varphi\lambda} \theta$

S.T $\varphi x_{k,t+1} - x_t\lambda \geq 0$

$-y_{k,t+1} + y_t\lambda \geq 0$

$\lambda \geq 0$

IV $\left[D_i^{t+1}(x_t, y_t)\right]^{-1} = \min_{\varphi\lambda} \theta$

S.T $\varphi x_{kt} - x_{t+1}\, \lambda \geq 0$

$-y_{kt} + y_{t+1}\lambda \geq 0$

$\lambda \geq 0$

Y_{kt} is a M×I vector of output quantities for the observation k at time t;

X_{kt} is a N×I vector input quantities for the observation k at time t;

$Y_{k,\ t+1}$ is a M×I vector of output quantities for the observation k at time t+1;

$X_{k,\ t+1}$ is a N×I vector of input quantities for the observation k at time t+1;

Y_t is a K×M matrix of output quantities for all observations at time t;

X_t is a K×N matrix of input quantities for all observations at time t;

λ is a K×I vector of weights and

φ is a scalar.

In the above formulation, is the efficiency score and take value between 0 and 1. The linear program may be solved k times, once for each observation in the sample.

In case of variable returns to scale, the Malmquist productivity change index can be further decomposed into three components:

$$M_i\left(x_{t+1}, y_{t+1}, x_t, y_t\right) = \text{TCH} * \text{PEFFCH} * \text{SEFFCH}$$

where TCH represents 'technological change', PEFFCH represents 'pure efficiency change' and SEFFCH represents 'scale efficiency change'. PEFFCH and SEFFCH are the components of EFFCH index relative to CRS technology. EFFCH index refers to efficiency change corresponding to CRS frontier (CCR Model). PEFFCH refers to pure efficiency change relative to VRS technology (BCC Model). Scale efficiency change is simply the ratio of $\text{EFFCH}_{\text{CRS}}/\text{PEFFCH}_{\text{VRS.}}$

Both the concepts have been illustrated in Figure 3.5 by adding two VRS frontiers. Pure TE change index is calculated in the same way as technical efficiency change index provided the production function technology is characterized by VRS frontier. Pure technical efficiency change depicts the movement of a firm/bank relative to the corresponding VRS frontier between two periods. On the other hand, scale efficiency change represents inter-period movement of an observed firm/bank from operating along VRS frontier to CRS frontier at the given level of output. We can derive following distance functions from the Figure 3.5.

$$\Delta\text{M} = \frac{D_v^{t+1}\left(x_{t+1}, y_{t+1}\right)}{D_v^t\left(x_t, y_t\right)}\left[\frac{D_c^{t+1}\left(x_{t+1}, y_{t+1}\right)}{D_v^{t+1}\left(x_{t+1}, y_{t+1}\right)} \cdot \frac{D_v^t\left(x_t, y_t\right)}{D_c^t\left(x_t, y_t\right)}\right]$$

(ΔP) (ΔS)

$$\left[\frac{D^t\left(x_{t+1}, y_{t+1}\right)}{D^{t+1}\left(x_{t+1}, y_{t+1}\right)} \cdot \frac{D^t\left(x_t, y_t\right)}{D^{t+1}\left(x_t, y_t\right)}\right]^{1/2}$$

(ΔT)

FIG. 3.5
Input-Oriented Malmquist Productivity Index under VRS

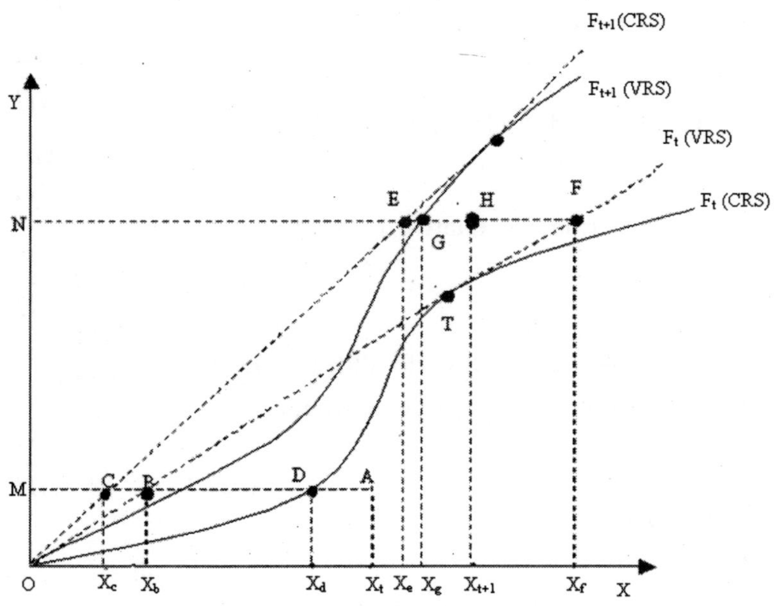

Adapted from Wu, S. (2005).

The first term, an index of pure TE change (ΔP) represents the effect of managerial decisions and managerial capabilities in the utilization of enhanced technological level between the periods t and t+1 under VRS technology. The second term (ΔS) captures the effect of scale between two periods t and t+1 under CRS and VRS technology. The last term (ΔT) measures the shift in the frontier due to innovations between period t and t+1 under CRS technology. As far as computation of scale efficiency index is concerned, it requires calculation of two additional distance functions: $D_v^t\left(x_t, y_t\right), D_v^{t+1}\left(x_{t+1}, y_{t+1}\right)$ with VRS technology by adding the following restriction: $\sum \lambda_k = 1$

Distance Functions with VRS Assumption

TE in period t relative to frontier t = $D_i^t(x_t, y_t) = \frac{MB}{MA}$

TE in period t+1 relative to frontier

t + 1= $D_i^{t+1}(x_{t+1}, y_{t+1}) = \frac{NE}{NH}$

TE in period t relative to frontier

t + 1 = $D_i^{t+1}(x_t, y_t) = \frac{MC}{MA}$

TE in period t+1 relative to frontier

t = $D_i^t(x_{t+1}, y_{t+1}) = \frac{NF}{NH}$

TE in period t relative to VRS t = $D_v^t(x_t, y_t) = \frac{MD}{MA}$

TE in period t+1 relative to frontier

t + 1 = $D_v^{t+1}(x_{t+1}, y_{t+1}) \frac{NG}{NH}$

Efficiency indices

$$\Delta E = \frac{D_i^{t+1}\left(x_t^{t+1}, y_t^{t+1}\right)}{D_i^t\left(x_t, y_t\right)} = \frac{NE}{NH} \times \frac{MA}{MB}$$

$$\Delta P = \frac{D_v^{t+1}\left(x_{t+1}, y_{t+1}\right)}{D_v^t\left(x_t, y_t\right)} = \frac{NG}{NH} \times \frac{MA}{MD}$$

$$\Delta S = \left[\frac{D_c^{t+1}\left(x_{t+1}, y_{t+1}\right)}{D_v^{t+1}\left(x_{t+1}, y_{t+1}\right)} \cdot \frac{D_c^t\left(x_t, y_t\right)}{D_v^t\left(x_t, y_t\right)}\right] = \left[\frac{NE}{NG} \cdot \frac{MB}{MD}\right]$$

$$\Delta T = \left[\left(\frac{D_i^t\left(x_{t+1}, y_{t+1}\right)}{D_i^{t+1}\left(x_{t+1}, y_{t+1}\right)}\right)\left(\frac{D_i^t\left(x_t, y_t\right)}{D_i^{t+1}\left(x_t, y_t\right)}\right)\right]^{\frac{1}{2}}$$

$$= \left[\left(\frac{NF}{NH}\times\frac{NH}{NE}\right)\times\left(\frac{MB}{MA}\times\frac{MA}{MC}\right)\right]^{\frac{1}{2}}$$

$$= \left[\frac{NF}{NE}\cdot\frac{MB}{MC}\right]^{\frac{1}{2}}$$

$$M_v = \Delta P * \Delta S * \Delta T$$

$$\Delta M = \frac{D_v^{t+1}(x_{t+1}, y_{t+1})}{D_v^t(x_t, y_t)}\left[\frac{D_c^{t+1}(x_{t+1}, y_{t+1})}{D_v^{t+1}(x_{t+1}, y_{t+1})}\cdot\frac{D_v^t(x_t, y_t)}{D_c^t(x_t, y_t)}\right]$$

$$\left[\frac{D^t(x_{t+1}, y_{t+1})}{D^{t+1}(x_{t+1}, y_{t+1})}\cdot\frac{D^t(x_t, y_t)}{D^{t+1}(x_t, y_t)}\right]^{1/2}$$

$$= \frac{NG}{NH}\times\frac{MA}{MD}\left[\frac{NE}{NG}\cdot\frac{MB}{MD}\right]\left[\frac{NF}{NE}\cdot\frac{MB}{MC}\right]^{\frac{1}{2}}$$

The additional input distance functions required constructing the VRS frontier could be calculated as follows:

I $\left[D_0^t(x_t, y_t)\right]^{-1} = \min_{\varphi\lambda}\theta$

S.T $\varphi x_{kt} - x_t\lambda \geq 0$

$-y_{kt} + y_t\lambda \geq 0$

$\sum \lambda_k = 1$

II $\left[D_i^{t+1}(x_{t+1}, y_{t+1})\right]^{-1} = \min_{\varphi\lambda}\theta$

S.T $\varphi x_{k,t+1} - x_{t+1}\lambda \geq 0$

$-y_{k,t+1} + y_{t+1}\ \lambda \geq 0$

$$\sum \lambda_k = 1$$

$$\lambda \geq 0$$

It should be noted that DEA based Malmquist productivity index assumes strong disposability of unwanted input and output that is a DMU can reduce its extra consumption of inputs costlessly. Inefficiency or input slack will emerge and this occurs when a DMU is operating on the sections of piecewise linear frontier which runs parallel to the axis. For instance, a DMU would be considered inefficient, if it could reduce additional input, still produce the same level of output and likewise increase its output without using any more inputs. However, Coelli and Rao (2001) explained that slacks are not important, if there are lots of data, as this would enable the DEA frontier to be a collection of many small facts providing a near smooth surface with minimal slack regional.

Scale Economies and X-Efficiency of Commercial Banks in India

On the onset of financial liberalization, the banking institutions are facing fast paced and highly dynamic economic environment, where efficiency and productivity growth have been recognized as the kingpin for survival. Therefore, the banking institutions of various nations are under pressure to improve their productive efficiency in order to survive and thrive in the global market. Historically, profitability was considered as the most important yardstick to gauge the performance of any business undertaking. But, banking is not merely an organization with profit motive; rather, it is a multi-purpose organization working to achieve some socio-economic objectives. Therefore, the performance of banks adjudged in terms of profitability cannot depict the multi-dimensional aspect of Indian banking sector. In light of this, the performance of the banks in terms of efficiency remains very high on the agenda of policy makers and researchers. And, it has been empirically examined that banks receiving higher efficiency scores are much more likely to survive than banks which have relatively low scores (Barr and Siems, 1996). In light of this, the notion of efficiency has attained priority to be analyzed by the researchers and policy-makers.

The assessment of efficiency has gained a lot of popularity by all the parties that participate in the banking industry. The regulators are interested in banks efficiency since it assists them to identify actual and potential problems in banking sector. Furthermore, it provides them the framework to assess the health of individual banks and to wipe out the complexities evolved in their working process. The efficiency scores provide the signal to investors and bank management regarding the soundness and managerial performance of the banking system. The banks efficiency also sheds light on the sustainability of banking sector, on the basis of which, decisions relating to mergers and acquisitions are taken. Banks are now more open to public examinations, on account of which, the banks are more likely to concentrate on their performance levels to sustain their position in the global market.

The present chapter has been devoted to analyze different measures of efficiency to have a comprehensive view of banks' performance. Therefore, overall efficiency (x-efficiency) takes into account the combined effect of allocative efficiency (AE) and technical efficiency (TE). Technical efficiency further takes into consideration the influence of scale efficiency (SE) and pure technical efficiency (PTE). To view this objective, linear programming-based Data Envelopment Analysis (DEA) approach has been applied on the balanced panel data set of 27 PSBs and 18 old private banks in India for the period 1985 to 2005-06. The entire study period has been classified into three distinct sub-periods: (i) Pre-liberalization period (1985 to 1991-92), (ii) Initial post-liberalization period (1992-93 to 1998-99) and (iii) Post-liberalization period (1999-00 to 2005-06). The analysis of pre-liberalization and post-liberalization period is justifiable on the ground that it assists us to analyze whether the liberalization program has favorably affected the efficiency of banks or not. To keep in lines with Howcroft and Attaullah (2006) and Zhao *et. al.* (2008), post-liberalization period has been further bifurcated into initial post-liberalization period or first-generation reforms period and post-liberalization period or second-generation reforms period. This attempt helps us to seek the change in the behavior of banks with the change in the degree of deregulation or liberalization. All the calculations related to DEA efficiency estimates have been computed through running DEAP software developed by Tim Coelli. In addition, Efficiency Measurement System (EMS) software developed by Holger Scheel has been used to calculate super-efficiency scores.

Empirical Evidence

The empirical results illustrate input-oriented efficiency scores obtained through running Charnes-Cooper-Rhodes (CCR) and Banker-Charnes-Cooper (BCC) model. It is important to note that input-oriented efficiency measures addresses the question: "By how much the input quantities can be proportionally reduced without altering the output quantities produced?" The empirical results illustrate an analysis of inter-temporal, ownership-wise and inter-bank comparison of x-efficiency (XE) and its components among commercial banks (CBs) in India for the period 1985 to 2005-06. Besides this, an attempt has been made to pinpoint the causes of inefficiency among commercial banks in India. Further, the empirical analysis seeks to explore the relationship between bank size and scale economies of commercial banks in India. In addition to it, this chapter focuses on identifying the super efficient banks and to rank them by the level of influence.

4.1 TEMPORAL PATTERN OF XE SCORES AND ITS COMPONENTS

4.1.1 XE Scores and Its Components

Table 4.1 presents temporal pattern of average XE scores and its components among commercial banks in India pertaining to various sub-periods. The empirical findings report that average cost x-efficiency has turned out to be 0.755 for all commercial banks (CBs) with standard deviation measure of 0.09. And, it ranged from the lowest figure of 0.657 in 1991-92 to the highest figure of 0.838 in 2002-03. The results, thus, imply that magnitude of cost inefficiency is to the tune of

TABLE 4.1

Temporal Pattern of Average X-Efficiency and its Components among Commercial Banks in India—1985 to 2005-06

Years	*Cost X-Efficiency*	*Technical Efficiency*	*Allocative Efficiency*	*Pure Technical Efficiency*	*Scale Efficiency*
1985	0.793	0.877	0.905	0.916	0.957
1986	0.798	0.897	0.890	0.924	0.970
1987	0.785	0.879	0.893	0.907	0.970
1988-89	0.740	0.848	0.873	0.889	0.954
1989-90	0.764	0.868	0.879	0.915	0.949
1990-91	0.675	0.768	0.883	0.821	0.937
1991-92	0.657	0.714	0.925	0.796	0.894
1992-93	0.685	0.724	0.947	0.761	0.943
1993-94	0.739	0.783	0.944	0.812	0.955
1994-95	0.775	0.803	0.965	0.851	0.940
1995-96	0.746	0.799	0.931	0.857	0.929
1996-97	0.688	0.750	0.919	0.836	0.894
1997-98	0.780	0.808	0.970	0.876	0.921
1998-99	0.752	0.810	0.931	0.885	0.912
1999-00	0.783	0.808	0.970	0.867	0.930
2000-01	0.765	0.814	0.942	0.886	0.918
2001-02	0.778	0.832	0.939	0.869	0.957
2002-03	0.838	0.863	0.971	0.905	0.953
2003-04	0.810	0.844	0.959	0.908	0.931
2004-05	0.755	0.785	0.963	0.888	0.886
2005-06	0.753	0.794	0.949	0.875	0.910
Averages					
1985/92	0.745	0.836	0.893	0.881	0.947
1993/99	0.738	0.782	0.944	0.840	0.928
2000/06	0.783	0.820	0.956	0.885	0.926
1985/06	0.755	0.813	0.931	0.869	0.934
S.D (1985/06)	0.090	0.087	0.030	0.081	0.050

Note : *S.D denotes standard deviations.

about 24.5 per cent among CBs in India. This suggests that, banks can, on an average, minimize their costs by eliminating the elements of inefficiencies with the help of best practices and can still produce the same level of outputs.

Looking at the components of XE, average TE score has worked out to be 0.813 with standard deviation of 0.087 and it ranged from the lowest figure of 0.714 in 1991-92 to the highest figure of 0.897 in 1986. In other words, the level of technical inefficiency of commercial banks tends out to be about (18.7 percent) in India. This suggests that, the banks can, on an average, curtail their expenditures on labor and loanable funds by at least 18.7 percent with the help of best practices without altering the level of outputs. Alternatively, the banks have the scope of producing 1.23 times (i.e., 1/0.813) as much as outputs from the same level of inputs.

The other component of XE reported 93.1 percent level of allocative efficiency with standard deviation measure of 0.03, varying from the lowest figure of 0.873 in the year 1988-89 to the highest figure of 0.971 in the year 2002-03. This implies that average AIE to the tune of about 6.9 percent is due to the choice of wrong mix of inputs to produce a given level of output. Thus, the empirical results suggest that, the banks can, on an average, reduce AIE through the use of optimal mix of inputs to produce a given level of outputs.

It is imperative to note that a considerable amount of x-inefficiency is due to the wastage of resources (18.7 percent) rather than the choice of wrong mix of input combinations (6.9 percent) to produce a given level of output. The results further imply that the bank managers are relatively good at selecting the optimum mix of inputs given the prices but they are not that good at using the minimum level of inputs to produce a given level of outputs. Therefore, it can safely be stated that technical inefficiency is the dominant source of x-inefficiency among CBs in India rather than allocative inefficiency in consistent to the findings of Rezvanian *et. al.* (2008).

4.1.2 Sources of Overall Technical (IN) Efficiency

As mentioned earlier, overall TE can be decomposed into two mutually exclusive and mutually exhaustive components viz., pure technical efficiency (PTE) and scale efficiency (SE).

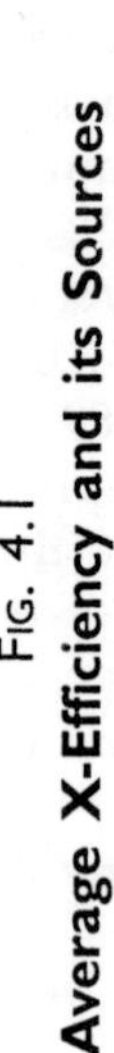

FIG. 4.1
Average X-Efficiency and its Sources

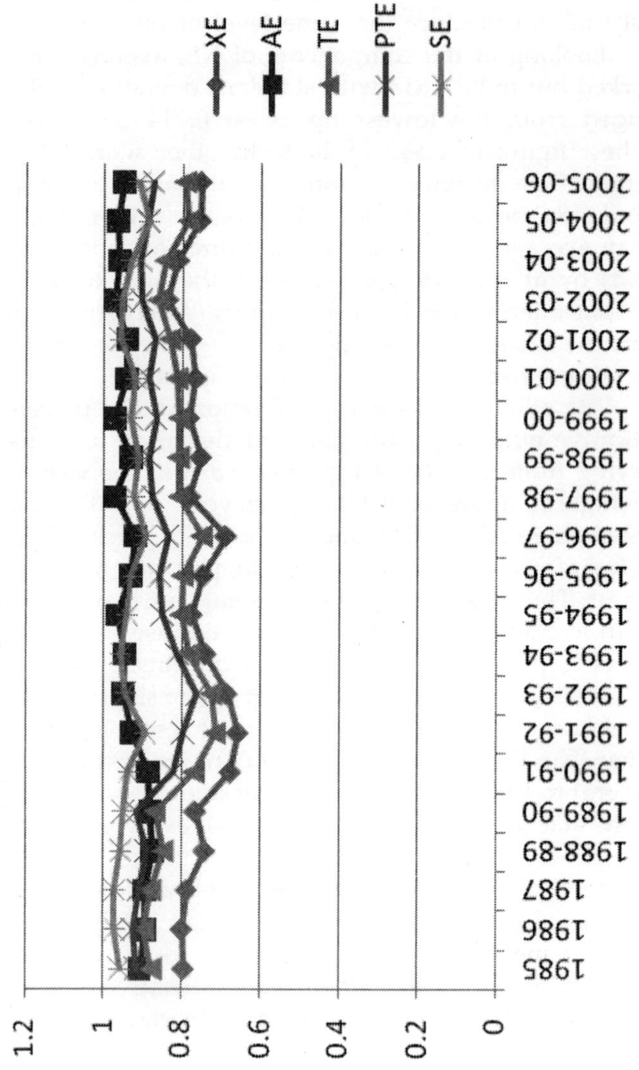

Like OTE, PTE also indicates the wastage of resources but unlike OTE, PTE is devoid of scale effects. PTE and SE scores have been computed through running BCC model for each year separately.

As depicted in Table 4.1, average PTE score of commercial banks has worked out to be 0.869 with standard deviation measure of 0.08. And, it fluctuated from the low value of 0.761 in the year 1992-93 to the high value of 0.924 in the year 1986. This in turn implies that average PTIE to the tune of about 13.1 percent is due to the inappropriate management practices in converting critical inputs into outputs. On the other hand, average scale efficiency score of CBs has noticed to be 0.934 with standard deviation of 0.05, varying from the low figure of 0.886 in 2004-05 to the high 0.970 in both the years of 1986 and 1987. This in turn implies that average SIE to the tune of about 6.6 percent is due to the choice of wrong scale of operation. Further, it is worth mentioning that a considerable portion of TIE (18.7 percent) is due to the inappropriate management practices in organizing the input resources (13 percent). However, the remaining part of the TIE can be attributed to the fact that the banks are either operating at below or above the optimum level. The connotation of the findings is that managerial irregularities have played a key role in emerging technical inefficiencies among CBs in India. And, these results are highly supported by the findings of Zhao *et. al.* (2008). Finally, the study suggests that concrete steps should be taken in order to improve the working of management. Although, scale-related problems are not found to be much serious as evidenced by the empirical findings. But, whatever amount of SIE has been worked out, appropriate steps should be taken to wipe it out so as to operate at the most productive scale size (MPSS).

4.1.3 X-Efficiency and its Decomposition : Period-wise Analysis

The comparative analysis of efficiency estimates of pre-reforms and first-generation reforms period highlights that average XE score of CBs has decelerated to 73.8 percent during 1993-99 in comparison to 74.5 percent during 1985-92. This further implies that the degree of x-inefficiency (XIE) has increased by (0.7 percent) between these periods. Looking at the decompositions of XE scores, the empirical findings divulge that average TE score of CBs has declined to 78.2 percent during 1993-99 as against 83.6 percent during 1985-92. This in turn infers that the degree of input waste (TIE) has increased by 5.4 percentage points between these periods.

However, somewhat contrasted picture has been portrayed in average AE estimates, where CBs experienced acceleration in efficiency scores to the level of 94.4 percent during first-generation reforms than that of 89.3 percent during pre-reforms period. This states that the degree of AIE has declined by (5.1 percent) during 1993-99 in comparison to 1985-92. Therefore, it can be stated that deregulatory policies have positive impact on the average allocative efficiency of banks.

As for the sources of TE, average PTE score of commercial banks declined to 84 percent during first-generation reforms in comparison to 88.1 during pre-reforms period. This in turn implies that the degree of inappropriate management practices of banks has increased by 4 percentage points between these periods. Similarly, the average SE score of CBs also noticed to be declined at 92.8 percent during the period 1993-99 as compared to 94.7 percent during the period 1985-92. This indicates a clear increase in the amount of scale inefficiency (SIE) by 2 percentage points between these periods. Overall, it has been noticed that first phase of reforms failed to exert positive impact on most of the DEA efficiency estimates of CBs in India (except AE). This may be due to the fact that the banks have to face significant and frequent policy changes during this period. But, banks could not suddenly adapt themselves according to the change in set standards and guidelines recommended by various committees during the study period.

In second-phase of liberalization period (1999-00 onwards), the average XE score of CBs accelerated to 78.3 percent as compared to initial-phase of liberalization period. This reveals a clear fall in the magnitude of XIE by 4.5 percentage points during the period 2000-06. Looking at the sources of XE the banks experienced similar pattern of acceleration in average TE and AE with efficiency measures of

(82 percent) and (95.6 percent) respectively during 2000-06. This clearly indicates a fall in the amount of TIE by (3.8 percent) and AIE by (1.2 percent) as against the first-generation reforms period.

As for the sources of TE, average PTE score of CBs accelerated to 88.5 percent, which implies fall in the degree of pure technical inefficiency (PTIE) by 4.5 percentage points during 2000-06. Similarly, average SE estimate of CBs decreased at the level of 92.6 percent during the period 2000-06, which indicates an increase in the amount of SIE by 0.2 percentage points as compared to the period 1993-99. Although, the degree of SE scores is noted to be higher than PTE scores in various sub-periods, but deregulatory policies failed to exert favorable dent on the average scale efficiency scores of sample banks in India.

Overall, it has been noticed that technical inefficiency is the major cause of concern for XIE rather than AIE as evidenced by various sub-periods' findings. Thus, bank managers should concentrate more upon the efficient utilization of resources at the given state of technology. As for the sources of TE, it can safely be concluded that inappropriate managerial practices are more responsible for emerging technical inefficiencies among CBs in India as compared to scale-related problems. And, this result is highly consistent to the findings of Das (1999-00) and Zhao *et. al.* (2008). Thus, the need of the hour is to evolve proper yardsticks to improve the managerial capabilities of labor force through various training programmes etc. It also emerges from the analysis is that improvement in DEA efficiency estimates is more apparent in second-generation reforms (1999-00 to 2005-06), which is consistent to the findings of RBI (2008). This may be primarily caused by the fact that banks are increasingly adopt the changes in set standards and prudential norms and thereby started to realize the benefits of high degree of liberalization in quantitative form during the period 2000-06.

Contrary to expectations, commercial banks are noted to be more efficient in pre-reforms period as compared to first-phase and second-phase of liberalisation period, which may possibly be attributed to the shift in accounting norms. According to these norms, any asset that have two consecutive quarterly defaults in interest accrual cannot be treated as income, rather till 1992, this item was considered as an income. The shift from *'Income on Accrual Basis'* to *'Income on Realization Basis'* has compressed the income level of the banks in India. Nevertheless, these results are highly consistent to the findings of Das (1997) and De, Prithwis Kumar (2004), where average efficiency scores of banks were noted to be lower in post-liberalization period than that of pre-liberalization period. These results are also found to be similar to the findings obtained by Zhao *et. al.* (2008), where the magnitude of input waste was estimated to be lower in second sub-period (1998-2004) than first sub-period (1992-97).

4.2 BANK OWNERSHIP AND X-EFFICIENCY

4.2.1 Bank Ownership and Period-wise Analysis of XE Estimates

In Table 4.2, we have presented average estimates of x-efficiency, allocative efficiency and technical efficiency of commercial banks in India for the period 1985-06. The commercial banks have been decomposed into two categories of PSBs and private banks. PSBs have been further bifurcated into two groups i.e., SBI group and NBs group.

If we look at the temporal performance of banks, (as shown in Table 4.2 and Figures 4.2, 4.3 and 4.4) no stable and consistent trend of XE, TE and AE scores has been observed among different forms of banks. The PSBs achieved the highest XE (0.838) in 2002-03 and lowest (0.637) in 1990-91. However, private banks noted the highest x-efficiency score (0.854) in 1985 and 1987 each and the lowest (0.662) in 1991-92.

Looking at the decompositions of XE, PSBs achieved the highest TE (0.880) in 1986 and lowest (0.675) in 1992-93. However, private banks recorded the highest TE (0.922) in 1985 and 1986 each and the lowest (0.715) in 1991-92.

Overall, PSBs have registered higher variations in the XE and TE scores as compared to private banks, which may be attributed to the improved practices of certain PSBs. On the other hand, lower variability in the efficiency scores of private banks may be attributed to the sudden and immediate response to new prudential norms and standards. Furthermore, according to the empirical findings, NBs group of

TABLE 4.2

Average Cost X-Efficiency, Technical Efficiency and Allocative Efficiency Scores of Commercial Banks in India : 1985 to 2005-06

	Cost-X Efficiency				*Technical Efficiency*				*Allocative Efficiency*			
Years	*NBs*	*SBI*	*PSBs*	*Private*	*NBs*	*SBI*	*PSBs*	*Private*	*NBs*	*SBI*	*PSBs*	*Private*
(1)	(2)	(3)	(4)	(5)	(6)	(7)	(8)	(9)	(10)	(11)	(12)	(13)
1985	0.737	0.789	0.753	0.854	0.858	0.820	0.847	0.922	0.859	0.963	0.890	0.927
1986	0.751	0.789	0.762	0.852	0.890	0.856	0.880	0.922	0.844	0.920	0.867	0.925
1987	0.723	0.778	0.739	0.854	0.876	0.832	0.863	0.904	0.824	0.939	0.858	0.946
1988-89	0.659	0.741	0.683	0.825	0.844	0.838	0.842	0.855	0.778	0.889	0.811	0.967
1989-90	0.685	0.761	0.707	0.849	0.853	0.850	0.852	0.892	0.800	0.896	0.828	0.954
1990-91	0.604	0.714	0.637	0.732	0.740	0.754	0.744	0.803	0.822	0.948	0.860	0.917
1991-92	0.58	0.829	0.653	0.662	0.644	0.878	0.714	0.715	0.916	0.944	0.924	0.927
1992-93	0.548	0.854	0.639	0.754	0.582	0.896	0.675	0.796	0.944	0.953	0.946	0.949
1993-94	0.604	0.852	0.677	0.831	0.634	0.914	0.717	0.881	0.950	0.932	0.945	0.943
1994-95	0.681	0.880	0.740	0.827	0.703	0.913	0.765	0.860	0.968	0.964	0.967	0.962
1995-96	0.642	0.827	0.697	0.819	0.692	0.924	0.761	0.857	0.925	0.895	0.916	0.954
1996-97	0.622	0.791	0.672	0.710	0.670	0.859	0.726	0.787	0.932	0.924	0.929	0.904
1997-98	0.731	0.923	0.788	0.781	0.746	0.952	0.807	0.810	0.976	0.970	0.975	0.963

(*Contd.*)

TABLE 4.2 (*Contd.*)

(1)	(2)	(3)	(4)	(5)	(6)	(7)	(8)	(9)	(10)	(11)	(12)	(13)
1998-99	0.694	0.902	0.756	0.747	0.747	0.923	0.799	0.826	0.935	0.977	0.948	0.905
1999-00	0.707	0.913	0.768	0.805	0.733	0.933	0.793	0.831	0.969	0.978	0.972	0.968
2000-01	0.719	0.916	0.777	0.748	0.758	0.925	0.808	0.824	0.954	0.991	0.965	0.908
2001-02	0.721	0.859	0.762	0.803	0.761	0.887	0.798	0.882	0.953	0.968	0.957	0.911
2002-03	0.817	0.888	0.838	0.839	0.840	0.905	0.859	0.869	0.974	0.982	0.977	0.964
2003-04	0.795	0.858	0.813	0.805	0.826	0.897	0.847	0.840	0.963	0.957	0.961	0.956
2004-05	0.786	0.834	0.800	0.687	0.809	0.849	0.821	0.731	0.974	0.985	0.977	0.942
2005-06	0.758	0.838	0.782	0.711	0.794	0.866	0.815	0.762	0.957	0.966	0.960	0.933
Averages												
1985/92	0.677	0.772	0.705	0.804	0.815	0.833	0.820	0.859	0.835	0.928	0.862	0.938
1993/99	0.646	0.861	0.710	0.781	0.682	0.912	0.750	0.831	0.947	0.945	0.947	0.940
2000/06	0.757	0.872	0.791	0.771	0.789	0.895	0.820	0.820	0.963	0.975	0.967	0.940
1985/06	0.693	0.835	0.735	0.785	0.762	0.880	0.797	0.837	0.915	0.950	0.925	0.939
S.D (1985/06)	0.075	0.040	0.093	0.080	0.083	0.046	0.090	0.077	0.027	0.017	0.029	0.031

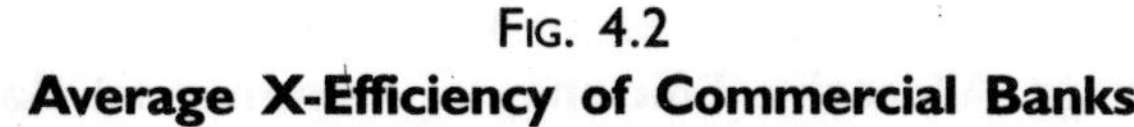

FIG. 4.2
Average X-Efficiency of Commercial Banks

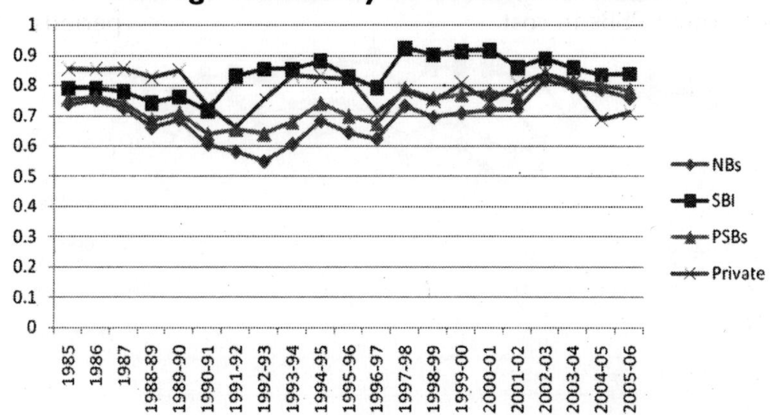

FIG. 4.3
Average Technical Efficiency of Commercial Banks

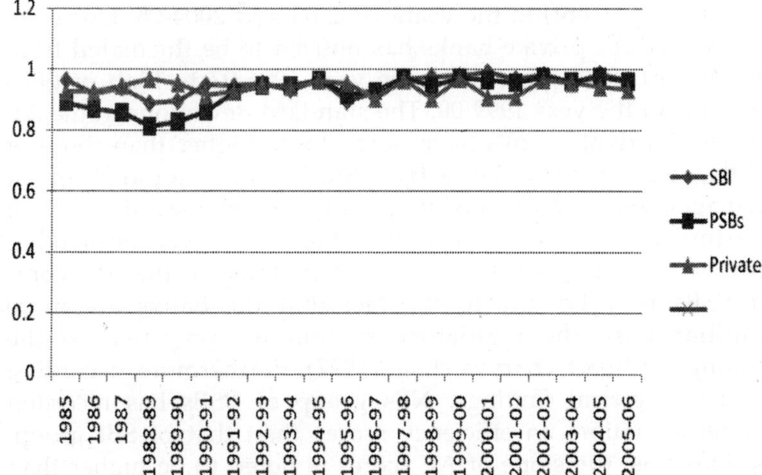

PSBs has recorded higher variations in efficiency scores than that of SBI group.

As for average AE measures PSBs reported average AE score from the low (81.1 percent) in the year 1988-89 to the

Fig. 4.4

Average Allocative Efficiency of Commercial Banks

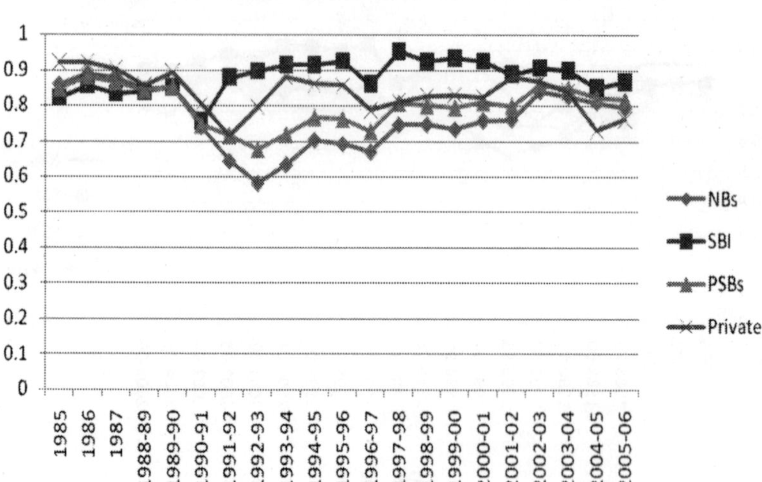

high (97.7 percent) in the years 2002-03 and 2004-05. However, average AE of private banks has noticed to be fluctuated from the low of (90.4 percent) in the year 1996-97 to high of (96.8 percent) in the year 1999-00. The standard deviations in the AE scores of private banks have noted to be higher than those of PSBs, which may be attributed to the separation of management and ownership as well as to the adoption of dissimilar practices by different banks in decision-making process. On the other hand, lower variability in the AE scores of PSBs may be due to the fact that the banks are more familiar with the regulatory system in consistent to the findings of Bhattacharyya *et. al.* (1997). Furthermore, according to the empirical findings, NBs group of PSBs has recorded higher variations in efficiency scores than that of SBI group. Besides this, the slope of AE scores is noted to be higher than TE scores in different forms of banks for most of the sample years.

Further, the empirical findings illustrate that the average XE of private banks is quite high at 78.5 percent followed by PSBs with efficiency measure of 73.5 percent during the period 1985-06. This indicates that private banks have the potential for cost saving by 21.5 percent while PSBs can cut their costs by 26.5 percent to become fully efficient banks and capture position on the *Best Practice Frontier*. Thus, it is obvious from the analysis that private banks have outperformed PSBs in cost savings with the given state of technology and these results are consistent with the findings of Rezvanian *et. al.* (2008). Despite larger cost efficiency gains by private banks, PSBs, especially the SBI group emerged to be the market leader with XE score of (83.5 percent) and lowest variability in performance levels (0.04) during the period 1985-06.

Turning towards the period-wise analysis, the average XE score of PSBs has noted to be accelerated at the level of (71.0 percent) during 1993-99 as against (70.5 percent) during 1985-92. This in turn provides the evidence of fall in the amount of XIE of PSBs by 0.5 percentage points during this period. However, average XE score of private banks declined to (78.1 percent) during 1993-99 as compared to (80.4 percent) during 1985-92. Further, the results imply that XIE of banks has increased by 2.3 percentage points between these periods. Despite insignificant dent of reforms on the average XE estimates of private banks, these banks performed better than its counterpart group (PSBs) in both the pre-reforms and first-generation reforms period.

In second-phase of liberalization period, the empirical findings reported that XE of PSBs has accelerated to (79.1 percent) in comparison to first-generation reforms. This states that PSBs have registered notable decline in the degree of XIE by (8.1 percent) between these periods. On the other hand, XE of private banks deteriorated, stood at the level of about (77.1 percent) as compared to first-generation reforms. This further infers that private banks have witnessed an increase in the amount of XIE by 1.1 percentage point between these periods. Thus, it can safely be stated that the PSBs have responded well to reformatory measures than their private sector counterparts in consistent to the findings of Bhaumik and Dimova (2004). As for the categories of PSBs, SBI group recorded tremendous fall in x-inefficiency by 8.9 percentage points from pre-reforms to first-generation reforms, but by just 1.1 percentage points from first-generation to second-generation reforms. On the whole, SBI group gained the most in XE than that of NBs group in distinct sub-periods.

4.2.2 Bank Ownership and Period-wise Analysis of Sources of X-(IN) Efficiency

It is obvious from Table 4.2 that the average TE of private banks is quite high at 83.7 percent, followed by PSBs (79.7 percent) during the period 1985-06. This indicates that private banks are more efficient in input utilization process to produce a given level of output than those of PSBs. Although, private banks outperformed PSBs in terms of technical efficiency but SBI group emerged to be market leader with average technical efficiency score of (88 percent) and variability in performance level of (0.046) during the period 1985-06. The empirical findings of TE scores are consistent with the findings of De, Prithwis Kumar (2004) as per time-variant efficiency scores for output measure Y_1 and Gunjan, M Sanjeev (2006), where private banks were found to be more technical efficient than PSBs. The dominance of SBI group over the NBs is consistent to the findings of Das (2000) and Kumar and Verma (2002-03).

The comparative analysis of pre-reforms and first-generation reforms divulges that the average TE score of private banks has decelerated to the level of 0.831 during 1993-99 in comparison to 0.859 during 1985-92. This in turn implies an increase in the amount of technical inefficiency of banks by 2.8 percentage points between these periods. PSBs also followed similar trend of fall in TE scores, stood at 0.750 during 1993-99 as against 0.820 during 1985-92. Stated differently, PSBs have experienced an increase in the amount of TIE by 7 percentage points between these periods. Overall, it has been observed that private banks have outperformed PSBs in both the pre-reforms and first-generation reforms period.

During the period 2000-06, the average TE score of private banks again decelerated to 0.820 relative to the period 1993-99. This, in turn, delineates an increase in the magnitude of TIE by 1.1 percentage points between these periods. However, average TE score of PSBs has noted to be increased at the level of 0.820 during the period 2000-06 as against the period 1993-99. Thus, the results imply that PSBs have noticed considerable fall in the amount of TIE i.e., by 7 percentage points between these periods. Further, the SBI group of PSBs has performed better than private banks in terms of technical efficiency during the sub-periods: 1993-99 and 2000-06. Although, SBI group of PSBs gained the most in TE during the sub-periods: 1993-99 and 2000-06 but it could not tend PSBs to become more efficient in input usages to produce a given level of output over the private banks. The empirical findings connote that PSBs have responded well than their private counterparts after the deregulatory policies came into practice (since 1992-93) in consistent to the findings of Bhaumik and Dimova (2004). Moreover, the empirical findings highlight that SBI group of PSBs has also outweighed the NBs group in terms of technical efficiency during various sub-periods.

In terms of allocative efficiency scores, although, SBI group of PSBs displayed its top most performance with efficiency measure of (95 percent) during 1985-06. But, it could not tend PSBs as a group to become more efficient than those of private banks. The empirical findings highlight that the average AE of private banks has turned out to (93.9 percent), followed by PSBs (92.5 percent) during the period 1985-06. Stated differently, private banks are found to be more efficient in selecting optimum input-combinations at the given input prices than those of PSBs. The results are found to be highly consistent with the findings of Rezvanian *et. al.* (2008), where private banks outperformed PSBs in terms of allocative efficiency.

Further, the period-wise analysis delineates that the average AE score of private banks has observed to be marginally increased at the level of 0.940 during 1993-99 as against 0.938 during 1985-92. This infers that AIE of private banks has declined by 0.2 percentage points between these periods. On the other hand, PSBs have experienced a notable improvement in AE scores at the level of 0.947 during 1993-99 in comparison to 0.862 during 1985-92. This indicates a substantial decline in the amount of AIE of PSBs by 8.5 percentage points between these periods.

During 2000-06, private banks did not register any change in AE estimates in comparison to 1993-99. However, PSBs experienced an increase with AE measure of 0.967 in comparison to the period 1993-99. This in turn signals that

PSBs have noticed fall in AIE by 2 percentage points between these periods. Similarly, SBI group of PSBs reported lower level of AIE than that of NBs group for most parts of the sub-periods. The connotation of the finding is that PSBs have become more efficient in selecting optimum mix of inputs to produce a given level of output on the eve of high degree of liberalization period. The allocative efficiency gains by PSBs may be attributed to the recovery of past NPAs and improvement in credit risk environment. Moreover, the wide disbursement of the banking business may be the other factor of higher efficiency gains among PSBs.

These results are highly supported by the findings of Singh and Kumar (2005) where average allocative efficiency of PSBs was noted to be higher than those of private banks. The results also highlight that private banks have not responded positively to the deregulatory policies as evinced by the findings of post-liberalization period, is highly supported by the findings of Bhaumik and Dimova (2004).

Overall, it has been observed that an improvement in efficiency scores is more pronounced in second-generation reforms period as compared to first-generation reforms period. In addition, private banks are found to be more efficient in inputs utilization process as compared to PSBs in various sub-periods. However, PSBs are noticed to be more efficient in selecting the optimum mix of inputs at the given prices. Further, the empirical findings substantiate that the magnitude of AE is higher among both the PSBs and private banks for most parts of the sub-periods. Thus, it can safely be concluded that allocative efficiency is the major source of x-efficiency among various forms of banks in distinct sub-periods. Finally, the empirical findings suggest that appropriate measures should be adopted to reduce the wastage of resources and to extract maximum possible returns at the given state of technology.

4.2.3 Bank Ownership and Sources of Technical (IN) Efficiency

In Table 4.3, average estimates of pure technical efficiency and scale efficiency of various forms of banks in India have been presented for the period 1985-06. Looking at the temporal

TABLE 4.3

Average Scale Efficiency and Pure Technical Efficiency Scores of Commercial Banks in India—1985 to 2005-06

	Pure Technical Efficiency				Scale Efficiency			
Years	NBs	SBI	PSBs	Private	NBs	SBI	PSBs	Private
(1)	(2)	(3)	(4)	(5)	(6)	(7)	(8)	(9)
1985	0.914	0.883	0.905	0.933	0.940	0.932	0.938	0.987
1986	0.908	0.933	0.915	0.938	0.980	0.920	0.962	0.982
1987	0.890	0.883	0.888	0.935	0.983	0.945	0.971	0.967
1988-89	0.877	0.889	0.88	0.902	0.963	0.944	0.958	0.948
1989-90	0.895	0.901	0.897	0.943	0.952	0.947	0.950	0.946
1990-91	0.794	0.815	0.800	0.853	0.935	0.931	0.934	0.941
1991-92	0.707	0.893	0.762	0.847	0.903	0.982	0.927	0.844
1992-93	0.626	0.911	0.710	0.837	0.918	0.985	0.938	0.950
1993-94	0.680	0.932	0.754	0.898	0.918	0.981	0.937	0.981
1994-95	0.751	0.922	0.801	0.926	0.930	0.990	0.947	0.928
1995-96	0.752	0.943	0.809	0.929	0.914	0.981	0.934	0.922
1996-97	0.743	0.901	0.790	0.906	0.894	0.954	0.912	0.867

(Contd.)

TABLE 4.3 (*Contd.*)

(1)	*(2)*	*(3)*	*(4)*	*(5)*	*(6)*	*(7)*	*(8)*	*(9)*
1997-98	0.785	0.973	0.841	0.928	0.945	0.979	0.955	0.871
1998-99	0.813	0.954	0.855	0.931	0.914	0.968	0.930	0.885
1999-00	0.788	0.958	0.838	0.911	0.929	0.975	0.943	0.910
2000-01	0.828	0.950	0.864	0.919	0.915	0.974	0.932	0.897
2001-02	0.810	0.898	0.836	0.918	0.941	0.987	0.954	0.962
2002-03	0.876	0.918	0.889	0.929	0.957	0.984	0.965	0.936
2003-04	0.867	0.942	0.889	0.937	0.951	0.954	0.952	0.899
2004-05	0.871	0.886	0.876	0.905	0.928	0.959	0.937	0.808
2005-06	0.835	0.879	0.848	0.914	0.950	0.986	0.961	0.834
Averages								
1985/92	0.855	0.885	0.864	0.907	0.951	0.943	0.949	0.945
1993/99	0.736	0.934	0.794	0.908	0.919	0.977	0.936	0.915
2000/06	0.839	0.919	0.863	0.919	0.939	0.974	0.949	0.892
1985/06	0.810	0.913	0.840	0.911	0.936	0.965	0.945	0.917
S.D (1985/06)	0.070	0.056	0.080	0.062	0.041	0.025	0.039	0.054

FIG. 4.5
Average SE of Commercial Banks

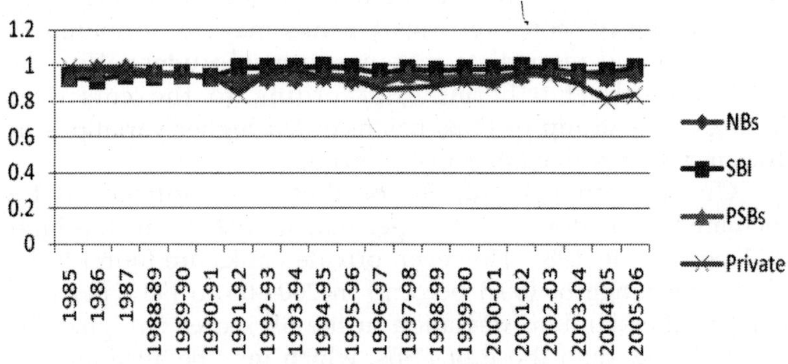

FIG. 4.6
Average PTE of Commercial Banks

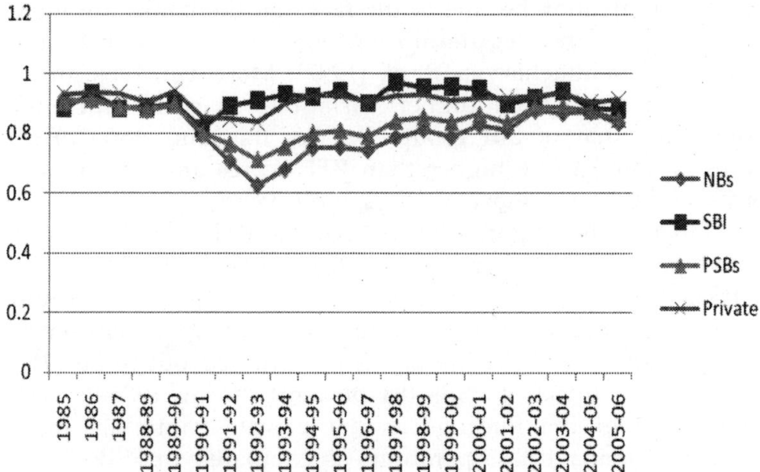

performance pattern of efficiency scores (as depicted in Table 4.3 and Figures 4.5 and 4.6), no stable and consistent trend of PTE and SE scores has been observed among different forms of banks. The PSBs achieved the highest PTE (0.915) in 1986 and lowest (0.710) in 1992-93. However, private banks noted the highest PTE score (0.943) in 1989-90 and the lowest (0.837) in 1992-93. Overall, it has been observed that the standard deviations in the PTE scores of PSBs are higher than those of private banks, which may be attributed to the improved practices of certain PSBs. On the other hand, lower variability in the efficiency scores of private banks may be attributed to the sudden and immediate response to new prudential norms and standards. Furthermore, according to the empirical findings, NBs group of PSBs has recorded higher variations in efficiency scores than that of SBI group.

On the other hand, SE of PSBs has noticed to be fluctuated from the low (91.2 percent) in 1996-97 to the high (97.1 percent) in 1987. However, private banks are found to be within the range of (80.8 percent) in 2004-05 to (98.7 percent) in 1985. The standard deviation in the SE scores is higher for private banks than those of PSBs, which may be attributed to the separation of management and ownership as well as to the adoption of dissimilar practices by different banks in decision making process. On the other hand, lower variability in the SE scores of PSBs may be due to the fact that the banks are more familiar with the regulatory system in consistent to the findings of Bhattacharyya *et. al.* (1997). Moreover, NBs group of PSBs has recorded higher variations in scale efficiency scores than that of SBI group. Besides this, the slope of SE scores is noted to be higher than PTE scores among different forms of banks for most of the sample years.

Table 4.3 highlights that the average PTE of SBI group is quite high at 91.3 percent during 1985-06. Although, SBI group of PSBs has attained the most in PTE scores, but, PSBs could not outperform private banks in terms of managerial efficiency. The average PTE of private banks has worked out to be (91.1 percent) than those of PSBs (84 percent) during 1985-06. The connotation of the findings is that private banks are more efficient in managerial operations as compared to PSBs.

Further, the period-wise analysis delineates that private banks have witnessed marginal improvement with average PTE measure of 0.908 during 1993-99 in comparison to 0.907 during 1985-92. This in turn indicates a meager decline in the amount of PTIE by (0.1 percent) between these periods. However, PSBs have experienced deceleration in average PTE score, stood at 0.794 during 1993-99 as compared to 0.864 during 1985-92. This further implies that PSBs have recorded an increase in the degree of PTIE by 7 percentage points between these periods.

During 2000-06, the average PTE score of private banks accelerated to 0.919 in comparison to the period 1993-99. This infers a clear fall in the amount of PTIE by 1.1 percentage points between these periods. Similarly, average PTE measure of PSBs sharply accelerated to 0.863 during 2000-06 as compared to 1993-99. This in turn signals that PSBs have recorded considerable fall in the amount of PTIE by 6.9 percentage points between these periods. The empirical findings connote that private banks are more efficient in managerial operations than those of PSBs in various sub-periods. It also emanates from the empirical analysis that SBI group has contributed more to the managerial efficiency of PSBs relative to NBs group in all the sub-periods.

As for scale efficiency estimates, PSBs have experienced efficiency to the tune of about (94.5 percent), followed by private banks (91.7 percent) during the period 1985-06. Stated differently, PSBs seems to be in a better position to reap substantial benefits of scale economies than those of private banks. Furthermore, SBI group of PSBs has emerged to be market leader with scale efficiency measure of (96.5 percent) during 1985-06. The connotation of the findings is that most of the PSBs are operating at an efficient scale of operation that that of private banks.

Further, the period-wise analysis delineates that SE of private banks has decreased to 0.915 during the period 1993-99 as against 0.945 during the period 1985-92. This in turn provides that SIE of banks has increased by 3.0 percentage points between these periods. Similarly, PSBs also registered declination with average SE score of 0.936 during 1993-99 in comparison to 0.949 during 1985-92. Stated differently, PSBs have experienced an increase in the amount of SIE by 1.3 percentage points between these periods.

In second-phase of liberalization period, the average SE of private banks again decelerated to 0.892 relative to initial-phase of liberalization period. This reflects an increase in the magnitude of SIE by 2.3 percentage points between these periods. In contrast, the average SE of PSBs accented to 0.949 during 2000-06 as compared to 1993-99. The results in turn provide that PSBs have witnessed a clear fall in the amount of SIE by 1.3 percentage points between these periods. Thus, PSBs are noted to be more scale efficient than those of private banks in distinct sub-periods. But whatever amount of scale inefficiency has been observed among PSBs, can be attributed to overstaffing as well as over branching. In addition, the scale inefficiency among PSBs may also be due to the fact that the banks are not allowed to close their unprofitable branches. Furthermore, according to the empirical findings, SBI group has performed better than NBs group in exhausting the benefits of scale economies for most parts of the sample periods.

Overall, it has been observed that second-phase of liberalization period does have perceptible impact on the improvement of SE and PTE scores in comparison to the initial-phase of liberalization period. Besides this, private banks are found to be more managerially efficient that that of PSBs in all the specified periods. However, PSBs are found to be operated at more efficient scale of operations than those of private banks in various sub-periods. Looking at the efficiency measures of SE and PTE, the magnitude of SE has noted to be higher among both the PSBs and private banks in most of the sub-periods. Thus, it can safely be concluded that scale efficiency is the major source of technical efficiency among various forms of banks as compared to managerial efficiency. Finally, the empirical findings suggest sharpening the managerial skills through various programmes to overcome the wastage of resources.

4.3 MANN-WHITNEY TEST

To investigate whether the change in DEA efficiency scores among different group of banks is statistically significant or not, Mann-Whitney U-Statistics rank test[1] has been applied. Through this test, following hypothesis has been tested for various sub-periods under consideration.

Under H_0 : The null-hypothesis is that there is no significant difference in the distribution of average efficiency scores among NBs v/s SBI, PSBs v/s private banks, SBI v/s private banks and NBs v/s private banks in various sub-periods.

Against H_1 : The alternative hypothesis is that there is significant difference in the distribution of average efficiency scores among NBs v/s SBI, PSBs v/s private banks, SBI v/s private banks and NBs v/s private banks in various sub-periods.

Now the null-hypothesis that both samples come from the same population can be tested using Z-test written as:

$$Z = \frac{U - \overline{U}}{s_u}$$

If $Z > Z_a$ (critical value of Z), then the null-hypothesis of common population is rejected, which signals significant efficiency differences among various bank groups in specified sub-periods and *vice-versa*. But, if the value of Z=0, then the null-hypothesis of common population is not defined, which means that there is no or negligible change in the efficiency score of banks in the specified periods.

Table 4.4 highlights the results of non-parametric Mann-Whitney U-statistics rank test for various ownership categories of CBs in India for the period 1985-06. The choice of Mann-Whitney test is motivated by its advantage over traditional t-test, which assumes that the parent population is normally distributed whereas the former is distribution free test. The Mann-Whitney test scores (as presented in Table 4.4) illustrate that no statistical significant difference has been noted when comparison is made between public v/s private banks for average XE, AE and TE scores for the period 1985-06. The results are supported by the results of Das (1997), which found no significant efficiency differences in any of the efficiency measures between public v/s private banks. However, this group differs for average SE and PTE scores during the period 1985-06. As for various sub-periods, this bank group recorded significant differences in XE and AE scores for pre-reforms, PTE scores for first-generation reforms and AE, SE and PTE scores for second-generation reforms period. However, the reverse holds to be true in rest of the DEA efficiency estimates. These results suggest that private banks are more efficient than

Table 4.4

Statistical Test of Equality between the Distribution of DEA Efficiency Scores of Bank Groups : An Application of Mann-Whitney U Test

			1985-92		1993-99		2000-06		1985-06	
XE	*N1*	*N2*	*U*	*Z*	*U*	*Z*	*U*	*Z*	*U*	*Z*
(1)	*(2)*	*(3)*	*(4)*	*(5)*	*(6)*	*(7)*	*(8)*	*(9)*	*(10)*	*(11)*
PSBs/ Pvt	27	18	116	-2.856*	191	-1.1	219	-0.445	170	-1.691
NBs/SBI	19	8	15	-3.239*	10	-3.505*	17	-3.133*	6	-3.717*
SBI/Pvt	8	18	57.5	-0.806	33	-2.167*	23	-2.722*	37	-1.944
NBs/Pvt	19	18	42.5	-3.905*	72	-3.008*	149	-0.669	63	-3.2*
AE	N1	N2	U	Z	U	Z	U	Z	U	Z
PSBs/ Pvt	27	18	85	-3.582*	222	-0.375	132	-2.482*	181	-1.436
NBs/SBI	19	8	17	-3.133*	74	-0.106	61	-0.797	18	-3.08*
SBI/Pvt	8	18	52	-1.111	67	-0.278	27.5	-2.473*	57	-0.833
NBs/Pvt	19	18	34	-4.163*	163	-0.243	89.5	-2.477*	94	-2.34*
OTE	N1	N2	U	Z	U	Z	U	Z	U	Z
PSBs/ Pvt	27	18	199	-0.913	181.5	-1.323	224.5	-0.316	180	-1.321
NBs/SBI	19	8	58	-0.956	6	-3.717*	26.5	-2.629*	20	-2.974*
SBI/Pvt	8	18	63	-0.5	38.5	-1.861	38	-1.889	43	-1.611
NBs/Pvt	19	18	119.5	-1.566	64	-3.251*	114.5	-1.717	85	-2.613*

SE	N1	N2	U	Z	U	Z	U	Z	U	Z
PSBs/ Pvt	27	18	200.5	-0.878	175.5	-1.463	134	-2.435*	158	-1.969*
NBs/SBI	19	8	60	-0.85	21.5	-2.894*	32	-2.337*	42	-1.805
SBI/Pvt	8	18	66	-0.33	28.5	-2.417*	24	-2.667*	26	-2.556*
NBs/Pvt	19	18	149	-0.669	162	-0.273	111	-1.823	132	-1.185
PTE	**N1**	**N2**	**U**	**Z**	**U**	**Z**	**U**	**Z**	**U**	**Z**
PSBs/ Pvt	27	18	177	-1.429	128	-2.575*	152	-2.01*	123	-2.78*
NBs/SBI	19	8	49.5	-1.407	6	-3.718*	38.5	-1.99*	21	-2.9*
SBI/Pvt	8	18	57.5	-0.807	62	-0.556	71	-0.056	71	-0.056
NBs/Pvt	19	18	104	-2.037*	38	-4.042*	79	-2.79*	52	-3.61*

Note : (1) *Signifies that the coefficient is significant at 5 percent significance level. The value of Z-statistics are compared with $Z_a = 1.96$.

PSBs in most of the DEA efficiency estimates during the sub-periods: 1985-92 and 1993-99 (with few exceptions). But, PSBs have become more efficient than private banks for most of the efficiency measures during the period 2000-06.

Further, the empirical findings highlight that NBs v/s SBI group has recorded significant differences in average XE, AE, OTE and PTE scores for the period 1985-06. Only SE differences significantly differ for this group. As for distinct sub-periods, NBs v/s SBI group registered significant differences in average XE and AE scores during 1985-92; XE, OTE, SE and PTE differences during 1993-99 and XE, TE, SE and PTE differences during 2000-06. The connotation of the findings is that SBI group is more efficient than NBs group for most of the efficiency estimates, although few exceptions exist.

In addition, SBI v/s private banks group did not report significant differences in XE, AE, TE and PTE scores for the entire study period. But, this group differs for SE estimates. Further, the period-wise analysis divulges that this bank group is found to be statistical significant for XE and SE scores in first-generation and for XE, AE and SE scores in second-generation reforms period. However, the reverse seems to be true in rest of the efficiency estimates in respective sub-periods. The results suggest that private banks as a group is more efficient than SBI group during pre-reforms period. But, SBI group has turned out to be more efficient than those of private banks after the deregulatory measures came into existence.

Besides it, NBs v/s private banks group recorded significant differences in most of the DEA efficiency estimates, but, this bank group differs for SE estimates in entire study period. The period-wise analysis presents that this bank group has noted statistically significant differences in XE, AE and PTE scores in pre-reforms period, XE, TE and PTE scores in first-generation and AE and PTE scores in second-generation reforms period. However, the opposite holds to be true for rest of the DEA efficiency estimates in respective sub-periods. The empirical findings connote that private banks have performed better than NBs group for most of DEA efficiency estimates in respective sub-periods (with few exceptions).

4.4 TEMPORAL PATTERN OF AVERAGE MINIMUM XE, TE AND AE SCORES AND BEST PRACTICE BANKS

Table 4.5 presents temporal pattern of the banks with minimum level of average XE, TE and AE scores and best practice banks for the period 1985-06. First of all, the empirical findings shed light on those banks, which registered minimum level of average efficiency scores in most of the sample years. United Bank of India reported minimum average XE score in six consecutive years, i.e., starting from 1991-92 to 1996-97. United Bank of India has been noted with minimum OTE score in five consecutive years starting from level of average to 1996-97 and two consecutive years i.e., from 1999-00 to 2000-01. Sangli Bank has emerged to be worst efficient bank in most of the times (i.e., 4 times in case of XE and 3 times in case of TE) during the entire study period. In addition, Bank of India and Ing Vysya Bank recorded minimum AE score in most of times (i.e., 4 times) over the entire study period.

Besides this, this part of the analysis also concentrates on identifying those banks that occupied position on the frontier in most of the sample years. The banks with efficiency score equal to 1 are considered as the most efficient banks. These banks together define the best-practice or efficient frontier and thus, form the reference set for inefficient banks. In DEA terminology, these banks are called peers and set an example of good operating practices for inefficient banks to emulate.

The empirical findings substantiate that Tamilnad Mercantile Bank (B34) dominates in entire study period as it occupied the position on XE, AE and TE frontier in most of the times (i.e., 16 times, 15 times and 18 times respectively) out of 21 sample years. The period-wise analysis divulges that Tamilnad Mercantile Bank (B34) has observed to be operating at XE frontier in most of the times (i.e., 7 times during 1985-92, 6 times during 1993-99 and 3 times during 2000-06). As for AE, it captured position on the frontier in most of the times (i.e., 6 times during 1985-92 and 1993-99 each and 3 times during 2000-06). Moreover, Tamilnad Mercantile Bank (B34) has noted to be on the TE frontier (7 times) in both the sub-periods: 1985-92 and 1993-99 and (4 times) in 2000-06. Bharat Overseas Bank (B28) has found to be on the TE frontier

TABLE 4.5

Average Minimum Level of XE, TE and AE Scores and Best Practice Banks in India : 1985 to 2005-06

Years	*Minimum Level of XE*	*Minimum Level of AE*	*Minimum Level of TE*
(1)	*(2)*	*(3)*	*(4)*
1985	State Bank of Patiala (0.567)	Bank of India (0.733)	State Bank of Patiala (0.610)
1986	State Bank of Patiala (0.485)	State Bank of Patiala (0.612)	State Bank of Travancore (0.773)
1987	Bank of India (0.518)	Bank of India (0.625)	State Bank of Patiala (0.733)
1988-89	Bank of India (0.448)	Bank of India (0.589)	State Bank of Patiala (0.687)
1989-90	Bank of India (0.457)	Bank of India (0.634)	United Commercial Bank (0.618)
1990-91	United Commercial Bank (0.468)	Lord Krishna Bank (0.501)	United Commercial Bank (0.542)
1991-92	United Bank of India (0.438)	Bank of Baroda (0.691)	United Commercial Bank (0.477)
1992-93	United Bank of India (0.201)	Ing Vysya Bank (0.751)	United Bank of India (0.203)
1993-94	United Bank of India (0.289)	Ing Vysya Bank (0.781)	United Bank of India (0.290)
1994-95	United Bank of India (0.316)	Ing Vysya Bank (0.701)	United Bank of India (0.352)
1995-96	United Bank of India (0.373)	State Bank of B & J (0.829)	United Bank of India (0.426)
1996-97	United Bank of India (0.319)	Lord Krishna Bank (0.717)	United Bank of India (0.344)
1997-98	Indian Bank (0.385)	Bharat Overseas Bank (0.812)	Indian Bank (0.423)

1998-99	Indian Bank (0.46)	Bharat Overseas Bank (0.737)	Indian Bank (0.485)
1999-00	Indian Bank (0.528)	Oriental Bank of Commerce (0.781)	United Bank of India (0.534)
2000-01	United Western Bank (0.497)	Jammu & Kashmir Bank (0.687)	United Bank of India (0.547)
2001-02	Indian Bank (0.571)	Ing Vysya Bank (0.807)	Indian Bank (0.578)
2002-03	Sangli Bank (0.537)	Syndicate Bank (0.896)	Sangli Bank (0.592)
2003-04	Sangli Bank (0.523)	Sangli Bank (0.836)	Sangli Bank (0.626)
2004-05	Sangli Bank (0.450)	Oriental Bank of Commerce (0.778)	United Western Bank (0.518)
2005-06	Sangli Bank (0.438)	Jammu & Kashmir Bank (0.750)	Sangli Bank and Bank of Rajasthan (0.530)

(Contd.)

TABLE 4.5 (*Contd.*)

Years	*Best Practice Banks (XE)*	*Best Practice Banks (AE)*	*Best Practice Banks (TE)*
(1)	*(5)*	*(6)*	*(7)*
1985	B34, B41	B3, B4, B41	B28, B34, B37, B39, B41, B44
1986	B34, B41	B34, B41	B13, B28, B32, B34, B36, B37, B41
1987	B28, B34	B28, B34	B6, B15, B28, B29, B32, B34
1988-89	B28, B34	B28, B34, B40	B6, B28, B32, B34
1989-90	B28, B34	B28, B34	B6, B28, B34, B37
1990-91	B34, B40	B34, B40	B3, B12, B28, B34, B40
1991-92	B34, B40	B25, B34	B25, B28, B34, B39
1992-93	B25, B34	B25, B34	B25, B28, B34, B39
1993-94	B25, B34	B8, B28, B34, B39, B44	B3, B23, B28, B34, B39, B41, B42, B44
1994-95	B34, B39, B41	B34, B39, B41	B23, B26, B28, B30, B34, B39, B41
1995-96	B30, B34	B30, B34	B23, B30, B34, B40
1996-97	B34	B34	B30, B34

1997-98	B34, B40	B3, B34, B40	B8, B21, B23, B24, B25, B34, B40
1998-99	B23, B41	B23, B41	B8, B12, B22, B23, B29, B34, B39, B41
1999-00	B25, B40, B41	B19, B25, B40, B41	B21, B22, B25, B40, B41, B45
2000-01	B21, B25, B41	B21, B25, B41	B8, B12, B21, B22, B25, B40, B41
2001-02	B25, B32, B42	B25, B32, B42	B12, B25, B32, B34, B42
2002-03	B23, B25, B32, B37	B6, B23, B25, B32, B37	B8, B12, B23, B24, B25, B30, B32, B37
2003-04	B23, B30, B34, B40	B23, B30, B32, B34, B40	B9, B12, B23, B30, B34, B40
2004-05	B2, B34	B1, B2, B23, B34	B2, B8, B21, B24, B34
2005-06	B9, B34, B40	B9, B34, B40	B8, B9, B24, B34, B40

(7 times) during the period 1985-92. As mentioned earlier, the best practice banks set example for inefficient banks, thus, lagging banks or inefficient banks should follow their practices to come ahead.

4.5 TEMPORAL PATTERN OF AVERAGE MINIMUM PTE AND SE SCORES, RETURNS TO SCALE AND BEST PRACTICE BANKS

Table 4.6 provides temporal pattern of average minimum level of PTE and SE scores, returns to scale (RTS) and best practice banks for the period 1985 to 2005-06. In first instance, the empirical findings (as shown in Table 4.6) concentrates on identifying those banks, which recorded minimum level of efficiency scores in most of the sample years. According to the empirical findings, Indian Bank has observed to be the bank with minimum efficiency score (i.e., 5 times) as per VRS technology over the study period. In addition, United Commercial Bank and Indian Overseas Bank registered minimum average PTE score in most of the times (i.e., 4 times) and United Western Bank did so (3 times) during the period 1985-06. United Bank of India is found to be the bank with minimum average scale efficiency score in five consecutive years, i.e., from 1992-93 to 1996-97. Sangli Bank noted minimum average scale efficiency score in seven consecutive years, i.e., from 1999-00 to 2005-06. Finally, the results suggest that the banks having most of times the minimum efficiency scores are not yet progressive in nature. So, these banks will have to incorporate substantial changes in their working set-up to keep in lines with international standards.

As far as returns to scale is concerned, the results illustrate that majority of 24 banks (i.e., 53 percent) during pre-reforms period, 31 banks (i.e., 70 percent) during first-generation reforms, 33 banks (i.e., 73 percent) during second-generation reforms and 29 banks (i.e., 65 percent) during the entire study period are found to be operating below their optimum scale size and thus, experiencing increasing returns-to-scale. These results are highly consistent to the findings of Rezvanian *et. al.* (2008), where about 77.75 percent banks were observed to operate below their optimum scale during the period 1998-2003. The results are also supported by the findings obtained by Noulas and Ketkar (1996). The findings connote that the banks in this category are operating at the decreasing portion of their long run average cost (LAC) curve and experiencing economies of scale. Thus, the empirical findings suggest that these banks can enhance their economic efficiency by expanding the size of their operations. Therefore, the closure of sick banks and mergers of the banks seem to be desirable in this direction. Moreover, the greater use of technology is more likely to generate substantial scale economies for most of the sample banks in India.

Furthermore, the empirical findings dwell that 15 (i.e., 33 percent) banks during the period 1985-92, 7 (i.e., 16 percent) banks during 1993-99, 6 banks (i.e., 13 percent) during 2000-06 and 10 banks (i.e., 21 percent) during 1985-06 are noted to be operating at above their optimum size and thus, experiencing decreasing returns-to-scale. These banks are likely to operate at the increasing portion of the LACs and therefore, experiencing diseconomies of scale. The banks are highly required to downsize the scale of their operations in order to overcome the diseconomies of scale. The improvement in asset quality and priority sector lending in addition to technological upgradation seem to be desirable in this direction. In addition to it, 6 banks (i.e., 14 percent) have been noticed to be operating at most productive scale size (MPSS) and thus, have minimum long-run average cost in distinct sub-periods.

Looking at the inter-period movement of the banks, it has been observed that the number of banks experiencing IRS continued to increase, however, the number of banks experiencing DRS continued to decrease. Thus, the empirical findings suggest that there is significant room for the banks to extract maximum possible output from the given level of resources by enhancing the size of the banks. Therefore, the strategy of scaling up the size of banks is recommended for majority of the sample banks.

As for best practice banks, the empirical findings highlight that Tamilnad Mercantile Bank (B34) has dominated during the entire study period as it occupied 18 times the position on SE frontier and 20 times on PTE frontier, thus emerged to be best practice bank in most of the sample years.

TABLE 4.6

Average Minimum Level of PTE and SE Scores, RTS and Best Practice Banks in India : 1985 to 2005-06

Years	*Minimum level of PTE Scores*	*Minimum level of SE Scores*	*Number of Banks having RTS*		
			IRS	*DRS*	*CRS*
(1)	*(2)*	*(3)*	*(4)*	*(5)*	*(6)*
1985	State Bank of Patiala (0.616)	Corporation Bank (0.894)	9	28	8
1986	Bank of Rajasthan (0.792)	State Bank of B&J (0.867)	10	28	7
1987	State Bank of Patiala (0.771)	Jammu & Kashmir Bank (0.859)	25	12	8
1988-89	Federal Bank (0.716)	State Bank of Saurashtra (0.829)	30	11	4
1989-90	United Commercial Bank (0.677)	Ratnakar Bank (0.805)	30	11	4
1990-91	United Commercial Bank (0.620)	Syndicate Bank (0.714)	31	9	5
1991-92	United Commercial Bank (0.558)	Ratnakar Bank (0.646)	32	8	5
1992-93	United Bank of India (0.386)	United Bank of India (0.526)	35	5	5
1993-94	United Bank of India (0.473)	United Bank of India (0.613)	25	11	9
1994-95	Indian Overseas Bank (0.532)	United Bank of India (0.620)	31	7	7
1995-96	Indian Bank and Indian Overseas Bank (0.530)	United Bank of India (0.719)	31	8	6
1996-97	Indian Overseas Bank (0.534)	United Bank of India (0.610)	37	6	2

1997-98	Indian Overseas Bank (0.594)	Dhanalakshmi Bank (0.710)	32	6	7
1998-99	Indian Bank (0.593)	Dhanalakshmi Bank (0.664)	29	8	9
1999-00	Indian Bank (0.615)	Sangli Bank (0.762)	28	11	6
2000-01	Indian Bank (0.654)	Sangli Bank (0.668)	32	6	7
2001-02	Indian Bank (0.585)	Sangli Bank (0.673)	29	8	8
2002-03	United Commercial Bank (0.737)	Sangli Bank (0.598)	35	2	8
2003-04	United Western Bank (0.660)	Sangli Bank (0.654)	35	5	5
2004-05	United Western Bank (0.648)	Sangli Bank (0.545)	37	3	5
2005-06	United Western Bank (0.634)	Sangli Bank (0.530)	35	5	5
Mean 1985/92			24	15	6
1993/99			31	7	6
2000/06			33	6	6
1985/06			29	10	6

(Contd.)

TABLE 4.6 (Contd.)

Years	Best Practice Banks (Scale Efficient)	Best Practice Banks (Pure Technical Efficient)
(1)	(7)	(8)
1985	B28, B34, B37, B38, B39, B40, B41, B44	B6, B15, B20, B23, B26, B28, B32, B34, B37, B39, B41, B44
1986	B13, B28, B32, B34, B36, B37, B41	B6, B13, B20, B26, B28, B29, B32, B34, B36, B37, B41
1987	B6, B8, B15, B27, B28, B29, B32, B34	B6, B15, B20, B26, B28, B29, B32, B34, B36, B39, B41
1988-89	B6, B28, B32, B34	B6, B15, B20, B26, B28, B32, B34, B41
1989-90	B6, B28, B34, B37	B6, B10, B20, B24, B25, B26, B28, B32, B34, B37, B38, B41, B44
1990-91	B3, B12, B28, B34, B40	B3, B6, B12, B20, B28, B32, B34, B40, B41, B42
1991-92	B8, B25, B28, B34, B39	B20, B25, B28, B32, B34, B39, B42
1992-93	B22, B25, B28, B34, B39	B20, B25, B28, B30, B32, B34, B39
1993-94	B3, B22, B23, B28, B34, B39, B41, B42, B44	B3, B10, B23, B28, B32, B34, B37, B39, B41, B42, B44
1994-95	B23, B26, B28, B30, B34, B39, B41	B3, B20, B23, B26, B28, B30, B32, B34, B37, B39, B41, B42
1995-96	B23, B26, B30, B34, B40, B45	B12, B20, B23, B28, B30, B32, B34, B40, B41, B42
1996-97	B30, B34	B8, B20, B23, B30, B31, B32, B34, B37, B41, B42, B45
1997-98	B8, B21, B23, B24, B25, B34, B40	B8, B20, B21, B23, B24, B25, B26, B30, B31, B33, B34, B37, B40, B41, B42. B43, B45
1998-99	B8, B12, B22, B23, B25, B29, B34, B39, B41	B8, B12, B20, B22, B23, B26, B29, B33, B34, B39, B40, B41, B42

1999-00	B21, B22, B25, B40, B41, B45	B8, B12, B20, B21, B22, B23, B25, B33, B40, B41, B42, B45
2000-01	B8, B12, B21, B22, B25, B40, B41	B8, B12, B20, B21, B22, B23, B25, B33, B34, B39, B40, B41, B42
2001-02	B12, B22, B25, B32, B34, B39, B40, B42	B12, B23, B25, B32, B33, B34, B39, B40, B42
2002-03	B8, B12, B23, B24, B25, B30, B32, B37	B8, B12, B23, B24, B25, B30, B32, B33, B34, B37, B39, B42
2003-04	B9, B12, B23, B30, B34, B40	B9, B12, B20, B23, B25, B30, B33, B34, B36, B37, B39, B40, B42, B44
2004-05	B2, B8, B21, B24, B34	B2, B8, B20, B21, B24, B28, B33, B34, B37, B42, B44
2005-06	B8, B9, B24, B34, B40	B8, B9, B20, B24, B33, B34, B40, B42, B43
Mean 1985/92		
1993/99		
2000/06		
1985/06		

Note : PTE denotes pure technical efficiency and SE denotes scale efficiency. RTS shows returns to scale, IRS denotes increasing returns to scale, DRS denotes diminishing returns to scale and CRS denotes constant returns to scale. 1985-92 period shows pre-reforms period, 1993-99 shows first generation and 2000-06 shows second-generation reforms period, 1985-06 denotes entire study period.

* The list of sample banks is shown in Appendix Table 1.

The period-wise analysis divulges that State Bank of India (B20), Bharat Overseas Bank (B28), Lord Krishna Bank (B32) and Tamilnad Mercantile Bank (B34) have found to be operating at the PTE frontier (7 times) during the pre-reforms period. Tamilnad Mercantile Bank (B34) has noted to be on PTE frontier (7 times) during first-generation reforms period. Besides this, Nainital Bank (B33) and Ratnakar Bank (B42) have occupied (7 times) the position on PTE frontier while Tamilnad Mercantile Bank did so in (6 times) during the second-generation reforms period.

As for SE frontier, Bharat Overseas Bank (B28) has noticed to be operating at the frontier (7 times) during the period 1985-92. Tamilnad Mercantile Bank (B34) has been found in most of the times (i.e., 7 times) on the SE frontier during the sub-periods: 1985-92 and 1993-99. Furthermore, Tamilnad Mercantile Bank (B34), Corporation Bank (B8), Oriental Bank of Commerce (B12) and State Bank of Patiala (B25) have been observed in most of the times (i.e., 4 times) on the SE frontier during the period 2000-06. Finally, the empirical findings connote that the best practice banks are more likely to be efficient in resource utilization process than that of other ones. Therefore, these banks set an example of good operating practices for inefficient banks to emulate.

4.6 INTER-PERIOD COMPARISON OF AVERAGE XE ESTIMATES AND ITS DECOMPOSITIONS

4.6.1 Inter-period Comparison of Average XE Scores

In order to test whether the degree of deregulation in various sub-periods can create significant efficiency differences between the banks, non-parametric Mann-Whitney U-Statistics rank test has been applied. Before applying this test, it is essential to ascertain the change (increase/decrease) in average efficiency scores of banks from pre-reforms to first-generation reforms and first-generation reforms to second-generation reforms period. Through this test, following hypothesis has been tested for various sample banks across various sub-periods.

Under H_0 : The null-hypothesis is that there is no significant difference in the distribution of efficiency scores of banks between pre-reforms v/s first-generation reforms and first-generation reforms v/s second-generation reforms.

Against H_1 : The alternative hypothesis is that there is significant difference in the distribution of efficiency scores of banks between pre-reforms v/s first-generation reforms and first-generation reforms v/s second-generation reforms.

Now the null-hypothesis that both samples come from the same population can be tested using Z-test written as:

$$Z = \frac{U - \overline{U}}{s_u}$$

If $Z > Z_\alpha$ (critical value of Z), then the null-hypothesis of common population is rejected, which signals significant efficiency differences between the specified sub-periods and vice-versa. But, if the value of Z=0, then null-hypothesis of common population is not defined, which means that there is no or negligible change in the efficiency scores of a specific bank between the specified sub-periods.

Table 4.7 provides average XE scores, Z-values and decision about null-hypothesis pertaining to various sub-periods. It is apparent from Table 4.7 that out of 45 sample banks, 22 banks viz., Allahabad Bank, Bank of Baroda, Bank of India, Corporation Bank, Dena Bank, Oriental Bank of Commerce, Punjab National Bank, Union Bank of India, State Bank of India, State Bank of B&J, State Bank of Hyderabad, State Bank of Indore, State Bank of Mysore, State Bank of Patiala, State Bank of Saurashtra, State Bank of Travancore, Karnataka Bank, Lord Krishna Bank, Jammu & Kashmir Bank, Lakshmi Vilas Bank, Ratnakar Bank and United Western Bank have experienced an acceleration in XE scores during first-generation reforms in comparison to the pre-reforms period. Contrarily, the banks that registered deterioration in x-efficiency scores are found to be Andhra Bank, Bank of Maharashtra, Canara Bank, Central Bank of India, Indian Bank, Indian Overseas Bank, Punjab and Sind Bank, Syndicate Bank, United Commercial Bank, United Bank of India, Vijaya Bank, Bharat Overseas Bank, City Union Bank, Ing Vysya Bank, Nainital Bank, Tamilnad Mercantile Bank, Bank of Rajasthan,

TABLE 4.7

Inter-Period Average XE Scores, Z-Values and Decision about null-hypothesis—1985 to 2005-06

Banks Name/Time Period	85-92 (1)	93-99 (2)	2000-06 (3)	Z (1/2)	Decision about H_0	Z(2/3)	Decision about H0
(1)	(2)	(3)	(4)	(5)	(6)	(7)	(8)
Allahabad Bank	0.601	0.605	0.755	-0.319	Accepted	-3.003	Rejected
Andhra Bank	0.657	0.605	0.820	-0.958	Accepted	-2.364	Rejected
Bank of Baroda	0.642	0.838	0.778	-2.747	Rejected	-1.086	Accepted
Bank of India	0.530	0.635	0.715	-2.236	Rejected	-1.597	Accepted
Bank of Maharashtra	0.666	0.648	0.701	-0.192	Accepted	-0.064	Accepted
Canara Bank	0.777	0.753	0.752	-0.575	Accepted	-0.319	Accepted
Central Bank of India	0.632	0.593	0.741	-0.575	Accepted	-2.108	Rejected
Corporation Bank	0.771	0.844	0.907	-1.214	Accepted	-1.471	Accepted
Dena Bank	0.742	0.766	0.844	-0.319	Accepted	-0.447	Accepted
Indian Bank	0.592	0.483	0.673	-2.814	Rejected	-5.239	Rejected
Indian Overseas Bank	0.646	0.605	0.754	-0.959	Accepted	-1.981	Rejected
Oriental Bank of Commerce	0.756	0.850	0.814	-2.364	Rejected	-0.958	Accepted
Punjab and Sind Bank	0.709	0.534	0.710	-1.853	Accepted	-2.622	Rejected
Punjab National Bank	0.613	0.713	0.801	-2.302	Rejected	-1.853	Accepted
Syndicate Bank	0.756	0.595	0.763	-2.108	Rejected	-3.13	Rejected

United Commercial Bank	0.601	0.469	0.632	-1.343	Accepted	-3.13	Rejected
Union Bank of India	0.714	0.718	0.738	-0.192	Accepted	-0.703	Accepted
United Bank of India	0.695	0.387	0.697	-2.622	Rejected	-2.875	Rejected
Vijaya Bank	0.760	0.633	0.796	-1.597	Accepted	-3.13	Rejected
State Bank of India	0.778	0.863	0.812	-1.853	Accepted	-1.853	Accepted
State Bank of B & J	0.779	0.827	0.940	-0.831	Accepted	-2.364	Rejected
State Bank of Hyderabad	0.791	0.906	0.891	-2.492	Rejected	-0.192	Accepted
State Bank of Indore	0.773	0.912	0.930	-2.619	Rejected	-0.706	Accepted
State Bank of Mysore	0.795	0.834	0.916	-1.086	Accepted	-2.108	Rejected
State Bank of Patiala	0.722	0.899	0.906	-1.919	Accepted	-0.719	Accepted
State Bank of Saurashtra	0.834	0.887	0.807	-1.281	Accepted	-1.727	Accepted
State Bank of Travancore	0.701	0.763	0.777	-1.727	Accepted	-0.834	Accepted
Bharat Overseas Bank	0.942	0.854	0.751	-1.292	Accepted	-0.831	Accepted
City Union Bank	0.845	0.798	0.808	-1.086	Accepted	-0.064	Accepted
Ing Vysya Bank	0.795	0.768	0.805	-1.214	Accepted	-0.384	Accepted
Karnataka Bank	0.769	0.784	0.744	-0.319	Accepted	-0.767	Accepted
Lord Krishna Bank	0.705	0.812	0.784	-1.725	Accepted	-0.064	Accepted
Nainital Bank	0.801	0.760	0.836	-0.831	Accepted	-1.343	Accepted
Tamilnad Mercantile Bank	1.000	0.993	0.947	-1	Accepted	-1.712	Accepted
Bank of Rajasthan	0.748	0.707	0.691	-1.597	Accepted	-0.192	Accepted

(Contd.)

TABLE 4.7 (*Contd.*)

(1)	*(2)*	*(3)*	*(4)*	*(5)*	*(6)*	*(7)*	*(8)*
Catholic Syrian Bank	0.828	0.604	0.751	-2.111	Rejected	-2.492	Rejected
Dhanalakshmi Bank	0.722	0.684	0.773	-0.704	Accepted	-1.087	Accepted
Federal Bank	0.771	0.665	0.766	-1.214	Accepted	-1.342	Accepted
Jammu & Kashmir Bank	0.795	0.938	0.737	-1.983	Accepted	-2.75	Rejected
Karur Vysya Bank	0.900	0.857	0.933	-0.896	Accepted	-1.68	Accepted
Lakshmi Vilas Bank	0.896	0.904	0.801	-0.065	Accepted	-1.227	Accepted
Ratnakar Bank	0.708	0.719	0.773	-0.448	Accepted	-0.575	Accepted
Sangli Bank	0.721	0.694	0.539	-0.703	Accepted	-2.619	Rejected
South Indian Bank	0.809	0.702	0.773	-1.214	Accepted	-1.469	Accepted
United Western Bank	0.715	0.818	0.665	-1.086	Accepted	-1.853	Accepted
Mean	0.745	0.738	0.783	-0.145	Accepted	-1.38	Accepted

Catholic Syrian Bank, Dhanalakshmi Bank, Federal Bank, Karur Vysya Bank, Sangli Bank and South Indian Bank.

Further, the empirical findings reported that the banks viz., Bank of Baroda, Bank of India, Indian Bank, Oriental Bank of Commerce, Punjab National Bank, Syndicate Bank, United Bank of India, State Bank of Hyderabad, State Bank of Indore and Catholic Syrian Bank have recorded significant differences in the distribution of XE scores between these periods (1985-92 and 1993-99). The empirical findings connote that deregulatory practices have significant impact on the efficiency measures of these banks, thus, null-hypothesis of no efficiency differences is strongly rejected. Except these banks, the null-hypothesis is accepted in remaining sample banks, as these banks did not illustrate any significant efficiency differences between these periods.

The number of banks that noted acceleration in average XE scores increased to 30 banks during the period 2000-06 as against 22 banks during the period 1993-99. These banks are Allahabad Bank, Andhra Bank, Bank of India, Bank of Maharashtra, Central Bank of India, Corporation Bank, Dena Bank, Indian Bank, Indian Overseas Bank, Punjab and Sind Bank, Punjab National Bank, Syndicate Bank, United Commercial Bank, Union Bank of India, United Bank of India, Vijaya Bank, State Bank of B&J, State Bank of Indore, State Bank of Mysore, State Bank of Patiala, State Bank of Travancore, City Union Bank, Ing Vysya Bank, Nainital Bank, Catholic Syrian Bank, Dhanalakshmi Bank, Federal Bank, Karur Vysya Bank, Ratnakar Bank and South Indian Bank. However, the banks that noted deceleration in XE scores are observed to be Bank of Baroda, Canara Bank, Oriental Bank of Commerce, State Bank of India, State Bank of Hyderabad, State Bank of Saurashtra, Bharat Overseas Bank, Karnataka Bank, Lord Krishna Bank, Tamilnad Mercantile Bank, Bank of Rajasthan, Jammu & Kashmir Bank, Lakshmi Vilas Bank, Sangli Bank and United Western Bank.

The banks that witnessed significant gaps in the distribution of XE scores are found to be Allahabad Bank, Andhra Bank, Central Bank of India, Indian Bank, Indian Overseas Bank, Punjab & Sind Bank, Syndicate Bank, United Commercial Bank, United Bank of India, Vijaya Bank, State

Bank of B&J, State Bank of Mysore, Catholic Syrian Bank, Jammu & Kashmir Bank and Sangli Bank. These banks have illustrated significant efficiency differences between the periods: 1993-99 and 2000-06, thus, suggest the rejection of null-hypothesis of the equality in the average XE estimates. It also emerges from the analysis that there is significant dent of reformatory measures on the x-efficiency scores of these banks. Except these banks, the reforms process failed to impart significant impact on the XE of remaining sample banks, which suggests the acceptance of null-hypothesis of no differences in XE estimates between these periods. As for aggregate level, null-hypothesis of the equality of efficiency distributions between various sub-periods under consideration is strongly accepted.

4.6.2 Inter-period Comparison of Average TE Scores

Table 4.8 provides inter-period average TE scores, Z-values and decision about null-hypothesis with respect to various sub-periods. It is clear from the empirical findings that out of 45 sample banks, 14 banks have experienced an improvement in TE scores during first-generation reforms as against pre-reforms period. The banks that recorded acceleration in efficiency estimates are noted to be Corporation Bank, State Bank of B&J, State Bank of Hyderabad, State Bank of Indore, State Bank of Mysore, State Bank of Patiala, State Bank of Saurashtra, State Bank of Travancore, Ing Vysya Bank, Karnataka Bank, Jammu & Kashmir Bank, Lakshmi Vilas Bank, Sangli Bank and United Western Bank. However, the banks that registered deceleration in TE scores are noticed to be Allahabad Bank, Andhra Bank, Bank of Baroda, Bank of India, Bank of Maharashtra, Canara Bank, Central Bank of India, Dena Bank, Indian Bank, Indian Overseas Bank, Oriental Bank of Commerce, Punjab & Sind Bank, Punjab National Bank, Syndicate Bank, United Commercial Bank, Union Bank of India, United Bank of India, Vijaya Bank, State Bank of India, Bharat Overseas Bank, City Union Bank, Lord Krishna Bank, Nainital Bank, Bank of Rajasthan, Catholic Syrian Bank, Dhanalakshmi Bank, Federal Bank, Karur Vysya Bank, Ratnakar Bank and South Indian Bank. It is unique Tamilnad Mercantile Bank which recorded no change in technical efficiency scores between these periods, thus emerged to be best practice bank in both the pre-reforms and first-generation reforms period.

Besides this, the empirical findings highlight that the null-hypothesis of no significant efficiency differences between the periods: 1985-92 and 1993-99 is strongly rejected in case of Allahabad Bank, Bank of India, Canara Bank, Central Bank of India, Indian Bank, Indian Overseas Bank, Punjab & Sind Bank, Syndicate Bank, United Commercial Bank, United Bank of India, Vijaya Bank, State Bank of B&J, State Bank of Hyderabad, State Bank of Indore, State Bank of Mysore, State Bank of Saurashtra, Bharat Overseas Bank, Ing Vysya Bank, Catholic Syrian Bank and Dhanalakshmi Bank. Except these banks (including Tamilnad Mercantile Bank the best practice bank), the null-hypothesis of no significant efficiency differences is strongly accepted for all the remaining sample banks between these periods.

During the period 2000-06, the number of banks that noted acceleration in technical efficiency scores increased to 28 banks in comparison to first-generation reforms. The banks that recorded an improvement in TE scores are found to be Allahabad Bank, Andhra Bank, Bank of India, Bank of Maharashtra, Central Bank of India, Corporation Bank, Dena Bank, Indian Bank, Indian Overseas Bank, Oriental Bank of Commerce, Punjab and Sind Bank, Punjab National Bank, Syndicate Bank, United Commercial Bank, Union Bank of India, United Bank of India, Vijaya Bank, State Bank of B&J, State Bank of Mysore, State Bank of Patiala, City Union Bank, Nainital Bank, Catholic Syrian Bank, Dhanalakshmi Bank, Federal Bank, Karur Vysya Bank, Ratnakar Bank and South Indian Bank. However, the banks that recorded deterioration in efficiency scores are noticed to be Bank of Baroda, Canara Bank, State Bank of India, State Bank of Hyderabad, State Bank of Indore, State Bank of Saurashtra, State Bank of Travancore, Bharat Overseas Bank, Ing Vysya Bank, Karnataka Bank, Lord Krishna Bank, Tamilnad Mercantile Bank, Bank of Rajasthan, Jammu and Kashmir Bank, Lakshmi Vilas Bank, Sangli Bank and United Western Bank.

The banks that witnessed significant gaps in the distribution of TE scores are found to be Allahabad Bank,

TABLE 4.8

Inter-Period Average TE Scores, Z-Values and Decision about Null-hypothesis —1985 to 2005-06

Banks Name/Time Period	*1985-92 (1)*	*1993-99 (2)*	*2000-06 (3)*	*Z (1/2)*	*Decision about H_0*	*Z(2/3)*	*Decision about H_0*
(1)	(2)	(3)	(4)	(5)	(6)	(7)	(8)
Allahabad Bank	0.751	0.628	0.767	-2.619	Rejected	-2.364	Rejected
Andhra Bank	0.769	0.640	0.846	-1.597	Accepted	-2.875	Rejected
Bank of Baroda	0.929	0.892	0.794	-0.767	Accepted	-0.831	Accepted
Bank of India	0.787	0.656	0.728	-2.492	Rejected	-1.597	Accepted
Bank of Maharashtra	0.750	0.704	0.713	-0.319	Accepted	-1.981	Rejected
Canara Bank	0.943	0.777	0.763	-2.57	Rejected	-0.319	Accepted
Central Bank of India	0.776	0.627	0.771	-1.981	Rejected	-2.108	Rejected
Corporation Bank	0.835	0.901	0.976	-1.343	Accepted	-1.396	Accepted
Dena Bank	0.823	0.806	0.857	-0.831	Accepted	-0.448	Accepted
Indian Bank	0.872	0.522	0.694	-3.13	Rejected	-2.492	Rejected
Indian Overseas Bank	0.798	0.620	0.767	-2.236	Rejected	-1.981	Rejected
Oriental Bank of Commerce	0.927	0.906	0.982	-0.064	Accepted	-1.633	Accepted
Punjab and Sind Bank	0.792	0.561	0.746	-1.981	Rejected	-2.622	Rejected
Punjab National Bank	0.764	0.743	0.824	-0.831	Accepted	-1.981	Rejected

Syndicate Bank	0.840	0.652	0.798	-2.108	Rejected	-2.875	Rejected
United Commercial Bank	0.684	0.508	0.650	-2.108	Rejected	-3.13	Rejected
Union Bank of India	0.792	0.738	0.785	-1.469	Accepted	-1.214	Accepted
United Bank of India	0.806	0.407	0.722	-2.747	Rejected	-2.875	Rejected
Vijaya Bank	0.847	0.668	0.803	-2.364	Rejected	-3.13	Rejected
State Bank of India	0.940	0.902	0.826	-0.767	Accepted	-2.492	Rejected
State Bank of B & J	0.822	0.920	0.982	-2.364	Rejected	-2.455	Rejected
State Bank of Hyderabad	0.827	0.940	0.907	-2.942	Rejected	-0.835	Accepted
State Bank of Indore	0.843	0.971	0.938	-2.548	Rejected	-1.16	Accepted
State Bank of Mysore	0.826	0.904	0.965	-2.108	Rejected	-1.938	Accepted
State Bank of Patiala	0.809	0.925	0.932	-1.604	Accepted	-0.598	Accepted
State Bank of Saurashtra	0.854	0.944	0.823	-2.619	Rejected	-2.619	Rejected
State Bank of Travancore	0.741	0.786	0.783	-1.214	Accepted	-0.192	Accepted
Bharat Overseas Bank	1.000	0.937	0.855	-2.241	Rejected	-1.733	Accepted
City Union Bank	0.891	0.821	0.843	-1.279	Accepted	-0.447	Accepted
Ing Vysya Bank	0.811	0.936	0.868	-2.374	Rejected	-0.849	Accepted
Karnataka Bank	0.800	0.831	0.807	-0.064	Accepted	-0.512	Accepted
Lord Krishna Bank	0.941	0.902	0.809	-1.861	Accepted	-0.831	Accepted
Nainital Bank	0.815	0.813	0.899	-0.32	Accepted	-1.471	Accepted

(Contd.)

Table 4.8 (*Contd.*)

(1)	(2)	(3)	(4)	(5)	(6)	(7)	(8)
Tamilnad Mercantile Bank	1.000	1.000	0.985	0	Not Defined	-1.867	Accepted
Bank of Rajasthan	0.756	0.722	0.702	-1.086	Accepted	-0.064	Accepted
Catholic Syrian Bank	0.868	0.626	0.788	-2.492	Rejected	-2.492	Rejected
Dhanalakshmi Bank	0.925	0.748	0.794	-2.374	Rejected	-0.64	Accepted
Federal Bank	0.808	0.725	0.809	-1.597	Accepted	-0.831	Accepted
Jammu & Kashmir Bank	0.837	0.958	0.892	-1.531	Accepted	-1.764	Accepted
Karur Vysya Bank	0.929	0.905	0.973	-0.193	Accepted	-1.296	Accepted
Lakshmi Vilas Bank	0.929	0.931	0.812	-0.327	Accepted	-1.372	Accepted
Ratnakar Bank	0.770	0.765	0.802	-0.703	Accepted	-0.384	Accepted
Sangli Bank	0.753	0.760	0.606	-0.064	Accepted	-2.236	Rejected
South Indian Bank	0.879	0.727	0.816	-1.537	Accepted	-1.469	Accepted
United Western Bank	0.750	0.847	0.696	-1.342	Accepted	-1.597	Accepted
Mean	0.836	0.782	0.820	-1.646	Accepted	-1.069	Accepted

Andhra Bank, Bank of Maharashtra, Central Bank of India, Indian Bank, Indian Overseas Bank, Punjab & Sind Bank, Punjab National Bank, Syndicate Bank, United Commercial Bank, United Bank of India, Vijaya Bank, State Bank of India, State Bank of B&J, State Bank of Saurashtra, Catholic Syrian Bank and Sangli Bank between first-phase of reforms and second-phase of reforms period. Thus, the empirical findings suggest the rejection of null-hypothesis of no significant differences in average TE scores between these sub-periods. The results also imply significant dent of reforms on the technical efficiency scores of above-mentioned banks. However, the remaining sample banks did not illustrate significant efficiency differences between these periods, which suggests the acceptance of null-hypothesis. On aggregate level, the null-hypothesis of no any significant technical efficiency gaps is strongly accepted between various sub-periods under consideration.

4.6.3 Inter-period Comparison of Average AE Scores

Table 4.9 reports average AE scores, Z-values and decision about null-hypothesis for various sub-periods. The empirical findings divulge that out of 45 sample banks, 33 banks have experienced an improvement in AE scores during first-generation reforms in comparison to pre-reforms period. These banks are Allahabad Bank, Andhra Bank, Bank of Baroda, Bank of India, Bank of Maharashtra, Canara Bank, Central Bank of India, Corporation Bank, Dena Bank, Indian Bank, Indian Overseas Bank, Oriental Bank of Commerce, Punjab and Sind Bank, Punjab National Bank, Syndicate Bank, United Commercial Bank, Union Bank of India, United Bank of India, Vijaya Bank, State Bank of India, State Bank of Hyderabad, State Bank of Indore, State Bank of Patiala, State Bank of Travancore, City Union Bank, Lord Krishna Bank, Catholic Syrian Bank, Dhanalakshmi Bank, Jammu & Kashmir Bank, Lakshmi Vilas Bank, Ratnakar Bank, South Indian Bank and United Western Bank. However, the banks that recorded deterioration in AE estimates are estimated to be State Bank of B&J, State Bank of Mysore, State Bank of Saurashtra, Bharat Overseas Bank, Ing Vysya Bank, Karnataka Bank, Nainital

TABLE 4.9

Inter-Period Average AE Scores, Z-Values and Decision about Null-hypothesis —1985 to 2005-06

Banks Name/Time Period	*85-92 (1)*	*93-99 (2)*	*2000-06 (3)*	Z (1/2)	*Decision about H_0*	Z(2/3)	*Decision about H_0*
(1)	(2)	(3)	(4)	(5)	(6)	(7)	(8)
Allahabad Bank	0.801	0.963	0.984	-3.13	Rejected	-1.791	Accepted
Andhra Bank	0.862	0.944	0.968	-2.239	Rejected	-1.727	Accepted
Bank of Baroda	0.690	0.939	0.979	-3.13	Rejected	-1.215	Accepted
Bank of India	0.674	0.970	0.983	-3.13	Rejected	-0.576	Accepted
Bank of Maharashtra	0.890	0.918	0.982	-0.831	Accepted	-2.366	Rejected
Canara Bank	0.825	0.969	0.985	-2.878	Rejected	-1.537	Accepted
Central Bank of India	0.823	0.945	0.962	-2.364	Rejected	-0.831	Accepted
Corporation Bank	0.924	0.942	0.929	-1.087	Accepted	-0.959	Accepted
Dena Bank	0.904	0.949	0.984	-2.111	Rejected	-2.366	Rejected
Indian Bank	0.680	0.930	0.973	-3.13	Rejected	-1.151	Accepted
Indian Overseas Bank	0.811	0.974	0.983	-3.003	Rejected	-0.192	Accepted
Oriental Bank of Commerce	0.818	0.942	0.828	-2.494	Rejected	-2.305	Rejected
Punjab and Sind Bank	0.900	0.950	0.954	-2.108	Rejected	0	Not Defined
Punjab National Bank	0.805	0.960	0.973	-3.13	Rejected	-0.447	Accepted
Syndicate Bank	0.903	0.913	0.958	-0.319	Accepted	-1.853	Accepted

United Commercial Bank	0.876	0.920	0.974	-0.831	Accepted	-2.366	Rejected
Union Bank of India	0.905	0.972	0.943	-2.494	Rejected	-0.064	Accepted
United Bank of India	0.869	0.951	0.968	-2.558	Rejected	-0.321	Accepted
Vijaya Bank	0.899	0.946	0.993	-1.215	Accepted	-3.137	Rejected
State Bank of India	0.828	0.958	0.983	-3.003	Rejected	-1.471	Accepted
State Bank of B & J	0.950	0.898	0.958	-2.108	Rejected	-2.108	Rejected
State Bank of Hyderabad	0.955	0.963	0.983	-0.128	Accepted	-1.727	Accepted
State Bank of Indore	0.917	0.939	0.991	-0.831	Accepted	-2.328	Rejected
State Bank of Mysore	0.962	0.922	0.949	-2.366	Rejected	-1.086	Accepted
State Bank of Patiala	0.891	0.970	0.968	-1.791	Accepted	-0.98	Accepted
State Bank of Saurashtra	0.976	0.939	0.979	-1.855	Accepted	-1.599	Accepted
State Bank of Travancore	0.947	0.970	0.992	-1.153	Accepted	-2.115	Rejected
Bharat Overseas Bank	0.942	0.907	0.881	-0.775	Accepted	-0.575	Accepted
City Union Bank	0.950	0.973	0.958	-1.086	Accepted	-0.706	Accepted
Ing Vysya Bank	0.980	0.824	0.922	-1.857	Accepted	-1.535	Accepted
Karnataka Bank	0.964	0.942	0.925	-0.128	Accepted	-0.959	Accepted
Lord Krishna Bank	0.748	0.900	0.968	-2.364	Rejected	-2.118	Rejected
Nainital Bank	0.982	0.930	0.931	-1.597	Accepted	0	Not Defined
Tamilnad Mercantile Bank	1.000	0.993	0.962	-1.000	Accepted	-1.564	Accepted
Bank of Rajasthan	0.989	0.978	0.985	-2.049	Rejected	-0.959	Accepted

(Contd.)

TABLE 4.9 (*Contd.*)

(1)	(2)	(3)	(4)	(5)	(6)	(7)	(8)
Catholic Syrian Bank	0.952	0.966	0.953	-0.576	Accepted	-0.192	Accepted
Dhanalakshmi Bank	0.782	0.911	0.973	-2.364	Rejected	-1.279	Accepted
Federal Bank	0.955	0.917	0.948	-0.128	Accepted	-0.512	Accepted
Jammu & Kashmir Bank	0.948	0.978	0.826	-1.793	Accepted	-2.817	Rejected
Karur Vysya Bank	0.968	0.947	0.959	-0.578	Accepted	-0.388	Accepted
Lakshmi Vilas Bank	0.964	0.971	0.986	-0.194	Accepted	-1.098	Accepted
Ratnakar Bank	0.923	0.942	0.961	-0.575	Accepted	-1.023	Accepted
Sangli Bank	0.960	0.914	0.886	-2.047	Rejected	-1.087	Accepted
South Indian Bank	0.917	0.963	0.948	-1.981	Rejected	-0.958	Accepted
United Western Bank	0.954	0.964	0.955	-0.895	Accepted	-0.447	Accepted
Mean	0.893	0.944	0.956	-2.865	Rejected	-2.95	Rejected

Bank, Tamilnad Mercantile Bank, Bank of Rajasthan, Federal Bank, Karur Vysya Bank and Sangli Bank.

Besides this, the empirical findings highlight that the null-hypothesis of no significant efficiency differences between the periods: 1985-92 and 1993-99 is strongly rejected in case of Allahabad Bank, Andhra Bank, Bank of Baroda, Bank of India, Canara Bank, Central Bank of India, Dena Bank, Indian Bank, Indian Overseas Bank, Oriental Bank of Commerce, Punjab & Sind Bank, Punjab National Bank, Union Bank of India, United Bank of India, State Bank of India, State Bank of B&J, State Bank of Mysore, Lord Krishna Bank, Bank of Rajasthan, Dhanalakshmi Bank, Sangli Bank and South Indian Bank. Except these banks, the null-hypothesis of no significant efficiency differences is strongly accepted for all the remaining sample banks between these periods.

The movement of the banks from first-generation reforms to second-generation reforms provide that Allahabad Bank, Andhra Bank, Bank of Baroda, Bank of India, Bank of Maharashtra, Canara Bank, Central Bank of India, Dena Bank, Indian Bank, Indian Overseas Bank, Punjab and Sind Bank, Punjab National Bank, Syndicate Bank, United Commercial Bank, United Bank of India, Vijaya Bank, State Bank of India, State Bank of B&J, State Bank of Hyderabad, State Bank of Indore, State Bank of Mysore, State Bank of Saurashtra, State Bank of Travancore, Ing Vysya Bank, Lord Krishna Bank, Nainital Bank, Bank of Rajasthan, Dhanalakshmi Bank, Federal Bank, Karur Vysya Bank, Lakshmi Vilas Bank and Ratnakar Bank have recorded comparative acceleration in AE scores between these periods. However, the banks that experienced deceleration in AE estimates are observed to be Corporation Bank, Oriental Bank of Commerce, Union Bank of India, State Bank of Patiala, Bharat Overseas Bank, City Union Bank, Karnataka Bank, Tamilnad Mercantile Bank, Catholic Syrian Bank, Jammu & Kashmir Bank, Sangli Bank, South Indian Bank and United Western Bank

Besides this, the empirical findings highlight that the null-hypothesis of the equality of AE distributions is strongly rejected in case of Bank of Maharashtra, Dena Bank, Oriental Bank of Commerce, United Commercial Bank, Vijaya Bank, State Bank of B&J, State Bank of Indore, State Bank of

Travancore, Lord Krishna Bank and Jammu & Kashmir Bank between first-generation and second-generation reforms. Thus, it emerges from the empirical findings that deregulatory measures do have significant impact on the allocative efficiency of these banks. Except these banks (and Punjab & Sind Bank and Nainital Bank as best practice banks), the empirical findings suggests the acceptance of null-hypothesis in all other sample banks as no significant efficiency differences have been noticed between these periods. As for aggregate basis, the banks have illustrated significant efficiency differences between these periods, thus, the empirical findings support the rejection of null-hypothesis.

4.6.4 Inter-period Comparison of Average PTE Scores

Table 4.10 represents average PTE scores, Z-values and decision about null-hypothesis relating to various sub-periods. The empirical findings highlight that out of 45 sample banks, only 15 banks have experienced an improvement in PTE scores during first-generation reforms as against pre-reforms period. These banks are Corporation Bank, State Bank of B&J, State Bank of Hyderabad, State Bank of Indore, State Bank of Mysore, State Bank of Patiala, State Bank of Travancore, Ing Vysya Bank, Karnataka Bank, Nainital Bank, Jammu & Kashmir Bank, Lakshmi Vilas Bank, Ratnakar Bank, Sangli Bank and United Western Bank. On the other hand, the banks that registered a fall in PTE scores are noted to be Allahabad Bank, Andhra Bank, Bank of Baroda, Bank of India, Bank of Maharashtra, Canara Bank, Central Bank of India, Dena Bank, Indian Bank, Indian Overseas Bank, Oriental Bank of Commerce, Punjab & Sind Bank, Punjab National Bank, Syndicate Bank, United Commercial Bank, Union Bank of India, United Bank of India, Vijaya Bank, State Bank of India, State Bank of Saurashtra, Bharat Overseas Bank, City Union Bank, Lord Krishna Bank, Bank of Rajasthan, Catholic Syrian Bank, Federal Bank, Karur Vysya Bank and South Indian Bank.

Besides this, the empirical findings report that the hypothesis of the equality of PTE distributions is strongly rejected in case of Allahabad Bank, Bank of India, Canara Bank, Indian Bank, Punjab & Sind Bank, Syndicate Bank, United Bank of India, Vijaya Bank, State Bank of Indore, City

Union Bank, Ing Vysya Bank and Sangli Bank between pre-reforms and first-generation reforms period. Thus, it can be stated that these banks have witnessed significant variations in efficiency scores on account of liberalization. Except these banks (and Tamilnad Mercantile Bank as best practice bank), the null-hypothesis is accepted in the remaining sample banks as no significant efficiency differences have been detected between these periods.

Further, the number of banks that recorded acceleration in efficiency scores increased to 29 banks during second-generation reforms as against 15 banks during first-generation reforms period. The banks that witnessed an acceleration in efficiency estimates as per VRS technology are estimated to be Allahabad Bank, Andhra Bank, Bank of India, Bank of Maharashtra, Central Bank of India, Corporation Bank, Dena Bank, Indian Bank, Indian Overseas Bank, Oriental Bank of Commerce, Punjab and Sind Bank, Punjab National Bank, Syndicate Bank, United Commercial Bank, Union Bank of India, United Bank of India, Vijaya Bank, State Bank of B&J, State Bank of Mysore, State Bank of Patiala, City Union Bank, Nainital Bank, Bank of Rajasthan, Catholic Syrian Bank, Federal Bank, Karur Vysya Bank, Ratnakar Bank, Sangli Bank and South Indian Bank. Contrarily, the banks that recorded deterioration in PTE estimates are noted to be Bank of Baroda, Canara Bank, State Bank of India, State Bank of Hyderabad, State Bank of Indore, State Bank of Saurashtra, State Bank of Travancore, Bharat Overseas Bank, Ing Vysya Bank, Karnataka Bank, Lord Krishna Bank, Tamilnad Mercantile Bank, Dhanalakshmi Bank, Jammu & Kashmir Bank, Lakshmi Vilas Bank and United Western Bank, Punjab & Sind Bank, Syndicate Bank, United Commercial Bank, Union Bank of India, United Bank of India, Vijaya Bank, State Bank of Saurashtra, Nainital Bank, Catholic Syrian Bank, Lakshmi Vilas Bank and South Indian Bank. Thus, the empirical findings imply the rejection of null-hypothesis of no significant efficiency differences between first-generation and second-generation reforms period.

In contrast, the remaining sample banks did not illustrate significant changes in PTE scores between these sub-periods; which supports the acceptance of null-hypothesis. On

TABLE 4.10

Inter-Period Average PTE Scores, Z-Values and Decision about Null-hypothesis—1985 to 2005-06

Banks Name/Time Period	*85-92 (1)*	*93-99 (2)*	*2000-06 (3)*	*Z (1/2)*	*Decision about H_0*	*Z(2/3)*	*Decision about H_0*
(1)	*(2)*	*(3)*	*(4)*	*(5)*	*(6)*	*(7)*	*(8)*
Allahabad Bank	0.854	0.746	0.909	-2.239	Rejected	-2.747	Rejected
Andhra Bank	0.807	0.714	0.903	-1.469	Accepted	-2.492	Rejected
Bank of Baroda	0.951	0.908	0.815	-0.578	Accepted	-1.601	Accepted
Bank of India	0.808	0.664	0.739	-2.686	Rejected	-1.725	Accepted
Bank of Maharashtra	0.798	0.777	0.820	-0.319	Accepted	-0.447	Accepted
Canara Bank	0.984	0.809	0.775	-2.859	Rejected	-0.447	Accepted
Central Bank of India	0.826	0.691	0.841	-1.853	Accepted	-2.492	Rejected
Corporation Bank	0.867	0.915	0.983	-0.707	Accepted	-1.274	Accepted
Dena Bank	0.865	0.851	0.952	-0.064	Accepted	-1.983	Accepted
Indian Bank	0.890	0.591	0.728	-3.13	Rejected	-2.364	Rejected
Indian Overseas Bank	0.825	0.665	0.783	-1.853	Accepted	-1.725	Accepted
Oriental Bank of Commerce	0.944	0.920	0.988	-0.193	Accepted	-1.569	Accepted
Punjab and Sind Bank	0.834	0.615	0.796	-2.364	Rejected	-2.619	Rejected
Punjab National Bank	0.795	0.770	0.854	-0.831	Accepted	-1.983	Accepted
Syndicate Bank	0.930	0.673	0.843	-2.374	Rejected	-3.13	Rejected

United Commercial Bank	0.739	0.626	0.720	-1.597	Accepted	-2.492	Rejected
Union Bank of India	0.816	0.770	0.848	-1.342	Accepted	-2.047	Rejected
United Bank of India	0.840	0.566	0.800	-2.619	Rejected	-2.747	Rejected
Vijaya Bank	0.873	0.708	0.853	-2.108	Rejected	-3.13	Rejected
State Bank of India	1.000	0.993	0.952	-1	Accepted	-0.8	Accepted
State Bank of B & J	0.873	0.942	0.987	-1.214	Accepted	-1.938	Accepted
State Bank of Hyderabad	0.878	0.945	0.919	-1.853	Accepted	-0.579	Accepted
State Bank of Indore	0.880	0.976	0.951	-2.115	Rejected	-0.622	Accepted
State Bank of Mysore	0.885	0.919	0.976	-0.767	Accepted	-1.938	Accepted
State Bank of Patiala	0.838	0.930	0.946	-1.035	Accepted	-0.887	Accepted
State Bank of Saurashtra	0.966	0.958	0.830	-0.708	Accepted	-2.631	Rejected
State Bank of Travancore	0.762	0.807	0.791	-0.958	Accepted	-0.447	Accepted
Bharat Overseas Bank	1.000	0.959	0.929	-1.867	Accepted	-1.111	Accepted
City Union Bank	0.944	0.866	0.896	-2.246	Rejected	-0.958	Accepted
Ing Vysya Bank	0.832	0.984	0.891	-3.071	Rejected	-1.844	Accepted
Karnataka Bank	0.871	0.899	0.889	-0.512	Accepted	-0.32	Accepted
Lord Krishna Bank	1.000	0.984	0.899	-1.468	Accepted	-1.842	Accepted
Nainital Bank	0.899	0.914	1.000	-0.831	Accepted	-2.606	Rejected
Tamilnad Mercantile Bank	1.000	1.000	0.990	0	Not Defined	-1	Accepted
Bank of Rajasthan	0.783	0.773	0.818	-1.469	Accepted	-1.725	Accepted

(*Contd.*)

TABLE 4.10 (*Contd.*)

(1)	(2)	(3)	(4)	(5)	(6)	(7)	(8)
Catholic Syrian Bank	0.903	0.773	0.902	-1.601	Accepted	-2.111	Rejected
Dhanalakshmi Bank	0.972	0.972	0.969	-0.341	Accepted	-0.341	Accepted
Federal Bank	0.852	0.756	0.825	-1.597	Accepted	-1.214	Accepted
Jammu & Kashmir Bank	0.928	0.963	0.947	-0.887	Accepted	-0.212	Accepted
Karur Vysya Bank	0.961	0.927	0.981	-0.129	Accepted	-1.132	Accepted
Lakshmi Vilas Bank	0.990	0.994	0.934	-0.105	Accepted	-2.335	Rejected
Ratnakar Bank	0.915	0.965	1.000	-1.627	Accepted	-1	Accepted
Sangli Bank	0.795	0.900	0.962	-2.236	Rejected	-1.663	Accepted
South Indian Bank	0.905	0.846	0.961	-1.091	Accepted	-2.056	Rejected
United Western Bank	0.782	0.865	0.751	-0.831	Accepted	-1.733	Accepted
Mean	0.881	0.840	0.885	-1.119	Accepted	-1.469	Accepted

aggregate level, the hypothesis of equality in the PTE distributions between various sub-periods is accepted.

4.6.5 Inter-period Comparison of Average SE Scores

Table 4.11 presents average SE scores, Z-values and decision about null-hypothesis pertaining to various sub-periods. It is clear from the analysis that out of 45 sample banks, only 20 banks have experienced an improvement in SE estimates during first-generation reforms in comparison to pre-reforms period. The banks that recorded efficiency increase are noted to be Bank of Baroda, Bank of India, Canara Bank, Corporation Bank, Dena Bank, Punjab National Bank, Syndicate Bank, State Bank of B&J, State Bank of Hyderabad, State Bank of Indore, State Bank of Mysore, State Bank of Patiala, State Bank of Saurashtra, State Bank of Travancore, City Union Bank, Karnataka Bank, Federal Bank, Jammu & Kashmir Bank, Karur Vysya Bank and United Western Bank. On the other hand, the banks that experienced deceleration in SE scores are found to be Allahabad Bank, Andhra Bank, Bank of Maharashtra, Central Bank of India, Indian Bank, Indian Overseas Bank, Punjab and Sind Bank, United Commercial Bank, Union Bank of India, United Bank of India, Vijaya Bank, State Bank of India, Bharat Overseas Bank, Ing Vysya Bank, Lord Krishna Bank, Nainital Bank, Bank of Rajasthan, Catholic Syrian Bank, Dhanalakshmi Bank, Lakshmi Vilas Bank, Ratnakar Bank, Sangli Bank and South Indian Bank.

The empirical findings further demonstrate that the banks viz., Andhra Bank, Indian Bank, Oriental Bank of Commerce, United Commercial Bank, United Bank of India, State Bank of Hyderabad, State Bank of Indore, State Bank of Mysore, State Bank of Saurashtra, Bharat Overseas Bank, Catholic Syrian Bank and Dhanalakshmi Bank have witnessed inequality in the efficiency distributions between pre-reforms and first-generation reforms period, which strictly rejects the null-hypothesis to be stated. It also emanates from the analysis that these banks have registered significant scale efficiency differences on account of deregulatory measures. Except these banks (including Tamilnad Mercantile Bank as the best practice bank), null-hypothesis of no efficiency differences is strongly accepted in remaining sample banks between these periods.

TABLE 4.11

Inter-Period Average SE Scores, Z-Values and Decision about null-hypothesis—1985 to 2005-06

Banks Name/ Time Period	85-92 (1)	93-99 (2)	2000-06 (3)	Z (1/2)	Decision about H_0	Z(2/3)	Decision about H_0
(1)	(2)	(3)	(4)	(5)	(6)	(7)	(8)
Allahabad Bank	0.881	0.845	0.843	-1.214	Accepted	-0.064	Accepted
Andhra Bank	0.945	0.892	0.935	-2.236	Rejected	-1.535	Accepted
Bank of Baroda	0.976	0.982	0.974	-0.064	Accepted	-1.023	Accepted
Bank of India	0.973	0.987	0.984	-1.473	Accepted	-0.514	Accepted
Bank of Maharashtra	0.936	0.899	0.870	-1.725	Accepted	-1.342	Accepted
Canara Bank	0.958	0.964	0.986	-0.578	Accepted	-1.086	Accepted
Central Bank of India	0.936	0.905	0.916	-1.214	Accepted	-0.128	Accepted
Corporation Bank	0.965	0.984	0.993	-0.84	Accepted	-1.13	Accepted
Dena Bank	0.947	0.950	0.900	-0.256	Accepted	-1.217	Accepted
Indian Bank	0.980	0.883	0.951	-2.561	Rejected	-1.597	Accepted
Indian Overseas Bank	0.969	0.935	0.978	-2.108	Accepted	-2.492	Rejected
Oriental Bank of Commerce	0.983	0.983	0.994	-0.192	Rejected	-1.177	Accepted
Punjab and Sind Bank	0.939	0.906	0.938	-0.958	Accepted	-0.831	Accepted
Punjab National Bank	0.960	0.965	0.964	-0.512	Accepted	-0.319	Accepted

Syndicate Bank	0.907	0.969	0.947	-1.215	Accepted	-2.113	Rejected
United Commercial Bank	0.920	0.812	0.904	-2.364	Rejected	-2.108	Rejected
Union Bank of India	0.968	0.961	0.925	-0.128	Accepted	-1.597	Accepted
United Bank of India	0.951	0.695	0.898	-2.747	Rejected	-2.175	Rejected
Vijaya Bank	0.970	0.943	0.940	-1.725	Accepted	-0.447	Accepted
State Bank of India	0.940	0.908	0.870	-0.767	Accepted	-1.214	Accepted
State Bank of B & J	0.943	0.977	0.995	-1.535	Accepted	-1.617	Accepted
State Bank of Hyderabad	0.944	0.995	0.986	-2.827	Rejected	-0.665	Accepted
State Bank of Indore	0.960	0.995	0.985	-2.548	Rejected	-1.569	Accepted
State Bank of Mysore	0.933	0.984	0.989	-3.13	Rejected	-1.165	Accepted
State Bank of Patiala	0.966	0.995	0.985	-1.876	Accepted	-0.341	Accepted
State Bank of Saurashtra	0.886	0.986	0.992	-2.561	Rejected	-0.259	Accepted
State Bank of Travancore	0.973	0.975	0.990	-0.064	Accepted	-1.222	Accepted
Bharat Overseas Bank	1.000	0.977	0.920	-2.241	Rejected	-2.503	Rejected
City Union Bank	0.941	0.946	0.940	-0.256	Accepted	-0.128	Accepted
Ing Vysya Bank	0.974	0.952	0.972	-1.091	Accepted	-0.196	Accepted
Karnataka Bank	0.916	0.926	0.905	-0.192	Accepted	-0.447	Accepted
Lord Krishna Bank	0.941	0.915	0.891	-1.733	Accepted	-0.064	Accepted
Nainital Bank	0.905	0.891	0.899	-0.32	Accepted	-0.064	Accepted
Tamilnad Mercantile Bank	1.000	1.000	0.995	0	Not Defined	-1.867	Accepted

(*Contd.*)

TABLE 4.11 (*Contd.*)

(1)	(2)	(3)	(4)	(5)	(6)	(7)	(8)
Bank of Rajasthan	0.965	0.931	0.855	-0.767	Accepted	-1.214	Accepted
Catholic Syrian Bank	0.955	0.812	0.875	-2.503	Rejected	-1.215	Accepted
Dhanalakshmi Bank	0.948	0.772	0.821	-2.503	Rejected	-0.575	Accepted
Federal Bank	0.943	0.956	0.982	-0.128	Accepted	-0.319	Accepted
Jammu & Kashmir Bank	0.900	0.995	0.943	-1.928	Accepted	-2.224	Rejected
Karur Vysya Bank	0.966	0.976	0.991	-0.581	Accepted	-1.433	Accepted
Lakshmi Vilas Bank	0.938	0.937	0.869	-0.196	Accepted	-0.719	Accepted
Ratnakar Bank	0.848	0.793	0.802	-0.958	Accepted	0	Not Defined
Sangli Bank	0.945	0.847	0.633	-1.535	Accepted	2.747	Rejected
South Indian Bank	0.968	0.859	0.850	-1.535	Accepted	-0.128	Accepted
United Western Bank	0.956	0.982	0.919	-1.086	Accepted	-1.217	Accepted
Mean	0.947	0.928	0.927	-0.262	Accepted	-0.117	Accepted

The movement of the CBs from first-generation reforms to second-generation reforms delineates that the banks namely Andhra Bank, Canara Bank, Central Bank of India, Corporation Bank, Indian Bank, Indian Overseas Bank, Oriental Bank of Commerce, Punjab & Sind Bank, United Commercial Bank, United Bank of India, State Bank of B&J, State Bank of Mysore, State Bank of Saurashtra, State Bank of Travancore, Ing Vysya Bank, Nainital Bank, Catholic Syrian Bank, Dhanalakshmi Bank, Federal Bank, Karur Vysya Bank and Ratnakar Bank have recorded comparative acceleration in efficiency estimates. In contrast to this, the banks that experienced comparative deceleration in SE scores are found to be Allahabad Bank, Bank of Baroda, Bank of India, Bank of Maharashtra, Dena Bank, Punjab National Bank, Syndicate Bank, Union Bank of India, Vijaya Bank, State Bank of India, State Bank of Hyderabad, State Bank of Indore, State Bank of Patiala, Bharat Overseas Bank, City Union Bank, Karnataka Bank, Lord Krishna Bank, Tamilnad Mercantile Bank, Bank of Rajasthan, Jammu & Kashmir Bank, Lakshmi Vilas Bank, Sangli Bank, South Indian Bank and United Western Bank.

Further, the empirical findings divulge that the null-hypothesis of no efficiency differences is rejected in the banks viz., Indian Overseas Bank, Syndicate Bank, United Commercial Bank, United Bank of India, Bharat Overseas Bank, Jammu & Kashmir Bank and Sangli Bank between first-generation and second-generation reforms period. Thus, it can safely be stated that there is significant dent of reformatory measures on the scale efficiency of these banks. Except these banks (and Ratnakar Bank as the best practice bank), the null-hypothesis of no efficiency differences is accepted between these sub-periods in rest of the sample banks. Thus, it safely be stated that banking reforms failed to impart significant impact on the scale efficiency of these banks. According to empirical findings, the null-hypothesis of no efficiency differences is accepted between the sub-periods under consideration at aggregate level too.

4.7 BANK SIZE AND SCALE ECONOMIES

In order to explore the relationship between bank size (in

terms of total assets) and scale economies of commercial banks in India, the sample banks have been classified into three size classes, labeled as small, medium and large banks for the period 1985-06. Small-sized banks consists those banks having total assets less than equal to Rs. 100 billion. The medium-sized banks includes all the banks which have total assets more than Rs. 100 billion but less than or equal to Rs. 500 billion. The third category of large-sized banks covers all the banks, which have total assets exceeding Rs. 500 billion. Table 4.12 presents average scale economies by bank size for various sub-periods and its plots are given in Figure 4.7.

TABLE 4.12
Average Scale Economies by Assets Size (1985 to 2005-06)

Bank Size (in Rs. Billion)	*1985-92*	*1993-99*	*2000-06*	*1985-06*
0-100	0.947	0.929	0.886	0.921
100-500	0.949	0.921	0.945	0.938
Above 500	0.94	0.932	0.952	0.941

FIG. 4.7
Bank Size and Scale Economies

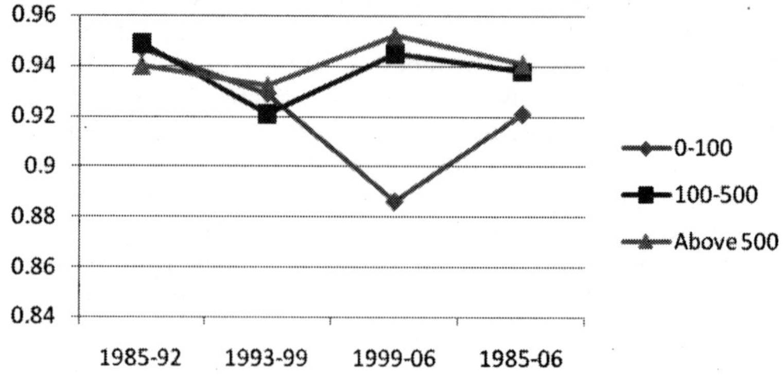

The empirical findings represent that large-sized banks have realized maximum level of scale economies (0.941), followed by medium-sized banks (0.938) and small-sized banks (0.921) during the period 1985-06. Thus, it emanates from the analysis that scale economies tend to increase with an increase in the size of banks. This may be due to the fact that the banks have witnessed several mergers and acquisitions during this period. The merged banks invariably enhanced the size of operations and thus, enabled to reap the maximum benefits of scale economies. Moreover, large-sized banks are expected to be highly involved in the diversification of banking activities and therefore, enjoy significant scale economies in lieu of costs spread across the products.

The above findings are found to be consistent up to some extent across distinct sub-periods. During pre-reforms period, medium-sized banks gained the most i.e., (94.9 percent) level of scale economies, followed by small-sized banks (94.7 percent) and large-sized banks (94 percent). The results clearly indicate that large-sized banks could not realize substantial scale economies during this period. This may be due to the fact that most of the large-sized banks are operating in the region of diminishing returns to scale, while the converse seems to be possibly true in case of small-sized as well as medium-sized banks during pre-reforms period.

Further, the empirical findings illustrate that large-sized banks have experienced highest level of scale economies (93.2 percent), followed by small-sized banks (92.9 percent) and medium-sized banks (92.1 percent) during the period 1993-99. The small degree of difference in average scale economies observed in various bank-sized groups highlights that size is somewhat unrelated to the scale efficiency scores during the sub-periods: 1985-92 and 1993-99. However, this relationship seems to be dominant during the period 2000-06, where large-sized banks gained the most, i.e., (95.2 percent) level of scale economies, followed by medium-sized banks (94.5 percent) and small-sized banks (88.6 percent). The connotation of the findings is that large-sized banks are in better position to reap the benefits of scale economies as compared to medium-sized and small-sized banks during the period 2000-06. This may be attributed to the recommendations of Narasimham Committee Report II, which laid more emphasis on mergers and acquisitions of the banks in India. In response to these recommendations, large-sized banks may have registered substantial amount of scale economies as compared to its counterpart groups.

4.8 SUPER EFFICIENCY

As alluded earlier, CCR model allows the ranking of only inefficient banks by means of their efficiency scores and assigns efficiency score equal to unity to all the efficient banks. Thus, the basic CCR model fails to discriminate and strictly rank the efficient banks. In light of this, Andersen and Petersen developed *super-efficiency* DEA model to get more clear idea about the efficient banks. Therefore, this part of the analysis does not throw light only on the ranking of efficient banks but also assists to identify the positions of inefficient banks on the super-efficiency scale.

Table 4.13 divulges *super–efficiency* scores and respective ranks of the commercial banks in India, obtained through applying Andersen and Petersen's *super-efficiency* DEA model for the period 1985 to 2006. Tamilnad Mercantile Bank has noted to be the most efficient bank with average *super–efficiency* score of 1.118. Bharat Overseas Bank attained second rank with average *super–efficiency* score of 1.005. The banks viz., United Commercial Bank (0.614), United Bank of India (0.644), Indian Bank (0.696), Punjab & Sind Bank (0.704), Sangli Bank (0.707), Allahabad Bank (0.715), Bank of Maharashtra (0.723), Bank of India (0.724), Central Bank of India (0.725), Bank of Rajasthan (0.727) and Indian Overseas Bank (0.728) are found to be at the lower end of *super-efficiency* scale.

Turning towards the period-wise analysis, Bharat Overseas Bank attained top most rank with average *super-efficiency* score of (1.183), followed by Tamilnad Mercantile Bank (1.156) and Lakshmi Vilas Bank (1.036) during pre-reforms period. However, the banks viz., United Commercial Bank (0.684), State Bank of Travancore (0.740), Bank of Maharashtra (0.750), United Western Bank (0.750), Allahabad Bank (0.751), Sangli Bank (0.754), Bank of Rajasthan (0.756), Punjab National Bank (0.765), Andhra Bank (0.769), Ratnakar Bank (0.770), Central Bank of India (0.777) and Bank of India

TABLE 4.13

Ranking of Commercial Banks in India according to Andersen and Petersen's Super-Efficiency Model

1985 to 1991-92		*1992-93 to 1998-99*	
Bank Name	*Super Efficiency*	*Bank Name*	*Super Efficiency*
(1)	(2)	(3)	(4)
Bharat Overseas Bank	1.183	Tamilnad Mercantile Bank	1.167
Tamilnad Mercantile Bank	1.156	Ing Vysya Bank	1.006
Lakshmi Vilas Bank	1.036	State Bank of Indore	1.001
Karur Vysya Bank	0.986	Jammu & Kashmir Bank	1.000
Canara Bank	0.974	Lakshmi Vilas Bank	0.985
Dhanalakshmi Bank	0.960	Bharat Overseas Bank	0.977
Lord Krishna Bank	0.959	Karur Vysya Bank	0.952
Bank of Baroda	0.953	State Bank of Saurashtra	0.945
State Bank of India	0.939	State Bank of Patiala	0.945
Oriental Bank of Commerce	0.932	State Bank of Hyderabad	0.941
City Union Bank	0.898	Corporation Bank	0.93
South Indian Bank	0.884	State Bank of B & J	0.929

(*Contd.*)

TABLE 4.13 (*Contd.*)

(1)	(2)	(3)	(4)
Jammu & Kashmir Bank	0.876	Oriental Bank of Commerce	0.907
Indian Bank	0.873	State Bank of Mysore	0.904
Catholic Syrian Bank	0.869	State Bank of India	0.902
State Bank of Saurashtra	0.854	Lord Krishna Bank	0.901
Vijaya Bank	0.847	Bank of Baroda	0.898
Syndicate Bank	0.844	United Western Bank	0.848
State Bank of Indore	0.842	Karnataka Bank	0.831
State Bank of Patiala	0.836	City Union Bank	0.824
Corporation Bank	0.835	Nainital Bank	0.813
State Bank of Hyderabad	0.828	Dena Bank	0.806
State Bank of Mysore	0.826	State Bank of Travancore	0.786
Dena Bank	0.824	Canara Bank	0.778
State Bank of B & J	0.822	Ratnakar Bank	0.767
Nainital Bank	0.815	Sangli Bank	0.76
Ing Vysya Bank	0.811	Dhanalakshmi Bank	0.748
Federal Bank	0.809	Punjab National Bank	0.743

United Bank of India	0.805	Union Bank of India	0.738
Punjab and Sind Bank	0.805	South Indian Bank	0.733
Karnataka Bank	0.799	Federal Bank	0.725
Indian Overseas Bank	0.797	Bank of Rajasthan	0.723
Union Bank of India	0.792	Bank of Maharashtra	0.705
Bank of India	0.787	Vijaya Bank	0.668
Central Bank of India	0.777	Bank of India	0.656
Ratnakar Bank	0.770	Syndicate Bank	0.652
Andhra Bank	0.769	Andhra Bank	0.641
Punjab National Bank	0.765	Allahabad Bank	0.628
Bank of Rajasthan	0.756	Central Bank of India	0.627
Sangli Bank	0.754	Catholic Syrian Bank	0.627
Allahabad Bank	0.751	Indian Overseas Bank	0.620
United Western Bank	0.750	Punjab and Sind Bank	0.562
Bank of Maharashtra	0.750	Indian Bank	0.523
State Bank of Travancore	0.740	United Commercial Bank	0.508
United Commercial Bank	0.684	United Bank of India	0.406

(*Contd.*)

Table 4.13 (*Contd.*)

1999-00 to 2005-06		*1985 to 2005-06*	
Bank Name	*Super Efficiency*	*Bank Name*	*Super Efficiency*
(5)	*(6)*	*(7)*	*(8)*
Oriental Bank of Commerce	1.047	Tamilnad Mercantile Bank	1.118
Corporation Bank	1.043	Bharat Overseas Bank	1.005
Tamilnad Mercantile Bank	1.031	Karur Vysya Bank	0.984
Karur Vysya Bank	1.014	Oriental Bank of Commerce	0.962
State Bank of Patiala	1.010	Lakshmi Vilas Bank	0.956
State Bank of B & J	1.005	State Bank of Indore	0.937
State Bank of Mysore	0.992	Corporation Bank	0.936
State Bank of Indore	0.968	State Bank of Patiala	0.930
Ing Vysya Bank	0.914	Jammu & Kashmir Bank	0.924
State Bank of Hyderabad	0.910	State Bank of B& J	0.919
Nainital Bank	0.899	Lord Krishna Bank	0.914
Jammu & Kashmir Bank	0.897	Ing Vysya Bank	0.910
Lord Krishna Bank	0.882	State Bank of Mysore	0.907
Andhra Bank	0.872	State Bank of Hyderabad	0.893
Dena Bank	0.861	State Bank of India	0.889
Bharat Overseas Bank	0.855	Bank of Baroda	0.882

Lakshmi Vilas Bank	0.848	State Bank of Saurashtra	0.874
City Union Bank	0.843	City Union Bank	0.855
State Bank of India	0.826	Nainital Bank	0.843
Ratnakar Bank	0.824	Canara Bank	0.838
Punjab National Bank	0.824	Dhanalakshmi Bank	0.835
State Bank of Saurashtra	0.823	Dena Bank	0.831
South Indian Bank	0.816	Karnataka Bank	0.812
Federal Bank	0.809	South Indian Bank	0.811
Karnataka Bank	0.807	Ratnakar Bank	0.787
Vijaya Bank	0.802	Federal Bank	0.781
Dhanalakshmi Bank	0.799	Punjab National Bank	0.777
Syndicate Bank	0.798	Vijaya Bank	0.773
Bank of Baroda	0.794	United Western Bank	0.772
Catholic Syrian Bank	0.788	Union Bank of India	0.772
Union Bank of India	0.785	State Bank of Travancore	0.770
State Bank of Travancore	0.783	Syndicate Bank	0.765
Central Bank of India	0.771	Catholic Syrian Bank	0.761
Indian Overseas Bank	0.767	Andhra Bank	0.761
Allahabad Bank	0.767	Indian Overseas Bank	0.728
Canara Bank	0.763	Bank of Rajasthan	0.727

(Contd.)

TABLE 4.13 (*Contd.*)

(5)	(6)	(7)	(8)
Punjab and Sind Bank	0.746	Central Bank of India	0.725
Bank of India	0.728	Bank of India	0.724
United Bank of India	0.722	Bank of Maharashtra	0.723
United Western Bank	0.718	Allahabad Bank	0.715
Bank of Maharashtra	0.713	Sangli Bank	0.707
Bank of Rajasthan	0.703	Punjab and Sind Bank	0.704
Indian Bank	0.694	Indian Bank	0.696
United Commercial Bank	0.650	United Bank of India	0.644
Sangli Bank	0.606	United Commercial Bank	0.614

(0.787) are found to be lowest efficient banks during the period 1985-92.

Further, Tamilnadu Mercantile Bank with *super–efficiency* score of (1.167) has turned out to be the most *super-efficient* bank during the period 1993-99. Ing Vysya Bank and State Bank of Indore achieved second and third highest place with average *super–efficiency* score of 1.006 and 1.001 respectively. The banks viz., United Bank of India (0.406), United Commercial Bank (0.508), Indian Bank (0.523), Punjab & Sind Bank (0.562), Indian Overseas Bank (0.620), Catholic Syrian Bank (0.627), Central Bank of India (0.627), Allahabad Bank (0.628), Andhra Bank (0.641), Syndicate Bank (0.652) and Bank of India (0.656) are noticed to be at the lower end of *super-efficiency* scale during this period.

The number of *super-efficient* banks increased to six during second-generation reforms as against three during first-generation reforms. The banks that got first six ranks are found to be Oriental Bank of Commerce, Corporation Bank, Tamilnad Mercantile Bank, Karur Vysya Bank, State Bank of Patiala and State Bank of Bikaner and Jaipur with average *super-efficiency* score of 1.047, 1.043, 1.031, 1.014, 1.010 and 1.005 respectively. On the other hand, the lowest super-efficiency score has been accounted for Sangli Bank (0.606), United Commercial Bank (0.650), Indian Bank (0.694), Bank of Rajasthan (0.703), Bank of Maharashtra (0.713), United Western Bank (0.718), United Bank of India (0.722), Bank of India (0.728), Punjab and Sind Bank (0.746), Canara Bank (0.763), Allahabad Bank (0.767) and Indian Overseas Bank (0.767) during the period 2000-06.

The lowest efficient banks as identified in various sub-periods are somewhat supported by the findings of Saha and Ravishankar (2002), which highlighted the banks viz., Punjab & Sind Bank, United Bank of India, United Commercial Bank, Syndicate Bank and Central Bank of India at the lower end of the efficiency scale. The results are also similar to the findings of Das (1999-00) and Kumar and Verma (2002-03) to some extent, which reported United Commercial Bank and United Bank of India as the poor performer while Corporation Bank and Oriental Bank of Commerce as the best performer banks.

Looking at the inter-period shift of the banks, it has been noticed that rankings change considerably across the various sub-periods. Stated differently, most of the sample banks could not maintain their positions or ranks on the *super-efficiency* scale across various sub-periods. The comparative analysis of pre-reforms and first-generation reforms period presents that Bharat Overseas Bank reported shift from top most rank to sixth rank, Tamilnad Mercantile Bank from second to top most rank, Lakshmi Vilas Bank from third to fifth rank and Karur Vysya Bank from fourth to seventh rank between these periods.

During second-generation reforms period, Tamilnad Mercantile Bank and Karur Vysya Bank replaced to third and fourth positions as against seventh and first position during first-generation reforms period respectively. However, Bharat Overseas Bank and Lakshmi Vilas Bank recorded a significant down to sixteenth and seventeenth position in comparison of sixth and fifth position during first-generation reforms period. According to the empirical findings, it is the unique Tamilnad Mercantile Bank, which maintained its position consistently on first three ranks in the sub-periods under consideration. The super efficient banks are expected to utilize their resources up to maximum possible extent at the given state of technology. Therefore, the empirical findings suggest laggard banks (banks at the lower end of efficiency scale) to concentrate more upon minimizing the wastage of resources at the given state of technology like super-efficient banks.

CONCLUSIONS

In the present study, an endeavor has been made to analyze inter-temporal, ownership-wise and inter-bank measures of overall efficiency among CBs in India for the period 1985-06. To view this objective, non-parametric, Data Envelopment Analysis approach has been applied. According to the empirical findings, average cost x-efficiency has turned out to be 0.755 for all CBs, which imply that magnitude of cost inefficiency is to the tune of about 24.5 per cent. This suggests that, banks can, on an average, minimize their costs by eliminating the elements of inefficiencies with the help of best practices and can still produce the same level of outputs.

Further, the empirical findings illustrate that a considerable amount of x-inefficiency is due to the wastage of resources (18.7 percent) rather than the choice of wrong mix of input combinations (6.9 percent) to produce a given level of output. Thus, the results imply that the bank managers are relatively good at selecting the optimum mix of inputs given the prices but they are not that good at using the minimum level of inputs to produce a given level of outputs.

As for the sources of TIE, it has been observed that a considerable portion of TIE (18.7 percent) is due to the inappropriate management practices in organizing the input resources (13 percent). However, the remaining part of the TIE may be attributed to the fact that the banks are either operating at below or above the optimum level. The connotation of the findings is that managerial irregularities have played a key role in emerging technical inefficiencies among CBs in India.

Turning towards the period-wise analysis, CBs have recorded negative trend in various DEA efficiency scores in the first-half of post-reforms period and positive trend in the second-half of post-reforms period (with few exceptions). Therefore, an improvement in DEA efficiency scores is more apparent during second-generation reforms than that of first-generation reforms period. This may be primarily caused by the fact that banks are increasingly adopt the changes in set standards and prudential norms and thereby started to realize the benefits of high degree of liberalization in quantitative form during the period 2000-06. The empirical findings further illustrate that technical inefficiency is the major cause of concern for XIE rather than AIE across various sub-periods. Moreover, inappropriate managerial practices are noted to be more responsible for emerging technical inefficiency among CBs in India than scale related problems across various sub-periods.

As for ownership wise analysis, the average XE of private banks is estimated to be quite high at 78.5 percent followed by PSBs (73.5 percent) during the period 1985-06. This indicates that private banks have the potential for cost saving by 21.5 percent while PSBs can cut their costs by 26.5 percent to capture the position on *Best Practice Frontier*. Despite larger cost efficiency gains by private banks, SBI group emerged to be the market leader with x-efficiency estimate of (83.5 percent) during the period 1985-06. Private banks are found to be more efficient than PSBs in most of DEA efficiency measures during the sub-periods: 1985-92 and 1993-99 but PSBs did so during 2000-06. Thus, it can safely be stated that PSBs have responded better to the liberalization, competitive forces and the change in set standards and prudential norms than those of private banks on the wake of liberalization.

Overall, it has been observed that private banks are more efficient in input utilization process as compared to PSBs in various sub-periods. However, PSBs are found to be more efficient in selecting the optimum mix of inputs at the given prices. Further, the results substantiate that the magnitude of AE has noted to be higher among different forms of banks for most parts of the sub-periods. Thus, it can safely be concluded that AE is the major source of XE than TE across various sub-periods. In addition, an improvement in efficiency scores is more pronounced among various forms of banks. during second-generation reforms as compared to first-generation reforms period. Besides this, large banks are more likely to enjoy the benefits of scale economies than that of small banks.

The results further divulge that majority of sample banks have been operating at below their optimum scale size and thus, experiencing increasing returns-to-scale. There is significant room for these banks to extract maximum possible advantages of scale economies by enhancing the size of the banks. Therefore, closure of sick banks and mergers of the banks seems to be desirable in this direction.

At disaggregated level, average XE has noted to be improved in 22 sample banks, TE in 14 banks, AE in 33 banks, PTE in 15 and SE in 20 banks during first-generation reforms relative to pre-reforms. On the other hand, average XE has observed to be improved in 30 sample banks, TE in 28 banks, AE in 32 banks, PTE in 29 and SE in 21 banks during 2000-06 relative to 1993-99. Therefore, it emanates from the empirical findings that second-phase of banking reforms have marked a significant dent on the efficiency measures of most of the banks.

Out of 45 sample banks, Tamilnad Mercantile Bank has been identified as "relatively efficient" with efficiency score equal to unity and thus, defined. "Best Practice Frontier". This bank dominates in entire study period as it found to be operating at TE and SE frontier (18 times), AE (15 times), XE frontier (16 times) and PTE frontier (20 times) out of 21 sample years. Tamilnad Mercantile Bank is also noted to be operating at the frontier in most of the times across various sub-periods.

The banks that recorded minimum DEA efficiency scores in most of the sample years are noted to be United Bank of India, Sangli Bank, Bank of India, United Commercial Bank and United Western Bank. Therefore, the results suggest that these banks will have to incorporate substantial changes in their policies to keep in lines with international standards.

The results of Andersen and Petersen's super-efficiency scores highlight that Tamilnad Mercantile Bank has captured top most position with average super-efficiency score of 1.118, followed by Bharat Overseas Bank (1.005) during 1985-92. The banks viz., Sangli Bank, Allahabad Bank, Bank of Maharashtra, Bank of India, Central Bank of India, Bank of Rajasthan and Indian Overseas Bank are found to be at the lower end of *super-efficiency* scale. Looking at the inter-period shift of the banks, it is worth to mention that most of the sample banks that captured super-efficiency score during pre-reforms period could not maintain their ranks on *super-efficiency* scale in subsequent periods. However, it is the unique Tamilnad Mercantile Bank, which maintained its position consistently on first three ranks in the specified sub-periods. Therefore, the empirical findings suggest laggard banks to concentrate more upon minimizing the wastage of resources at the given state of technology.

In sum, the policy implication of the aforementioned results is that although efficiency of CBs has improved in second half of the liberalization period, but still there are certain key areas of weaknesses which need quick or immediate redresses by the policy makers. According to the empirical findings of present study, the inefficient use of scarce resources and managerial irregularities are found to be the major cause of concern in emerging technical inefficiencies among CBs in India. To wipe it out, this calls for the need of effective and optimum use of scarce resources and sharpening the managerial skills through various training programmes. Although, scale related problems are not observed to be much serious, but, whatever amount of scale inefficiency has been worked out, appropriate steps should be taken to overcome it so as to operate at the most productive scale size. As majority of sample banks are found to be operating at below their optimum scale size, therefore, closure of sick banks and mergers of banks seem to be desirable to exhaust substantial scale economies. Moreover, the greater use of technology is more likely to generate substantial scale economies for most of the sample banks in India. Furthermore, the banks falling in the region of decreasing returns-to-scale are highly required to downsize the scale of their operations in order to overcome diseconomies of scale. Therefore, an improvement in asset quality and priority sector lending in addition to technological upgradation seem to be desirable in this direction. Overall, it is imperative to fine-tune all the key areas of weaknesses to even out the dismal performance of banks in India. In addition, banks are highly required to avail the maximum benefits from the productive opportunities of liberalization.

NOTES AND REFERENCES

1. The Mann-Whitney *U-test* is based upon the comparison of the rank of the values of one sample in an array of the combined values of the two samples. It is fairly obvious that if the two samples come from the same population, or two populations with equal means, average ranks for each sample should be equal. U is the sample statistic for the distribution of the sum of the ranks (R) for one of the samples.

$$U_1 = n_1 n_2 + \frac{n_1(n_1+1)}{2} - R_1$$

$$U_2 = n_1 n_2 + \frac{n_2(n_2+1)}{2} - R_2$$

Where, n_1 and n_2 are the sizes of sample 1 and sample 2, respectively. R_1 and R_2 are the sum of the ranks of the first sample and second sample, respectively. *U-statistics* is the lower value of U_1 or U_2. Assuming that n_1 and n_2 are sufficiently large (≥ 10), the sampling distribution of U can be normal with the parameters

$\overline{U} = \frac{n_1 n_2}{2}$ and $s_u = \sqrt{\frac{n_1 n_2 (n_1 + n_2 + 1)}{12}}$. Now the null-hypothesis that both samples come from the same population can be tested using *Z-test* written as: $Z = \frac{U - \overline{U}}{s_u}$.

2. The banks at the lower end of super efficiency scale have been identified on the basis-super efficiency score of the bank under observation < the value of first-quartile. Hence the value of Q1 = 0.791 for the period 1985 to 1992-93, Q_1 = 0.665 for 1992-93 to 1998-99, Q_1 = 0.770 for 1999-00 to 2005-06 and Q_1 = 0.753 for the period 1985 to 2005-06.

5

Total Factor Productivity Growth of Commercial Banks in India

As discussed in previous chapter, efficiency measures the bank's performance relative to a benchmark at a given point of time. A major problem associated with efficiency studies is that it does not throw light on the question whether efficiency improves or deteriorates over time. It is therefore in this context, the notion of productivity has gained renewed importance to measure bank's performance over time. Alternatively, if we want to ascertain the robustness of growth or see whether the banks are consistently facing steady state of growth, it is quintessential to ascertain productivity growth pattern of the banks. Productivity indices are recognized as a useful tool in economic forecasting and determining the most effective allocation of resources. Moreover, productivity indices assist to set realistic targets for monitoring activities during the developmental process through identifying the key areas of weaknesses and barriers to performance. In addition, it suggests us the remedial measures to wipe out the dismal performance of the banks.

Ahuluwalia (1985) has pointed out that in context to service sector in India, one need to look at the broader concept of total factor productivity growth, which is used to explain not merely the (productive) efficiency of labor and capital but also the way the management combines these and other factors to enhance the output of the unit. The productive efficiency in this approach is measured as the ratio of weighted output by weighted input, with weights assigned to various inputs and outputs on a heuristic basis. Technical progress, technology absorption/usage, managerial efficiency, distribution network, etc., or some of the other factors, which have a bearing in case of service sector, more so in the financial sector.

During the last four decades, a lot of research work has been undertaken on the measurement of productivity and its growth especially in developed nations. Nevertheless, the major emphasis was confined to agriculture and industrial sector of an economy. As far as bank productivity is concerned, even in developed nations like USA, the research work on productivity started in 1980s. The empirical evidence also suggests few studies on this emerging issue in context to Indian banking sector. However, banking being an important economic activity, can not afford to lose sight of the concept of productivity. So, there is a need to conduct such types of studies for the developing country like India.

The present chapter is an attempt in this direction to study the total factor productivity growth pattern of commercial banks in India. To view this objective, DEA based Malmquist Productivity Index (MPI) approach has been applied on balanced panel data set of 27 public sector banks and 18 old private sector banks in India for the period 1985 to 2005-06. The entire study period has been classified into three distinct sub-periods: (i) Pre-liberalization period (1985 to 1991-92) (ii) Initial post-liberalization period (1992-93 to 1998-99) and (iii) Post-liberalization period (1999-00 to 2005-06). The analysis of pre-liberalization and post-liberalization period is justifiable on the ground that it assists us to ascertain whether liberalization has favourably affected the productivity level of banks or not. To keep in lines with Howcroft and Attaullah (2006) and Zhao *et. al.* (2008), post-liberalization period has been further bifurcated into initial post-liberalization period or first-generation reforms and post-liberalization period or second-generation reforms period. This attempt helps us to analyze the change in the behaviour of TFP growth of banks with the change in the degree of deregulation. All the calculations related to Malmquist productivity index and its related indices have been computed through running DEAP software developed by Tim Coelli.

5.1 EMPIRICAL FINDINGS

The empirical findings present inter-temporal, ownership-wise and inter-bank analysis of TFP growth and its related indices among commercial banks (CBs) in India for the period 1985 to 2005-06, divided into distinct sub-periods. In addition, the relationship of bank size and TFP change along with its components has been explored among commercial banks in India. Besides this, an attempt has been made to discriminate the banks on the basis of TFP growth and its relative indices.

To discuss the empirical findings in a systematic manner, this chapter has been divided into two broad sections. Section I concentrates on the analysis of Malmquist productivity index (MPI) and its indices on aggregate basis (inter-temporal and ownership wise analysis). Section II elaborates the analysis of MPI and its indices on disaggregate basis (inter-bank analysis).

SECTION I

5.1.1 Temporal Pattern of MPI and its Components

As stated earlier, this paper applies DEA-based MPI to compute TFP growth and its related indices among CBs in India for the period 1985 to 2005-06, reclassified into distinct sub-periods. Table 5.1 highlights temporal pattern of Malmquist productivity index and its components among commercial banks in India. The TFP ascertains the growth of an individual bank relative to the best practice banks in the sample. To estimate the TFP growth rate, one is subtracted from the TFP index and then value is multiplied by 100 to express the growth rate in percentage. A TFPCH index greater than 1 indicates productivity gain, while a TFPCH index lesser than 1 denotes productivity loss. The same procedure has been

TABLE 5.1
Temporal Pattern of TFP Growth and its Components among Commercial Banks in India : 1985 to 2005-06

Years	*TCH*	*G.R.*	*EFFCH*	*G.R.*	*SEFFCH*	*G.R.*	*PEFFCH*	*G.R.*	*TFP*	*G.R.*
(1)	*(2)*	*(3)*	*(4)*	*(5)*	*(6)*	*(7)*	*(8)*	*(9)*	*(10)*	*(11)*
1986	1.025	2.5	1.024	2.4	1.013	1.3	1.011	1.1	1.05	5.0
1987	1.043	4.3	0.980	-2.0	0.999	-0.1	0.980	-2.0	1.022	2.2
1988-89	1.372	37.2	0.963	-3.7	0.983	-1.7	0.980	-2.0	1.321	32.1
1989-90	0.912	-8.8	1.023	2.3	0.994	-0.6	1.029	2.9	0.933	-6.7
1990-91	1.128	12.8	0.879	-12.1	0.986	-1.4	0.891	-10.9	0.992	-0.8
1991-92	1.487	48.7	0.917	-8.3	0.951	-4.9	0.965	-3.5	1.364	36.4
1992-93	0.884	-11.6	0.995	-0.5	1.056	5.6	0.942	-5.8	0.880	-12.0
1993-94	0.966	-3.4	1.089	8.9	1.013	1.3	1.075	7.5	1.052	5.2
1994-95	1.081	8.1	1.041	4.1	0.984	-1.6	1.059	5.9	1.126	12.6
1995-96	1.064	6.4	0.996	-0.4	0.990	-1.0	1.006	0.6	1.059	5.9
1996-97	1.074	7.4	0.936	-6.4	0.959	-4.1	0.976	-2.4	1.005	0.5
1997-98	0.954	-4.6	1.085	8.5	1.033	3.3	1.050	5.0	1.035	3.5
1998-99	0.923	-7.7	1.002	0.2	0.988	-1.2	1.013	1.3	0.925	-7.5

(Contd.)

TABLE 5.1 (*Contd.*)

(1)	(2)	(3)	(4)	(5)	(6)	(7)	(8)	(9)	(10)	(11)
1999-2000	1.090	9.0	1.003	0.3	1.023	2.3	0.980	-2.0	1.093	9.3
2000-01	1.035	3.5	1.010	1.0	0.987	-1.3	1.024	2.4	1.045	4.5
2001-02	1.152	15.2	1.024	2.4	1.044	4.4	0.981	-1.9	1.179	17.9
2002-03	1.020	2.0	1.040	4.0	0.995	-0.5	1.044	4.4	1.061	6.1
2003-04	1.052	5.2	0.977	-2.3	0.975	-2.5	1.002	0.2	1.028	2.8
2004-05	0.956	-4.4	0.924	-7.6	0.947	-5.3	0.976	-2.4	0.884	-11.6
2005-06	0.982	-1.8	1.012	1.2	1.028	2.8	0.984	-1.6	0.994	-0.6
Averages										
1986/92	1.144	14.4	0.963	-3.7	0.987	-1.3	0.975	-2.5	1.102	10.2
1993/99	0.990	-1.0	1.019	1.9	1.003	0.3	1.016	1.6	1.009	0.9
2000/06	1.039	3.9	0.998	-0.2	0.999	-0.1	0.998	-0.2	1.037	3.7
1986/06	1.051	5.1	0.995	-0.5	0.997	-0.3	0.998	-0.2	1.046	4.6
S.D (86/06)	0.021	—	0.018	—	0.008	—	0.007	—	0.024	—

Note : All the indices are relative to previous year, therefore, no results for the initial sample year (1985).

FIG. 5.1
TFP Growth and its Components

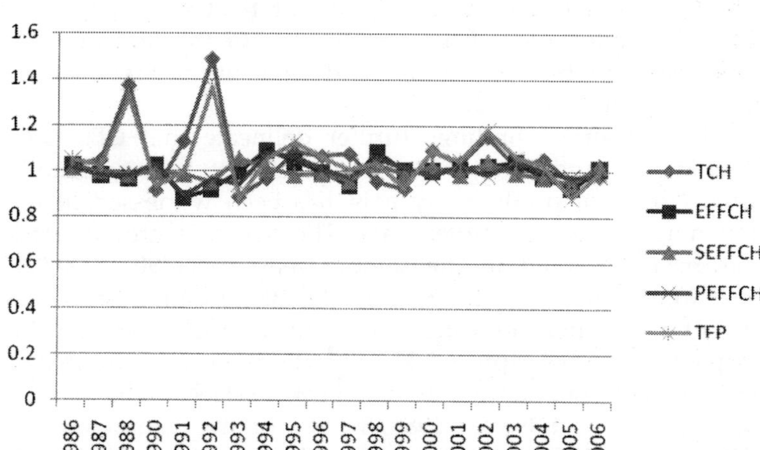

extended to calculate the growth rates of the related indices of Malmquist productivity index. It is note worthy that the productivity growth and its related indices are relative to previous year, therefore, no figures exist for the initial sample year 1985.

The empirical findings illustrate that commercial banks have experienced total factor productivity (TFP) growth at the rate of 4.6 percent per annum during the period 1986-06. Over this period, TFP growth has been realized on account of (5.1 percent) growth rate of technological progress and (–0.5 percent) growth rate of technical efficiency. Thus, it is apparent from the analysis that catching up phenomenon is fragile (as observed when technological change is greater than efficiency change) among the sample banks. The weak catching up effect (deterioration in technical efficiency) can be the result of poor diffusion process of new technology and a little accumulation of knowledge through learning by doings. On the basis of this ground, failure of CBs in achieving technological mastery can safely be stated.

Looking at the yearly averages of MPI and its indices (as shown in Table 5.1 and Figure 5.1), no stable and consistent year-to-year trend of MPI and its indices is discernable from the empirical analysis. The range of the growth rates of MPI and its indices has recorded significant fluctuations through out the sample years. This may be due to the fact that the banks have to face significant and frequent policy changes during the study period.

The empirical findings further delineate that CBs have experienced productivity loss in six out of twenty sample years. However, productivity gain has been witnessed in the remaining fourteen sample years. The negative growth rates have been observed in the sample years 1989/90, 1990/91, 1992/93, 1998/99, 2004/05 and 2005/06, ranging from 0.6 percent to 12 percent during the entire study period. The sample banks have captured TFP growth at an alarming rate of (36.4 percent) per annum in the year 1991/92, followed by (32.1 percent) in the year 1988/89. As for the components of MPI, the sample banks have witnessed technological progress in thirteen sample years and accordingly, technological regress in remaining seven sample years. The CBs reported tremendous growth in terms of TCH index in the years 1991/92 and 1988/89 at the rate of (48.7 percent) and (37.2 percent) respectively. As for EFFCH index, the commercial banks experienced efficiency increase in eleven sample years; however, efficiency decrease in remaining nine sample years. The CBs achieved highest efficiency increase in 1993-94 at the rate of 8.9 percent per annum. Thus, it emanates from the analysis that the range of growth rates of technological change and TFP change has recorded significant fluctuations through out the sample years as compared to EFFCH index and its related indices (SEFFCH and PEFFCH index). In addition, the sample banks have realized TFP growth either due to technological progress or improvement in technical efficiency in most of the sample years. But, both the technological progress and efficiency increase positively influenced the TFP growth of banks in six sample years. Similarly, an improvement in both the components of scale efficiency and pure technical efficiency has been observed in the sample years of 1986, 1993/94 and 1997/98.

The period-wise analysis delineates that sample banks have experienced TFP growth at the rate of (10.2 percent) per annum during pre-reforms period. Over the period, technological change (frontier effect) increased the TFP growth of CBs by (14.4 percent) per annum, however, the negative growth of technical efficiency (catching up effect) lowered down the level of TFP growth by (3.7 percent) per annum. Thus, strong frontier effect has emerged out to be the major driver of TFP gains rather catching up effect is found to be missing during pre-reforms period.

The inter-period shift of the banks presents deceleration in TFP growth at the rate of (0.9 percent) per annum due to the technical change (-1.0 percent) and efficiency change (1.9 percent) during the period 1993-99 in comparison of the period 1986-92. The surprising result that emerges from the analysis is that whatever amount of productivity has been realized during 1993-99 is exclusively due to strong catching up effect which was completely absent during 1986-92. The positive catch up effect signals that the banks have started to use the existing technologies during the period 1993-99. On the other hand, weak frontier effect may be attributed to the absence of technological upgradation, shocks (financial crisis), changes in market structure (high concentration due to M&As) and regulatory policies (financial deregulation), etc.

In second-phase of liberalization period, banks have witnessed a clear acceleration in TFP growth at the rate of (3.7 percent) per annum. This increase in TFP growth of CBs can exclusively be attributed to technological change at the rate of (3.9 percent) per annum rather than efficiency change (-0.2 percent) per annum. The results suggest that poor diffusion process of the technology is most probably the consequent factor of fragile catching up effect. Drake (2001) advocated a similar explanation when he conducted a study to measure TFP growth of retail banks in U.K during the period 1984-95. He illustrated that the evidence of negative catchup may be attributable to the intensification of competition in retail banking in U.K over this time period. While this may have been a force producing technical change, it may also have produced a greater disparity in performance across banks, with some remaining on the frontier but others falling farther away from the shifting frontier and thereby exhibiting negative catchup efficiency.

As for various sources of technical efficiency, the empirical findings highlight that both the negative growth of scale efficiency and pure technical efficiency indices has slowed down the level of technical efficiency. This finding seems to be true during the sub-periods: 1986/92 and 2000/06. However, the contrasted picture has been observed during the sub-period 1993/99, where both the components favorably contributed to the efficiency change of CBs in India.

Overall, it has been observed that TFP growth of banks has declined during first-phase and second-phase of liberalization period in comparison of pre-liberalization period. After liberalization, the reason of fall in TFP growth may possibly be on account of the introduction of prudential accounting norms into the Indian banking system in 1992. According to these norms, any asset that have two consecutive quarterly defaults in interest accrual cannot be treated as income, rather till 1992, this item was considered as an income. The shift from *'Income on Accrual Basis'* to *'Income on Realization Basis'* has compressed the income level of the banks in India. In addition, the TFP growth of banks is more pronounced during second-generation reforms as compared to first-generation reforms in consistent to the findings of Zhao *et. al.* (2008). These results are also in lines with the results obtained by Howcroft and Attaullah (2006) where TFP growth of banks has noticed to be higher in post-deregulation period as compared to initial post-deregulation period.

5.1.2 Bank Ownership-wise Analysis

5.1.2.1 TFP and its related Indices by Ownership Groups

In Table 5.2, we have presented average estimates of TFP growth, technical efficiency change and technological change of commercial banks in India for the period 1985-06. The commercial banks have been decomposed into two categories of PSBs and private banks. PSBs have been further divided into two groups, i.e., SBI group and NBs group.

If we look at the temporal performance of the banks, (as shown in Table 5.2 and Figure 5.2, 5.3 and 5.4), no stable and consistent trend of TFP growth and its indices has been observed among different forms of banks. The PSBs achieved

TABLE 5.2

Average Technical Efficiency Change, Technological Change and Total Factor Productivity Change of Commercial Banks in India —1985 to 2005-06

Years	*Technical Efficiency Change*				*Technological Change*				*Total Factor Productivity Change*			
	NBs	*SBI*	*PSBs*	*Pvt*	*NBs*	*SBI*	*PSBs*	*Pvt*	*NBs*	*SBI*	*PSBs*	*Pvt*
(1)	(2)	(3)	(4)	(5)	(6)	(7)	(8)	(9)	(10)	(11)	(12)	(13)
1986	1.037	1.050	1.040	1.000	1.043	1.041	1.043	0.999	1.081	1.093	1.085	1.000
1987	0.983	0.972	0.980	0.980	1.054	1.055	1.054	1.027	1.036	1.025	1.032	1.006
1988-89	0.964	1.005	0.976	0.944	1.365	1.393	1.373	1.370	1.316	1.400	1.340	1.293
1989-90	1.006	1.014	1.008	1.045	0.938	0.912	0.930	0.886	0.943	0.925	0.938	0.926
1990-91	0.864	0.887	0.871	0.892	1.128	1.111	1.123	1.136	0.975	0.986	0.978	1.013
1991-92	0.858	1.159	0.938	0.887	1.518	1.432	1.492	1.481	1.302	1.659	1.399	1.313
1992-93	0.880	1.027	0.922	1.116	0.969	0.837	0.928	0.823	0.853	0.859	0.855	0.918
1993-94	1.094	1.022	1.073	1.114	0.974	0.957	0.969	0.962	1.066	0.978	1.039	1.072
1994-95	1.129	0.996	1.088	0.975	1.077	1.075	1.076	1.088	1.216	1.070	1.171	1.062
1995-96	0.987	1.015	0.995	0.997	1.066	1.075	1.069	1.055	1.053	1.090	1.064	1.053
1996-97	0.964	0.926	0.953	0.911	1.082	1.090	1.084	1.058	1.043	1.010	1.033	0.964
1997-98	1.126	1.110	1.121	1.032	0.905	0.861	0.892	1.057	1.019	0.956	1.000	1.091

(*Contd.*)

TABLE 5.2 (*Contd.*)

(1)	(2)	(3)	(4)	(5)	(6)	(7)	(8)	(9)	(10)	(11)	(12)	(13)
1998-99	1.001	0.970	0.992	1.016	0.966	0.973	0.968	0.860	0.967	0.944	0.960	0.874
1999-00	0.990	1.009	0.995	1.014	1.047	1.018	1.039	1.173	1.036	1.028	1.034	1.189
2000-01	1.035	0.991	1.022	0.992	1.064	1.028	1.053	1.009	1.101	1.019	1.076	1.001
2001-02	1.007	0.957	0.992	1.074	1.078	1.096	1.083	1.263	1.085	1.049	1.074	1.356
2002-03	1.105	1.021	1.079	0.983	1.029	1.010	1.023	1.016	1.136	1.031	1.104	0.998
2003-04	0.982	0.993	0.985	0.965	1.080	1.062	1.075	1.018	1.061	1.055	1.059	0.983
2004-05	0.978	0.944	0.968	0.862	0.969	0.936	0.959	0.952	0.948	0.884	0.929	0.821
2005-06	0.982	1.019	0.993	1.042	0.978	0.942	0.967	1.005	0.960	0.961	0.960	1.047
Averages												
1986/92	0.949	1.011	0.967	0.956	1.158	1.142	1.153	1.131	1.099	1.155	1.115	1.082
1993/99	1.022	1.008	1.018	1.021	1.003	0.976	0.995	0.981	1.026	0.984	1.013	1.001
2000/06	1.010	0.990	1.004	0.988	1.034	1.012	1.027	1.057	1.045	1.002	1.032	1.045
1986/06	0.996	1.003	0.998	0.990	1.059	1.036	1.052	1.051	1.054	1.039	1.050	1.040
S.D (86/06)	0.007	0.008	0.008	0.010	0.015	0.010	0.017	0.026	0.018	0.011	0.018	0.031

FIG. 5.2
Technical Efficiency Change of Commercial Banks

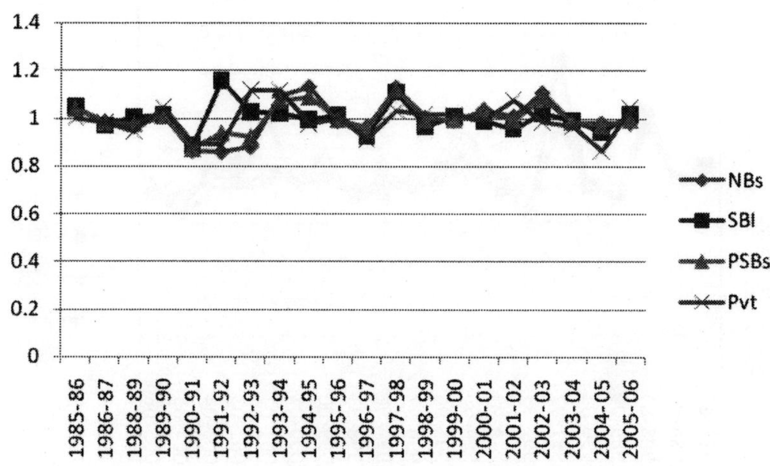

FIG. 5.3
Technological Change of Commercial Banks

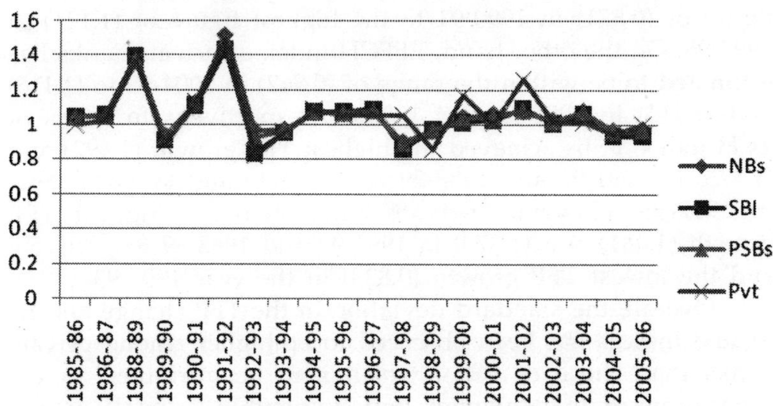

the highest TFP growth (1.399) and (1.340) in 1991-92 and 1988-89 respectively and lowest (0.855) in 1992-93. However, private banks have highest TFP growth (1.356), (1.313) and (1.293) in 2001-02, 1991-92 and 1988-89 respectively and the lowest (0.821) in 2004-05.

FIG. 5.4
Total Factor Productivity Growth of Commercial Banks

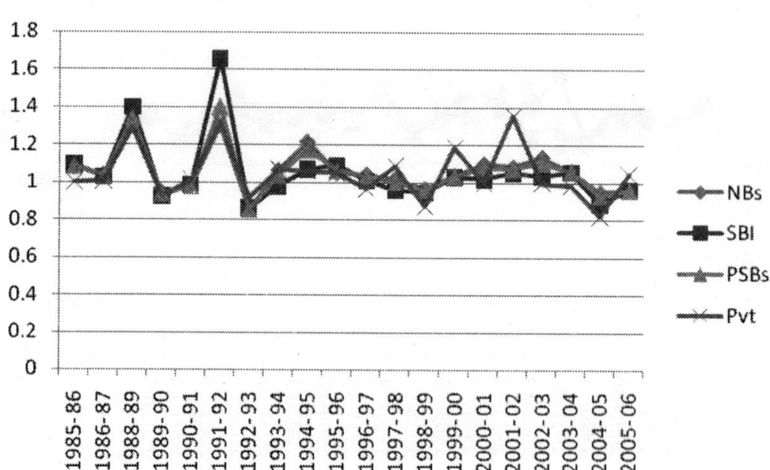

Looking at the decompositions of TFP growth, the EFFCH index of PSBs has estimated to be varying from the lowest figure of (0.871) in 1990-91 to the highest figure of (1.121) in 1997-98. On the other hand, EFFCH index of private banks has estimated to be within the range of (0.862) in 2004-05 to (1.116) and (1.114) in 1992-93 and 1993-94, respectively. In terms of TCH index, PSBs achieved the highest TFP growth (1.492) and (1.373) in 1991-92 and 1988-89 respectively and lowest (0.892) in 1997-98. However, private banks realized highest TFP growth (1.481) and (1.370) in 1991-92 and 1988-89 respectively and the lowest TFP growth (0.823) in the year 1992-93.

Overall, the standard deviation in the TFP change and its related indices has been observed to be higher among private banks than those of PSBs, which may be attributed to the separation of management and ownership as well as the adoption of dissimilar practices by different banks in decision making process. On the other hand, lower variability in the TFP change and its indices among PSBs may be due to the fact that the banks are more familiar with the regulatory system in consistent to the findings of Bhattacharyya *et. al.* (1997). Furthermore, NBs group of PSBs recorded higher level of variations in TCH index and TFP change index than that of SBI group; however, the opposite holds true for EFFCH index.

As evident in Table 5.2, PSBs are observed to grow at the rate of (5 percent) per annum, followed by private banks (4.0 percent) during the period 1986-06. The productivity gains of PSBs outweigh those of private banks in consistent to the findings of Kumbhakar and Sarkar (2003), Mohan and Ray (2004), Howcroft and Attaullah (2006) as per loan based model and Rezvanian *et. al.* (2008). Further, the results provide that productivity gains of PSBs and private sector banks have originated more due to the frontier effect of (5.2 percent) and (5.1 percent) per annum respectively. However, the deterioration in efficiency has decelerated the level of TFP growth of private banks by (-1.0 percent) and PSBs (-0.2 percent) per annum over the period. The results are highly supported by the findings of Subrahmanyam, G. (1993), RBI (2008) and Zhao *et. al.* (2008), which highlighted the dominance of TCH index over the EFFCH index to TFP growth.

As for various categories of PSBs, NBs group experienced TFP growth at the rate of (5.4 percent) per annum, followed by SBI group (3.9 percent). Further, it has been observed that both the improved technologies (3.6 percent) and the efficient use of these technologies (0.3 percent) have exerted positive impact on the TFP growth of SBI group. However, NBs group has experienced most of the productivity gain on account of TCH at the rate of (5.9 percent) per annum than EFFCH at the rate of (-0.4 percent) per annum over the period 1986-06.

The period-wise analysis highlights that PSBs have emerged to be more productive than private banks during pre-reforms and first-generation reforms period. However, the comparative analysis of growth rates illustrates that PSBs have experienced a significant deceleration in TFP growth at the rate of (1.3 percent) per annum during first-generation reforms as against (11.5 percent) during pre-reforms period. This deceleration in TFP growth has originated more due to the reverse change in the rate of TCH (i.e., from 15.3 percent to -0.5 percent) rather than EFFCH (i.e., from -3.3 percent to 1.8 percent) per annum. On the other hand, private banks experienced TFP growth at the rate of (8.2 percent) per annum during 1986-92 but it significantly declined to (0.1 percent) during 1993-99. This was on account of the movement of both the indices in opposite direction i.e., [EFFCH (-4.4 percent to 2.1 percent] and TCH [(13.1 percent to (-1.9 percent)], which cancelled out the affect of each other. As far as categories of PSBs are concerned, NBs also reported fall in productivity scores (i.e., 9.9 percent to 2.6 percent) more due to the fall in TCH index (i.e., from 15.8 percent to 0.3 percent) rather than efficiency change (-5.1 percent to 2.2 percent) during these periods. On the other hand, SBI group also registered tremendous fall in productivity scores (i.e., from 15.5 percent to -1.6 percent) on account of technological change (i.e., 14.2 percent to -2.4 percent) and efficiency change (i.e., from 1.1 percent to 0.8 percent) during these periods. It is worth specifying that TCH index, the major driver of productivity growth during the period 1986-92, failed to impart significant impact on the TFP growth of different forms of banks during 1993-99. Therefore, it can be concluded that TFP growth of banks has primarily emanated on account of effective diffusion process of technologies during first-generation reforms. The results also imply that banks have started catching up each other to achieve highest level of TFP growth. These results are in lines with the findings of Galagedera *et. al.* (2004), which noticed the dominance of efficiency change over the technological change among private banks in India for the period 1995-02. The results are also supported by the findings of Zhao *et. al.* (2008), which highlighted the dominance of EFFCH index over the TCH index for the first sub-period (1992-97).

In second-phase of liberalization period, private banks witnessed acceleration in TFP growth at the rate (4.5 percent) per annum in comparison of first-generation reforms. Most of the productivity gain can be attributed to technological progress at the rate of (5.7 percent) rather than efficiency change at the rate of (-1.2 percent) per annum. Thus, the empirical evidence highlights an important role of advanced technologies to the TFP gain; however, the absence of technological mastery to absorb these enhanced technologies can safely be stated. The above finding is found to be consistent to the findings of Zhao *et. al.* (2008), where TFP growth was realized more due to the advancement in technologies than efficiency change in second sub-period (1998-04).

On the other hand, PSBs recorded acceleration in TFP at the growth rate of (3.2 percent) per annum during 2000-06 as against (1.3 percent) during 1993-99. It has also been observed that both the forces of catching up effect (0.4 percent) and frontier effect (2.7 percent) have favorably contributed to the TFP growth of PSBs during 2000-06. But, the dominance of frontier effect over the catching up effect is visible from the empirical analysis. The strong frontier effect among PSBs can be attributed to the heavy investment in computerization of branches, installation of ATMs, core banking solutions and IT technologies, etc. But, the weak catching up effect reflects the failure of PSBs to catch up the best practices available in the banking industry. Furthermore, it emanates from the analysis that PSBs are more likely to make serious attempts to utilize scarce resources in order to get maximum returns out of it than those of private sector counterpart.

As for various categories of PSBs, NBs have witnessed TFP growth at the rate of (4.5 percent) per annum more due to the technological change (3.4 percent) per annum rather than efficiency change (1.0 percent) per annum during the period 2000-06. SBI group performed poorly than that of NBs group and has been noted to be growing at the rate of (0.2 percent) per annum. This growth can be attributed more to the advancement in technologies (1.2 percent) rather than efficient use of these technologies (-1.0 percent). Therefore, improved technologies (innovations) have emerged to be the major driver of TFP growth in SBI group of PSBs during 2000-06. On the other hand, the empirical evidence suggests the inability of the SBI group to catch up the best practices available in banking industry. In this context, Kalirajan and Shand (1997) stated that the adoption of new technology by 'best practice firm' in turn leads to an improvement in technical efficiency but if high rate of technological progress is co-existed with low rate of technical efficiency change, it may reflect failures in achieving technological mastery. It may also reflect higher levels of technological dynamism but with higher degree of obsolescence. Moreover, the empirical findings highlight that an improvement in TFP growth is highly pronounced during second-generation reforms than that of first-generation reforms period, which is consistent to the findings of Kumbhakar and Sarkar (2003) and Zhao *et. al.* (2008).

5.1.2.2 Sources of Efficiency Change Index by Ownership Groups

In Table 5.3, we have presented average estimates (geometric averages) of pure technical efficiency and scale efficiency change of various forms of banks in India for the period 1985-06. Looking at the temporal performance pattern of efficiency scores (as depicted in Table 5.3 and Figures 5.5 and 5.6), no stable and consistent trend of SE change and PTE change has been observed among different forms of banks through out the sample years. The PSBs achieved the highest PTE change (1.074), (1.073) and (1.067) in 1994-95, 1993-94 and 1997-98 respectively and lowest (0.887) in 1990-91. However, private banks noted the highest PTE change (1.078) in 1993-94 and the lowest (0.897) in 1990-91. Overall, it has been observed that the standard deviation in the PTE change of PSBs is higher than those of private banks, which may be attributed to the improved practices of certain PSBs. On the other hand, lower variability in the PTE change of private banks may be attributed to their sudden and immediate response to new prudential norms and standards. Furthermore, standard deviation in the PTE change of SBI group has been observed to be higher than that of NBs group.

On the other hand, the scale efficiency change index of PSBs fluctuated widely from the low (0.974) in the years 1996-97 and 1998-99 each to the high (1.051) in the year 1997-98. And, SEFFCH of private banks has been noted to be varying from the low (0.893) in the year 1991-92 to the high (1.132) in the year 1992-93. The standard deviation in the SEFFCH index of the private banks is higher than those of PSBs, which may be attributed to the separation of management and ownership as well as to the adoption of dissimilar practices by different banks in decision-making process. On the other hand, lower variability in the SEFFCH of PSBs may be due to the fact that the banks are more familiar with the regulatory system in India. Furthermore, the standard deviation in the SE change of

TABLE 5.3

Average Scale Efficiency Change and Pure Technical Efficiency Change Index of Commercial Banks in India—1985 to 2005-06

Years	*Scale Efficiency Change*				*Pure Technical Efficiency Change*			
	NBs	*SBI*	*PSBs*	*Pvt.*	*NBs*	*SBI*	*PSBs*	*Pvt.*
(1)	(2)	(3)	(4)	(5)	(6)	(7)	(8)	(9)
1986	1.043	0.986	1.026	0.995	0.993	1.065	1.014	1.006
1987	1.002	1.028	1.010	0.984	0.981	0.946	0.970	0.996
1988-89	0.980	0.999	0.986	0.980	0.984	1.006	0.991	0.964
1989-90	0.987	1.002	0.992	0.997	1.019	1.012	1.017	1.048
1990-91	0.981	0.984	0.981	0.994	0.881	0.902	0.887	0.897
1991-92	0.965	1.056	0.991	0.893	0.889	1.097	0.946	0.993
1992-93	1.011	1.002	1.009	1.132	0.870	1.025	0.914	0.986
1993-94	1.001	0.996	1.000	1.034	1.093	1.026	1.073	1.078
1994-95	1.015	1.009	1.013	0.941	1.113	0.987	1.074	1.036
1995-96	0.986	0.991	0.988	0.995	1.001	1.025	1.008	1.002
1996-97	0.974	0.972	0.974	0.936	0.990	0.953	0.979	0.972
1997-98	1.061	1.026	1.051	1.007	1.061	1.082	1.067	1.025

(*Contd.*)

TABLE 5.3 (*Contd.*)

(1)	(2)	(3)	(4)	(5)	(6)	(7)	(8)	(9)
1998-99	0.967	0.990	0.974	1.011	1.036	0.980	1.019	1.006
1999-00	1.018	1.006	1.015	1.036	0.972	1.003	0.981	0.979
2000-01	0.983	0.999	0.988	0.985	1.053	0.992	1.034	1.007
2001-02	1.029	1.014	1.025	1.074	0.978	0.944	0.968	1.000
2002-03	1.019	0.998	1.012	0.971	1.084	1.024	1.066	1.013
2003-04	0.993	0.967	0.985	0.960	0.989	1.027	1.000	1.006
2004-05	0.974	1.006	0.984	0.894	1.004	0.938	0.984	0.964
2005-06	1.025	1.029	1.026	1.031	0.958	0.990	0.967	1.011
Averages								
1986/92	0.993	1.009	0.997	0.973	0.956	1.002	0.970	0.983
1993/99	1.002	0.998	1.001	1.006	1.020	1.010	1.017	1.014
2000/06	1.006	1.003	1.005	0.991	1.005	0.988	1.000	0.997
1986/06	1.001	1.003	1.001	0.991	0.995	1.000	0.997	0.999
S.D 86/06	0.004	0.002	0.003	0.009	0.007	0.009	0.008	0.007

FIG. 5.5
Scale Efficiency Change of Commercial Banks

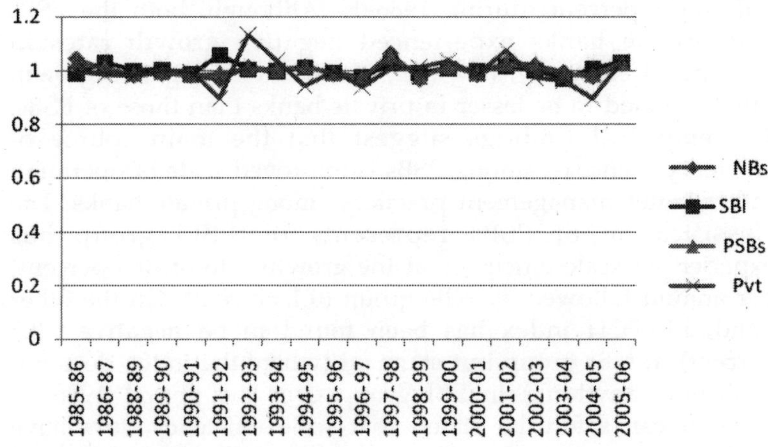

FIG. 5.6
Pure Techical Efficiency Change of Commercial Banks

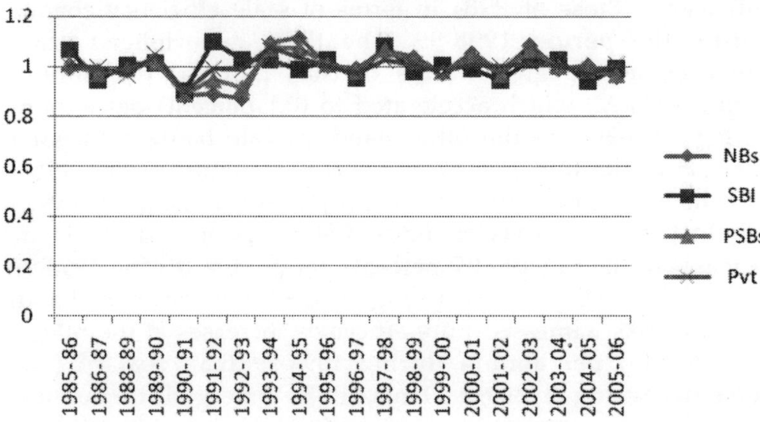

NBs group has been observed to be higher than SBI group.

The empirical findings (as shown in Table 5.3) highlight that PSBs outweigh those of private banks in terms of scale efficiency change during the period 1986-06. PSBs exhibited scale efficiency at the growth rate of (0.1 percent) per annum, followed by private banks (-0.9 percent) per annum during the period 1986-06. On the other hand, private banks experienced pure efficiency at the growth rate of (-0.1 percent), followed by PSBs (-0.3 percent) during 1986-06. Although, both the PSBs and private banks experienced negative growth rates in managerial efficiency; however, the extent of negative growth rate has noted to be lesser in private banks than those of PSBs. The empirical findings suggest that the main source of efficiency increases among PSBs is improved scale of operation rather better management practices among private banks. The classification of PSBs represents that SBI group has experienced scale efficiency at the growth rate of (0.3 percent) per annum followed by NBs group (0.1 percent). On the other hand, PEFFCH index has been found to be negative (-0.5 percent) in NBs group but stagnant (where the index does not contribute anything) in SBI group over the period 1986-06. Thus, it can safely be stated that scale efficiency does have profound impact on the efficiency change of both the NBs and SBI group of PSBs.

The comparative analysis of pre-reforms and first-generation reforms period illustrates that private banks have outweighed those of PSBs in terms of scale efficiency change during the period 1998-99. The PSBs experienced scale efficiency at the growth rate of (-0.3 percent) per annum during 1986-92, which accelerated to (0.1 percent) per annum during 1993-99. On the other hand, private banks witnessed SEFFCH at the rate of (-1.7 percent) per annum during 1986-92, which increased notably to (0.6 percent) during 1993-99.

In terms of PEFFCH index, PSBs experienced efficiency increases at the rate of (1.7 percent) per annum during 1993-99 contrary to (-3.0 percent) during 1986-92. On the other hand, private banks witnessed pure efficiency increases at the rate of (1.4 percent) per annum during 1993-99 than that of (-1.7 percent) during 1986-92. Thus, PSBs emerged to be out-performers in terms of managerial efficiency change index than those of private banks during the period 1993-99.

Further, the empirical findings substantiate that NBs group has recorded acceleration in scale efficiency and pure technical efficiency with the respective growth rates of (0.2 percent) and (2.0 percent) per annum during 1993-99 as compared to negative growth rates during 1986-92. On the other hand, SBI group registered decline in SEFFCH at the rate of (-0.2 percent) per annum during first-generation reforms than that of (0.9 percent) per annum during pre-reforms period. But, SBI group recorded an increase in pure efficiency at the growth rate of (1.0 percent) during first-generation reforms as compared to (0.2 percent) during pre-reforms period. Thus, it emanates from the analysis that both the NBs group and SBI group has performed better during first-generation reforms in comparison to pre-reforms period (with few exceptions). Overall, it has been observed that initial-phase of reforms has exerted positive influence on the scale of operation and managerial capabilities of the banks so as to have optimum use of resources. But, the dominance of better management practices to the technical efficiency increases is clear from the empirical analysis during first-generation reforms period.

Further, the empirical findings substantiate that PSBs have experienced acceleration in the scale efficiency at the growth rate of (0.5 percent) during second-generation reforms as compared to first-generation reforms. But, private banks have witnessed tremendous fall at the rate of (-0.9 percent) per annum between these periods. As far as PEFFCH index is concerned, private banks have recorded considerable fall at the rate of (-0.3 percent) per annum while PSBs reported no growth between these periods. Thus, the results suggest that improved scale of operations has enhanced the level of efficiency increases among PSBs during the period 2000-06. Nevertheless, management practices could not contribute anything to efficiency increases. Further, the results present that NBs group has out-performed SBI group in both the terms of SEFFCH and PEFFCH index. SBI group and NBs group experienced an accelerative pattern of scale efficiency at the respective growth rates of (0.6 percent) and (0.3 percent) per annum during the period 2000-06. As for PEFFCH index, NBs experienced efficiency increases at the rate of (0.5 percent) per annum, followed by SBI group (-1.2 percent) per annum during the period 2000-06. Thus, it emerges from the analysis that NBs group has out-performed SBI group in terms of improved scale of operations and managerial efficiency after the deregulatory policies came into force (since 2000-06). Finally, the empirical findings suggest that PSBs have responded well to deregulatory practices however, private banks failed to get efficiency increases under the high degree of deregulation. Also, NBs group seems to follow the similar trend of growth of PSBs during second-generation reforms period.

5.1.3 Percentage of PSBs, Private Banks and all CBs with TFP Gain/Loss and Efficiency Increase/Decrease

5.1.3.1 Percentage of PSBs with TFP Gain/Loss and Efficiency Increase/Decrease

Table 5.4 illustrates productivity gain (loss) and efficiency increase (decrease) of PSBs along with its components for the period 1986-06. The results highlight that about (61 percent) PSBs have experienced TFP gain while (39 percent) banks have witnessed TFP loss during the period 1986-06. Most of the productivity gain have stemmed from technological progress (67 percent banks experienced technical progress) rather than efficiency increase (46 percent). And, most of the productivity loss in banks can be attributed to the decline in technical efficiency (50 percent banks reported decline in technical efficiency) rather than technological regress (33 percent). Of the banks that captured efficiency increase (decrease), 47 percent (48 percent) owe it mostly to scale efficiency increase (decrease) rather 43 percent (46 percent) owe it to pure efficiency increase (decrease). Thus, it has been observed that improved scale of operation has favorably influenced the technical efficiency of banks than that of managerial efficiency. Moreover, 4 percent PSBs did not report any change in efficiency during the period 1986-06.

The comparative analysis of PSBs in various sub-periods reports that 69 percent (31 percent) banks have faced productivity gain (loss) in pre-reforms period. Most of the banks have experienced productivity gain due to technological progress (83 percent banks reported technical progress) rather than efficiency increase (38 percent). Contrarily, most of the banks have faced productivity loss on account of efficiency declinations (60 percent) rather than technological regress (16

TABLE 5.4

Percentage of PSBs with TFP Gain/Loss and Efficiency Increase/Decrease

Years	TFP Growth		TFP Gain due to		TFP Loss due to		No Change in TFP	TE Inc due to		TE Dec. due to		No Change in TE
	TFP Gain	TFP Loss	Tech Progress	TE Inc	Tech Regress	TE Dec.		PTE Inc	SE Inc	PTE Dec.	SE Dec.	
(1)	(2)	(3)	(4)	(5)	(6)	(7)	(8)	(9)	(10)	(11)	(12)	(13)
1986	93	7	93	78	4	22	0	44	78	44	22	0
1987	74	26	96	37	4	63	0	22	59	67	41	0
1988-89	100	0	100	22	0	70	0	33	19	48	78	7
1989-90	19	81	11	44	85	52	0	44	33	44	59	4
1990-91	26	74	100	15	0	85	0	19	26	74	70	0
1991-92	100	0	100	33	0	67	0	33	48	63	52	0
1992-93	22	78	26	37	74	59	0	37	59	56	37	4
1993-94	56	44	11	63	89	37	0	63	59	37	30	0
1994-95	89	11	100	67	0	30	0	67	52	26	44	4
1995-96	67	33	93	41	7	56	0	52	26	41	67	4
1996-97	63	33	100	30	0	70	4	30	30	59	70	0
1997-98	41	59	11	89	89	11	0	70	89	19	11	0
1998-99	33	67	44	41	56	52	0	41	19	44	70	7

(Contd.)

TABLE 5.4 (*Contd.*)

(1)	(2)	(3)	(4)	(5)	(6)	(7)	(8)	(9)	(10)	(11)	(12)	(13)
1999-00	33	67	81	48	19	48	0	37	59	44	33	4
2000-01	89	11	85	52	15	37	0	48	41	22	48	11
2001-02	78	19	85	44	15	48	4	33	52	56	37	7
2002-03	89	11	59	70	41	22	0	70	56	15	37	7
2003-04	81	19	100	37	0	56	0	48	33	41	59	7
2004-05	30	70	11	44	89	56	0	44	33	52	67	0
2005-06	30	67	33	26	67	67	4	22	70	67	22	7
Averages												
1986/92	69	31	83	38	16	60	0	33	44	57	54	2
1993/99	53	47	55	53	45	45	1	51	48	40	47	3
2000/06	61	38	65	46	35	48	1	43	49	42	43	6
1986/06	61	39	67	46	33	50	1	43	47	46	48	4

percent) during the period 1986-92. Of the banks that experienced efficiency increase (decrease), 44 percent (54 percent) owe it mostly to scale efficiency increase (decrease) rather 33 percent (57 percent) owe it to pure efficiency increase (decrease). Thus, improved scale of operation has emerged to be the responsible factor of efficiency increase among sample banks as compared to managerial efficiency.

The percentage of banks that recorded productivity gain (loss) stood at 53 percent (47 percent) during the period 1993-99 as against the period 1986-92. Most of the banks have experienced productivity gain due to technical progress (55 percent banks reported technical progress) rather than an improvement in efficiency (53 percent). Contrarily, most of the banks have faced productivity loss on account of decline in efficiency and technological regress (45 percent) each during the period 1993-99. Of the banks that witnessed efficiency increase (decrease), 51 percent (40 percent) owe it to pure technical efficiency increase (decrease) and 48 percent (47 percent) owe it to scale efficiency increase (decrease). Thus, improved management practices seem to the major factor of efficiency increase among sample banks rather than improved scale of operation.

The percentage of banks that recorded productivity gain (loss) came out to be 61 percent (38 percent) during the period 2000-06. The productivity gain in the banks can be attributed to technical progress (65 percent banks encountered technological progress) and efficiency increase (46 percent). On the other hand, productivity loss among PSBs is more due to the deterioration in efficiency (48 percent) rather than technological regress (35 percent). Of the banks that experienced efficiency increase (decrease), 49 percent (43 percent) owe it to the scale efficiency increase (decrease) and 43 percent (42 percent) owe it to pure technical efficiency increase (decrease). Thus, the empirical findings highlight scale of operation as the major determinant of efficiency increase/ decrease among sample banks in India during this period.

The results suggest that most of the banks have improved their productivity growth due to technological progress rather an inefficient use of these enhanced technologies can safely be stated. Looking at the components of efficiency change, somewhat mixed picture of the contribution of scale efficiency and pure technical efficiency has been observed across various sub-periods. Therefore, the results suggest that banks are required to adopt suitable measures in order to develop the managerial skills and to have improved scale of operation so as to catch up the best practices available in Indian banking industry.

5.1.3.2 Percentage of Private Sector Banks with TFP Gain/Loss and Efficiency Increase/Decrease

Table 5.5 highlights productivity gain (loss) and efficiency increase (decrease) and its components for private sector banks during the period 1986-06. The results delineate that about (57 percent) private sector banks have experienced TFP gain while (43 percent) banks have witnessed TFP loss during the period 1986-06. Most of the productivity gain has originated from technological progress (64 percent banks encountered technical progress) relative to efficiency increase (45 percent). And, most of the productivity loss can be attributed to the decline in technical efficiency (44 percent banks reported decline in technical efficiency) rather than technological regress (36 percent). Of the banks that captured efficiency increase (decrease), 39 percent (49 percent) owe it mostly to scale efficiency increase (decrease) and 35 percent (38 percent) owe it to pure efficiency increase (decrease). Thus, it has been observed that improved scale of operation has favorably influenced the technical efficiency of banks than that of managerial efficiency. In addition, 12 percent private banks did not register any change in efficiency during the period 1986-06.

The period-wise analysis highlights that 57 percent (43 percent) banks have faced productivity gain (loss) during the period 1986-92. Most of the productivity gain has been realized due to advanced technologies (70 percent banks exhibited technical progress) rather than efficient use of these technologies (40 percent). On the other hand, most of the productivity loss in the banks can be attributed to the decline in technical efficiency (45 percent banks experienced deterioration in efficiency) rather than technological regress (29 percent). Of the banks that experienced efficiency increase (decrease), 28 percent (56 percent) owe it mostly to scale efficiency increase (decrease) and 30 percent (45 percent) owe it to pure efficiency increase (decrease). Thus, scale of operation has emerged to be the responsible factor of efficiency increase/decrease among sample banks as compared to managerial efficiency.

The percentage of banks that recorded productivity gain (loss) worked out to be 51 percent (49 percent) during first-generation reforms. Most of the productivity gain has occurred on account of technological progress (62 percent banks exhibited technical progress) rather than efficiency increase (48 percent). On the other hand, most of the productivity loss in sample banks may be attributed to decline in technical efficiency (40 percent banks experienced deterioration in efficiency) rather than technological regress (37 percent). Of the banks that witnessed efficiency increase (decrease), 43 percent (44 percent) may be attributed to scale efficiency increase (decrease) and 37 percent (33 percent) to pure technical efficiency increase (decrease). Thus, scale of operation seems to be the major driver of efficiency increase and decrease among the sample banks.

The percentage of banks that recorded productivity gain (loss) noted as 62 percent (38 percent) during the period 2000-06. Most of the productivity gain among the banks are the result of technological progress (60 percent banks have experienced technical progress) relative to efficiency increase (47 percent). In contrast to it, most of the productivity loss has originated on account of efficiency decrease (47 percent banks reported fall in efficiency) rather than technological regress (40 percent).

Of the banks that experienced efficiency increase (decrease), 38 percent (37 percent) owe it to the pure technical efficiency increase (decrease) and 45 percent (48 percent) owe it to the scale efficiency increase (decrease). Thus, the empirical findings highlight scale of operation as the major determinant of efficiency increase/decrease among sample banks in India during this period.

TABLE 5.5
Percentage of Private Sector Banks with TFP Gain/Loss and Efficiency Increase/Decrease

Years	TFP Growth		TFP Gain due to		TFP Loss due to		No Change in TFP	TE Inc due to		TE Dec. due to		No Change in TE
	TFP Gain	TFP Loss	Tech Progress	TE Inc	Tech Regress	TE Dec.		PTE Inc	SE Inc	PTE Dec.	SE Dec.	
(1)	(2)	(3)	(4)	(5)	(6)	(7)	(8)	(9)	(10)	(11)	(12)	(13)
1986	50	50	50	44	50	33	0	44	39	28	39	22
1987	44	56	89	17	6	61	0	28	22	39	61	22
1988-89	100	0	100	11	0	72	0	17	28	61	56	17
1989-90	17	83	0	72	100	17	0	61	44	17	33	11
1990-91	44	56	83	11	17	78	0	11	28	67	61	11
1991-92	89	11	100	83	0	6	0	17	6	61	83	11
1992-93	28	72	83	72	11	11	0	22	78	56	6	17
1993-94	67	33	11	56	89	28	0	50	61	28	22	17
1994-95	78	22	100	39	0	39	0	39	22	22	56	22
1995-96	72	28	83	44	17	44	0	39	39	28	50	11
1996-97	33	67	89	11	11	78	0	22	11	50	78	11
1997-98	61	39	56	61	44	33	0	44	44	17	50	6
1998-99	17	83	11	50	89	44	0	39	44	33	50	6
1999-00	89	11	89	44	11	50	0	28	50	50	44	6

2000-01	61	39	50	61	50	28	0	56	39	22	44	11
2001-02	100	0	94	72	6	22	0	33	89	39	6	6
2002-03	50	50	67	33	33	61	0	44	28	28	67	6
2003-04	50	50	56	44	44	50	0	44	33	22	61	6
2004-05	17	83	22	11	78	83	0	17	17	56	78	6
2005-06	67	33	44	61	56	33	0	44	61	39	33	6
Averages												
1986/92	57	43	70	40	29	45	0	30	28	45	56	16
1993/99	51	49	62	48	37	40	0	37	43	33	44	13
2000/06	62	38	60	47	40	47	0	38	45	37	48	7
1986/06	57	43	64	45	36	44	0	35	39	38	49	12

The results suggest that most of the banks have realized productivity gain on technological grounds but the optimum use of these enhanced technological measures is likely to be missing. Therefore, the banks are highly required to incorporate the necessary changes in the scale of operation and managerial skills to avail maximum benefits of enhanced technologies or innovations.

5.1.3.3 Percentage of all Commercial Banks with TFP Gain/ Loss and Efficiency Increase/Decrease

Table 5.6 highlights productivity gain (loss) and efficiency increase (decrease) along with its sources for all sample banks in India. The empirical results highlight that about (59 percent) banks have experienced productivity gain during the period 1986-06. Most of the TFP gain can be attributed to technological progress (67 percent of the banks have witnessed technological gain) and an improvement in efficiency (46 percent). On the other hand, about (41 percent) banks have incurred productivity loss, which can be attributed to the declination in technical efficiency (48 percent banks experienced fall in efficiency) rather than technological regress (33 percent). Of the banks that captured efficiency increase (decrease), 44 percent (48 percent) owe it to scale efficiency increase (decrease) and 40 percent (43 percent) owe it to the pure efficiency increase (decrease). Thus, it has been observed that scale of operation has influenced the technical efficiency of banks to larger extent than that of managerial efficiency. Moreover, 7 percent sample banks did not report any change in technical efficiency during the period 1986-06.

The period-wise analysis presents that 64 percent (36 percent) banks have faced productivity gain (loss) during the period 1986-92. Most of the productivity gain has been realized due to technological progress (78 percent) rather than efficiency increase (39 percent) during this period. And, most of the productivity loss can be attributed to decline in technical efficiency (54 percent) rather than technological regress (20 percent). Of the banks that experienced efficiency increase

Table 5.6
Percentage of all Commercial Banks with TFP Gain/Loss and Efficiency Increase/Decrease

Years	TFP Growth		TFP Gain due to		TFP Loss due to		No Change in TFP	TE Inc due to		TE Dec. due to		No Change in TE
	TFP Gain	TFP Loss	Tech Progress	TE Inc	Tech Regress	TE Dec.		PTE Inc	SE Inc	PTE Dec.	SE Dec.	
(1)	(2)	(3)	(4)	(5)	(6)	(7)	(8)	(9)	(10)	(11)	(12)	(13)
1986	76	24	76	64	22	27	0	44	62	38	29	9
1987	62	38	93	29	4	62	0	24	44	56	49	9
1988-89	100	0	100	18	0	71	0	27	22	53	69	11
1989-90	18	82	7	56	91	38	0	51	38	33	49	7
1990-91	33	67	93	13	7	82	0	16	27	71	67	4
1991-92	96	4	100	53	0	42	0	27	31	62	64	4
1992-93	24	76	49	51	49	40	0	31	67	56	24	9
1993-94	60	40	11	60	89	33	0	58	60	33	27	7
1994-95	84	16	100	56	0	33	0	56	40	24	49	11
1995-96	69	31	89	42	11	51	0	47	31	36	60	7
1996-97	51	47	96	22	4	73	2	27	22	56	73	4
1997-98	49	51	29	78	71	20	0	60	71	18	27	2
1998-99	27	73	31	44	69	49	0	40	29	40	62	7

(Contd.)

TABLE 5.6 (*Contd.*)

(1)	*(2)*	*(3)*	*(4)*	*(5)*	*(6)*	*(7)*	*(8)*	*(9)*	*(10)*	*(11)*	*(12)*	*(13)*
1999-00	56	44	84	47	16	49	0	33	56	47	38	4
2000-01	78	22	71	56	29	33	0	51	40	22	47	11
2001-02	87	11	89	56	11	38	2	33	67	49	24	7
2002-03	73	27	62	56	38	38	0	60	44	20	49	7
2003-04	69	31	82	40	18	53	0	47	33	33	60	7
2004-05	24	76	16	31	84	67	0	33	27	53	71	2
2005-06	44	53	38	40	62	53	2	31	67	56	27	7
Averages												
1986/92	64	36	78	39	20	54	0	31	37	52	54	7
1993/99	52	48	58	50	42	43	0	45	46	37	46	7
2000/06	62	38	62	47	38	47	1	41	48	40	45	6
1986/06	59	41	67	46	33	48	0	40	44	43	48	7

(decrease), 37 percent (54 percent) owe it mostly to scale efficiency increase (decrease) and 31 percent (52 percent) owe it to pure efficiency increase (decrease). Thus, scale of operation has emerged to be the responsible factor of efficiency change among sample banks as compared to management practices.

The percentage of banks that recorded productivity gain (loss) noted down to be 52 percent (48 percent) in first-generation reforms period. Most of the productivity gain in the banks has been observed due to technical progress (58 percent) rather than efficiency increase (50 percent). In contrast, most of the productivity loss among banks has noted to be on account of efficiency decrease (43 percent) rather than technological regress (42 percent). Of the banks that experienced efficiency increase (decrease), 46 percent (46 percent) may be attributed to scale efficiency increase (decrease) and 45 percent (37 percent) to pure efficiency increase (decrease). Thus, scale efficiency change seems to be the major factor of efficiency change among the sample banks.

The percentage of banks that recorded productivity gain (loss) stood at 62 percent (38 percent) in second-generation reforms period. The percentage of banks that exhibited technical progress (regress) turned out to be 62 percent (38 percent) and efficiency increase (decrease) to be 47 percent (47 percent) during the period 2000-06. Of the banks that experienced efficiency increase (decreases), 41 percent (40 percent) owe it to pure technical efficiency increase (decrease) and 48 percent (45 percent) owe it to the scale efficiency increase (decrease). Thus, the empirical findings highlight scale of operation as the major determinant of efficiency change among sample banks in India during this period.

The results suggest that the all commercial banks have realized TFP more due to the technological progress than that of efficiency increase. Whatever amount of improvement (deterioration) in technical efficiency has been realized, that is more due to effective (ineffective) scale of operation in most parts of the sub-periods. Therefore, the empirical findings suggest that appropriate steps should be taken in order to have improved scale of operation. Moreover, suitable measures should also be adopted in order to reduce the input wastages to produce a prescribed level of output. This will in turn improve the level of efficiency as well as TFP growth of CBs in India.

5.2 TOTAL FACTOR PRODUCTIVITY GROWTH BY BANK SIZE

In order to explore the relationship among bank size and productivity, the TFP and its related indices have been arranged in accordance to the size of the banks. The banks have been classified into three groups of small, medium and large banks. Small-sized banks comprises those banks having total assets less than equal to Rs. 100 billion. The medium-sized group includes all the banks which have assets more than Rs. 100 billion but less than or equal to Rs. 500 billion. The large-sized group consists of those banks, which have total assets exceeding Rs. 500 billion. Table 5.7 reports TFP growth and its components among CBs in India for the study period 1985-06 and its plots are given in Figure 5.7.

It has been observed from the analysis that average TFP increases with an increase in the size of banks. It is clear from Table 5.7 that large-sized banks have experienced TFP growth at the rate of (5.6 percent), followed by medium-sized banks (4.9 percent) and small-sized banks (4.2 percent) per annum during the study period. The average TFP growth of CBs has originated exclusively due to technological progress in India. Over the period, technological progress has enhanced the level of TFP growth of small-sized banks by (5.1 percent) per annum

TABLE 5.7

Average Total Factor Productivity Growth and its Indices with Respect to Assets Size (1985 to 2005-06)

Bank Size (Rs. Billion)	*Technical Change*	*Technical Efficiency Change*	*Total Factor Productivity Growth*
Small	1.051	0.992	1.042
Medium	1.060	0.990	1.049
Large	1.060	0.999	1.056

FIG. 5.7

TFP and its Indices with Bank Size

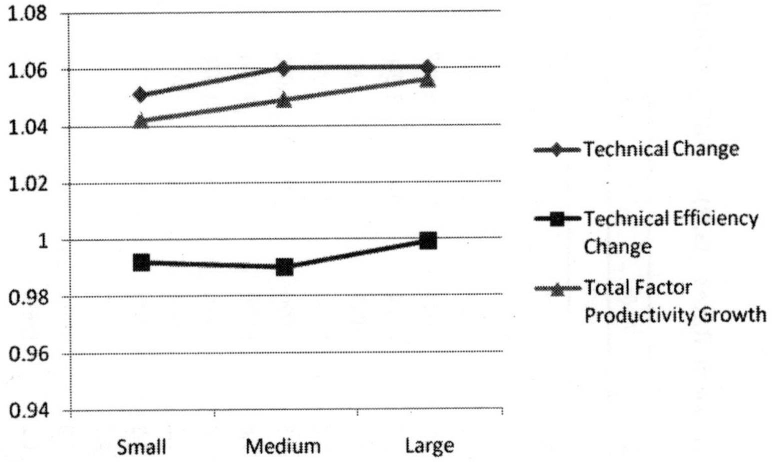

and medium-sized and large-sized banks by (6.0 percent) per annum each. In contrast to this, the efficiency decrease has lowered down the level of TFP growth of small-sized, medium-sized and large-sized banks by (-0.8 percent), (-1.0 percent) and (-0.1 percent) per annum respectively through out the study period. Thus, the results imply that technologies (innovations) have played a key role in deriving TFP gains; however the use of existing technologies is likely to be missing among various size groups of banks.

SECTION II

5.3 DISAGGREGATED ANALYSIS OF TFP GROWTH AND ITS COMPONENTS

5.3.1 Disaggregated Analysis of TFP Growth

Coming to the disaggregated analysis of banks as shown in Table 5.8, it has been observed that all the sample banks have experienced positive TFP growth pattern during the period 1985-06. Ing Vysya, an old private bank has experienced TFP growth at an exciting rate of (11.3 percent), followed by

TABLE 5.8

Inter-Bank Malmquist Productivity Index and their Growth Rates (G.R)—1985 to 2005-06

Banks Name/Indices	*1986-92*	*G.R*	*1993-99*	*G.R*	*2000-06*	*G.R*	*1986-06*	*G.R*
(1)	*(2)*	*(3)*	*(4)*	*(5)*	*(6)*	*(7)*	*(8)*	*(9)*
Allahabad Bank	1.117	11.7	1.031	3.1	1.027	2.7	1.055	5.5
Andhra Bank	1.065	6.5	1.053	5.3	1.033	3.3	1.050	5.0
Bank of Baroda	1.149	14.9	1.038	3.8	1.023	2.3	1.064	6.4
Bank of India	1.159	15.9	1.029	2.9	1.004	0.4	1.057	5.7
Bank of Maharashtra	1.076	7.6	1.047	4.7	1.004	0.4	1.040	4.0
Canara Bank	1.172	17.2	0.985	-1.5	1.011	1.1	1.047	4.7
Central Bank of India	1.075	7.5	1.038	3.8	1.014	1.4	1.040	4.0
Corporation Bank	1.114	11.4	1.075	7.5	1.090	9.0	1.092	9.2
Dena Bank	1.069	6.9	1.018	1.8	1.039	3.9	1.041	4.1
Indian Bank	1.158	15.8	0.958	-4.2	1.116	11.6	1.070	7.0
Indian Overseas Bank	1.106	10.6	1.022	2.2	1.094	9.4	1.072	7.2
Oriental Bank of Commerce	1.168	16.8	1.032	3.2	1.105	10.5	1.097	9.7
Punjab and Sind Bank	1.029	2.9	1.042	4.2	1.062	6.2	1.045	4.5
Punjab National Bank	1.130	13.0	1.030	3.0	0.994	-0.6	1.046	4.6
Syndicate Bank	1.072	7.2	1.012	1.2	1.009	0.9	1.029	2.9
United Commercial Bank	1.031	3.1	1.034	3.4	1.033	3.3	1.033	3.3

Union Bank of India	1.125	12.5	0.993	-0.7	1.076	7.6	1.060	6.0
United Bank of India	1.021	2.1	1.034	3.4	1.077	7.7	1.045	4.5
Vijaya Bank	1.069	6.9	1.029	2.9	1.049	4.9	1.048	4.8
State Bank of India	1.166	16.6	0.976	-2.4	1.025	2.5	1.047	4.7
State Bank of B & J	1.161	16.1	0.968	-3.2	0.996	-0.4	1.033	3.3
State Bank of Hyderabad	1.175	17.5	0.998	-0.2	1.009	0.9	1.052	5.2
State Bank of Indore	1.150	15.0	1.007	0.7	1.005	0.5	1.047	4.7
State Bank of Mysore	1.129	12.9	1.002	0.2	0.990	-1.0	1.034	3.4
State Bank of Patiala	1.245	24.5	0.937	-6.3	1.002	0.2	1.045	4.5
State Bank of Saurashtra	1.110	11.0	1.000	0.0	0.964	-3.6	1.019	1.9
State Bank of Travancore	1.108	10.8	0.986	-1.4	1.027	2.7	1.036	3.6
Bharat Overseas Bank	1.156	15.6	1.009	0.9	1.116	11.6	1.089	8.9
City Union Bank	1.077	7.7	1.007	0.7	1.054	5.4	1.044	4.4
Ing Vysya Bank	1.132	13.2	1.091	9.1	1.118	11.8	1.113	11.3
Karnataka Bank	1.085	8.5	1.005	0.5	1.063	6.3	1.049	4.9
Lord Krishna Bank	0.995	-0.5	1.063	6.3	0.998	-0.2	1.019	1.9
Nainital Bank	1.120	12.0	0.994	-0.6	1.006	0.6	1.035	3.5
Tamilnad Mercantile Bank	1.105	10.5	1.020	2.0	1.073	7.3	1.063	6.3
Bank of Rajasthan	1.114	11.4	0.944	-5.6	1.003	0.3	1.013	1.3
Catholic Syrian Bank	1.039	3.9	0.926	-7.4	1.055	5.5	1.003	0.3

(*Contd.*)

TABLE 5.8 (*Contd.*)

(1)	*(2)*	*(3)*	*(4)*	*(5)*	*(6)*	*(7)*	*(8)*	*(9)*
Dhanalakshmi Bank	1.005	0.5	0.981	-1.9	1.044	4.4	1.010	1.0
Federal Bank	1.055	5.5	1.055	5.5	1.092	9.2	1.068	6.8
Jammu & Kashmir Bank	1.212	21.2	0.974	-2.6	1.080	8.0	1.078	7.8
Karur Vysya Bank	1.081	8.1	1.016	1.6	1.071	7.1	1.055	5.5
Lakshmi Vilas Bank	1.046	4.6	1.025	2.5	0.966	-3.4	1.010	1.0
Ratnakar Bank	1.098	9.8	0.957	-4.3	1.032	3.2	1.024	2.4
Sangli Bank	1.108	10.8	0.948	-5.2	0.991	-0.9	1.009	0.9
South Indian Bank	1.023	2.3	0.990	-1.0	1.063	6.3	1.025	2.5
United Western Bank	1.043	4.3	1.038	3.8	1.001	0.1	1.027	2.7

Oriental Bank of Commerce (9.7), Corporation Bank (9.2) and Bharat Overseas Bank (8.9 percent) per annum during the period 1986-06. However, the banking industry of Catholic Syrian Bank and Sangli Bank has noted to be least productive, growing at the rate of less than 1 percent per annum. Among PSBs, State Bank of Saurashtra registered productivity growth at the pity rate of (1.9 percent) per annum during the entire study period.

The comparative analysis of pre-reforms and first-generation reforms illustrates that banking industry of Punjab & Sind Bank, United Commercial Bank and United Bank of India has witnessed comparative acceleration in TFP growth rates. However, the banking industry of Allahabad Bank, Andhra Bank, Bank of Baroda, Bank of India, Bank of Maharashtra, Central Bank of India, Corporation Bank, Dena Bank, Indian Overseas Bank, Oriental Bank of Commerce, Punjab National Bank, Syndicate Bank, Vijaya Bank, State Bank of Indore, State Bank of Mysore, State Bank of Saurashtra, Bharat Overseas Bank, City Union Bank, Ing Vysya Bank, Karnataka Bank, Tamilnad Mercantile Bank, Karur Vysya Bank, Lakashmi Vilas Bank and United Western Bank has witnessed comparative deceleration in TFP growth rates. Although, Ing Vysya Bank and Corporation Bank have witnessed comparative deceleration in TFP growth rates during the period 1993-99 but these banks attained TFP growth at an alarming rate of (9.1 percent) and (7.5 percent) per annum respectively. The banking industry of Canara Bank, Indian Bank, Union Bank of India, State Bank of India, State Bank of B & J, State Bank of Hyderabad, State Bank of Patiala, State Bank of Travancore, Nainital Bank, Bank of Rajasthan, Catholic Syrian Bank, Dhanalakhmi Bank, Jammu & Kashmir Bank, Ratnakar Bank, Sangli Bank and South Indian Bank registered negative growth rate during first-generation reforms contrary to positive growth rate during pre-reforms period. Among these banks, the banking industry of State Bank of Patiala and Jammu & Kashmir Bank experienced TFP growth at an alarming rate of (24.5 percent) and (21.2 percent) per annum during pre-reforms period but the growth rates tend out to be negative during first-generation reforms. The banking industry of State Bank of Patiala and Catholic Syrian Bank is found to be least productive with respective growth rates of (-6.3 percent) and (-7.4 percent) per annum respectively during the period 1993-99. It is only the Lord Krishna Bank that witnessed positive TFP growth during Initial-phase of liberalization period contrary to negative TFP growth during pre-liberalization period. Overall, a notable change in the magnitude of growth rates has been witnessed between these periods.

In second-phase of liberalization period, the banking industry of Punjab National Bank, State Bank of Mysore, State Bank of Saurashtra, Lord Krishna Bank and Lakshmi Vilas Bank registered negative growth rate contrary to a positive growth rate during 1993-99. Among these banks, State Bank of Saurashtra and Lakshmi Vilas Bank are found to be least productive banks with respective growth rates of (-3.6 percent) and (-3.4 percent) per annum during 2000-06. The banking industry of Canara Bank, Indian Bank, Union Bank of India, State Bank of India, State Bank of Hyderabad, State Bank of Patiala, State Bank of Travancore, Nainital Bank, Bank of Rajasthan, Catholic Syrian Bank, Dhanalakhmi Bank, Jammu & Kashmir Bank, Ratnakar Bank and South Indian Bank recorded positive growth rate during 2000-06 in comparison to negative growth rates during 1993-99. It is worth mentioning that the banking industry of Indian Bank and Bharat Overseas Bank has been found to be growing at striking rate of (11.6 percent) per annum each during second-generation reforms. The banking industry of State Bank of B&J and Sangli Bank experienced negative growth rate during 1993-99 and continued to be negative during 2000-06. However, the extent of negative growth rate has noticed to be lesser than that of the period 1993-99. The banks, which realized comparative deceleration in TFP growth rates are noted to be Allahabad Bank, Andhra Bank, Bank of Baroda, Bank of India, Bank of Maharashtra, Central Bank of India, Syndicate Bank, United Commercial Bank, State Bank of Indore and United Western Bank. And, the banks that experienced comparative acceleration in TFP growth rates are noticed to be Corporation Bank, Dena Bank, Indian Overseas Bank, Oriental Bank of Commerce, Punjab & Sind Bank, United Bank of India, Vijaya Bank, Bharat Overseas Bank, City Union Bank, Ing Vysya

Bank, Karnataka Bank, Tamilnad Mercantile Bank, Federal Bank and Karur Vysya Bank. Among these banks, the banking industry of Ing Vysya has observed to be growing at an exiting rate of (11.8 percent) per annum during the period 2000-06. Overall, positive upshot of banking sector reforms is pronounced during second-generation reforms that that of first-generation reforms period.

5.3.2 Sources of Total Factor Productivity Growth

5.3.2.1 Disaggregated Analysis of EFFCH Index

As previously mentioned, the Malmquist productivity index decomposes TFP change into technical efficiency change and technological change. The term efficiency change represents the movement of the banks either closer to the frontier (catching up) or farther away from the frontier. The second term TCH defines the change in technology or the shift in the frontier from period t to t+1. Thus, TFP growth is the combined effect of both the technical efficiency change and technological change.

It is apparent from Table 5.9 that State Bank of Patiala has experienced EFFCH at the rate of (1.2 percent), followed by Nainital Bank (0.7 percent) per annum during the period 1986-06. On the other hand, Lakshmi Vilas Bank and United Western Bank have registered efficiency at the lowest growth rate of (-2.5 percent) and (-2.4 percent) per annum respectively. Among PSBs, United Commercial Bank has emerged to poor performer with growth rate of efficiency (-1.5 percent) per annum. Out of 45 sample banks, majority of 20 banks followed negative trend of the growth rate of technical efficiency during the entire study period. Thus, it can safely be stated that most of the sample banks are lagging behind in terms of catching up effect.

The comparative analysis of growth rates of pre-reforms and first-generation reforms illustrates that banking industry of Indian Overseas Bank, Bank of Rajasthan, Catholic Syrian Bank, Dhanalakshmi Bank and Sangli Bank has experienced negative growth rate of technical efficiency between these periods, however, the extent of negative growth rates has noted to be comparatively declined. Among these banks,

TABLE 5.9

Inter-Bank Growth Rates (G.R.) of EFFCH and TCH index in India—1985 to 2005-06

Banks Name/Indices	1986-92		1993-99		2000-06		1986-06	
	EFFCH	TCH	EFFCH	TCH	EFFCH	TCH	EFFCH	TCH
(1)	(2)	(3)	(4)	(5)	(6)	(7)	(8)	(9)
Allahabad Bank	-1.5	13.4	0.2	2.8	1.1	1.6	0.0	5.4
Andhra Bank	-9.0	17.0	6.5	-1.2	1.4	1.8	-0.1	5.0
Bank of Baroda	-0.4	15.3	0.6	3.2	-2.7	5.2	-0.9	7.4
Bank of India	1.9	13.8	-1.8	4.8	-2.1	2.6	-0.8	6.6
Bank of Maharashtra	-7.2	16.0	5.7	-1.0	-2.7	3.2	-1.3	5.3
Canara Bank	-1.1	18.4	0.0	-1.5	-2.5	3.7	-1.2	6.0
Central Bank of India	-8.9	17.9	5.3	-1.5	0.6	0.9	-0.8	4.8
Corporation Bank	-3.8	15.9	6.0	1.4	0.0	9.0	0.9	8.2
Dena Bank	-7.2	15.2	5.7	-3.6	2.2	1.7	0.4	3.6
Indian Bank	0.8	14.8	-8.0	4.2	6.7	4.5	-0.4	7.4
Indian Overseas Bank	-2.5	13.5	-2.0	4.3	5.0	4.2	0.2	6.9
Oriental Bank of Commerce	-2.1	19.4	3.1	0.0	-0.9	11.4	0.1	9.5
Punjab and Sind Bank	-11.2	15.9	5.1	-0.8	3.0	3.0	-0.8	5.3
Punjab National Bank	-6.1	20.3	6.1	-2.9	-1.3	0.7	-0.2	4.9
Syndicate Bank	-6.8	15.1	1.6	-0.4	1.3	-0.4	-1.1	4.0

United Commercial Bank	-8.4	12.6	2.4	1.0	0.8	2.5	-1.5	4.9
Union Bank of India	-3.4	16.5	2.4	-3.0	1.6	6.0	0.3	5.7
United Bank of India	-10.8	14.5	2.1	1.3	7.2	0.5	-0.3	4.8
Vijaya Bank	-6.9	14.7	2.8	0.1	1.6	3.3	-0.6	5.4
State Bank of India	0.5	16.1	-1.8	-0.6	1.5	1.0	0.0	4.7
State Bank of B & J	2.9	12.8	-0.3	-3.0	0.0	-0.4	0.8	2.4
State Bank of Hyderabad	2.0	15.2	1.5	-1.7	-1.2	2.1	0.7	4.5
State Bank of Indore	-0.3	15.4	1.7	-1.0	-2.4	3.0	-0.4	5.1
State Bank of Mysore	-0.8	13.9	2.4	-2.2	1.1	-2.1	1.0	2.4
State Bank of Patiala	8.6	14.6	-0.9	-5.4	-2.7	2.9	1.2	3.2
State Bank of Saurashtra	-0.3	11.3	0.9	-0.8	-4.4	0.8	-1.3	3.2
State Bank of Travancore	-3.2	14.4	3.1	-4.3	0.4	2.3	0.2	3.3
Bharat Overseas Bank	0.0	15.6	-1.4	2.3	-0.6	12.3	-0.7	9.7
City Union Bank	-3.3	11.4	3.7	-2.9	-2.7	8.2	-0.7	5.1
Ing Vysya Bank	-2.7	16.3	3.6	5.3	-0.2	12.0	0.4	10.9
Karnataka Bank	-5.0	14.2	3.1	-2.5	-0.5	6.9	-0.7	5.6
Lord Krishna Bank	-5.9	5.8	4.4	1.8	-5.4	5.5	-2.2	4.3
Nainital Bank	-4.8	17.7	5.9	-6.2	0.5	0.1	0.7	2.7
Tamilnad Mercantile Bank	0.0	10.5	0.0	2.0	0.0	7.3	0.0	6.3
Bank of Rajasthan	-2.7	14.4	-0.4	-5.3	-2.6	2.9	-1.9	3.2

(*Contd.*)

TABLE 5.9 (*Contd.*)

(1)	(2)	(3)	(4)	(5)	(6)	(7)	(8)	(9)
Catholic Syrian Bank	-7.1	11.9	-2.5	-5.0	5.4	0.0	-1.2	1.6
Dhanalakshmi Bank	-7.3	8.4	-0.1	-1.8	1.4	2.9	-1.8	2.8
Federal Bank	-8.2	14.9	6.2	-0.7	-0.2	9.5	-0.5	7.4
Jammu & Kashmir Bank	0.0	21.2	0.0	-2.6	-2.3	10.6	-0.8	8.7
Karur Vysya Bank	-4.2	12.8	3.1	-1.5	0.9	6.2	0.1	5.3
Lakshmi Vilas Bank	-3.5	8.4	3.1	-0.6	-7.1	3.9	-2.5	3.6
Ratnakar Bank	-4.2	14.6	1.9	-6.1	-0.2	3.4	-0.7	3.1
Sangli Bank	-3.6	15.0	-0.6	-4.7	-2.5	1.7	-2.2	3.2
South Indian Bank	-7.4	10.5	1.3	-2.2	1.5	4.8	-1.3	3.9
United Western Bank	-8.2	13.6	6.7	-2.7	-5.7	6.3	-2.4	5.1

Catholic Syrian Bank has noted to be bank with lowest negative growth rate of technical efficiency (-2.5 percent) per annum during 1993-99. The banking industry of Bank of India, Indian Bank, State Bank of India, State Bank of B & J, State Bank of Patiala and Bharat Overseas Bank experienced negative growth rates of EFFCH index during first-generation reforms as against positive growth rates during pre-report period. It is imperative to state that State Bank of Patiala experienced efficiency change at an exiting rate of (8.6 percent) per annum during pre-reforms period, which turned out to be negative during first-generation reforms. The banking industry of Indian Bank experienced substantial efficiency decreases at the growth rate of (-8.0 percent) per annum during 1993-99. The banking industry of State Bank of Hyderabad experienced comparative deceleration in the growth rate of efficiency during 1993-99. The banks viz., Allahabad Bank, Andhra Bank, Bank of Baroda, Bank of India, Bank of Maharashtra, Central Bank of India, Corporation Bank, Dena Bank, Oriental Bank of Commerce, Punjab & Sind Bank, Punjab National Bank, Syndicate Bank, United Commercial Bank, Union Bank of India, United Bank of India, Vijaya Bank, State Bank of Indore, State Bank of Mysore, State Bank of Saurashtra, State Bank of Travancore, City Union Bank, Ing Vysya Bank, Karnataka Bank, Lord Krishna Bank, Nainital Bank, Federal Bank, Karur Vyasa Bank, Lakshmi Vilas Bank, Ratnakar Bank, South Indian Bank and United Western Bank experienced positive growth rates during 1993-99 in comparison to the negative growth rates during 1986-92. Among these banks, Punjab and Sind Bank experienced efficiency decrease at the lowest growth rate of (-11.2) per annum during 1986-92, but it turned out to be efficiency increase during 1993-99. It is imperative to state that the banking industry of United Western Bank experienced EFFCH at the highest growth rate of (6.7 percent) per annum, followed by Andhra Bank (6.5 percent) during first-generation reforms. The empirical findings also divulge that the banking industry of Tamilnad Mercantile Bank and Jammu & Kashmir Bank has registered stagnant growth in technical efficiency between these periods.

Further, the empirical findings provide that the banking industry of Bank of India, State Bank of Patiala, Bharat Overseas Bank, Bank of Rajasthan and Sangli Bank has registered negative growth rate during first-phase of reforms and continued to be negative during second-phase of reforms. However, the magnitude of negative growth rates has been found to be higher among the banks namely Bank of India, State Bank of Patiala, Bank of Rajasthan and Sangli Bank; however, lesser in case of Bharat Overseas Bank during second-phase of reforms. The banking industry of Bank of Baroda, Bank of Maharashtra, Canara Bank, Oriental Bank of Commerce, Punjab National Bank, State Bank of Hyderabad, State Bank of Indore, State Bank of Saurashtra, City Union Bank, Ing Vysya Bank, Karnataka Bank, Lord Krishna Bank, Federal Bank, Jammu & Kashmir Bank, Lakshmi Vilas Bank, Ratnakar Bank and United Western Bank experienced negative growth rate during 2000-06 as compared to positive growth rate during 1993-99. Among these banks, the banking industry of Lakhmi Vilas Bank and State Bank of Saurashtra registered a substantial decline in EFFCH at the highest rate of (-7.1 percent) and (-4.4 percent) per annum respectively during the period 2000-06. The empirical findings further substantiate that Allahabad Bank, United Bank of India and South Indian Bank have witnessed comparative acceleration in EFFCH index as compared to 1993-99. Among these banks, the banking an industry of United Bank of India witnessed EFFCH at alarming rate of (7.2 percent) per annum during 2000-06. The banks viz., Indian Bank, Indian Overseas Bank, State Bank of India, Catholic Syrian Bank and Dhanalakshmi Bank registered positive growth rates during second-generation reforms contrary to negative growth rates during first-generation reforms. Among these banks, the banking industry of Catholic Syrian Bank has experienced EFFCH at the rate of (5.4 percent) per annum during the period 2000-06. Contrarily, the banking industry of Andhra Bank, Central Bank of India, Corporation Bank, Dena Bank, Punjab & Sind Bank, Syndicate Bank, United Commercial Bank, Union Bank of India, Vijaya Bank, State Bank of Mysore, State Bank of Travancore, Nainital Bank, Karur Vysya Bank has experienced comparative deceleration during 2000-06. Besides this, the banking industry of Tamilnad

Mercantile Bank recorded stagnant growth in technical efficiency between these periods. Overall, it has been noticed that the banks have started to catch up the best practices available in banking industry as evidenced by the findings of first-generation reforms. However, the degree of growth rates is noted to be higher during 2000-06 as compared to 1993-99. Therefore, the empirical evidence suggests somewhat mixed impact of the reforms on the efficiency change of CBs in India during post-liberalization period.

5.3.2.2 Disaggregated Analysis of TCH Index

Table 5.9 highlights inter-bank and inter-period comparison of the growth rates of technological change index for the study period 1985-06. The empirical findings represent that the banking industry of Ing Vysya Bank and Oriental Bank of Commerce has registered TCH at an exiting rate of (10.9 percent) and (9.5 percent) per annum respectively during 1985-06. Contrarily, Catholic Syrian Bank has noted TCH at the lowest rate of (1.6 percent) per annum. Among PSBs, the banking industry of State Bank of B&J and State Bank of Mysore has witnessed TCH at the lowest rate of (2.4 percent) per annum each. Moreover, the empirical findings provide that all the sample banks have experienced technological progress during the period 1986-06, which in turn implies that most of the sample banks are operating with advanced technologies in India.

The comparative analysis of growth rates of pre-reforms and first-generation reforms illustrates that although, Allahabad Bank, Bank of Baroda, Bank of India, Corporation Bank, Indian Bank, Indian Overseas Bank, Oriental Bank of Commerce, United Commercial Bank, United Bank of India, Vijaya Bank, Bharat Overseas Bank, Ing Vysya Bank, Lord Krishna Bank and Tamilnad Mercantile Bank have witnessed positive growth rate, but, these banks have noted a comparative deceleration in the growth rate of technology index. Among these banks, the banking industry of Ing Vysya Bank and Bank of India has experienced TCH at the highest rate of (5.3 percent) and (4.8 percent) per annum during the period 1993-99. The banking industry of Andhra Bank, Bank of Maharashtra, Canara Bank, Central Bank of India, Dena Bank,

Punjab & Sind Bank, Punjab National Bank, Syndicate Bank, Union Bank of India, State Bank of India, State Bank of B&J, State Bank of Hyderabad, State Bank of Indore, State Bank of Mysore, State Bank of Patiala, State Bank of Saurashtra, State Bank of Travancore, City Union Bank, Karnataka Bank, Nainital Bank, Bank of Rajasthan, Catholic Syrian Bank, Dhanalakhmi Bank, Federal Bank, Jammu & Kashmir Bank, Karur Vysya Bank, Lakshmi Vilas Bank, Ratnakar Bank, Sangli Bank, South Indian Bank and United Western Bank has witnessed negative growth rates of TCH index during 1993-99 as against positive growth rates during 1986-92. Among these banks, Jammu & Kashmir Bank and Punjab National Bank have registered negative growth rates during 1993-99 contrary to exiting growth rate of (21.2 percent) and (20.3 percent) respectively during 1986-92. And, the banking industry of State Bank of Saurashtra experienced TCH at the lowest growth rate of (11.3 percent) per annum during 1986-92. But, the magnitude of lowest growth rate seems to be varying tremendously as evidenced by Nainital Bank (-6.2 percent) and State Bank of Patiala (-5.4 percent) per annum during the period 1993-99.

In second-generation reforms period, although, Syndicate Bank, State Bank of B&J and State Bank of Mysore have experienced negative growth rates; but, the extent of negative growth rates is found to be comparatively lesser than that of first-generation reforms. Nevertheless, State Bank of Mysore noted significant slow down in technological change at the rate of (-2.1 percent) per annum while Catholic Syrian Bank reported stagnant growth during 2000-06. Except Catholic Syrian Bank, all the remaining private banks experienced positive growth rates of technology during 2000-06. The banks that witnessed comparative acceleration in the growth rate of TCH are noted to be Bank of Baroda, Corporation Bank, Indian Bank, Oriental Bank of Commerce, United Commercial Bank, Vijaya Bank, Bharat Overseas Bank, Ing Vysya Bank, Lord Krishna Bank and Tamilnad Mercantile Bank. Among these banks, the banking industry of Bharat Overseas Bank and Oriental Bank of Commerce has recorded TCH at an exiting rate of (12.3 percent) and (11.4 percent) per annum respectively during second-generation reforms. Contrarily, the banking industry of Allahabad Bank, Bank of India, Indian Overseas Bank and United Bank of India, has witnessed comparative deceleration in the growth rates of TCH index. The banking industry of Andhra Bank, Bank of Maharashtra, Canara Bank, Central Bank of India, Dena Bank, Punjab & Sind Bank, Punjab National Bank, Union Bank of India, State Bank of India, State Bank of Hyderabad, State Bank of Indore, State Bank of Patiala, State Bank of Saurashtra, State Bank of Travancore, City Union Bank, Karnataka Bank, Lord Krishna Bank, Nainital Bank, Bank of Rajasthan, Dhanalakhmi Bank, Federal Bank, Jammu & Kashmir Bank, Karur Vysya Bank, Lakshmi Vilas Bank, Ratnakar Bank, Sangli Bank, South Indian Bank and United Western Bank has witnessed positive growth rates of technology during 2000-06 in comparison of negative growth rates during 1993-99. Overall, it has been observed that the positive impact of technologies is more pronounced during second-phase of liberalization among various sample banks than that of initial-phase of liberalization.

After scrutinize the disaggregated analysis of the components of TFP growth as portrayed in Table 5.8 and 5.9, it has been observed that improved technologies has played a key role in augmenting productivity gains among various sample banks in India for the study period 1985-06. Even for period-wise analysis too, the improved technologies have contributed a lot in deriving productivity gains among various sample banks in India for most parts of the sub-periods (except 1993-99). However, the absorption of these technologies is likely to be missing due to the poor diffusion process and a little accumulation of knowledge through learning by doings. This demands the need of substantial changes in the working processes and sharpening of the managerial skills through various training programmes.

5.4 CLASSIFICATION OF BANKS

In addition to get an idea about the inter-period change in the behavior of TFP change and its indices, an attempt has been made to discriminate all the sample banks into four distinct categories. These categories are: (1) Best Performers; (2) Middle Robust Banks; (3) Low Robust Banks; and (4) Worst

Performers. For this, we utilized the values of first quartile, median and third quartile of TFP growth, EFFCH and TCH index of commercial banks in India for various sub-periods (as given in Table 5.10).

TABLE 5.10

Criterion for the Classification of Commercial Banks on the basis of TFP Growth and its Indices

Periods	*TFP*	*TCH*	*EFFCH*
Pre-Reforms Period	$Q_3 = 1.149$,	$Q_3 = 1.041$,	$Q_3 = 0.996$,
	$Q_2 = 1.108$,	$Q_2 = 1.028$,	$Q_2 = 0.965$,
	$Q_1 = 1.069$	$Q_1 = 1.022$	$Q_1 = 0.929$
First-Generation	$Q_3 = 1.034$,	$Q_3 = 1.034$,	$Q_3 = 1.037$,
Reforms Period	$Q_2 = 1.012$,	$Q_2 = 1.018$,	$Q_2 = 1.021$,
	$Q_1 = 0.985$	$Q_1 = 1.003$	$Q_1 = 1.000$
Second-Generation	$Q_3 = 1.071$,	$Q_3 = 1.063$,	$Q_3 = 1.014$,
Reforms Period	$Q_2 = 1.032$,	$Q_2 = 1.052$,	$Q_2 = 1.000$,
	$Q_1 = 1.004$	$Q_1 = 1.042$	$Q_1 = 0.976$
Entire Study Period	$Q_3 = 1.057$,	$Q_3 = 1.057$,	$Q_3 = 1.001$,
	$Q_2 = 1.045$,	$Q_2 = 1.048$,	$Q_2 = 0.994$,
	$Q_1 = 1.033$	$Q_1 = 1.037$	$Q_1 = 0.988$

Best Performers (TFP, TCH and EFFCH = Q_3)
Middle Robust Banks (Q_2 = TFP, TCH and EFFCH < Q_3)
Low Robust Banks (Q_1 = TFP, TCH and EFFCH < Q_2)
Worst Performers (TFP, TCH and EFFCH < Q_1)

The banks that attained TFP growth, TCH and EFFCH index above the value of third quartile are included in the category of 'Best Performers'. The category of 'Middle Robust Banks' constitutes those banks, which experienced TFP growth, TCH and EFFCH index above the value of median but lesser than the value of third quartile. The category of 'Low Robust Banks' includes those banks which registered TFP growth, TCH and EFFCH index lesser than the value of median but greater than the value of first quartile. The 'Worst Performers' category comprises of those banks, which recorded TFP growth, TCH and EFFCH index below the value of first quartile. The results have been summarized in Appendix Tables 5.6, 5.7, 5.8 and 5.9.

The banks that come under the category of 'Best Performers' are supposed to be operating with high level of TFP growth, EFFCH and TCH index in respective sub-periods. The banks in this group should rely more upon the advancement in technologies with a little bit improvement in the resource utilization process to achieve sustainable and technology driven growth. Further, the banks that get placed in the category of 'Middle Robust Banks' have the potential to grow at a faster rate by overcoming the distortions come in the way of efficient working (e.g., lack of managerial expertise and improper scale of operation, etc.). Moreover, the use of sophisticated technological measures may help these banks to experience high TFP growth rates in future. The banks that fall in the group of 'Low Robust Banks' are more likely to experience productivity loss due to inability in extracting maximum possible returns from the given level of resources. Thus, an improvement in technical efficiency or say technological mastery becomes a prerequisite for these banks to achieve sustainable growth. Besides this, the affiliate banks of 'Worst Performer' group are likely to be highly inefficient in the use of scarce resources to derive maximum benefits out of it. Therefore, these banks are highly required to focus more and more upon reducing the excessive use of resources at the given state of technology to achieve higher TFP gains in near future, which in turn demands trained and skilled workforce.

CONCLUSIONS

This chapter attempts to empirically examine the total factor productivity growth and its related indices among commercial banks in India for the period 1985 to 2005-06. The TFP growth has been computed through applying DEA-based MPI for the balanced panel data set of 27 PSBs and 18 old private banks in India. The empirical findings illustrate that commercial banks have experienced TFP growth at the rate of (4.6 percent) per annum on account of (5.2 percent) growth rate of technological progress and (–0.5 percent) of efficiency change during the period 1986-06. Thus, technological progress has emerged to be the major driver of TFP growth, but the failure of banks in achieving technological mastery can safely be stated.

The inter-period shift of the banks divulges deceleration in TFP growth at the rate of (0.9 percent) per annum during 1993-99 as against (10.2 percent) per annum during 1986-92. Further it has been observed that whatever amount of productivity has been realized during first-generation reforms is exclusively due to strong catching up effect, which was completely absent during pre-reforms period. In second-generation reforms, banks have witnessed acceleration in TFP growth at the rate of (3.7 percent) per annum, which may be attributed more to technological change (3.9 percent) rather than efficiency change (-0.2 percent) per annum.

The results suggest that poor diffusion process of new technology is responsible for fragile catching up effect during this period. Besides this, TFP growth of banks is more pronounced during second-generation reforms as compared to first-generation reforms.

The ownership-wise analysis of banks represents that PSBs are observed to be growing at the rate of (5 percent) per annum, followed by private banks (4.0 percent) during 1986-06. And, most of the productivity gains have originated due to strong frontier effect rather than weak catching up effect. PSBs are found to be more productive than those of private banks during the sub-periods: 1986-92 and 1993-99, however, the reverse holds true during the period 2000-06. Further, the empirical findings highlight that private banks are more efficient in managerial operations; however, PSBs have improved scale of operations in most parts of the sub-periods (except 1993-99). The empirical evidence also divulges an important role of technologies to the TFP growth in most parts of the sub-periods (except during 1993-99); however, the absence of technological mastery to absorb the technologies can safely be stated among various forms of banks. Besides this, large banks are found to be more productive than medium and small banks.

At disaggregated levels, all the sample banks have recorded significant variations in TFP growth and its components across various sub-periods. The empirical findings further illustrate that Ing Vysya Bank has experienced TFP growth at an exciting rate of (11.3 percent) per annum however, Catholic Syrian Bank and Sangli Bank noted to be least productive, growing at the rate of less than 1 percent during the entire study period. The comparative growth rates of pre-reforms and first-generation reforms period illustrates that 24(3) banks have witnessed comparative deceleration (acceleration) in TFP growth during 1993-99. The empirical findings reported that the number of banks that registered negative growth rate during 1993-99 in comparison to a positive growth rate during pre-reforms period stood at 16. Overall, a notable change in the magnitude of growth rates has been witnessed between these periods. In second-generation reforms period, only 5 banks have registered negative growth rate as against positive growth rate during 1993-99. The number of banks that recorded positive growth rates during 2000-06 as against negative growth rates during 1993-99 stood at 14. Overall, it has been noticed that banking sector reforms failed to impart significant dent on the performance level of sample banks during 1993-99 in comparison to 2000-06. As for various sources of TFP growth at disaggregated level, it has been noticed that improved technologies has played a key role in deriving productivity gains among various sample banks in India for most parts of the sub-periods (except 1993-99). However, the absorption of these technologies is likely to be missing due to poor diffusion process and little accumulation of knowledge through learning by doings.

Further, the discrimination of the banks on the basis of TFP growth and its related indices illustrates that best performer banks are likely to operate at high level of TFP growth, EFFCH and TCH index in various sub-periods. Thus, banks in this group should rely more upon the advancement in technologies. Further, the results provide that middle robust banks have the potential to grow at a faster rate, therefore the use of sophisticated technological measures is recommended to experience high TFP gains in future. The low robust banks are more likely to experience productivity loss due to the inability to use existing resources in an optimum manner. Thus, the efficient use of existing technologies becomes a prerequisite for these banks to achieve sustainable growth. Besides this, worst performer banks are likely to be highly inefficient in the use of scarce resources; therefore, the main thrust of these banks should be on reducing the wastage of resources, which in turn demands trained and skilled workforce.

The policy implication of the aforementioned results is that although TFP growth of CBs has improved in later parts of study period (1999-00 to 2005-06), but still most of the banks in India are lagging behind due to inefficient use of the scarce resources. This in turn reflects inability of the banks to catch up best practices available in banking industry. This demands substantial changes in the working processes and sharpening the managerial skills through various training programmes. Therefore, large investments will have to be made in information technology and human resources development programmes for imparting knowledge and inculcating special skills among workforce. The bank managers should pay key attention to make proper and optimum use of existing as well as the enhanced technologies in order to augment productivity gains. Furthermore, appropriate steps should be taken in order to have improved scale of operation. Besides this, the banks should become conscious in availing the productive opportunities offered to them in terms of various relaxations and removal of the barriers to the performance.

6

Determinants of Efficiency and Convergence/Divergence among Commercial Banks in India

In this chapter, an endeavor has been made to investigate the environmental factors affecting the efficiency of commercial banks in India and to test whether the phenomenon of convergence or divergence exists in Indian banking industry. In light of this, this chapter has been divided into two broad sections. Section I focuses on the detailed explanation of environmental factors affecting the efficiency of banks in general and Indian banking sector in particular. Section II explains the theoretical exposition of the concept of catching up or convergence/divergence and its empirical application among commercial banks in India.

SECTION I

The empirical findings outlined in chapter four illustrates that the efficiency of commercial banks in India has changed during the study period. However, according to the empirical results, the magnitude of efficiency differences is found to be dissimilar across the sample banks. Some banks have witnessed an improvement in efficiency scores while the others did not. This may be attributed to the difference of the consequences of deregulation (liberalization) and internal bank-specific factors across the banks. In addition, the economic environment is also likely to be different across the banks and these differences induce bank efficiency differences through different channels. For instance, size, profitability, asset quality, market structure, ownership structure, gross domestic product (GDP), per capita income, stock market capitalization, inflation ratio and liberalization can produce significant differences (gaps) in the efficiency of banks.

The performance of banks highly depends upon the environment in which they are working. Accordingly, the banks working with favorable internal and external environment may outperform the banks working with unfavorable internal and external environment. Therefore, it is imperative to investigate the factors that can explain variations or differences in the efficiency of banks.

6.1 DETERMINANTS OF BANK EFFICIENCY

In the empirical economic variables literature, there are diversity of socio-economic, which have significant association with the efficiency of banks. These factors can broadly be categorized into three groups, inter alia, internal bank-specific factors, external environmental factors and other factors. The internal bank-specific factors include endogenous factors which are under the control of management such as capital employed, size of banks, management styles, work methods, ownership and organizational structure, asset/liability structure, age, cost/earning ratios, etc. and exogenous factors like market share, which may be beyond the control of management under certain circumstances.

The external environmental factors such as GDP, per capita income, stock market capitalization, inflation ratio and liberalization may have significant impact on the performance

TABLE 6.1
Internal Bank-Specific, External Environment and Other Factors affecting Banks Efficiency

Variables	*Study*
	Internal Bank-Specific Factors
(1)	*(2)*
Size	Favero and Papi (1995), Fat and Hua (1998), Dogan and Fausten (2002), Doshit *et. al.* (2003), Isik and Hasan (2003), Hauner (2004), Kumar and Verma (2002-03), Maghyereh (2004), Attaullah and Lee (2006), Kwan (2006), Rezvanian *et. al.* (2007), Suffian *et. al.* (2007)
Return on Assets	Doshit *et. al.* (2003), Kumar and Verma (2002-03), Maghyereh (2004), Attaullah and Lee (2006), Rezvanian *et. al.* (2007), Suffian *et. al.* (2007), Ketkar and Ketkar (2008)
Quality of Staff	Hauner (2004), Suffian *et. al.* (2007)
Exposure to Off-Balance Sheet Activities	Kwan (2006)
Loan to Total Assets	Dogan and Fausten (2002), Isik and Hasan (2002), Isik and Hasan (2003)
Business per Employee	Doshit *et. al.* (2003), Kumar and Verma (2002-03)
Risk	Isik and Hasan (2002), Isik and Hasan (2003), Hauner (2004)
Market Power	Favero and Papi (1995), Dogan and Fausten (2002), Kumar and Verma (2002-03), Isik and Hasan (2003), Maghyereh (2004)
Capital Adequacy Ratio	Grigorian and Manole (2002), Doshit *et. al.* (2003), Kumar and Verma (2002-03)
Problem Loans	Pastor (2002), Isik and Hasan (2003), Maghyereh (2004)
Non-Performing Loans to Total Loans	Doshit *et. al.* (2003), Kumar and Verma (2002-03), Kwan (2006), Ketkar and Ketkar (2008)
Priority Sector Lending	Kumar and Verma (2002-03), Ketkar and Ketkar (2008)

(Contd.)

TABLE 6.1 (*Contd.*)

(1)	*(2)*
	External Environment Factors
Inflation Ratio	Grigorian and Manole (2002)
Stock Market Capitalization	Grigorian and Manole (2002)
Per Capita Income	Grigorian and Manole (2002)
Liberalization	Maghyereh (2004)
GDP	Grigorian and Manole (2002), Hauner (2004), Rezvanian *et. al.* (2007)
	Other Factors
Specialization	Favero and Papi (1995), Dogan and Fausten (2002)
Ownership	Isik and Hasan (2003), Hauner (2004), Maghyereh (2004), Rezvanian *et. al.* (2007)
Location	Favero and Papi (1995)
Number of Branches	Kumar and Verma (2002-03)

measures of banks. There are also some other non-economic factors like specialization, ownership, location and number of branches, which may have strong influence on the performance measures of banks.

In most of the studies, the authors have taken into account either only the internal bank-specific factors or the internal as well as external factors to keep in view the objective of the study. But, more specifically, they have given priority to investigate the impact of internal bank-specific (regulatory) factors such as capital adequacy ratio, problem loans, size, profitability, asset quality, market structure, ownership structure, risk and quality of staff, etc. [Favero and Papi (1995), Doshit *et. al.* (2003), Isik and Hasan (2003), Kumar and Verma (2002-03), Maghyereh (2004)]. Table 6.1 depicts some of the factors, which have been considered in existing studies.

Further, it was observed that the opening up of more branches reduced the level of cost efficiency but did not negatively affect the profit efficiency because higher costs of more branches is roughly offsetted by higher profits. Moreover, banks in large rural markets were found to be more cost efficient. The local banks that had installed a broad ATM network were found to be relatively cost efficient. Finally, the empirical findings concluded that local banks can improve their efficiency through a careful choice of main and branch offices and location of ATMs when bank specific, market specific and macroeconomic variables do not play role.

Haunar (2004) employed Tobit regression model in order to explain cost efficiency differences in German and Austrian banks. The results highlighted that cost efficiency is positively related to size, scope and quality of staff. No significant differences have been detected in the cost efficiency of privately owned .and cooperative banks. However, independent saving banks were found to be significantly less cost efficient banks. State owned banks emerged to be more cost efficient than other banks, which can largely be due to the state guarantees that give access to cheaper funds. Besides this, both the cooperative and private banks registered same level of average cost efficiency.

Maghyereh (2004) employed panel data Tobit model to investigate the influence of environmental factors affecting DEA efficiency scores of banks in Jordan. As per empirical findings, various measures of DEA efficiency scores were better explained by bank size and profitability, rather poorly by capital adequacy ratio and market power. In addition, liberalization variable was found to be positively associated to the efficiency of Jordanian banks.

Fries and Taci (2005) considered cost efficiency estimates as dependant variable and regressed on a set of explanatory variables. They stated that country level factors such as lower nominal interest rates; a greater share of majority foreign-owned banks and a higher intermediation ratio have positive impact on cost efficiency. The banks with larger market share were found to be more efficient than smaller ones. Privatized banks with majority of foreign ownership were appeared to be more cost efficient followed by newly established domestic and foreign-owned private banks. Privatized banks with majority of domestic ownership were noticed to be least cost efficient but still better than state owned banks. The banking systems with higher capital to total assets ratios and banks with lower loan losses tend to have lower costs, which might be associated with lower risks in banking sectors.

Attaullah and Le (2006) constructed two DEA models to derive technical efficiency estimates of commercial banks in India. Further, they considered the resultant efficiency score as dependent variable and regressed on a range of explanatory variables using ordinary least square method and general moment method. They highlighted that efficiency of previous year is significantly and positively related to the efficiency of current year in both the models. The relationship between size and efficiency was noted to be positive however; the degree of significance seemed to be varied in both the models. The higher investments to total assets ratio reported positive impact on efficiency as per Model A and negative impact as per Model B. Furthermore, it was observed that return on asset ratio negatively affected the banks' efficiency as per Model A, however positively as per Model B. In addition, the empirical findings highlighted negative association between GDP and efficiency of banks as per Model A and Model B.

Kwan (2006) applied fixed effect model to analyze the impact of bank-specific variables affecting x-efficiency of banks in Hong Kong. The empirical findings reported that bank size has strong negative impact on the efficiency scores of full sample banks and small banks, but to lesser extent on the efficiency scores of large banks. The relationship between x-efficiency and loss loan provisions was estimated to be negative but statistical insignificant for the full sample banks and large banks. Furthermore, off-balance sheet activities registered significant positive impact on the x-efficiency of large banks, small banks and all banks group. In addition, loan growth rate was noted to be significantly negatively related to x-efficiency estimates of both the large and small banks.

Sufian and Majid (2007) fitted Tobit regression model to investigate the impact of various determinants on the efficiency of banks in Singapore. According to the empirical results, bank size was noted to be insignificantly negatively related to efficiency measures obtained from both the DEA models. The variable profitability was found to be significantly positively associated to efficiency as per Model 2. The capitalization variable has been observed to be insignificantly positively related to banks' efficiency for both the models. In addition, the empirical findings provided that higher overheads cost resulted in better bank performance in Singapore as per Model 1. Besides this, the level of loan quality was found to be negatively related to the efficiency of banks for both the Model 1 and Model 2.

The review of the empirical studies presents a mixed evidence of the factors affecting efficiency of banking sector. Nevertheless, the impact of variables is highly sensitive to the differences in choice of techniques, alternative set of input and output variables, measurement of those variables and differences in regulatory and economic environments. Therefore, the empirical evidence suggests somewhat dissimilar or inconsistent relationship of the same environmental variables with efficiency estimates.

6.3 MODEL DEVELOPMENT

In literature, most of the studies have applied two-stage procedural technique to analyze the impact of various environmental factors on the efficiency of banks. Following literature, at the first stage, the point efficiency estimates of each sample bank in each sample year have been derived through non-parametric DEA approach. At the second stage, the resultant efficiency scores are regressed on a range of explanatory variables.

As eluded earlier, the point efficiency estimates may be dissimilar across the banks. These inter-firm (bank) differences can arise due to the differences in factors like size, profitability, asset quality, market structure, ownership structure and external factors. Financial analysts are often interested to identify whether these differences are significant or not in a statistical sense. This can be identified by using regression analysis. But the simple linear model is not appropriate here because the dependent variable (efficiency scores) obtained from DEA model is censored in nature (i.e., lie between zero and one). Therefore, a simple application of ordinary least square (OLS) method may produce biased results. In such cases, the appropriate regression model is known as a Tobit or censored regression model, which handles data that is skewed and truncated [Avkiran, (1999)].

Baltagi (2001) explained that panel data Tobit models could include fixed or random effects. The first type models the individual, farm-specific effects as fixed parameters; that is; the method would be equivalent to creating as many dummy variables as the number of farms (units) to control for their fixed time-variant effect in the model. In the random effects panel data model, the individual specific effects are allowed to be random; thus allowing for variation of these influences across the 'representative population'.

In the present study, panel data model has been estimated using a bank specific fixed effect Tobit regression model. The standard Tobit model can be defined as:

$$y_{it}^{*} = \beta^{T} x_{it} + \varepsilon_{it}$$

$$y_{it} = y_{it}^{*} \text{ if } y_{it}^{*} > 0, \text{ and} \quad i = 1, 2, \text{——} N, \ t = 1, 2, \text{——} T$$

$$y_{it} = 0, \text{ otherwise,}$$

where bank is indexed by i and time is indexed by *t*. $\varepsilon_{it} \sim N(0, \sigma^2)$, x_{it}, and β are vectors of explanatory variables and unknown parameters, respectively. The y_{it}^{*} is a latent variable and y_i is the dependent variable. Following Kumar and Verma (2002-03), the dependent variable y_{it} is defined as one minus cost x-efficiency score (i.e., y_{it} = (1-XE)). It is possible to estimate the unknown parameter vector β in the Tobit model in several ways. In the present study, the econometric software package Eviews 5 has been used to estimate the parameters by the method of maximum likelihood.

6.4 DETERMINANTS OF BANKS COST X-EFFICIENCY IN INDIA

As previously mentioned, the existing literature has studied the impact of three types of variables on the estimated efficiency scores. The existing empirical findings provided that the banking system with favorable environmental is more efficient and productive as compared to banking system with unfavorable environmental factors. Therefore, it is important to investigate the impact of various factors affecting the efficiency of commercial banks in India. Nevertheless, this study concentrates on bank-specific variables to study their expected relationship with estimated cost inefficiency scores since these variables are more specific to individual banks.

In second-stage regression analysis, the explanatory variables that have been taken into account to explain DEA cost-x inefficiency are Size (log of total assets), ROA (net profit/total earning assets), exposure to off-balance-sheet activities (non-interest income/total assets), quality of staff (establishment expenses/total number of employees) and operational risk as (total loans/total assets). In addition to this, 44 bank-specific and 2 period dummies (PD_1 and PD_2) have been incorporated in the regression equations. PD_1 denotes dummy variable equals to 1 for first-generation reforms period and 0 for otherwise. Similarly, PD_2 denotes dummy variable equal to 1 for second-generation reforms period and 0 for otherwise as depicted in Table 6.2. To address it, three left-censored Tobit regression equations have been fitted for PSBs, private sector banks and all sample banks separately.

To check the specified hypothesis, following Tobit regression equation has been estimated.

$$(1-\theta_i) = \beta_0 + \beta_1 \text{ Size} + \beta_2 \text{ ROA} + \beta_3 \text{ Overheads} + \beta_4 \text{ LOAN–TA} + \beta_5 \text{ Off BALANCE} + \beta_6 \text{ PD1} + \beta_7 \text{ PD2} + \varepsilon_1$$

It is pertinent to note that dependant variable in the above model is x-inefficiency, computed by transforming DEA x-efficiency scores. Therefore, the present study has used 'inefficiency' rather than 'efficiency' in the above model. Accordingly, a positive sign of regression coefficient implies an association with inefficiency increases or decreased efficiency whereas negative coefficient indicates an association with inefficiency decline or increased efficiency.

The preliminary estimates of the model suggest that the results are quite sensitive to the inclusion and exclusion of the explanatory variable. This may be due to the fact that the explanatory variables are highly correlated with each other. Although, there has been considerable attention provided to pre-testing procedures in applied econometrics, there is no specific criterion regarding the selection of variables in final model. Thus, final model has been selected on the basis of two considerations: (1) the statistical significance of regression coefficients, (2) an agreement of signs of regression coefficients with *a priori* expectations.

It is hypothesized that the explanatory variable *'Size'* may have either positive or negative association with x-inefficiency scores. Besides this, all the other explanatory variables such as profitability, off-balance-sheet activities, quality of staff and operational risk are expected to have negative sign or positive relationship with x-inefficiency scores.

TABLE 6.2

Description of the Variables Affecting Cost X-Inefficiency Scores

Predictor	*Symbol*	*Proxy Variable*
Size	SIZE	log (Total Assets)
Profitability	ROA	$\frac{\text{Net Profit}}{\text{Total Earning Assets}}$
Quality of Staff	OVERHEADS	$\frac{\text{Establishment Expenses}}{\text{Total Number of Employees}}$
Exposure to Off-Balance Sheet Activities	OFFBALANCE	$\frac{\text{Non-nterest Income}}{\text{Total Assets}}$
Operational Risk	LOAN-TA	$\frac{\text{Total Loans}}{\text{Total Assests}}$
First-Generation Reforms Period	PD_1	Dummy variable = 1 for First-Generation Reforms Period and 0 for otherwise
Second-Generation Reforms period	PD_2	Dummy variable = 1 for Second-Generation Reforms Period and 0 for otherwise

The empirical results of Tobit regression model have been presented in Table 6.3. It has been observed that barring a few, in all the regression equations, the signs of the estimated regression coefficients are in line with priori expectations. Also, most of the regression coefficients are noted to be statistically significant at five percent or one percent level of significance.

6.5 EMPIRICAL RESULTS

Profitability: This study has applied return on total earning assets as a proxy for banks' profitability. Profitability indicates the ability of a bank to earn in excess to the expenditures incurred on handling all the related operations. The proposition that high levels of profitability as proxied by the explanatory variable (ROA) leads to higher efficiency seems to apply in commercial banks operating in India. Since the value of ROA coefficient has worked out to be (-0.035373) for all CBs, (-0.033382) for PSBs and (-0.048571) for private sector banks as shown in Table 6.3. The value of coefficients has expected negative sign and also the coefficients are found to be highly significant at one percent level of significance for different forms of banks. Therefore, ROA has proved to be a major determinant of XIE of banks in India. The results imply that higher the level of profitability of banks leads to lower the level of x-inefficiency and *vice versa*. The empirical findings also reflect that banks are more efficient in intermediation process between savers and borrowers with given level of resources. The efficiency in intermediation process lowers down the cost of bank operations and in turn, enhances the profitability of the banks. These results are highly supported by the findings of Jackson and Fethi (2000) and Kumar and Verma (2002-03), which stated that profitable banks are more technically efficient. Nevertheless, the empirical evidence suggests somewhat mixed or inconsistent relationship of profitability and efficiency measures. For instance, Casu and Girardone (2004) reported negative and statistically significant relationship between profits and efficiency in Italy. Attaullah and Lee (2006) reported that the strong negative and positive impact of ROA on efficiency measures depends upon the specification of the model.

Size: The present study has considered logarithm of total assets as a proxy variable for Size. Table 6.3 shows that the value of SIZE coefficient has worked out to be (0.103765) for all CBs, (0.078811) for PSBs and (0.078672) for private sector banks i.e., the coefficient is having positive sign. Further, SIZE coefficient is noted to be highly significant at one percent level of significance for various forms of banks. The empirical findings illustrates that the explanatory variable 'Size' has strong positive association with XIE estimates. This suggests that efficiency of small banks is higher than that of large ones, which perhaps supports 'divisibility theory'. According to Maghyereh (2004), the divisibility theory states that there will be no such operational advantages accruing to large banks, if the technology is divisible, that is, small scale banks can produce financial services at costs per unit output comparable to those of large banks, suggesting no (or negative) association between size and efficiency. Alternatively, higher efficiency of small banks over the larger ones may also be attributed to close and cordial relationships of the top-level management with customers and other officers. On the other hand, lower efficiency of large banks over the small banks may arise due to the reason that bank managers fail to handle all the operational details with an increase in the size of banks due to the lack of sufficient expertise. Therefore, negative relationship exists between size and XIE estimates of commercial banks in India. These results are consistent with the results obtained by Doshit *et. al.* (2003), Kumar and Verma (2002-03) and Kwan (2006), which highlighted negative relationship between size and efficiency.

Exposure to Off-Balance Sheet Activities: The present study has applied non-interest income to total assets ratio to investigate the influence of exposure to off-balance sheet activities on XIE estimates of CBs in India. Since the value of OFFBALANCE coefficient is (-0.104599) for all CBs, (-0.093925) for PSBs and (-0.103829) for private sector banks as depicted in Table 6.3. The value of coefficients has expected negative sign and further, the coefficients are observed to be highly significant at one percent level of significance for different ownership groups of banks. Therefore, OFFBALANCE has emerged to be one of the major determinants affecting XIE of

TABLE 6.3

Relationship between Cost X-Inefficiency and Bank Characteristics in India : Tobit Regression Analysis (1985 to 2005-06)

Banks	*All Banks*	*PSBs*	*Private Banks*
Explanatory Variables	*Coefficient*	*Coefficient*	*Coefficient*
Intercept	-0.317425*	-0.050260	-0.093503
	[0.0022]	[0.7568]	[0.4221]
ROA	-0.035373*	-0.033382*	-0.048571*
	[0.0000]	[00000]	[0.0000]
Size	0.103765*	0.078811*	0.078672*
	(0.0000]	[0.0000]	[0.0000]
Off-Balance	-0.104599*	-0.093925*	-0.103829*
	[0.0000]	[0.0000]	[0.0000]
Overheads Quality of Staff	-0.029163* [0.0066]	-0.01972 [0.1188]	-0.017266 [0.4074]
Loan-TA	-0.004230*	-0.005043*	-0.004054*
	[0.0000]	[0.0000]	[0.0004]
PD1	-0.019685	-0.042679*	0.037883
	[0.0946]	[0.0045]	[0.0647]
PD2	-0.027870	-0.052079**	0.048214
	[0.1526]	[0.0277]	[0.1604]
R-squared	0.593704	0.648927	0.509949
Adjusted R-squared	0.570019	0.62649	0.475144
S.E. of regression	0.093164	0.087121	0.098653
Sum squared residual	7.742189	4.037902	3.425807
Log likelihood	797.8616	563.5597	258.3424
Avg. log likelihood	0.844298	0.993932	0.683445

Notes : 1. The values in parentheses are p-values.

2. * indicates the level of significance at 1% level of significance, and ** indicates the level of significance at 5% level of significance.

commercial banks in India. The empirical findings have highlighted strong negative impact of off-balance activities on the XIE scores of various categories of banks in India. Thus, the results imply that banks are increasingly engaging themselves in recent and modern banking activities to have an edge over the others. Accordingly, the income from off-balance sheet business items such as commission, exchange, fees, brokerage plus other receipts has substantially increased particularly after the deregulatory policies came into practice in India. Thus, it emanates from the analysis that banks have experienced decline in the amount of cost inefficiency with an increase in the exposure to off-balance sheet activities. The above finding is consistent to the findings of Kwan (2006), which highlighted strong positive impact of exposure to off-balance sheet activities on the efficiency of banks.

Quality of Staff: Quality of staff is another major determinant of x-inefficiency of commercial banks in India. Overhead has been considered as the proxy variable of quality of staff. Table 6.3 highlights that the value of overhead coefficient is (-0.029163) for all CBs, (-0.019720) for PSBs and (-0.017266) for private sector banks. The results delineate that negative sign of the coefficient of overheads is in accordance to the priori expectations. Further, the coefficients are observed to be highly significant at one percent level of significance for CBs but insignificant for PSBs and private sector banks. The negative relationship between overheads and XIE estimates may be attributed to the fact that commercial banks bear higher overheads cost, which results in higher bank performance. The empirical findings also imply that employees take more initiative to handle all the operations in a productive manner with minimum usage of resources whereby adequate remuneration is paid-off to them. Sathye (2001) suggested that management that is more professional might require high remuneration and thus a highly significant positive relationship with efficiency measures is natural. These results are in line with the results obtained by Sufian and M. Zulkhibri (2006).

Operational Risk: Operational risk can be regarded as another important variable affecting X-inefficiency of CBs in India. In most of studies in literature, standard deviation of return on asset (i.e., SD of ROA) has been considered as the proxy variable for risk. Following Seelanatha, S.L. (2007), the present study has applied total loans to total assets ratio as proxy variable for operational risk. This variable can also be considered as a measure of risk taking behavior of the bank management. Profit-seeking banks generally get involved in high risk lending portfolios to get higher earning portfolios. The higher loan to asset ratio may lead to wider interest margins and to large loan losses. But, interest margin thinned out on account of higher costs involved in handling all the related operations to loans administration. The increased cost in maintaining the large loan level adversely affects the future lending potential. On the other hand, the risk takers may prefer to explore more productive investment opportunities while reducing the other overhead costs. Thus, these banks can increase their operational efficiency by keeping a significant portion of funds in income generating assets. As such, positive relationship between size and cost inefficiency can be expected.

Table 6.3 provides that the value of operational risk coefficient is found to be (-0.004230) for all CBs, (-0.005043) for PSBs and (-0.004054) for private sector banks. The value of coefficients has expected negative sign and also the coefficients are found to be highly significant at one percent level of significance for different forms of banks. Therefore, operational risk has proved to be a major determinant affecting XIE of various ownership categories in India. The policy implication of the results is that higher the investment in productive or high income yielding assets has improved banks' cost efficiency. In addition, the risk taking banks are emerged to be more cost efficient than that of the banks less indulged in risk taking activities.

Pre-Reforms Period: Table 6.3 indicates that the value of intercept coefficient is worked out to be (-0.317425) for all CBs, (-0.050260) for PSBs and (-0.093503) for private sector banks. The results delineate that negative sign of the intercept coefficient is in accordance to the prior expectations. Further, the coefficients are observed to be highly significant at one percent level of significance for CBs, though, the degree of significance varies for PSBs and private sector banks.

The results provided the evidence of negative and statistically significant association of XIE estimates for CBs during pre-reforms period. Thus, the results provide the signal that CBs have attained the most in cost savings in this period. This finding also holds true in case of PSBs and private banks, though, the results are not found to be significant.

First-Generation and Second-Generation Reform Period

Table 6.3 reported that the value of PD_1 coefficient, proxy variable of first-generation reforms period, is estimated to be (-0.019685) for all CBs, (-0.042679) for PSBs and (0.037883) for private sector banks. Similarly, the value of PD_2 coefficient, proxy variable of second-generation reforms period has worked out to be (-0.027870) for all CBs, (-0.052079) for PSBs and (0.048214) for private sector banks.

The results reported the evidence of negative but statistically insignificant association with XIE estimates in both the first-generation and second-generation reforms period for CBs. Thus, it is clear from the analysis that banks could not get maximum benefits of liberalization in these periods. Further, the findings highlighted negative relationship with XIE estimates in case of PSBs at one percent level of statistical significance for first-generation reforms and at five percent level for second-generation reforms period. However, this result is found completely different for private banks. Thus, the results imply that PSBs have improved their efficiency response to banking sector reforms, however, private banks could not get maximum benefits of deregulatory practices in these periods. Stated differently, liberalization has strong positive impact on the X-efficiency of PSBs in India unlike private banks.

The predictive performance of the model can be judged by R^2 and adjusted R^2. In the present model, the value of adjusted R^2 is 0.57 for all CBs in India, which indicates that 57 percent of the variations in banks' efficiency are due to size, profitability, exposure to off balance sheet activities, quality of staff, operational risk and liberalization measures (PD_1 and PD_2). The value of adjusted R^2 worked out to be 0.63 for PSBs in India, which delineates that the bank-specific variables explain 63 percent variation of the total variations in the model. In addition, the value of adjusted R^2 has come out to be (0.475) for private banks in India, which highlights that the bank-specific variables explain 47.5 percent variations of the total variations in the specified model.

6.6 CONCLUSION

In the first part of the chapter, the empirical findings shed light on the environmental factors affecting x-inefficiency of commercial banks in India. To view this objective, bank-specific fixed effect panel data Tobit regression model has been applied for PSBs, private banks and all sample banks separately. The explanatory variables that have been used to explain x-inefficiency are size, ROA, exposure to off balance sheet activities, quality of staff and operational risk. In addition, two period dummies (PD_1 and PD_2) have been incorporated in the regression equations to study the impact of liberalization on the x-inefficiency estimates of CBs in India.

According to the empirical findings, the x-efficiency of all the forms of banks is best explained by ROA, quality of staff, off-balance sheet activities and operational risk but poorly explained by size. This implies that higher profitability levels, extensive exposure to off-balance sheet activities, quality of staff and higher operational risk have a strong negative impact on the x-inefficiency of commercial banks in India. However, the explanatory variable size has significant positive impact on the XIE estimates of CBs in India, which perhaps supports divisibility theory. Further, the results highlight that CBs have attained the most in terms of cost savings in pre-reforms period. This finding also holds true in case of PSBs and private banks' group, though, the results are not found to be significant. Moreover, according to the empirical findings, commercial banks could not get maximum benefits of deregulatory policies in first-generation and second-generation reforms period. In contrast to it, PSBs have improved their efficiency levels in response to banking sector reforms, however, the completely reverse holds true for private banks during these periods.

6.7 CONVERGENCE/DIVERGENCE

6.7.1 Introduction

In the empirical literature on economic growth, the economic convergence across the nations (developed and developing countries) is one of the most important factors of catching up hypothesis. According to this hypothesis, the developing countries should grow at faster rate on average than those of developed countries. The first reason is due to technology transfer. In recent times, the developing countries are not required to reinvent the technology because that has already been invented by developed countries. The developing countries have to simply follow the historical stages of innovations. This would enable the developing economies to 'leapfrog' over some of the developed economies, which had to invent the technology for growth purpose. This is the reason why developing economies took lesser time to attain highest level of productivity growth. For instance, British doubled its output per person in first 60 years of its industrial revolution, America did so in 45 years and South Korea did so in 11 years.

The second reason of convergence is 'factor accumulation'. The developed nations generally have higher levels of physical and human resources, which lead to higher level of output per person. But, the marginal product of capital and investments would be lower in developed nations due to the application of law of diminishing marginal returns. Contrarily, an additional unit of capital would comparatively generate more output in developing nations where capital is scarce. This may also be due to the fact that these nations are yet operating at increasing returns to scale.

On account of given one or both of the conditions, i.e., technology transfer and rapid capital accumulation, the income gaps of the developed and developing nations would decline in long-run, as the faster growing developing countries would be catching up the slower growing developed countries.

In a cross-section context, the convergence term has been used to state that the income gaps between the economies have declined overtime. We have empirically applied the same concept of convergence to understand the efficiency/ productivity dynamics in banking.

Lee et. al. (1996) discussed three types of convergence. With cross-section data, convergence involves the investigation of relationship between growth rates and initial efficiency/ productivity levels. Unconditional or absolute β-convergence exists when regressing a growth measure, such as efficiency change, on initial efficiency gives a negative and significant coefficient. If other, conditioning variables are included, they should be jointly insignificant, for absolute convergence to hold. Conditional convergence will also require a negative coefficient on initial efficiency, after controlling for the effects of other explanatory variables, at least some of which prove to be significant.

SECTION II

6.7.2 Methods of Convergence

In banking sector, if the banks with low levels of efficiency at the beginning of the study period grow more rapidly than the banks with high level of efficiency in initial sample year, convergence occurs. The literature spells out mainly two different types of convergence : 1. σ-Convergence, and 2. β-Convergence. The σ-convergence addresses the question whether the gaps between efficient and inefficient banks have declined over the time or not. The concept of σ-convergence exists in case the efficiency gaps of efficient and inefficient banks decline over the time and if otherwise, the concept of σ-divergence is said to exist. The σ-convergence can be tested by regressing the standard deviations of the efficiency score of various cross sections (banks) overtime on trend variable. Using data for the standard deviations in technical efficiency scores (see Appendix Table 4.2), following regression equations can be fitted for testing σ-convergence:

$$SD_{1985\text{-}92} = a + \sigma_{1985\text{-}92} + \varepsilon_t \qquad \ldots\ 6.1$$
$$SD_{1993\text{-}06} = a + \sigma_{1993\text{-}06} + \varepsilon_t \qquad \ldots\ 6.2$$
$$SD_{1985\text{-}06} = a + \sigma_{1985\text{-}06} + \varepsilon_t \qquad \ldots\ 6.3$$

where a is constant, SD denotes standard deviations of the banks over pre-reforms period (1985-92), post-reforms period (1993-06) and entire study period (1985-06) as shown in equation 6.1, 6.2 and 6.3 respectively. A negative and significant slope coefficient (σs) signals that the dispersion in the efficiency of banks has narrowed down or declined overtime and vice versa. Stated differently, the estimated value of (σs) coefficient indicates whether the phenomenon of σ-convergence or catching up effect is present in banking sector or not.

As for β-convergence, the relationship between the initial level of efficiency of banks and change in efficiency scores (growth rates) over the study period is tested. The negative relationship between both signifies the existence of β–convergence i.e., originally inefficient banks are leapfrogging over the originally efficient ones. In other words, the inefficient banks are growing at a rapid rate than that of efficient ones overtime. Using the data given for technical efficiency (see Appendix Table 4.2) and average efficiency change (see Appendix Table 5.1) for distinct sub-periods, following regression equations can be fitted for testing β-convergence:

$$\text{AEFFCH}_{1986\text{-}92} = \sigma_1 + \beta_1 \text{ Efficiency}_{1985} + \varepsilon_1 \quad \ldots 6.4$$

$$\text{AEFFCH}_{1993\text{-}06} = \sigma_2 + \beta_2 \text{ Efficiency}_{1992\text{-}93} + \varepsilon_2 \quad \ldots 6.5$$

$$\text{AEFFCH}_{1986\text{-}06} = \sigma_3 + \beta_3 \text{ Efficiency}_{1985} + \varepsilon_3 \quad \ldots 6.6$$

where, AEFFCH is average efficiency change over the period 1986-92, 1993-06 and 1986-06 and efficiency is the initial efficiency score of pre-reforms period (1985), post-reforms period (1992-93) and entire study period (1985) as shown in equation 6.4, 6.5 and 6.6. The εs and βs are regression coefficients and σs are error terms. A negative and significant slope coefficient (βs) indicates that the banks with low level of efficiency in initial year of the study period have experienced high average efficiency change over the study period. In other words, it implies that catching up and leapfrogging is taking place in the efficiency/productivity growth of banks.

Both the σ-convergence and β-convergence are related to each other, but both are not the same. In particular, β-convergence is necessary but not the sufficient condition for σ-convergence (Sala-i-Martin, 1996). Koski and Majumdar (2000) stated that both the β-convergence and σ-convergence should be used simultaneously to draw a conclusion about the presence of catching up and leapfrogging phenomenon. They listed four distinct possibilities as given in Table 6.4.

The first possibility is that both the '*σ-convergence* and *β-convergence*' occurs. This means that the originally inefficient banks converge towards the originally efficient ones. Moreover, the originally inefficient banks grow at such a rate that they overtake the well-performing banks.

The second possibility of the existence of '*σ-convergence without β-convergence*' demonstrates that the performance gaps between the banks declines overtime, however, the poor-performing banks do not grow at such a rate that they may overtake the well-performing banks. This implies that catching up process occurs but not the leapfrogging.

The third possibility '*β-convergence without σ-convergence*' highlights the importance of *β-convergence in addition to σ-convergence*. Catching up may occur even if the variability in the distribution of efficiency measures increase overtime. This happens when originally poor-performing banks grow at such a fast paced rate that they overtake the originally well performing banks. This in turn increases the variability in the distribution of performance measures.

The fourth option of 'No *β-convergence and No σ-convergence*' dwells that the inefficient banks diverge from the efficient ones overtime (no catching up), moreover, the originally inefficient banks do not grow at such a rate that they may overtake the well-performing banks.

6.8 EMPIRICAL RESULTS AND DISCUSSIONS

6.8.1 In the Table 6.5, we have estimated three regression equations for the pre-liberalization period (1985-92), post-liberalization period (1993-06) and entire study period (1985-06). The dependant variable is taken as the natural logarithm of the standard deviation of technical efficiency scores of all the sample banks overtime, which is regressed on time variable t in each of these regression equations.

Table 6.5 illustrates that the value of slope coefficient (σ) has worked out to be (0.120) in pre-liberalization period. The coefficient has positive sign and also the coefficient is statistically significant at five percent level of significance. This implies that originally inefficient banks did not converge significantly to originally efficient ones, i.e., the efficiency gaps between efficient and inefficient banks have increased over the pre-liberalization period. Therefore, the empirical findings rule out the possibility of σ-convergence phenomenon among commercial banks operating in India.

Further, the empirical findings substantiate that the value of slope coefficient (σ) has noticed to be (-0.0412) in post-liberalization period (1993-06). The value of coefficient has negative sign, which is statistically significant at five percent level of significance. This clearly indicates that dispersion and inequalities of the distribution of TE scores between efficient and inefficient banks has declined overtime. The result also signifies the presence of σ-convergence, which states that inefficient banks are converging towards the efficient ones in post-reforms period. Therefore, it can safely be stated that there is significant dent of reforms on the performance measures of banks in this period.

In the case of entire worked out period study, period the value of slope coefficient (σ) has to be (0.01621). The value of coefficient is having positive sign, which is statistically insignificant at five percent level of significance. Accordingly, the dispersion between the efficiencies of banks has increased over the time span of 21 years, but this increase has not observed to be significant. In other words, empirical findings signify the presence of divergence at the place of convergence but divergence is not found to be much serious on account of the positive impact of reformatory measures in post-liberalization period.

On the whole, the above regression estimates reveal that the elements of leaning by doing and the process of catching up is absent among commercial banks in India in pre-reforms period. Nevertheless, the reformatory measures have exerted favorable impact on the efficiency and productivity growth of low efficient banks in post-reforms period. On the whole, it can be stated that inefficient banks are trying their best to converge towards efficient ones.

6.8.2 For testing β-convergence, we have estimated three regression equations where average efficiency change has been taken as dependant variable and regressed on initial years'

TABLE 6.4

The Implications of β-Convergence and σ-Convergence for Catching Up and Leapfrogging

	σ-Convergence: Yes	*σ-Convergence: No*
β-Convergence: Yes	Catching Up Leapfrogging	Catching Up Leapfrogging
β-Convergence: No	Catching Up No Leapfrogging	No Catching Up No Leapfrogging

TABLE 6.5

Regression Results about σ-Convergence

Period	*Intercept*	*Slope*	*R-square*	*F-Ratio*	*Decision about Convergence*
(Dependent Variable = σ)					
Pre-Liberalization Period	-2.815 [-20.928]	0.120 [3.983*]	0.13	0.612	Divergence
Post- Liberalization Period	-1.650 [-26.925]	-0.0412 [-5.938*]	0.01	0.625	Convergence
Entire Study Period	-2.262 [-16.652]	0.01621 [1.589]	0.12	2.523	Divergence

Notes : (i) Figures in the parentheses of type [ ] are the *t*-values, and
(ii) The decision about convergence is based upon the sign and significance of slope parameter.

technical efficiency scores. As is evident from Table 6.6, the value of (β) coefficient has worked out to be (-0.158) during pre-reforms period, (-0.0606) during post-reforms period and (-0.0452) during entire study period. The value of (βs) coefficients has negative sign and the coefficients are found to be significant at five percent level of significance. This indicates that efficiency scores of the banks in beginning year (i.e., 1985 for pre-reforms and for entire study period each and 1992-93 for post-reforms period) and average efficiency change [i.e., the time span of 1986 to 1991-92 for pre-reforms period, 1992-93 to 2005-06 for post-reforms period and 1986 to 2005-06 for entire study period] have strong negative association with each other. The empirical findings, thus, imply that originally inefficient banks are catching up the originally efficient ones in various sub-periods under consideration. This also reflects that formerly poor-performing banks are growing at such a faster rate than that of previous leaders that they have overtaken them. In other words, the empirical evidence suggests that inter-bank efficiency/productivity differences (gaps) have significantly declined overtime.

As per the terminology of Koski and Majumdar (2000), the empirical findings fall in third category, i.e., 'β-convergence without σ-convergence' for pre-reforms period and entire study period. This illustrates that catching up may occur even if the variability in the distribution of efficiency measures increases overtime. This happens when originally poor-performing banks grow at such a rate that they overtake the originally well-performing banks. Thus, it can safely be concluded that catching up process is taking place among CBs in India during these periods. On the other hand, the empirical findings of post-reforms period fall in first category, i.e., 'β-convergence' and 'σ-convergence'. This substantiates that the originally inefficient banks are not only catching up the originally efficient banks, but also, they are also growing at such a rate that they have overtaken the originally efficient banks during the post-liberalization period. Therefore, it can be concluded that the process of catching up and leapfrogging is present among commercial banks in India.

6.9 CONCLUSION

In this chapter, an attempt has been made to empirically test the phenomenon of catching up or convergence (σ-convergence and β-convergence) in the efficiency/productivity scores of commercial banks in India. The σ-convergence addresses the question whether the gap between efficient and inefficient banks has declined over the time or not. It has been tested by regressing the standard deviations of the efficiency score of various cross-sections (banks) overtime on trend variable. The concept of σ-convergence exists in case the efficiency gaps of efficient and inefficient banks decline over the time. As for β-convergence, the relationship between the initial level of efficiency of banks and change in efficiency scores (growth rates) over the study period has been tested. The negative relationship between both signifies the presence of β-convergence, i.e., originally inefficient banks are leapfrogging over the originally efficient ones.

As per σ-regression estimates, the empirical findings substantiate that the elements of leaning by doings and the process of catching up is absent among commercial banks in India during pre-reforms period. Nevertheless, the reformatory measures have exerted favorable impact on the efficiency and productivity growth of low efficient banks as evidenced in post-reforms period. Overall, the empirical findings provide the evidence of divergence at the place of convergence but divergence is not found to be much serious during the entire study period, which may be attributed to the positive impact of liberalization during 1993-06. Thus, it can safely be stated that inefficient banks are trying their best to converge towards efficient ones.

The β-convergence results highlight that the banks with low efficiency level in initial year of the sample period have experienced high efficiency change in all the specified periods. Therefore, the banks, which were previously lagging behind, are growing at such rate, that these banks have overtaken the

TABLE 6.6

Regression Results about σ-Convergence

Period	*Intercept*	*Slope*	*R-square*	*F-Ratio*	*Decision about Convergence*
Pre-Liberalization Period	1.102 [18.132]	-0.158 [-2.286*]	0.108	5.23	Convergence
Post-Liberalization Period	1.053 [132.4]	-0.0606 [-5.6*]	0.431	32.585	Convergence
Entire Study Period	1.034 [65.9]	-0.0452 [-2.9*]	0.16	8.554	Convergence

Notes : (i) Figures in the parentheses of type [ ] are the *t*-values, and
(ii) The decision about convergence is based upon the sign and significance of slope parameter.

well performing banks. Banking sector reforms have contributed a lot in detecting efficiency and productivity gaps among efficient and inefficient banks. Despite an increase in the variability of efficiency scores over the time span of 1985-92 and 1985-06, the high paced growth of less efficient banks over the originally efficient ones supports the possibility of the phenomenon of catching up in the efficiency/productivity growth of CBs in India during these periods. As per post-reforms' findings, the originally inefficient banks are not only found to be catching up the originally efficient banks, but also the inefficient banks are growing at such a faster rate that these banks have overtaken the originally efficient banks. Therefore, the empirical findings provided the evidence of the process of catching up and leapfrogging among commercial banks in India in post-reforms period.

Conclusions

I

Banking sector, considered as the prime driver of economic growth, has brought tectonic swings in the economic landscape of the nation. It has turned Indian economy to be more opened, liberalized and one of the fastest growing economies of the world, where efficiency and productivity growth have been considered as the kingpin for survival. Therefore, the banking institutions of various countries are under pressure to improve their productive efficiency. Moreover, it has been empirically examined that banks receiving higher efficiency scores are much more likely to survive than banks, which have relatively low scores (Barr and Siems, 1996). In light of this, efficiency and productivity growth measurement remain very high on the agenda of policy-makers and researchers.

The banks efficiency has gained a lot of popularity by all the parties that participate in the banking industry. The regulators are interested in banks efficiency since it assists them to identify actual and potential problems in banking sector. Furthermore, it provides them the framework to assess the health of individual banks and to wipe out the complexities evolved in their working process. The efficiency scores provide the signal to investors and bank management regarding the soundness and managerial performance of the banking system. The banks efficiency also sheds light on the sustainability of banking sector, on the basis of which, decisions relating to mergers and acquisitions are taken. Banks are now more open to public examinations, on account of which, the banks are more likely to concentrate on their performance levels to sustain their position in global market. On the other hand, productivity indices are recognized as a useful tool in economic forecasting and determining the most effective allocation of resources. Moreover, productivity indices assist to set realistic targets for monitoring activities during the developmental process through identifying the key areas of weaknesses and barriers to performance. In addition, it suggests us the remedial measures to wipe out the dismal performance of the banks.

The contribution of present study to the literature on efficiency and productivity growth of commercial banks in India is manifold. Firstly, most of the empirical work done so far have been concentrated at the aggregate (macro) level and therefore, they do not shed light on the empirical analysis of banks at disaggregate (micro) level. Secondly, most of the empirical studies are confined to the empirical analysis of banks pertaining to either the pre-liberalization or the post-liberalization period. Thus, a few studies have been found in existing literature considering both the pre-liberalization and post-liberalization period. In addition, no subsequent attempt has been made to bifurcate the post-liberalization period into initial-phase of liberalization and post-liberalization period to show how the magnitude of efficiency and productivity scores vary with the change in the degree of deregulation or liberalization. Thirdly, little attempts have been made in existing literature to test the phenomenon of catching up or convergence in the efficiency/productivity growth of commercial banks in India with the use of σ-convergence and β-convergence. Fourthly, most of the studies relating to banks' efficiency in India paid negligible attention to compute super-efficiency scores and ranking of the efficient banks. As, no in-depth and comprehensive study has been conducted on the above-said issues in India, thus, the present study is an endeavor in this direction to enrich the existing literature on the efficiency and productivity growth of commercial banks in India.

OBJECTIVES OF THE STUDY

The main objective of the present study is to analyze scale economies, x-efficiency and total factor productivity growth of commercial banks in India during pre-reforms and post-reforms period. Specifically, the following are the key objectives of the study:

1. To examine x-efficiency and its sources among commercial banks in India;
2. To measure scale economies and pure technical efficiency of commercial banks in India;
3. To pinpoint the sources of inefficiency among commercial banks in India;
4. To rank the efficient banks on the basis of their performance;
5. To examine total factor productivity growth and its sources among commercial banks in India;
6. To analyze the impact of ownership and banking reforms on the efficiency and total factor productivity growth of commercial banks in India;
7. To study the impact of environmental factors affecting x-efficiency of commercial banks in India; and
8. To test the phenomenon of convergence/divergence in the performance level of banks in India.

Data Base

The study is based upon secondary data and it is confined to the period 1985 to 2005-06. The entire study period has been classified into three distinct sub-periods: (i) Pre-liberalization period (1985 to 1991-92), (ii) Initial post-liberalization period (1992-93 to 1998-99), and (iii) post-liberalization period (1999-00 to 2005-06). The analysis of pre-liberalization and post-liberalization period assists us to ascertain whether the liberalization program has favorably affected the efficiency and productivity of banks or not. Further, the bifurcation of post-liberalization period into first-generation reforms and second-generation reforms period seeks us to analyze the change in the behavior of efficiency and productivity growth of banks with the change in the degree of deregulation. As far as, sample banks are concerned, this study has considered balanced panel data set of 19 nationalized banks (NBs), State Bank of India (SBI) and its 7 subsidiaries and 18 old private sector banks in India. The sample includes only those banks, which have been continuously operating since 1985 to 2006. The relevant data have been extracted from 'Performance Highlights of Banks' and 'Financial Analysis of Banks' (Volume I & II)—annual publications of Indian Banks' Association and 'Statistical Tables Relating to Banks in India', 'Annual Accounts of Banks', 'Report on Trend & Progress in Banking' and 'Reserve Bank of India Bulletins'—annual publications of Reserve Bank of India. In addition, the requisite data have been culled out from 'National Income Statistics' published by Center for Monitoring Indian Economy.

Measurement of Input and Output Variables

In banking literature, measurement of inputs and outputs underscores a prominent and controversial issue. Although, a variety of approaches has been followed, but there are two most commonly used approaches (production and intermediation) in banking. The production approach views banks as the producers of deposits and loans with the use of labor and physical capital. The deposits and various categories of assets are defined in terms of number of accounts. This approach takes into account only the operating cost; however, interest cost does not form the part of total cost. On the other hand, the intermediation approach views the banks as the producers of various categories of bank assets using deposits together with purchased inputs. Outputs are measured in monetary values and total costs include all the operating expenses and interest expenses. In literature, most of the researchers have adopted intermediation approach (IA) to measure input and output variables for a specific bank.

Following intermediation approach, the input variables that have been taken into account in the present study are labor (measured as the full time personnel) and loanable fund (measured as the sum of deposits and borrowings) for a given period. On the other hand, output parameters have been defined in terms of spread (measured as the difference between interest earned and interest expanded) and non-interest income (measured as the difference between total income and interest income) for a given period. The treatment of output variables is in lines suggested by Das (1997 and 2000), and Kumar and Verma (2002-03) and particularly applicable in Indian banking industry. All the input and output variables except staff have been measured in Rs. crore. Further, GDP price deflator has been used to deflate two outputs viz., spread and other income and loanable fund input. Moreover, the expenditure incurred on employees has been deflated by consumer price index for urban non-manual employees. All the nominal data has been converted into real prices (base 1999-00 = 100) to mitigate the impact of rise in price level. Further, the real values of input and output variables except staff have been divided by number of branches to reduce the effects of random noise due to the measurement error in inputs and outputs.

Methodology

As mentioned earlier, the main objective of the study is to analyze scale economies, x-efficiency and total factor productivity growth of commercial banks in India. Thus, Data Envelopment Analysis (DEA), non-parametric frontier approach has been utilized for estimating different measures of efficiency. Further, Mann-Whitney U-statistics rank test has been executed to study whether the efficiency differences of banks are significant or not across various sub-periods. To ascertain TFP growth and its related indices' pattern among CBs in India, DEA-based Malmquist productivity index (MPI) approach has been employed. The subsequent second-stage fixed effect Tobit regression model has been applied to analyze the impact of various environmental factors on x-inefficiency estimates of banks. Besides this, the traditional regression approach has been used to identify the presence of convergence/divergence among CBs in India.

Chapter Scheme

The present study has been organized into seven chapters.

1. Introduction
2. Review of Studies Made
3. Methodology for Analysis
4. Scale Economies and X-Efficiency of Commercial Banks in India
5. Total Factor Productivity Growth of Commercial Banks in India
6. Determinants of Efficiency and Convergence/ Divergence among Commercial Banks in India
7. Summary and Conclusions

Plan of the Study

Chapter 1 is introductory in nature concentrating on the importance of banking, role of banks in economic development, its evolution and detailed analysis of banking sector reforms in India. It further outlines objectives, rationale of the study and plan of the study.

Chapter 2 reviews the literature focusing on the key issues viz., scale economies, x-efficiency and total factor productivity growth of banks. This chapter includes the studies both of national and International character.

Chapter 3 illustrates database, various issues related to the measurement of variables in banking sector and the selection of variables for present study. It also discusses methodological framework of the applied techniques to examine efficiency and productivity growth of commercial banks in India.

Chapter 4 elaborates inter-temporal, ownership-wise and inter-bank analysis of x-efficiency and its decompositions among CBs in India for the period 1985 to 2005-06, divided into distinct sub-periods. In addition, it sheds light on the relationship of bank size and scale economies among commercial banks in India. Besides this, this chapter focuses on identifying the super efficient banks and ranking them by the level of influence.

Chapter 5 illustrates inter-temporal, ownership-wise and inter-bank analysis of TFP growth and its related indices among CBs in India for the period 1985 to 2005-06, divided into various sub-periods. Besides this, the relationship of bank size and TFP change along with its indices has been explored among commercial banks in India. Moreover, an attempt has been made to discriminate the banks on the basis of TFP growth, technological change and efficiency change.

Chapter 6 highlights the impact of various environmental factors on the x-inefficiency scores of commercial banks in India. Moreover, this chapter throws light on the question whether the phenomenon of convergence or divergence exists in the efficiency/productivity growth of commercial banks in India or not.

Seventh 7 summarizes the study and concludes with the scope for further research.

II

EMPIRICAL RESULTS

Chapter IV: X-Efficiency and Scale Economies of Commercial Banks in India

The empirical results demonstrate input-oriented DEA efficiency scores obtained through running Charnes-Cooper-Rhodes (CCR) and Banker-Charnes-Cooper (BCC) model. Further, an analysis aims to pinpoint the sources of inefficiency existing among commercial banks in India. To study whether the efficiency differences of banks are significant or not across various sub-periods, Mann-Whitney U-statistics test has been executed. In addition, the relationship of bank size and scale economies among commercial banks in India has been investigated. Besides this, this chapter focuses on identifying the super efficient banks and ranking them by the level of influence.

Empirical Findings

4.1 The average cost x-efficiency of all CBs has turned out to be 0.755, ranging from 0.657 to 0.838 during the entire study period. The results, thus, imply that the magnitude of cost inefficiency is to the tune of about (24.5 per cent) among CBs in India. This suggests that, the banking industry can, on an average, minimize their costs by eliminating the elements of inefficiencies with the help of best practices and still produce the existing level of outputs.

4.2 Looking at the components of XE, the average TE score has been estimated to be 0.813 for the period 1985-06. This indicates that the level of technical inefficiency of commercial banks has turned out to be about (18.7 per cent) in India. Thus, the empirical findings suggest that, the banks can, on an average, curtail their expenditures on labor and loanable funds by atleast (18.7 percent) with the help of best practices and still produce the same level of outputs. Alternatively, the banks have the scope of producing 1.23 times (i.e., 1/0.813) as much outputs from the same level of inputs to produce a given level of output. On the other hand, average AE of banks has worked out to be (93.1 percent) during the study period. This implies that the average allocative inefficiency (AIE) to the tune of about (6.9 percent) is due to the choice of wrong mix of inputs. Thus, the empirical findings suggest that banks can reduce AIE through the use of correct input combinations to produce a given level of output at the given prices

4.3 It is pertinent to note that a considerable amount of x-inefficiency (XIE) is due to the wastage of resources (18.7 percent) rather than due to the wrong mix of input combinations (6.9 percent) to produce a given level of output. The results thus imply that the managers of banks are relatively good at choosing the optimum combinations of inputs at the given input prices but they are not that good at using the minimum level of inputs to produce a given level of output.

4.4 As far as sources of TE are concerned, the average PTE score of commercial banks has noted to be 0.869 during the period 1985-06. This in turn implies that average PTIE to the tune of about 13.1 percent is due to the inappropriate management practices in converting critical inputs into outputs. On the other hand, CBs have experienced average scale efficiency to the tune of about 0.934, which in turn delineates an increase in the magnitude of SIE by 6.6 percentage points, that is, due to the choice of wrong scale of operation. Therefore, it emanates from the analysis that 13 percentage points of 18.7 percent technical inefficiency (TIE) is due to the incapability of the management to convert critical inputs into outputs. However, the rest part of the TIE may be attributed to the fact that the banks are either operating at below or above the optimal scale. The connotation of the findings is that managerial irregularities have played a key role in emerging technical inefficiencies existing among CBs in India.

4.5 The comparative analysis of pre-reforms and first-generation reforms period substantiates that the sample banks have witnessed an increase in average XIE by (0.7 percent), TIE by (5.4 percent), PTIE by (4 percent), and SIE by (2 percent) but the decline in AIE scores by (5.1 percent). In contrast to it, CBs have experienced deceleration in XIE, TIE, AIE and PTIE estimates by (4.5 percent), (3.8 percent), (1.2 percent) and (4.5 percent) respectively but acceleration in SIE scores by (0.2 percent) in second-generation reforms period. Overall, improvement in DEA efficiency scores is more pronounced in second-generation reforms period. This may be attributed to the fact that banks have started to adapt themselves in accordance to the guidelines issued by various committees and therefore have gained from the productive opportunities of liberalization.

4.6 Contrary to expectations, commercial banks are noted to be more efficient and productive in pre-reforms period as compared to first-phase and second-phase of post-liberalization period, which may possibly be attributed to the shift in accounting norms.

4.7 The ownership-wise analysis of x-efficiency and its sources provides that average XE of private banks is quite high at (78.5 percent), followed by PSBs (73.5 percent) during the 1985-06 period. This indicates that private banks have the potential for cost savings by (21.5 percent) while PSBs can cut their costs by (26.5 percent) to become fully efficient banks and to capture the position on the Best Practice Frontier.

4.8 As for sources of x-efficiency, private banks have reported average AE in tune of about (93.9 percent), followed by PSBs (92.5 percent) during the period 1985-06. Thus, private banks are found to be more efficient in selecting optimal input-combinations at the given input prices than those of PSBs. On the other hand, average TE of private banks worked out to be (83.7 percent), followed by PSBs (79.7 percent), which indicates that private banks are more efficient in inputs utilization process than PSBs to produce a given level of output.

4.9 As for the sources of TE, the average PTE of private banks has noted out to be (91.1 percent) higher than those of PSBs (84 percent) during 1985-06. In contrast, PSBs experienced SE to the tune of (94.5 percent) followed by private banks (91.7 percent) during the entire study period. Thus, the empirical findings connote that private banks are more managerially efficient in their operations as compared to PSBs, however, PSBs are in a better position to reap substantial scale economies than those of private banks.

4.10 Also, it is worth noting that, despite larger efficiency gains by private banks, SBI group gained the most in

XE, TE, AE, SE and PTE scores with least variability in performance levels during the period 1985-06.

4.11 The period-wise analysis dwells that PSBs have recorded higher amount of XIE, TIE and PTIE during the sub-periods: 1985-92 and 1993-99 than those of private banks. Contrarily, private banks have registered higher amount of XIE during the period 2000-06 as compared to PSBs, however, the opposite holds true in case of PTIE estimates. In addition, the amount of TIE of both the PSBs and private banks worked out to be same during 2000-06. The connotation of the findings is that PSBs have started to realize the benefits of liberalization in quantitative form during the period 2000-06 than that of private sector counterparts.

4.12 As for AE estimates, private banks registered lesser amount of inefficiency than that of PSBs during 1985-92, but the opposite holds true during the sub-periods: 1993-99 and 2000-06. This clearly indicates that PSBs have become more efficient in choosing optimum inputs combinations to produce a given level of output after the deregulatory policies came into practice (since 1992-93).

4.13 Further, PSBs experienced comparatively lesser amount of SIE as compared to private banks in all the sub-periods. The connotation of the findings is that PSBs are not much infected with scale-related problems like private banks. Further, SBI group of PSBs are noted to be more scale efficient than NBs in most parts of the sub-periods.

4.14 An improvement in efficiency scores among various forms of banks is more pronounced in second-generation reforms as compared to first-generation reforms period.

4.15 Further, it has been observed that the standard deviation of XE, TE and PTE for the PSBs is higher than that of private banks, which may be attributed to the improved practices of certain PSBs. On the other hand, lower variability of the efficiency of private banks may be attributed to their sudden and immediate response to new prudential norms and standards.

4.16 The standard deviation of AE and SE for the private banks is higher than that of PSBs, which may be attributed to the separation of management and ownership as well as to the adoption of dissimilar practices by different banks in decision-making process. On the other hand, lower variability of the efficiency of PSBs may be due to the fact that the banks are more familiar with the regulatory system of Indian banking industry.

4.17 The empirical findings reported that the average (XE, AE and TE) differences of public/private group are found to be statistically significant for the period 1985-06. As for various sub-periods, this bank group recorded significant differences in XE and AE scores for pre-reforms, PTE scores for first-generation reforms and AE, SE and PTE scores for second-generation reforms. These results suggest that private banks are more efficient than PSBs in most of the DEA efficiency scores during the sub-periods: 1985-92 and 1993-99 (with few exceptions). However, PSBs have become more efficient than private banks during the period 2000-06.

4.18 NBs v/s SBI group has recorded significant differences in average OTE, PTE, XE and AE scores for the period 1985-06. For various sub-periods, this group registered significant differences in average XE and AE scores during 1985-92; XE, OTE, SE and PTE differences during 1993-99 and XE, TE, SE and PTE differences during 2000-06. The connotation of the findings is that SBI group is more efficient than NBs group for most of the efficiency estimates.

4.19 SBI v/s private banks group did not report significant differences in XE, AE, TE and PTE scores for the entire study period. However, this bank group is found to be statistical significant for XE and SE scores in first-generation and for XE, AE and SE scores in second-generation reforms. This suggests that private banks, as a group is more efficient than SBI group during pre-reforms period. Nevertheless, SBI group has turned out to be more efficient than private banks after the deregulation measures came into existence (since 1992-93).

4.20 NBs v/s private banks group recorded significant differences in most of the DEA efficiency estimates in entire study period. As for period-wise analysis, this bank group has recorded significant differences in XE, AE and PTE scores in pre-reforms period, XE, TE and PTE scores in first-generation and AE and PTE scores in second-generation reforms. The empirical findings connote that private banks have performed better than NBs group for most of the DEA efficiency estimates in respective sub-periods (with few exceptions).

4.21 The average XE has improved in 22 sample banks, TE in 14 banks, AE in 33 banks, PTE in 15 and SE in 20 banks during first-generation reforms relative to pre-reforms. Contrarily, the average XE has declined in 23 sample banks, TE in 30 banks, AE in 12 banks, PTE in 28 and SE in 23 banks during 1993-99 as against 1985-92. Besides this, the number of banks that observed significant efficiency differences are noticed to be 10 banks in XE, 20 in TE, 22 in AE, 12 in PTE and 12 in SE scores during these periods. Therefore, null hypothesis of no significant efficiency differences between these periods is strongly rejected for these banks.

4.22 During 2000-06, the average XE has improved in 30 sample banks, TE in 28 banks, AE in 32 banks, PTE in 29 and SE in 21 banks as against of 1993-99. In contrast, the average XE has declined in 15 sample banks, TE in 17 banks, AE in 13 banks, PTE in 16 and SE in 24 banks during 2000-06 as against 1993-99. Besides this, the number of banks that observed significant efficiency differences are noticed to be 15 banks in XE, 17 in TE, 10 in AE, 15 in PTE and 7 in SE scores during these periods. Therefore, null hypothesis of no significant efficiency differences between these periods is strongly rejected for these banks.

4.23 On aggregate basis, commercial banks have not illustrated significant XE, TE, SE and PTE differences between pre-reforms v/s first-generation and first-generation v/s second-generation reforms period. However, the completely reverse holds true for AE differences.

4.24 As for best practice banks, Tamilnad Mercantile Bank has been found to be operating at the TE and SE frontier in most of the times (i.e., 18 times); at AE frontier (15 times); at XE frontier (16 times) and at the PTE frontier (20 times).

4.25 Furthermore, the banks that registered the position on the frontier in most of the times are found to be Tamilnad Mercantile Bank (i.e., 7 times in XE and TE each and 6 times in AE), Tamilnad Mercantile Bank and Bharat Overseas Bank (7 times in SE) and State Bank of India, Bharat Overseas Bank, Lord Krishna Bank and Tamilnad Mercantile Bank (7 times in PTE) in pre-reforms period.

4.26 Tamilnad Mercantile Bank has been found to be operated at the frontier in most of times (i.e., 6 times in XE and AE each and 7 times in TE, SE and PTE each) during first-generation reforms period.

4.27 During 2000-06, State Bank of Patiala, Karur Vyaya Bank and Tamilnad Mercantile Bank are found to be operating at the frontier in most of times (i.e., 3 times in XE and AE each and 4 times in TE). Karur Vyaya Bank occupied the position on the SE frontier (5 times) and State Bank of Patiala and Tamilnad Mercantile Bank (4 times) each during 2000-06. Nainital Bank and Ratnakar Bank are found to be at the PTE frontier in most of the times (i.e., 7 times) and Tamilnad Mercantile Bank did so (6 times) during this period.

4.28 Out of 21 sample years, United Bank of average India has been noted to be the bank with minimum efficiency score in most of the times (i.e., 7 times in OTE, 6 times in XE and 5 times in SE) during 1985-

06. Sangli Bank has emerged to be lowest efficient bank in most of the times (i.e. 4 times in case of XE, 3 times in TE and 7 times in SE). Bank of India and Ing Vysya Bank registered minimum AE score in most of (4 times) over the study period. Besides this, Indian Bank registered minimum PTE score in most of (5 times), United Commercial Bank and Indian Overseas Bank (4 times) each and United Western Bank did so (3 times) during the period 1985-06. Finally, the results suggest that these banks will have to incorporate substantial changes in their working set-up to keep in lines with international standards.

4.29 As far as returns to scale is concerned, the results substantiate that majority of banks (i.e., 65 percent), are operating at below their optimal scale size and thus, experiencing increasing returns-to-scale (IRS) during the study period. The banks in this category are operating at the decreasing portion of their long-run average cost (LAC) curve and experiencing economies of scale. These banks can enhance their overall efficiency by scaling up the size of their operations. Therefore, closure of sick banks, mergers of banks and modernization programs seem to be desirable in this direction.

4.30 Furthermore, the empirical findings dwell that 10 banks (i.e., 21 percent) are operating at above their optimal size and thus, experiencing decreasing returns-to-scale (DRS) during 1985-06. These banks are likely to operate at the increasing portion of the LACs and therefore, experiencing diseconomies of scale. The banks are required to downsize the scale of their operations to overcome diseconomies of scale. Thus, improvement in asset quality and priority sector lending in addition to technological upgradation seems to be desirable in this direction.

4.31 In addition to this, six sample banks (i.e., almost 14 percent) are found to be operating at most productive scale size and thus, have minimum long-run average cost in all the sub-periods.

4.32 Further, it has observed that the percentage of banks experiencing IRS continued to increase while the percentage of the banks experiencing DRS continued to decrease over the study period. Thus, the empirical findings suggest that there is significant room for the banks to extract maximum benefits of scale economies. Therefore, the strategy of scaling up the size of banks is recommended for majority of the sample banks.

4.33 The relationship of bank size and scale economies delineates that the average level of scale economies tends out to be 0.921 for small, 0.938 for medium and 0.941 for large banks during the period 1985-06. Thus, the empirical findings suggest that scale economies tend to increase with an increase in the size of banks. This may be attributed to the fact that banks have witnessed several mergers and acquisitions in Indian banking industry during this period. The merged banks invariably enhanced the size of operations and thus, enabled to reap the maximum benefits of scale economies. The same relationship is found to be consistent up to some extent across distinct sub-periods.

4.34 The results of Andersen and Petersen's super-efficiency scores highlight that Tamilnad Mercantile Bank captured top most position with super-efficiency score of 1.118, followed by Bharat Overseas Bank 1.005 during 1985-06. The banks viz., Allahabad Bank, Sangli Bank, Punjab & Sind Bank, Indian Bank, United Bank of India, United Commercial Bank are found to be at the lower end over this period.

4.35 The period-wise analysis dwells that Bharat Overseas Bank has attained top most rank with average super efficiency score of 1.183, followed by Tamilnad Mercantile Bank 1.156 and Lakshmi Vilas Bank 1.036 in pre-reforms period. On the other hand, Sangli Bank, Allahabad Bank, United Western Bank, Bank of Maharashtra, State Bank of Travancore and United Commercial Bank are found to be lowest efficient banks in pre-reforms period.

4.36 Tamilnad Mercantile Bank with super-efficiency score equals to 1.167 turned out to be the most efficient bank during the period 1993-99. Ing Vysya Bank and State Bank of Indore achieved second and third highest place with super-efficiency score of 1.006 and 1.001 respectively. The banks viz., Catholic Syrian Bank, Indian Overseas Bank, Punjab & Sind Bank, Indian Bank, United Commercial Bank and United Bank of India noted least super efficiency score.

4.37 The number of super efficient banks increased to six during 2000-06 as compared to three banks during 1993-99. Oriental Bank of Commerce, Corporation Bank, Tamilnad Mercantile Bank, Karur Vysya Bank, State Bank of Patiala and State Bank of Bikaner & Jaipur got first six ranks with average super efficiency score equal to 1.047, 1.043, 1.031, 1.014, 1.010 and 1.005 respectively. Contrarily, the banks viz., Bank of Rajasthan, Indian Bank, United Commercial Bank and Sangli Bank turned out to be poor performers during 2000-06. Finally, the empirical findings suggest the laggard banks to concentrate more and more upon minimizing the wastage of resources at the given state of technology.

4.38 Looking at the inter-period shift of the banks, it has been noticed that rankings of banks change considerably across various sub-periods. Stated differently, most of the sample banks could not maintain their positions or ranks on the *super-efficiency* scale across various sub-periods. Rather, it is the unique Tamilnad Mercantile Bank, which maintained its position consistently on first three ranks in the specified sub-periods.

Chapter V: Total Factor Productivity Growth of Commercial Banks in India

The empirical results demonstrate input-oriented total factor productivity growth (TFP) and its relative indices computed through applying DEA-based Malmquist productivity index. The empirical findings present inter-temporal, ownership-wise and inter-bank analysis of TFP growth and its related indices among CBs in India. In addition, the relationship between bank size and TFP change with its relative indices has been explored. In addition, the sample banks have been discriminated on the basis of TFP growth, efficiency change and technological change.

Empirical Findings

5.1. The empirical results illustrate that commercial banks have experienced total factor productivity (TFP) growth at the rate of (4.6 percent) per annum during the period 1985-06. Over the period, TFP growth has been realized on account of (5.1 percent) growth rate of technological progress and (–0.5 percent) of efficiency change. Thus, it is apparent from the analysis that catching up phenomenon is fragile (as observed when technological change is greater than efficiency change) among sample banks in India. On the basis of this ground, the failure of commercial banks in achieving technological mastery can safely be stated.

5.2. Looking at the yearly averages of MPI and its indices, no stable year-to-year trend of MPI and its indices is discernable from the analysis. The range of the growth rate of MPI and its indices has recorded significant fluctuations in all the sample years. This may be due to the fact that the banks have to face significant and frequent policy changes time to time.

5.3. The inter-period shift of the banks has reported deceleration in TFP growth at the rate of (0.9 percent) per annum during 1993-99 as against (10.2 percent) per annum during 1986-92. Thus, whatever amount of productivity has been realized during 1993-99, is exclusively due to strong catching up effect, which was completely absent during 1986-92. On the other hand, the frontier effect could not contribute to the TFP gains during 1993-99, which seems to be dominant during 1986-92.

5.4. In second-generation reforms, banks have witnessed acceleration in TFP growth at the rate of (3.7 percent) per annum, which can be attributed to technological change (3.9 percent) than efficiency change (-0.2 percent). The results suggest that poor diffusion process of new technology is the consequent factor of fragile catching up effect. In addition, the CBs have experienced negative growth of both the scale efficiency and pure technical efficiency index in most parts of the sub-periods (except 1993-99). Besides this, TFP growth and the growth of its related indices is more pronounced during second-generation reforms as compared to first-generation reforms.

5.5. As for ownership analysis, PSBs are observed to be growing at the rate of (5 percent) per annum, followed by private banks (4.0 percent) during the period 1986-06. Further, the results provide that productivity gains of PSBs and private banks have originated more due to strong frontier effect (5.2 percent) and (5.1 percent) respectively. However, technical efficiency has decelerated the level of TFP growth of private banks by (-1.0 percent) and PSBs (-0.2 percent) per annum over the period.

5.6. The period-wise analysis highlight that PSBs have emerged to be more productive than private banks during pre-reforms and first-generation reforms period. However, the comparative analysis of growth rates between these periods illustrates that PSBs have experienced a significant deceleration in TFP growth at the rate of (1.3 percent) per annum during first-generation reforms as against (11.5 percent) during pre-reforms period. On the other hand, private banks experienced TFP growth at the rate of (8.2 percent) per annum during 1986-92 but it significantly declined to (0.1 percent) during 1993-99. In addition, NBs and SBI groups also reported considerable fall in productivity scores during these periods. It is worth specifying that improved technologies has emerged to be the major driver of productivity gain during the period 1986-92, which failed to mark significant dent on the TFP growth of different forms of banks during 1993-99.

5.7. In second-phase of liberalization period, private banks witnessed acceleration in TFP growth at the rate (4.5 percent) per annum as compared to first-generation reforms. Thus, the empirical evidence highlights an important role of advanced technologies to the TFP growth; however, the absence of technological mastery to absorb these enhanced technologies can safely be stated. On the other hand, PSBs recorded acceleration in TFP at the growth rate of (3.2 percent) per annum during 2000-06 as against (1.3 percent) per annum during 1993-99. It has also been observed that both the forces of catching up (0.4 percent) and frontier effect (2.7 percent) have favorably contributed to the TFP growth of PSBs during 2000-06. But, the dominance of frontier effect over the catching up effect is visible from the empirical analysis. The strong frontier effect among PSBs may be attributed to the heavy investment in computerization of branches, installation of ATMs, core banking solutions and IT technologies, etc. But, the weak catching up effect reflects the failure of PSBs to catch up the best practices available in the banking industry. Moreover, it emerges from the empirical analysis that most of the PSBs are likely to make serious attempts to utilize the scarce resources in order to get maximum returns out of it than those of private banks. The dominance of TCH over the EFFCH also holds true in case of SBI group and NBs group of PSBs group.

5.8. The empirical findings substantiate that the main source of efficiency increases among PSBs is improved scale of operation rather better management practices among private banks over the period 1986-06. NBs and SBI group of PSBs group also exhibited efficiency increase exclusively due to scale efficiency increase.

5.9. The period-wise analysis presents that both the PSBs and private banks have improved their scale efficiency and pure technical efficiency change during first-generation reforms relative to pre-reforms period. In addition, both the NBs group and SBI group have performed well during 1993-99 in comparison to 1986-92 (with few exceptions). Private banks outweighed those of PSBs in terms of pure technical efficiency change rather PSBs did so in terms of scale efficiency change during 1993-99. It has also been observed that efficient managerial practices have contributed more to the efficiency increase than effective scale of operation among various forms of banks during 1993-99.

5.10. During 2000-06, PSBs provided the evidence of higher scale efficiency and pure efficiency change than those of private banks. Scale efficiency change is found to be the prime factor of efficiency change during this period. In addition, NBs group has performed well than SBI group during 2000-06 (with few exceptions).

5.11. The results also provided the evidence that majority of the PSBs, private banks and all CBs have improved their productivity levels on account of advanced technologies but absorption of these technologies is likely to be missing in various sub-periods. Thus, optimum use of these resources is indispensable to wipe out the productivity gaps among the banks. For this, the banks are required to adopt suitable measures in order to improve the scale of operation and to sharpen managerial skills.

5.12. The relationship of bank size and TFP growth with its indices highlight that large-sized banks have experienced TFP growth at the rate of (5.6 percent), followed by medium-sized banks (4.9 percent) and small-sized banks (4.2 percent) per annum during 1986-06. Over the period, technological progress has enhanced the level of TFP growth of small-sized banks by (5.1 percent) and medium-sized and large-sized banks by (6.0 percent) each. In contrast, the deterioration in technical efficiency has lowered down the level of TFP growth of small-sized (-0.8 percent), medium-sized (-1.0 percent) and large-sized banks (-0.1 percent) throughout the study period. Thus, the results imply that technologies (innovations) have played a key role in deriving TFP gains; however, the efficient use of these technologies is likely to be missing in all bank-sized groups.

5.13. At disaggregate level, Ing Vysya Bank has experienced TFP growth at an exciting rate of (11.3 percent), followed by Oriental Bank of Commerce (9.7), Corporation Bank (9.2) and Bharat Overseas Bank (8.9 percent) per annum during the period 1986-06. However, the banking industry of Catholic Syrian Bank and Sangli Bank is noted to be least productive, growing at the rate of less than 1 percent. Among PSBs, State Bank of Saurashtra registered productivity growth at the lowest rate of (1.9 percent) per annum.

5.14. The comparative analysis of the growth rates of pre-reforms and first-generation reforms illustrates that banking industry of Punjab & Sind Bank, United Commercial Bank and United Bank of India has witnessed comparative acceleration in TFP growth rates. However, the number of banks that experienced comparative deceleration in TFP growth during 1993-99 stood at 24. In addition, the number of banks that registered negative growth rates during 1993-99 in comparison to a positive growth rates during pre-reforms period stood at 16. Among these banks, the banking industry of State Bank of Patiala and Jammu & Kashmir Bank is found to be growing at an alarming rate of (24.5 percent) and (21.2 percent) per annum respectively during pre-reforms period but the growth rates tend out to be negative during first-generation reforms. The banking industry of Ing Vysya Bank and Corporation Bank experienced TFP growth at an alarming rate of (9.1 percent) and (7.5 percent) per annum respectively during 1993-99. Contrarily, State Bank of Patiala and Catholic Syrian Bank are found to be the least productive banks with respective growth rates of (-6.3 percent) and (-7.4 percent) per annum during 1993-99. It is only the Lord Krishna Bank that witnessed positive TFP growth during 1993-99 contrary to negative TFP growth during 1986-92. Overall, a notable change in the magnitude of growth rates has been witnessed between these periods.

5.15. In second-phase of reforms, the banking industry of Punjab National Bank, State Bank of Mysore, State Bank of Saurashtra, Lord Krishna Bank and Lakshmi Vilas Bank registered negative growth rates contrary to positive growth rates during 1993-99. Among these banks, State Bank of Saurashtra and Lakshmi Vilas Bank are found to be least productive banks with respective growth rates of (-3.6 percent) and (-3.4 percent) per annum during 2000-06. The number of banks that recorded positive growth rates during 2000-06 as against negative growth rates during 1993-99 stood at 14. Further, the banking industry of Indian Bank and Bharat Overseas Bank are found to be growing at striking rate of (11.6 percent) per annum each during this period. The banking industry of State Bank of B&J and Sangli Bank experienced negative growth rate during 1993-99 and continued to be negative during 2000-06. However, the extent of negative growth rate has noticed to be lesser than the period 1993-99. The banks, which realized comparative deceleration in TFP growth rates are noted to be Allahabad Bank, Andhra Bank, Bank of Baroda, Bank of India, Bank of Maharashtra, Central Bank of India, Syndicate Bank, United Commercial Bank, State Bank of Indore, Karnataka Bank, and United Western Bank during 2000-06.

5.16. As for the sources of TFP growth, State Bank of Patiala has experienced efficiency change at the rate of (1.2 percent) per annum while Lakshmi Vilas Bank recorded lowest growth rate of (-2.5 percent) per annum for the period 1986-06. The empirical findings further illustrate that majority of the sample banks have witnessed negative growth rates of technical efficiency during 1986-06. Thus, it can safely be said that most of the sample banks are lagging behind in terms of catching up effect.

5.17. The comparative analysis of growth rates of pre-reforms and first-generation reforms illustrates that only 5 banks have exhibited negative growth rate of efficiency change. Among these banks, Catholic Syrian Bank has recorded lowest negative growth rate of technical efficiency (-2.5 percent) per annum during 1993-99. The banking industry of Bank of India, Indian Bank, State Bank of India, State Bank of B & J, State Bank of Patiala and Bharat Overseas Bank experienced negative growth rates of EFFCH index during 1993-99 as against positive growth rates during 1986-92. The banking industry of Indian Bank experienced substantial efficiency decreases at the growth rate of (-8.0 percent) per annum during 1993-99. The banks that experienced positive growth rates during 1993-99 contrary to the negative growth rates during 1986-92 stood at 30. The banking industry of United Western Bank experienced EFFCH at the rate of (6.7 percent) per annum, followed by Andhra Bank (6.5 percent) during first-generation reforms. Overall, a notable change has been witnessed in the magnitude of EFFCH index between these periods.

5.18. During 2000-06, the empirical findings reported that 17 banks have experienced negative growth rates contrary to positive growth rates during 1993-99. Further, the empirical findings substantiate that only 3 banks have witnessed comparative acceleration in technical efficiency. In contrast, the number of banks that experienced comparative deceleration in the growth rates of technical efficiency stood at 12 during 2000-06. The number of banks that registered positive growth rates during second-generation reforms as against negative growth rate during first-generation reforms stood at 5. The banking industry of Tamilnad Mercantile Bank recorded stagnant growth between these periods. Overall, it has been noticed that the banks have started to catch up best practices available in banking industry as evidenced by the findings of first-generation reforms. However, the degree of growth rates is noted to be higher during 2000-06 as compared to 1993-99. Therefore, the empirical evidence suggests somewhat mixed impact of the reforms on the efficiency change of CBs in India during post-liberalization period.

5.19. As for TCH index, the empirical findings represents that Ing Vysya Bank and Oriental Bank of Commerce have registered TCH at an exiting rate of (10.9 percent) and (9.5 percent) per annum respectively during 1985-06. Contrarily, Catholic Syrian Bank has recorded TCH at the lowest rate of (1.6 percent) per annum. Furthermore, all the sample banks have witnessed positive growth rate of technologies during this period, which in turn implies positive impact of improved technologies on the productivity growth of banks.

5.20. The comparative analysis of growth rates of pre-reforms and first-generation reforms illustrates that 14 banks have experienced a comparative deceleration in the growth rate of TCH index. The number of banks that witnessed positive to negative growth rates between these periods stood at 31. The banking industry of State Bank of Saurashtra registered TCH at the lowest rate of (11.3 percent) per annum during 1986-92. The magnitude of lowest growth rate seems to be varying tremendously as evidenced by Nainital Bank (-6.2 percent) and State Bank of Patiala (-5.4 percent) during the period 1993-99.

5.21. Further, it has been observed that only 3 banks have experienced negative growth rates during 2000-06. Among these banks, State Bank of Mysore has noted a significant slow down in TCH at the rate of (-2.1 percent) per annum. Except Catholic Syrian Bank, all the remaining private banks followed a positive trend of growth rates of technology. The banks that witnessed comparative acceleration/deceleration in the growth rates of TCH index stood at 10/4 in number. In addition, 28 banks have followed positive trend in the growth rate of TCH index contrary to a negative trend during 1993-99.

5.22. On the whole at disaggregate level, it has been noticed that improved technologies has played a key role in augmenting productivity gains among various sample banks in India for most parts of the sub-periods (except 1993-99). However, the absorption of these technologies is missing due to the poor diffusion process and little accumulation of knowledge through learning by doings.

5.23. The empirical findings related to the discrimination of banks states that best performer banks are likely to be operating at high level of TFP, EFFCH and TCH index in various sub-periods. Thus, banks in this group should rely more upon the advancement in technologies. Further, the results provide that middle robust banks have the potential to grow at a faster rate, therefore, the use of sophisticated technological measures is recommended to augment high TFP gains in future. The low robust banks are more likely to experience productivity loss due to the inability to use existing resources in an optimum manner. Thus, the efficient use of existing technologies becomes a prerequisite for these banks to achieve sustainable growth. Besides this, worst performer banks are more likely to be inefficient in the use of scarce resources; therefore, the main thrust of these banks should be on reducing the wastage of resources through managerial expertise.

Chapter VI : Determinants of Efficiency and Convergence/ Divergence among Commercial Banks in India

In this chapter, the empirical results shed light on the factors affecting x-inefficiency of CBs in India. To view this, three left-censored Tobit regression equations have been fitted for PSBs, private banks and all commercial banks. The explanatory variables that have been used to explain x-inefficiency are Size (log of total assets), ROA (net profit/ total earning assets), exposure to off balance sheet activities (non-interest income/total assets), quality of staff (establishment expenses per employee ratio) and operational risk (total loans to total assets ratio). In addition to this, 44 bank-specific and 2 period dummies (PD_1 and PD_2) have been incorporated in the regression equations. PD_1 denotes dummy variable equals to 1 for first-generation reforms and 0 for otherwise. Similarly, PD_2 considers dummy variable equals to 1 for second-generation reforms and 0 for otherwise. Further, an attempt has been made to test whether the phenomenon of convergence or divergence exists among CBs in India.

6.1 FINDINGS OF THE STUDY

6.1.1 Profitability

This study has applied return on total assets as a proxy for banks' profitability. Since the value of ROA coefficient has turned out to be (-0.035373) for all CBs, (-0.033382) for PSBs and (-0.048571) for private banks. Therefore, ROA has proved to be a major determinant of XIE of banks in India. The results imply that higher the level of profitability of banks leads to lower the level of x-inefficiency and *vice versa*. The empirical findings also reflect that banks are more efficient in intermediation process between savers and borrowers with the given level of resources. The efficiency in intermediation process lowers down the cost of bank operations and in turn, enhances the profitability of banks in India.

6.1.2 Size

The present study has taken into account the logarithm of total assets as a proxy variable for size. The value of size coefficient has worked out to be (0.103765) for all CBs, (0.078811) for PSBs and (0.078672) for private banks. The coefficient is having positive sign, which is noted to be highly significant at one percent level of significance. This suggests that efficiency of small banks is higher than that of large ones, which perhaps supports divisibility theory. The divisibility theory states that there will be no such operational advantages accruing to large banks, if the technology is divisible. In addition, the higher efficiency of small banks over the larger ones may be attributed to close and cordial relationships of the top-level management with customers and other officers. Alternatively, the lower efficiency of large banks over the small banks reflects the failure of bank managers in handling all the operational details with an increase in the size of banks due to the lack of sufficient expertise.

6.1.3 Exposure to Off-Balance Sheet Activities

Exposure to off-balance sheet activities (measured as non-interest income to total assets ratio) is one of the major determinants of x-inefficiency among CBs in India. Since the value of off-balance coefficient is (-0.104599) for all CBs, (-0.093925) for PSBs and (-0.103829) for private sector banks. The value of coefficients has expected negative sign and further, the coefficients are observed to be highly significant at one percent level of significance. Thus, the results imply that banks are increasingly engaging themselves in recent and modern banking activities to have an edge over the others. Consequently, the income from off-balance sheet business items such as commission, exchange, fees, brokerage plus other receipts have substantially increased particularly after the deregulatory policies came into practice in India. Thus, it emanates from the analysis that banks have experienced fall in cost inefficiency with an increase in the exposure to off-balance sheet activities.

6.1.4 Quality of Staff

The present study has considered overhead as the proxy variable of quality of staff. The value of overhead coefficient is (-0.029163) for all CBs, (-0.019720) for PSBs and (-0.017266) for private banks. The coefficient has negative sign and highly significant in case of CBs but insignificant in PSBs and private banks. The negative relationship between overheads and XIE estimates may be attributed to the fact that commercial banks bear higher overheads cost, which results in higher bank performance. The empirical findings also imply that employees take more initiative to handle all the operations in a productive manner with the minimum usage of resources whereby adequate remuneration is paid-off to them.

6.1.5 Operational Risk

The present study has applied total loans to total assets ratio as proxy variable for operational risk. The value of operational risk coefficient is found to be (-0.004230) for all CBs, (-0.005043) for PSBs and (-0.004054) for private sector banks. The value of coefficients has expected negative sign and the coefficients are found to be highly significant at one percent level of significance. Therefore, operational risk has proved to be a major determinant affecting XIE of various ownership categories of banks in India. The empirical findings suggest that the risk taking banks are more cost efficient than the banks less indulged in risk taking activities. In addition, higher the investment in productive or high income yielding assets also improves the banks' cost efficiency.

6.1.6 Pre-Reforms Period

The value of intercept coefficient has estimated to be (-0.317425) for all CBs, (-0.050260) for PSBs and (-0.093503) for private banks. The results provided the evidence of negative and statistically significant association of XIE estimates for CBs during pre-reforms period. Thus, the results provide the signal that CBs have attained the most in cost savings in this period. This finding also holds true in case of PSBs and private sector banks, though, the results are not found to be significant.

6.1.7 First-Generation and Second-Generation Reforms Period

The empirical findings also demonstrate that the value of PD_1 coefficient, proxy variable of first-generation reforms has noted to be (-0.019685) for all CBs, (-0.042679) for PSBs and (0.037883) for private banks. Similarly, the value of PD_2 coefficient, proxy variable of second-generation reforms has worked out to be (-0.027871) for all CBs, (-0.052079) for PSBs and (0.048214) for private banks. The results reported the evidence of negative but statistically insignificant association with XIE estimates in PD_1 and PD_2 for CBs. This indicates that banks could not get maximum benefits of deregulatory practices in these periods. Further, the findings highlight that PSBs have improved their efficiency scores in response to banking reforms, however, the completely reverse holds true for private banks during these periods.

Further, the empirical findings report that the value of adjusted R^2 is 0.57 for all CBs, 0.63 for PSBs and 0.475 for private banks in India. This indicates that 57 percent of the variations in CBs' efficiency, 63 percent in PSBs' efficiency and 47.5 percent in private banks' efficiency can be explained by size, profitability, exposure to off-balance sheet activities, quality of staff, operational risk and liberalization measure (PD_1 and PD_2).

6.2 EMPIRICAL RESULTS OF CATCHING UP AND CONVERGENCE/DIVERGENCE

6.2.1 The empirical findings illustrate that the value of slope coefficient (σ) has worked out to be (0.120) in pre-reforms period. The coefficient has positive sign and the coefficient is statistically significant at five percent level of significance. This implies that originally inefficient banks did not converge significantly to originally efficient ones i.e., the efficiency gaps between efficient and inefficient banks have increased over the pre-liberalization period. Therefore, the empirical findings rule out the possibility of σ-convergence phenomenon among commercial banks in India.

Further, the empirical findings substantiate that the value of slope coefficient (σ) has noticed to be (-0.0412) in post-liberalization period. The value of coefficient has negative sign, which is statistically significant at five percent level of significance. This indicates that dispersion and inequalities of the distribution of TE scores between efficient and inefficient banks has declined overtime. Thus, the result signifies the presence of σ-convergence, which states that inefficient banks are converging towards the efficient ones in post-reforms period. Moreover, banking reforms seem to mark a significant dent on the performance measures of banks in post-reforms period.

In case of entire study period, the value of slope coefficient (σ) has been noted to be (0.01621). The value of coefficient is having positive sign, which is statistically insignificant at five percent level of significance. This states that the dispersion between the efficiency of banks has insignificantly increased over the period. Thus, it in turn indicates the presence of divergence at the place of convergence but divergence is not found to be much serious on account of positive impact of liberalization in later part of the study period.

Overall, the above regression estimates reveal that the elements of leaning by doing and the process of catching up is absent among commercial banks in India in pre-reforms period. Nevertheless, the reformatory measures have exerted favorable impact on the efficiency and productivity growth of low efficient banks as evidenced in post-reforms period. Overall, it can be stated that inefficient banks have started to try their best to converge towards efficient ones.

6.2.2 The empirical findings highlighted that value of (β) coefficient has worked out to be (-0.158) in pre-reforms period, (-0.0606) in post-reforms period and (-0.0452) in entire study period. The value of (βs) coefficients has negative sign and the coefficients are found to be significant at five percent level of significance. The findings connote that the banks with low efficiency level in initial year of the sample period have experienced high efficiency change in both the pre-reforms and post-reforms period. The banks, which were previously lagging behind, are growing at such rate, that these banks have overtaken the well performing banks. Banking sector reforms have contributed a lot in detecting efficiency and productivity gaps among efficient and inefficient banks.

Overall, it can be concluded that although the variance in efficiency measures of banks has increased over the time span of 21 years, but the high-paced growth of less efficient banks over the originally efficient ones supports the possibility of the process of catching up or convergence in the efficiency/ productivity growth of CBs in India.

The Study thus Concludes as Follows

- The banks have experienced deceleration in most of the DEA efficiency estimates and total factor productivity growth in initial phase of the post-reforms period in comparison to the pre-reforms period. Thus, first-phase of banking reforms failed to mark a significant dent on the performance level of banks in India. However, an improvement in DEA efficiency scores and productivity growth is pronounced during second half of the post-reforms period. This may be primarily caused by the fact that banks are increasingly adopt the changes in set standards and prudential norms and thereby started to realize the benefits of high degree of liberalization in quantitative form during the period 2000-06.
- The empirical findings highlight that a considerable amount of x-inefficiency has originated due to the inefficient use of scarce resources to produce a given level of output rather than selecting the incorrect combination of inputs to produce a given level of output at the given input prices. Thus, the results imply that bank managers are relatively good at selecting the optimum mix of inputs given the prices but they are not that good at using the minimum level of inputs to produce a given level of output.
- Further, the empirical findings provide that managerial irregularities have played a key role in emerging technical inefficiencies, however, the scale-related problems are not found to be much serious among commercial banks in India.
- It is worth noting that, despite larger efficiency gains by private banks, SBI group of PSBs gained the most in XE, TE, AE, SE and PTE estimates with least variability in performance levels after the

deregulation measures came into practice.

- It also emanates from the analysis that PSBs have responded better to the competitive forces and the changes in set standards and accounting norms than those of private banks on the wake of liberalization.
- Majority of sample banks have been found to be operating at below their optimum scale size and thus, experiencing increasing returns-to-scale. Therefore, there is a significant room for these banks to extract maximum possible advantages of scale economies by enhancing the size of the banks.
- The empirical evidence suggests that size has positive association with scale economies. Therefore, scale economies tend to increase with an increase in the size of banks. This may be due to the fact that the banks have witnessed several mergers and acquisitions during the study period. The merged banks invariably enhanced the size of the operations and thus, enabled to reap the benefits of scale economies.
- The empirical findings reported that commercial banks have experienced total factor productivity growth more due to the technological progress (strong frontier effect) rather than efficiency change (poor catching up effect) in most parts of the study period. Thus, failure of the banks in achieving technological mastery can safely be stated. Further, TFP growth of banks is more apparent during second-generation reforms contrary to first-generation reforms.
- PSBs are found to be more productive than private banks during the sub-periods: 1986-92 and 1993-99 but private banks did so during 2000-06. The empirical evidence also highlights an important role of technologies to the TFP gains (except during 1993-99); however, the poor diffusion process and little accumulation of knowledge through learning by doings can safely be stated among various forms of banks to absorb the enhanced technologies. Further, TFP growth of various forms of banks is more

pronounced during second-generation reforms as compared to first-generation reforms. Besides this, large banks are found to be more productive than medium and small banks.

- At disaggregate level, the empirical findings provide the evidence of significant variations in different measures of efficiency and productivity growth across distinct sub-periods. Overall, it has been observed that second-phase of liberalization have illustrated a favorable influence on the productivity growth of banks relative to initial-phase of reforms.
- Further, it has been observed that average XIE scores of CBs are significantly negatively associated with profitability, exposure to off-balance sheet activities, quality of staff and operational risk. Nevertheless, the average XIE scores are found to be significantly positively associated to size. These results also hold true among PSBs and private banks; however, the degree of statistical significance varies in a few cases.
- The σ-convergence and β-convergence results indicate the presence of catching up phenomenon among commercial banks in India. The gap between efficient and inefficient banks has noted to be declined over the time in response to liberalization. The results also highlight that the banks with low efficiency score in initial year of sample period have experienced high efficiency change in the specified sub-periods. Moreover, the banks, which were previously lagging behind, are growing at such a rate, that these banks have overtaken the well performing banks. Banking reforms have contributed a lot in detecting efficiency and productivity gaps among efficient and inefficient banks.

Suggestions

In the light of the above-mentioned empirical results, the following suggestions have been put forward:

- The empirical findings highlight that a substantial amount of XIE has occurred due to wastage of resources to produce a given level of output during various sub-periods. Therefore, appropriate steps should be taken in order to make the effective and optimum use of scarce resources.

- Further, it has been noticed that managerial irregularities have played a key role in emerging technical inefficiencies among CBs in India. This calls for the need of sharpening the managerial skills through various training programmes.
- Scale-related problems are not observed to be much serious, but, whatever amount of scale inefficiency has been worked out, appropriate steps should be taken to wipe it out to operate at the most productive scale size.
- The best practice banks are likely to be more efficient in resource utilization process than that of other ones. These banks set an example of good operating practices for inefficient banks to emulate. Therefore, the empirical findings suggest laggard banks (banks at the lower end of efficiency scale) to follow their practices to converge the efficiency gaps among the banks.
- The results further divulge that majority of the sample banks are noted to be operating at below their optimum scale size and thus, experiencing increasing returns-to-scale. As there is significant room for these banks to extract maximum possible advantages of scale economies by enhancing the size of the banks, therefore, closure of sick banks and mergers of the banks seem to be desirable in this direction. Moreover, the greater use of technology is likely to generate substantial amount of scale economies for most of the sample banks in India.
- Furthermore, the banks falling in the region of decreasing returns-to-scale are highly required to downsize the scale of their operations in order to overcome diseconomies of scale. The improvement in asset quality and priority sector lending in addition

to technological upgradation seem to be desirable for these banks.

- Although, TFP growth of CBs has improved in later parts of the study period (2000-06), but still most of the banks in India are lagging behind due to the inefficient use of scarce resources. This in turn reflects inability of the banks to catch up the best practices available in Indian banking industry. Therefore, it demands substantial changes in the working processes and sharpening of the managerial skills through various training programmes. Therefore, large investments will have to be made in information technology and human resource development programmes for imparting knowledge and inculcating special skills among workforce. The bank managers should pay key attention to make proper and optimum use of the enhanced technologies in order to augment the productivity gains. Besides this, the empirical findings suggest that appropriate steps should be undertaken in order to have improved scale of operation.
- The empirical findings further suggest the banks, come under the category of 'Best Performers' to rely more upon the advancement in technologies with a little bit improvement in the resource utilization process to achieve sustainable and technology driven growth.
- The banks that are placed in the category of 'Middle Robust Banks' have the potential to grow at a faster rate by overcoming the distortions come in the way of smooth working (e.g., lack of managerial expertise and sub-optimal or supra-optimal scale of operation, etc.). Moreover, the use of sophisticated technological measures may help these banks to augment TFP gains in future.
- The empirical findings suggest an improvement in technical efficiency or say technological mastery for those banks that fall in the category of 'Low Robust Banks'.

- The banks that come in the category of 'Worst Performers' are highly required to develop the managerial skills among the workforce to make the optimum use of resources and in turn to attain the higher productivity gains in near future.
- In today's scenario, if banks have to become effective, efficient and competitive, they have to concentrate on the factors like profitability, exposure to off-balance sheet activities, quality of staff and operational risk, since these factors are directly linked to the banks' performance in India. The banks are also required to avail the maximum returns from the productive opportunities of liberalization.

Scope for further Research

This study has covered only efficiency and productivity growth of commercial banks in India. There are certain key issues like mergers and acquisitions of banks, market structure and competition, which are highly linked with the performance of banks. Therefore, it is proposed to conduct the future research on these key issues.

In recent studies (Pastor, 2002, Drake Hall and Simper, 2006 and etc.) suggest the use of three stage sequential technique based on DEA model to compute efficiency scores. These studies suggest the decomposition of risk into internal and external factors to get efficiency measures adjusted for risk and environment. However, the present study is confined to two-stage DEA procedural method to investigate the factors influencing x-inefficiency of commercial banks in India. Thus, the future research can be conducted with the use of three-stage procedural technique.

The conventional DEA models (CCR and BCC) provide radial measure of efficiency estimates and do not take into account input-output slacks. In recent times, the researchers have proposed several extended versions of basic DEA model. These models are non-radial in nature and directly take into account input-output slacks (Tone, 2001). Accordingly, future research can be concentrated on slack-based DEA models to compute efficiency and productivity scores.

APPENDICES

TABLE 3.1

Input and Output Variables used in Existing Studies

Author's Name	*Technique*	*Inputs*	*Outputs*	*Country (Year)*
(1)	*(2)*	*(3)*	*(4)*	*(5)*
Glass and Mckillop	Translog	Labor, Capital and Deposits.	Advances and Investments	Iran (1991)
Gropper	Translog	Labor, Capital, Funds	Total Loans and Trust Accounts	America (1991)
Hunter and Timme	Translog	Labor, Capital and Funds	Total Loans and Produced Deposits	U.S. (1991)
Berg *et. al.*	Malmquist Index	Labor, Materials	Short-term Loans, Long-term Loans and Produced deposits	Norway (1992)
Yue	DEA	Interest Expenses, Non-Interest Expenses, Transaction and Non-Transaction Deposit	Total Loans, Interest Income and Non-Interest Income	U.S. (1992)
Fukuyama	DEA	Labor, Capital and Funds	Loans and Revenue from business activities	Japan (1993)
Favero and Papi	DEA	Labor, Capital, Loanable Funds and Financial Capital	Loans, Investments and Non-Interest Income	Italy (1995)

Ray and Sanyal	Translog	Labor, Physical Capital, Loanable Funds	Deposits, Loan, Investment	1994-95 (India)
Zaim	DEA	Depreciation Expenses, Interest Expenses, Expenses on Materials, Labor	Demand Deposits, Time Deposits, Short-term Loan and Long-term Loans	Turkey (1995)
Bhattcharyya *et. al.*	DEA and SFA	Interest Expenses and Operating Expenses	Labor, Deposit, Investment	India (1997)
Chatterjee Gautam	Translog	Labor, Capital, Purchased Funds	Total Operating Cost	India (1997)
De Young	DFA	Physical Capital, Labor and Borrowed Funds	Total Loans, Transaction Deposits and Fee Based Incomes	U.S. (1997)
Altumbas *et. al.*	Stochastic Frontier	Loans, Securities and Off-Balance Sheet Business	Labor, Loanable Funds and Physical Capital	Europe (1999)
Mendas	Translog	Deposit, Labor and Other Materials	Deposits and Loans	Portugal (1999)
Das	DEA	Deposits, Borrowings and Number of Employees	Margin and other income	India (2000)
Dogan and Fausten	Malmquist Index	Labor, Capital	Investment Securities, Loans and Advances, Deposits	Malaysia (2002)
Grigorian and Manole	DEA	Labor,.Fixed Assets and Interest Expenses	Revenues, Deposits with Net Loans and Liquid Assets	Transition Countries (2002)

(*Contd.*)

TABLE 3.1 (*Contd.*)

(1)	(2)	(3)	(4)	(5)
Ray and Sanyal	Translog	Labor, Capital and Physical Capital	Loans and Other Earning Assets	India (2002)
Altanbus *et. al.*	Translog	Physical Capital, Labor and Deposits	Total Cost	Europe and U.S (2003)
Hasan and Marton	Translog	Labor and Borrowed Funds	Total Loans, Investments, Fee-related Income and Total Interest-bearing Borrowed Funds	Hungary (2003)
Kumar and Verma	DEA	Labor, Physical Capital, Loanable Funds	Spread, Non-Interest Income	India (2003)
Li, Hung and Chiu	Translog	Labor, Fixed Assets and Total Deposits	Loans, Investments and Non-Interest Income	Taiwan (2003)
Sathye, M.	DEA	Model A-Interest Expense, Non-Interest Expense, Model B-Deposit, Staff	Model A-Interest Income, Non-Interest Income; Model B-Net Loans, Non-Interest Income	India (2003)
De, Prithwis Kumar	SFA	Labor, Capital, Purchased Funds	Gross Income, Earning Assets	India (2004)
Haunar	DEA	Labor and Aggregate Funds	Loans and Securities	Germany and Australia (2004)

Mohan and Ray	Malmquist Index	Interest Cost and Operating Cost	Loans, Investment, Non-Interest Income	India (2004)
Penny Neal	Malmquist Index	Bank Branches, Loanable Funds	Labor, Deposit, Non-Interest Income	Australia (2004)
Shanmugam and Das	SFA	Net Interest Margin, Non-Interest Income, Credits and Investment	Labor, Deposits, Borrowings, Fixed Assets	India (2004))
Fries and Taci Countries (2005)	SFA	Labor, Capital	Loans, Deposits	European
Singh and Kumar	DEA	Deposits and Operating Costs	Loans, Investments and Other Incomes	India (2005)
Sanjeev, G.M	DEA	Interest Expenses and Non-Interest Expenses	Interest Income and Non-Interest Income	India (2006)

TABLE 4.1
List of Sample Banks

Sl. No.	Code No.	Banks Name	Type of Ownership
(1)	(2)	(3)	(4)
1.	B1	Allahabad Bank	Public
2.	B2	Andhra Bank	Public
3.	B3	Bank of Baroda	Public
4.	B4	Bank of India	Public
5.	B5	Bank of Maharastra	Public
6.	B6	Canara Bank	Public
7.	B7	Central Bank of India	Public
8.	B8	Corporation Bank	Public
9.	B9	Dena Bank	Public
10.	B10	Indian Bank	Public
11.	B11	Indian Overseas Bank	Public
12.	B12	Oriental Bank of Commerce	Public
13.	B13	Punjab & Sind Bank	Public
14.	B14	Punjab National Bank	Public
15.	B15	Syndicate Bank	Public
16.	B16	United Commercial Bank	Public
17.	B17	Union Bank of India	Public
18.	B18	United Bank of India	Public
19.	B19	Vijaya Bank	Public
20.	B20	State Bank of India	Public
21.	B21	State Bank of Bikaner & Mysore	Public
22.	B22	State Bank of Hyderabad	Public
23.	B23	State Bank of Indore	Public
24.	B24	State Bank of Mysore	Public
25.	B25	State Bank of Patiala	Public
26.	B26	State Bank of Saurashtra	Public
27.	B27	State Bank of Travancore	Public
28.	B28	Bharat Overseas Bank	Private

(*Contd.*)

TABLE 4.1 (*Contd.*)

(1)	*(2)*	*(3)*	*(4)*
29.	B29	City Union Bank	Private
30.	B30	Ing Vysya Bank	Private
31.	B31	Karnataka Bank	Private
32.	B32	Lord Krishna Bank	Private
33.	B33	Nainital Bank	Private
34.	B34	Tamilnad Mercantile Bank	Private
35.	B35	Bank of Rajasthan	Private
36.	B36	Catholic Syrian Bank	Private
37.	B37	Dhanalaksmi Bank	Private
38.	B38	Federal Bank	Private
39.	B39	Jammu & Kashmir Bank	Private
40.	B40	Karur Vysya Bank	Private
41.	B41	Laksmi Vilas Bank	Private
42.	B42	Ratnakar Bank	Private
43.	B43	Sangli Bank	Private
44.	B44	South Indian Bank	Private
45.	B45	United Western Bank	Private

TABLE 4.2
Inter-Bank Average Technical Efficiency Scores Over the Different Time Periods

Banks/Years	*1985*	*1986*	*1987*	*1988-89*	*1989-90*	*1990-91*	*1991-92*	*1992-93*	*1993-94*	*1994-95*	*1995-96*	*1996-97*	*1997-98*
(1)	*(2)*	*(3)*	*(4)*	*(5)*	*(6)*	*(7)*	*(8)*	*(9)*	*(10)*	*(11)*	*(12)*	*(13)*	*(14)*
Allahabad Bank	0.767	0.801	0.77	0.779	0.7	0.737	0.702	0.625	0.521	0.553	0.628	0.64	0.717
Andhra Bank	0.825	0.851	0.878	0.817	0.837	0.704	0.47	0.392	0.491	0.721	0.678	0.63	0.838
Bank of Baroda	0.911	0.975	0.958	0.916	0.853	1	0.889	0.876	1	0.99	0.886	0.767	0.797
Bank of India	0.78	0.85	0.83	0.761	0.722	0.692	0.872	0.518	0.6	0.687	0.661	0.632	0.729
Bank of Maharashtra	0.847	0.815	0.755	0.799	0.84	0.654	0.539	0.4	0.501	0.682	0.874	0.796	0.881
Canara Bank	0.913	0.971	1	1	1	0.86	0.856	0.88	0.722	0.899	0.778	0.659	0.646
Central Bank of India	0.882	0.97	0.82	0.767	0.811	0.68	0.505	0.482	0.414	0.604	0.71	0.668	0.781
Corporation Bank	0.844	0.891	0.928	0.913	0.905	0.698	0.667	0.7	0.807	0.934	0.882	0.981	1
Dena Bank	0.913	0.878	0.874	0.871	0.934	0.707	0.584	0.593	0.72	0.815	0.845	0.87	0.941
Indian Bank	0.825	0.843	0.889	0.851	0.981	0.849	0.868	0.67	0.552	0.547	0.466	0.514	0.423
Indian Overseas Bank	0.835	0.881	0.808	0.761	0.736	0.847	0.717	0.71	0.94	0.52	0.496	0.485	0.571
OBC	0.917	0.897	0.958	0.958	0.956	1	0.805	0.691	0.823	0.996	0.956	0.962	0.911
Punjab and Sind Bank	0.924	1	0.908	0.842	0.788	0.632	0.453	0.362	0.506	0.654	0.503	0.565	0.695
Punjab National Bank	0.825	0.802	0.819	0.808	0.848	0.68	0.566	0.681	0.709	0.677	0.753	0.724	0.799
Syndicate Bank	0.92	0.903	1	0.909	0.86	0.687	0.604	0.436	0.649	0.67	0.745	0.685	0.701

UCO	0.809	0.844	0.764	0.734	0.618	0.542	0.477	0.52	0.352	0.592	0.543	0.46	0.529
Union Bank of India	0.774	0.907	0.902	0.823	0.85	0.659	0.627	0.624	0.737	0.772	0.764	0.717	0.814
United Bank of India	0.893	0.912	0.847	0.84	0.986	0.712	0.449	0.203	0.29	0.352	0.426	0.344	0.718
Vijaya Bank	0.901	0.914	0.932	0.894	0.986	0.715	0.589	0.697	0.704	0.686	0.561	0.626	0.687
State Bank of India	0.959	0.971	0.965	0.978	0.865	0.854	0.986	0.899	0.876	0.978	0.983	0.844	0.863
State Bank of B&J	0.811	0.842	0.799	0.863	0.742	0.731	0.964	0.899	0.867	0.876	0.936	0.915	1
State Bank of Hyderabad	0.799	0.87	0.831	0.842	0.802	0.746	0.899	0.938	0.899	0.948	0.942	0.875	0.977
State Bank of Indore	0.909	0.812	0.844	0.832	0.863	0.747	0.891	0.827	1	1	1	0.97	1
State Bank of Mysore	0.824	0.878	0.826	0.8	0.964	0.707	0.784	0.831	0.92	0.83	0.907	0.915	1
State Bank of Patiala	0.61	0.793	0.733	0.687	0.972	0.869	1	1	0.952	0.892	0.885	0.808	1
State Bank of Saurashtra	0.902	0.91	0.876	0.829	0.821	0.756	0.887	0.973	0.951	1	0.919	0.842	0.981
State Bank of Travancore	0.749	0.773	0.785	0.871	0.767	0.623	0.616	0.8	0.849	0.777	0.822	0.699	0.794
Bharat Overseas Bank	1	1	1	1	1	1	1	1	1	1	0.941	0.824	0.891
City Union Bank	0.949	0.999	1	0.826	0.876	0.811	0.773	0.846	0.808	0.809	0.824	0.781	0.676
Ing Vysya Bank	0.816	0.871	0.828	0.787	0.905	0.773	0.695	0.873	0.979	1	1	1	0.812
Karnataka Bank	0.855	0.866	0.849	0.819	0.885	0.694	0.629	0.803	0.741	0.832	0.773	0.949	0.94
Lord Krishna Bank	0.976	1	1	1	0.972	0.966	0.676	0.98	0.97	0.944	0.957	0.883	0.667
Nainital Bank	0.846	0.836	0.901	0.846	0.848	0.799	0.63	0.762	0.698	0.699	0.841	0.818	0.931
Tamilnad Mercantile Bank	1	1	1	1	1	1	1	1	1	1	1	1	1
Bank of Rajasthan	0.771	0.788	0.778	0.789	0.772	0.737	0.657	0.733	0.803	0.934	0.687	0.617	0.644
Catholic Syrian Bank	0.933	1	0.947	0.937	0.961	0.699	0.601	0.602	0.794	0.651	0.644	0.589	0.6

(Contd.)

TABLE 4.2 (*Contd.*)

(1)	(2)	(3)	(4)	(5)	(6)	(7)	(8)	(9)	(10)	(11)	(12)	(13)	(14)
Dhanalakshmi Bank	1	1	0.961	0.966	1	0.91	0.635	0.802	0.868	0.85	0.714	0.663	0.71
Federal Bank	0.94	0.883	0.909	0.688	0.993	0.681	0.563	0.552	0.678	0.863	0.817	0.646	0.664
Jammu & Kashmir Bank	1	0.859	0.859	0.812	0.731	0.601	1	1	1	1	0.967	0.766	0.976
Karur Vysya Bank	0.98	0.973	0.967	0.908	0.92	1	0.758	0.791	0.765	0.922	1	0.915	1
Lakshmi Vilas Bank	1	1	0.974	0.861	0.873	0.991	0.807	0.879	1	1	0.998	0.838	0.804
Ratnakar Bank	0.835	0.85	0.819	0.743	0.754	0.745	0.646	0.59	1	0.703	0.758	0.735	0.831
Sangli Bank	0.821	0.833	0.77	0.716	0.805	0.664	0.659	0.719	0.951	0.75	0.802	0.61	0.858
South Indian Bank	1	0.97	0.909	0.909	0.976	0.76	0.631	0.641	1	0.739	0.826	0.556	0.64
United Western Bank	0.867	0.864	0.796	0.79	0.793	0.624	0.518	0.759	0.804	0.779	0.873	0.972	0.928
All CBs													
Mean	0.877	0.897	0.879	0.848	0.868	0.768	0.714	0.724	0.783	0.803	0.799	0.750	0.808
S.D	0.084	0.070	0.080	0.084	0.098	0.123	0.166	0.194	0.193	0.161	0.159	0.161	0.149
Q1	0.824	0.844	0.819	0.790	0.802	0.687	0.601	0.602	0.698	0.686	0.710	0.632	0.695
Q3	0.933	0.971	0.958	0.909	0.964	0.849	0.868	0.876	0.951	0.944	0.936	0.875	0.940
Median	0.882	0.881	0.876	0.840	0.863	0.737	0.667	0.733	0.807	0.815	0.824	0.766	0.812
PSBs													
Mean	0.847	0.880	0.863	0.842	0.852	0.744	0.714	0.675	0.717	0.765	0.761	0.726	0.807
S.D	0.074	0.062	0.075	0.074	0.100	0.107	0.180	0.210	0.207	0.176	0.174	0.167	0.158

Q1	0.810	0.843	0.814	0.800	0.795	0.684	0.575	0.519	0.537	0.662	0.645	0.631	0.709
Q3	0.910	0.911	0.918	0.883	0.945	0.802	0.880	0.854	0.888	0.917	0.897	0.857	0.959
Median	0.844	0.878	0.847	0.840	0.850	0.712	0.702	0.691	0.722	0.772	0.778	0.717	0.799
NBs													
Mean	0.858	0.890	0.876	0.844	0.853	0.740	0.644	0.582	0.634	0.703	0.692	0.670	0.746
S.D	0.054	0.059	0.076	0.073	0.108	0.119	0.153	0.175	0.190	0.168	0.160	0.163	0.143
Q1	0.825	0.847	0.820	0.789	0.800	0.680	0.522	0.459	0.504	0.598	0.552	0.596	0.691
Q3	0.912	0.913	0.930	0.902	0.945	0.792	0.761	0.694	0.730	0.794	0.812	0.746	0.826
Median	0.847	0.891	0.878	0.840	0.850	0.704	0.604	0.624	0.649	0.682	0.710	0.659	0.729
SBI													
Mean	0.820	0.856	0.832	0.838	0.850	0.754	0.878	0.896	0.914	0.913	0.924	0.859	0.952
S.D	0.109	0.065	0.069	0.081	0.084	0.079	0.127	0.072	0.051	0.083	0.056	0.082	0.079
Q1	0.787	0.807	0.796	0.822	0.793	0.725	0.861	0.830	0.874	0.865	0.902	0.834	0.949
Q3	0.904	0.886	0.852	0.865	0.890	0.781	0.970	0.947	0.951	0.984	0.952	0.915	1.000
Median	0.818	0.856	0.829	0.837	0.842	0.747	0.895	0.899	0.910	0.920	0.928	0.860	0.991
Pvt.													
Mean	0.922	0.922	0.904	0.855	0.892	0.803	0.715	0.796	0.881	0.860	0.857	0.787	0.810
S.D	0.080	0.077	0.082	0.098	0.092	0.139	0.148	0.144	0.119	0.120	0.116	0.148	0.138
Q1	0.848	0.860	0.833	0.789	0.816	0.695	0.630	0.723	0.796	0.757	0.780	0.650	0.669
Q3	1.000	1.000	0.972	0.930	0.975	0.952	0.769	0.878	1.000	0.986	0.965	0.907	0.930
Median	0.945	0.927	0.909	0.836	0.895	0.767	0.658	0.797	0.910	0.857	0.834	0.800	0.822

(Contd.)

TABLE 4.2 (Contd.)

Banks/Years	1998-99	1999-2000	2000-01	2001-02	2002-03	2003-04	2004-05	2005-06	1986-92	1993-99	2000-06	1985-06
(1)	(15)	(16)	(17)	(18)	(19)	(20)	(21)	(22)	(23)	(24)	(25)	(26)
Allahabad Bank	0.714	0.745	0.7	0.728	0.849	0.798	0.778	0.77	0.751	0.628	0.767	0.715
Andhra Bank	0.733	0.74	0.71	0.773	0.949	0.937	1	0.811	0.769	0.640	0.846	0.752
Bank of Baroda	0.928	0.768	0.804	0.793	0.782	0.826	0.823	0.763	0.929	0.892	0.794	0.872
Bank of India	0.767	0.694	0.818	0.754	0.802	0.741	0.625	0.663	0.787	0.656	0.728	0.724
Bank of Maharashtra	0.794	0.768	0.764	0.734	0.726	0.664	0.681	0.657	0.750	0.704	0.713	0.722
Canara Bank	0.856	0.752	0.81	0.755	0.779	0.769	0.761	0.716	0.943	0.777	0.763	0.828
Central Bank of India	0.729	0.742	0.685	0.697	0.863	0.812	0.84	0.756	0.776	0.627	0.771	0.725
Corporation Bank	1	0.974	1	0.902	1	0.957	1	1	0.835	0.901	0.976	0.904
Dena Bank	0.859	0.756	0.78	0.8	0.894	1	0.767	1	0.823	0.806	0.857	0.829
Indian Bank	0.485	0.543	0.606	0.578	0.722	0.839	0.802	0.765	0.872	0.522	0.694	0.696
Indian Overseas Bank	0.619	0.625	0.678	0.729	0.769	0.815	0.88	0.872	0.798	0.620	0.767	0.728
OBC	1	0.99	1	1	1	1	0.945	0.94	0.927	0.906	0.982	0.938
Punjab and Sind Bank	0.642	0.651	0.716	0.643	0.744	0.792	0.886	0.792	0.792	0.561	0.746	0.700
Punjab National Bank	0.859	0.773	0.768	0.771	0.954	0.891	0.827	0.784	0.764	0.743	0.824	0.777
Syndicate Bank	0.675	0.761	0.827	0.831	0.918	0.738	0.77	0.74	0.840	0.652	0.798	0.763
UCO	0.563	0.667	0.654	0.675	0.683	0.663	0.612	0.595	0.684	0.508	0.650	0.614
Union Bank of India	0.741	0.714	0.811	0.84	0.824	0.75	0.729	0.826	0.792	0.738	0.785	0.772

United Bank of India	0.518	0.534	0.547	0.728	0.81	0.785	0.807	0.841	0.806	0.407	0.722	0.645
Vijaya Bank	0.714	0.738	0.732	0.726	0.885	0.908	0.834	0.795	0.847	0.668	0.803	0.773
State Bank of India	0.868	0.827	0.821	0.759	0.788	0.781	0.84	0.967	0.940	0.902	0.826	0.889
State Bank of B&J	0.947	1	1	0.983	0.965	0.973	1	0.95	0.822	0.920	0.982	0.908
State Bank of Hyderabad	1	1	1	0.896	0.881	0.896	0.753	0.921	0.827	0.940	0.907	0.891
State Bank of Indore	1	0.984	0.992	0.993	1	1	0.757	0.841	0.843	0.971	0.938	0.917
State Bank of Mysore	0.925	0.968	0.947	0.903	1	0.937	1	1	0.826	0.904	0.965	0.898
State Bank of Patiala	0.939	1	1	1	1	0.94	0.809	0.776	0.809	0.925	0.932	0.889
State Bank of Saurashtra	0.944	0.932	0.83	0.85	0.825	0.853	0.783	0.691	0.854	0.944	0.823	0.874
State Bank of Travancore	0.763	0.754	0.806	0.715	0.781	0.794	0.849	0.785	0.741	0.786	0.783	0.770
Bharat Overseas Bank	0.904	0.783	0.905	0.923	0.755	0.812	0.942	0.864	1.000	0.937	0.855	0.931
City Union Bank	1	0.978	0.875	0.806	0.785	0.866	0.76	0.828	0.891	0.821	0.843	0.851
Ing Vysya Bank	0.888	0.875	0.736	0.901	1	1	0.687	0.876	0.811	0.936	0.868	0.872
Karnataka Bank	0.778	0.647	0.752	0.94	0.796	0.886	0.877	0.749	0.800	0.831	0.807	0.812
Lord Krishna Bank	0.916	0.755	0.828	1	1	0.909	0.548	0.622	0.941	0.902	0.809	0.884
Nainital Bank	0.943	0.897	0.787	0.916	0.975	0.913	0.831	0.975	0.815	0.813	0.899	0.842
Tamilnad Mercantile Bank	1	0.909	0.999	1	0.987	1	1	1	1.000	1.000	0.985	0.995
Bank of Rajasthan	0.638	0.715	0.796	0.8	0.838	0.702	0.536	0.53	0.756	0.722	0.702	0.727
Catholic Syrian Bank	0.504	0.676	0.743	0.737	0.947	0.921	0.765	0.729	0.868	0.626	0.788	0.761
Dhanalakshmi Bank	0.63	0.761	0.77	0.868	1	0.812	0.652	0.696	0.925	0.748	0.794	0.822
Federal Bank	0.856	0.775	0.803	0.849	0.816	0.819	0.761	0.842	0.808	0.725	0.809	0.781

(Contd.)

TABLE 4.2 (*Contd.*)

(1)	(15)	(16)	(17)	(18)	(19)	(20)	(21)	(22)	(23)	(24)	(25)	(26)
Jammu & Kashmir Bank	1	0.911	0.958	1	0.926	0.816	0.783	0.851	0.837	0.958	0.892	0.896
Karur Vysya Bank	0.939	1	1	1	0.911	1	0.898	1	0.929	0.905	0.973	0.936
Lakshmi Vilas Bank	1	1	1	0.846	0.81	0.789	0.641	0.598	0.929	0.931	0.812	0.891
Ratnakar Bank	0.737	0.796	0.813	1	0.873	0.68	0.72	0.729	0.770	0.765	0.802	0.779
Sangli Bank	0.633	0.656	0.644	0.657	0.592	0.626	0.537	0.53	0.753	0.760	0.606	0.706
South Indian Bank	0.69	0.819	0.824	0.812	0.859	0.937	0.694	0.764	0.879	0.727	0.816	0.807
United Western Bank	0.816	1	0.596	0.823	0.765	0.633	0.518	0.539	0.750	0.847	0.696	0.765
All CBs												
Mean	0.810	0.808	0.814	0.832	0.863	0.844	0.785	0.794	0.836	0.782	0.820	0.813
S.D	0.153	0.133	0.124	0.114	0.103	0.107	0.129	0.131	0.073	0.143	0.092	0.087
Q1	0.714	0.738	0.736	0.737	0.785	0.785	0.720	0.729	0.787	0.668	0.767	0.752
Q3	0.939	0.932	0.905	0.916	0.954	0.937	0.849	0.872	0.879	0.905	0.868	0.889
Median	0.856	0.768	0.806	0.823	0.859	0.826	0.783	0.785	0.823	0.786	0.809	0.812
PSBs												
Mean	0.799	0.793	0.808	0.798	0.859	0.847	0.821	0.815	0.820	0.750	0.820	0.797
S.D	0.153	0.141	0.131	0.112	0.099	0.099	0.105	0.111	0.063	0.158	0.094	0.091
Q1	0.714	0.726	0.713	0.728	0.782	0.783	0.764	0.760	0.782	0.634	0.765	0.724

Q3	0.934	0.950	0.889	0.873	0.952	0.937	0.865	0.897	0.845	0.903	0.882	0.889
Median	0.794	0.756	0.806	0.771	0.849	0.826	0.809	0.792	0.822	0.743	0.798	0.773
NBs												
Mean	0.747	0.733	0.758	0.761	0.840	0.826	0.809	0.794	0.815	0.682	0.789	0.762
S.D	0.147	0.113	0.114	0.093	0.095	0.101	0.107	0.107	0.067	0.136	0.084	0.083
Q1	0.659	0.681	0.693	0.727	0.774	0.760	0.764	0.748	0.773	0.624	0.737	0.719
Q3	0.858	0.765	0.811	0.797	0.906	0.900	0.860	0.834	0.844	0.760	0.813	0.802
Median	0.733	0.742	0.764	0.754	0.824	0.812	0.807	0.784	0.798	0.656	0.771	0.752
SBI												
Mean	0.923	0.933	0.925	0.887	0.905	0.897	0.849	0.866	0.833	0.912	0.895	0.880
S.D	0.077	0.093	0.089	0.108	0.098	0.081	0.100	0.110	0.055	0.055	0.074	0.046
Q1	0.911	0.906	0.828	0.827	0.816	0.838	0.777	0.783	0.819	0.903	0.825	0.885
Q3	0.960	1.000	1.000	0.986	1.000	0.948	0.887	0.954	0.846	0.941	0.945	0.901
Median	0.942	0.976	0.970	0.900	0.923	0.917	0.825	0.881	0.827	0.923	0.919	0.890
Pvt.												
Mean	0.826	0.831	0.824	0.882	0.869	0.840	0.731	0.762	0.859	0.831	0.820	0.837
S.D	0.155	0.120	0.116	0.100	0.111	0.120	0.144	0.156	0.082	0.103	0.092	0.077
Q1	0.702	0.757	0.757	0.815	0.800	0.795	0.644	0.641	0.802	0.751	0.796	0.779
Q3	0.942	0.911	0.898	0.985	0.968	0.919	0.819	0.861	0.928	0.925	0.865	0.889
Median	0.872	0.808	0.808	0.885	0.866	0.843	0.740	0.757	0.853	0.826	0.811	0.832

Note * : S.D denotes stanadard deviation, Q1 denotes first-quartile, Q3 denotes third quartile.

TABLE 4.3

Inter-Bank Average Pure Technical Effciency Scores Over the Different Time Periods

Banks/Years	*1985*	*1986*	*1987*	*1988-89*	*1989-90*	*1990-91*	*1991-92*	*1992-93*	*1993-94*	*1994-95*	*1995-96*	*1996-97*	*1997-98*
(1)	*(2)*	*(3)*	*(4)*	*(5)*	*(6)*	*(7)*	*(8)*	*(9)*	*(10)*	*(11)*	*(12)*	*(13)*	*(14)*
Allahabad Bank	0.786	0.849	0.845	0.875	0.845	0.919	0.859	0.681	0.583	0.691	0.773	0.818	0.807
Andhra Bank	0.848	0.861	0.89	0.853	0.875	0.719	0.605	0.468	0.564	0.788	0.758	0.717	0.879
Bank of Baroda	0.995	0.99	0.961	0.928	0.89	1	0.894	0.902	1	1	0.923	0.772	0.802
Bank of India	0.832	0.864	0.831	0.771	0.747	0.727	0.881	0.548	0.601	0.689	0.667	0.641	0.73
Bank of Maharashtra	0.87	0.841	0.811	0.825	0.889	0.708	0.639	0.454	0.607	0.777	0.932	0.881	0.925
Canara Bank	1	1	1	1	1	1	0.887	0.935	0.745	0.915	0.808	0.662	0.647
Central Bank of India	0.937	0.975	0.851	0.815	0.888	0.7	0.614	0.492	0.515	0.69	0.778	0.746	0.822
Corporation Bank	0.944	0.945	0.928	0.944	0.927	0.716	0.667	0.706	0.842	0.939	0.917	1	1
Dena Bank	0.939	0.898	0.905	0.917	0.97	0.747	0.68	0.606	0.73	0.868	0.901	0.934	0.974
Indian Bank	0.862	0.847	0.892	0.866	1	0.893	0.873	0.694	0.586	0.558	0.53	0.604	0.571
Indian Overseas Bank	0.916	0.896	0.81	0.774	0.762	0.897	0.72	0.805	1	0.532	0.53	0.534	0.594
OBC	0.967	0.907	0.958	0.984	0.982	1	0.809	0.729	0.823	0.998	1	0.977	0.915
Punjab and Sind Bank	0.974	1	0.919	0.866	0.824	0.672	0.586	0.454	0.524	0.67	0.578	0.649	0.726
Punjab National Bank	0.884	0.806	0.831	0.831	0.88	0.682	0.648	0.7	0.713	0.712	0.784	0.778	0.826
Syndicate Bank	1	0.941	1	1	0.996	0.962	0.614	0.44	0.65	0.7	0.761	0.726	0.721
UCO	0.89	0.85	0.788	0.791	0.677	0.62	0.558	0.54	0.499	0.685	0.653	0.631	0.654

Union Bank of India	0.794	0.917	0.903	0.844	0.877	0.683	0.691	0.634	0.742	0.781	0.786	0.787	0.839
United Bank of India	0.95	0.913	0.862	0.873	0.992	0.718	0.572	0.386	0.473	0.567	0.593	0.564	0.761
Vijaya Bank	0.984	0.945	0.933	0.901	0.99	0.724	0.631	0.723	0.715	0.702	0.624	0.694	0.728
State Bank of India	1	1	1	1	1	1	1	1	0.954	1	1	1	1
State Bank of B&J	0.904	0.972	0.837	0.914	0.744	0.767	0.974	0.901	0.87	0.907	0.983	0.968	1
State Bank of Hyderabad	0.878	0.998	0.914	0.862	0.825	0.754	0.916	0.938	0.9	0.95	0.954	0.893	0.978
State Bank of Indore	1	0.919	0.87	0.838	0.868	0.765	0.898	0.829	1	1	1	1	1
State Bank of Mysore	0.882	0.984	0.884	0.851	1	0.778	0.816	0.833	0.923	0.848	0.94	0.939	1
State Bank of Patiala	0.616	0.797	0.771	0.723	1	0.96	1	1	0.96	0.894	0.9	0.817	1
State Bank of Saurashtra	1	1	1	1	1	0.872	0.89	0.982	0.955	1	0.92	0.849	1
State Bank of Travancore	0.782	0.796	0.786	0.922	0.772	0.627	0.648	0.801	0.892	0.778	0.845	0.745	0.805
Bharat Overseas Bank	1	1	1	1	1	1	1	1	1	1	1	0.826	0.923
City Union Bank	0.97	1	1	0.92	0.948	0.867	0.905	0.855	0.84	0.851	0.881	0.864	0.772
Ing Vysya Bank	0.828	0.893	0.846	0.814	0.911	0.786	0.743	1	0.989	1	1	1	1
Karnataka Bank	0.879	0.892	0.873	0.88	0.951	0.818	0.802	0.84	0.76	0.879	0.849	1	1
Lord Krishna Bank	1	1	1	1	1	1	1	1	1	1	1	1	0.927
Nainital Bank	0.86	0.902	0.951	0.934	0.932	0.882	0.831	0.83	0.734	0.923	0.963	0.946	1
Tamilnad Mercantile Bank	1	1	1	1	1	1	1	1	1	1	1	1	1
Bank of Rajasthan	0.779	0.792	0.784	0.821	0.804	0.756	0.746	0.742	0.808	0.939	0.735	0.738	0.714
Catholic Syrian Bank	0.941	1	1	0.938	0.966	0.745	0.734	0.651	0.811	0.788	0.804	0.786	0.811
Dhanalakshmi Bank	1	1	0.968	0.996	1	0.936	0.907	0.868	1	1	0.983	1	1

(*Contd.*)

TABLE 4.3 (*Contd.*)

(1)	(2)	(3)	(4)	(5)	(6)	(7)	(8)	(9)	(10)	(11)	(12)	(13)	(14)
Federal Bank	0.94	0.891	0.977	0.716	1	0.728	0.712	0.613	0.685	0.866	0.822	0.697	0.745
Jammu & Kashmir Bank	1	0.969	1	0.936	0.902	0.688	1	1	1	1	0.976	0.784	0.98
Karur Vysya Bank	0.981	0.983	0.992	0.974	0.975	1	0.821	0.808	0.774	0.931	1	0.976	1
Lakshmi Vilas Bank	1	1	1	1	1	1	0.928	0.955	1	1	1	1	1
Ratnakar Bank	0.875	0.855	0.899	0.842	0.936	1	1	0.752	1	1	1	1	1
Sangli Bank	0.831	0.842	0.785	0.763	0.85	0.734	0.762	0.733	0.952	0.872	0.914	0.885	1
South Indian Bank	1	0.978	0.926	0.917	1	0.784	0.731	0.648	1	0.831	0.916	0.8	0.825
United Western Bank	0.914	0.893	0.83	0.791	0.798	0.63	0.62	0.762	0.811	0.787	0.874	1	1
All CBs													
Mean	0.916	0.924	0.907	0.889	0.915	0.821	0.796	0.761	0.812	0.851	0.857	0.836	0.876
S.D	0.084	0.068	0.076	0.082	0.089	0.128	0.142	0.180	0.169	0.138	0.140	0.140	0.132
Q1	0.870	0.864	0.845	0.831	0.868	0.719	0.667	0.648	0.713	0.777	0.778	0.738	0.772
Q3	1.000	0.998	0.992	0.944	1.000	0.960	0.905	0.902	0.989	1.000	0.983	0.977	1.000
Median	0.939	0.919	0.905	0.880	0.936	0.778	0.809	0.762	0.823	0.872	0.901	0.826	0.923
PSBs													
Mean	0.905	0.915	0.888	0.880	0.897	0.800	0.762	0.710	0.754	0.801	0.809	0.790	0.841
S.D	0.090	0.068	0.070	0.076	0.098	0.126	0.145	0.191	0.176	0.147	0.151	0.142	0.138
Q1	0.866	0.856	0.834	0.835	0.835	0.712	0.635	0.544	0.594	0.691	0.713	0.678	0.729

Q3	0.979	0.980	0.931	0.925	0.994	0.908	0.889	0.867	0.912	0.927	0.928	0.914	0.989
Median	0.916	0.917	0.890	0.866	0.889	0.754	0.720	0.706	0.742	0.781	0.808	0.778	0.826
NBs													
Mean	0.914	0.908	0.890	0.877	0.895	0.794	0.707	0.626	0.680	0.751	0.752	0.743	0.785
S.D	0.068	0.059	0.064	0.071	0.094	0.131	0.120	0.158	0.156	0.139	0.143	0.134	0.122
Q1	0.866	0.856	0.838	0.828	0.860	0.704	0.614	0.480	0.574	0.687	0.639	0.645	0.724
Q3	0.971	0.945	0.931	0.923	0.986	0.908	0.834	0.715	0.744	0.828	0.855	0.803	0.859
Median	0.937	0.907	0.892	0.866	0.889	0.724	0.667	0.634	0.650	0.702	0.773	0.726	0.802
SBI													
Mean	0.883	0.933	0.883	0.889	0.901	0.815	0.893	0.911	0.932	0.922	0.943	0.901	0.973
S.D	0.133	0.088	0.087	0.092	0.112	0.122	0.117	0.082	0.043	0.081	0.054	0.092	0.068
Q1	0.854	0.889	0.824	0.848	0.812	0.762	0.872	0.832	0.898	0.883	0.915	0.841	0.995
Q3	1.000	0.999	0.936	0.942	1.000	0.894	0.981	0.987	0.956	1.000	0.987	0.976	1.000
Median	0.893	0.978	0.877	0.888	0.934	0.773	0.907	0.920	0.939	0.929	0.947	0.916	1.000
Pvt.													
Mean	0.933	0.938	0.935	0.902	0.943	0.853	0.847	0.837	0.898	0.926	0.929	0.906	0.928
S.D	0.074	0.068	0.079	0.091	0.067	0.127	0.123	0.133	0.116	0.079	0.083	0.108	0.104
Q1	0.876	0.892	0.880	0.826	0.916	0.748	0.744	0.745	0.809	0.868	0.876	0.807	0.850
Q3	1.000	1.000	1.000	0.991	1.000	1.000	0.982	0.989	1.000	1.000	1.000	1.000	1.000
Median	0.956	0.974	0.973	0.927	0.959	0.843	0.826	0.835	0.971	0.935	0.970	0.961	1.000

(*Contd.*)

TABLE 4.3 (*Contd.*)

Banks/Years	*1998-99*	*1999-2000*	*2000-01*	*2001-02*	*2002-03*	*2003-04*	*2004-05*	*2005-06*	*1986-92*	*1993-99*	*2000-06*	*1985-06*
(1)	*(15)*	*(16)*	*(17)*	*(18)*	*(19)*	*(20)*	*(21)*	*(22)*	*(23)*	*(24)*	*(25)*	*(26)*
Allahabad Bank	0.869	0.863	0.862	0.866	0.95	0.93	0.935	0.956	0.854	0.746	0.909	0.836
Andhra Bank	0.821	0.776	0.832	0.849	0.969	0.984	1	0.908	0.807	0.714	0.903	0.808
Bank of Baroda	0.958	0.775	0.817	0.814	0.814	0.851	0.838	0.799	0.951	0.908	0.815	0.892
Bank of India	0.771	0.696	0.819	0.756	0.808	0.753	0.662	0.68	0.808	0.664	0.739	0.737
Bank of Maharashtra	0.864	0.854	0.868	0.833	0.823	0.801	0.831	0.729	0.798	0.777	0.820	0.798
Canara Bank	0.954	0.777	0.835	0.759	0.78	0.786	0.766	0.719	0.984	0.809	0.775	0.856
Central Bank of India	0.791	0.829	0.793	0.819	0.892	0.859	0.921	0.771	0.826	0.691	0.841	0.786
Corporation Bank	1	1	1	0.904	1	0.978	1	1	0.867	0.915	0.983	0.922
Dena Bank	0.947	0.817	0.984	0.907	0.987	1	0.967	1	0.865	0.851	0.952	0.889
Indian Bank	0.593	0.615	0.654	0.585	0.759	0.861	0.833	0.788	0.890	0.591	0.728	0.736
Indian Overseas Bank	0.66	0.665	0.71	0.738	0.788	0.821	0.885	0.874	0.825	0.665	0.783	0.758
OBC	1	1	1	1	1	1	0.964	0.954	0.944	0.920	0.988	0.951
Punjab and Sind Bank	0.707	0.691	0.769	0.697	0.803	0.84	0.963	0.806	0.834	0.615	0.796	0.748
Punjab National Bank	0.876	0.822	0.81	0.822	0.962	0.91	0.862	0.793	0.795	0.770	0.854	0.806
Syndicate Bank	0.716	0.809	0.893	0.882	0.932	0.769	0.819	0.796	0.930	0.673	0.843	0.816
UCO	0.72	0.775	0.758	0.691	0.737	0.716	0.693	0.669	0.739	0.626	0.720	0.695
Union Bank of India	0.818	0.775	0.87	0.901	0.868	0.818	0.815	0.889	0.816	0.770	0.848	0.811

United Bank of India	0.62	0.64	0.677	0.76	0.865	0.859	0.902	0.894	0.840	0.566	0.800	0.735
Vijaya Bank	0.769	0.786	0.782	0.808	0.915	0.932	0.9	0.849	0.873	0.708	0.853	0.811
State Bank of India	1	1	1	0.817	0.85	1	1	1	1.000	0.993	0.952	0.982
State Bank of B&J	0.965	1	1	0.985	0.969	0.989	1	0.963	0.873	0.942	0.987	0.934
State Bank of Hyderabad	1	1	1	0.896	0.9	0.901	0.795	0.938	0.878	0.945	0.919	0.914
State Bank of Indore	1	1	1	1	1	1	0.801	0.855	0.880	0.976	0.951	0.935
State Bank of Mysore	0.948	0.969	0.962	0.905	1	0.993	1	1	0.885	0.919	0.976	0.926
State Bank of Patiala	0.939	1	1	1	1	1	0.824	0.797	0.838	0.930	0.946	0.905
State Bank of Saurashtra	1	0.941	0.831	0.858	0.832	0.859	0.794	0.695	0.966	0.958	0.830	0.918
State Bank of Travancore	0.78	0.754	0.808	0.724	0.794	0.797	0.875	0.785	0.762	0.807	0.791	0.786
Bharat Overseas Bank	0.963	0.849	0.988	0.93	0.834	0.943	1	0.956	1.000	0.959	0.929	0.962
City Union Bank	1	0.98	0.908	0.814	0.833	0.931	0.915	0.893	0.944	0.866	0.896	0.902
Ing Vysya Bank	0.898	0.881	0.74	0.902	1	1	0.812	0.902	0.832	0.984	0.891	0.902
Karnataka Bank	0.964	0.807	0.877	0.948	0.845	0.908	0.935	0.906	0.871	0.899	0.889	0.886
Lord Krishna Bank	0.961	0.935	0.873	1	1	0.931	0.767	0.788	1.000	0.984	0.899	0.961
Nainital Bank	1	1	1	1	1	1	1	1	0.899	0.914	1.000	0.938
Tamilnad Mercantile Bank	1	0.927	1	1	1	1	1	1	1.000	1.000	0.990	0.997
Bank of Rajasthan	0.733	0.796	0.899	0.832	0.895	0.766	0.762	0.774	0.783	0.773	0.818	0.791
Catholic Syrian Bank	0.757	0.799	0.878	0.762	0.959	1	0.967	0.948	0.903	0.773	0.902	0.859
Dhanalakshmi Bank	0.95	0.951	0.957	0.907	1	1	1	0.966	0.972	0.972	0.969	0.971
Federal Bank	0.861	0.782	0.81	0.852	0.828	0.829	0.803	0.868	0.852	0.756	0.825	0.811

(Contd.)

TABLE 4.3 (Contd.)

(1)	(15)	(16)	(17)	(18)	(19)	(20)	(21)	(22)	(23)	(24)	(25)	(26)
Jammu & Kashmir Bank	1	0.915	1	1	1	1	0.826	0.886	0.928	0.963	0.947	0.946
Karur Vysya Bank	1	1	1	1	0.923	1	0.943	1	0.961	0.927	0.981	0.956
Lakshmi Vilas Bank	1	1	1	0.864	0.866	0.938	0.928	0.944	0.990	0.994	0.934	0.973
Ratnakar Bank	1	1	1	1	1	1	1	1	0.915	0.965	1.000	0.960
Sangli Bank	0.947	0.861	0.964	0.975	0.99	0.957	0.986	1	0.795	0.900	0.962	0.886
South Indian Bank	0.903	0.916	0.944	0.895	0.99	1	1	0.981	0.905	0.846	0.961	0.904
United Western Bank	0.819	1	0.705	0.84	0.767	0.66	0.648	0.634	0.782	0.865	0.751	0.799
All CBs												
Mean	0.885	0.867	0.886	0.869	0.905	0.908	0.888	0.875	0.875	0.875	0.875	0.875
S.D	0.119	0.114	0.104	0.101	0.086	0.094	0.100	0.106	0.072	0.126	0.082	0.081
Q1	0.791	0.782	0.810	0.814	0.832	0.840	0.815	0.793	0.826	0.756	0.820	0.806
Q3	1.000	1.000	1.000	0.948	1.000	1.000	0.986	0.963	0.944	0.945	0.952	0.935
Median	0.947	0.861	0.878	0.866	0.915	0.931	0.902	0.893	0.873	0.866	0.899	0.889
PSBs												
Mean	0.855	0.838	0.864	0.836	0.889	0.889	0.876	0.848	0.864	0.794	0.863	0.840
S.D	0.129	0.125	0.108	0.103	0.087	0.090	0.095	0.105	0.066	0.132	0.084	0.080
Q1	0.770	0.775	0.801	0.760	0.811	0.820	0.817	0.787	0.820	0.682	0.798	0.786
Q3	0.962	0.985	0.992	0.903	0.969	0.987	0.964	0.946	0.888	0.920	0.948	0.916

Median	0.869	0.817	0.835	0.833	0.892	0.861	0.875	0.849	0.865	0.777	0.848	0.816
NBs												
Mean	0.813	0.788	0.828	0.810	0.876	0.867	0.871	0.835	0.855	0.736	0.839	0.810
S.D	0.125	0.103	0.098	0.095	0.087	0.086	0.096	0.101	0.062	0.109	0.079	0.069
Q1	0.718	0.736	0.776	0.758	0.806	0.810	0.825	0.780	0.812	0.664	0.789	0.753
Q3	0.912	0.826	0.869	0.874	0.956	0.931	0.949	0.901	0.882	0.793	0.879	0.846
Median	0.818	0.777	0.819	0.819	0.868	0.859	0.885	0.806	0.840	0.714	0.841	0.808
SBI												
Mean	0.954	0.958	0.950	0.898	0.918	0.942	0.886	0.879	0.885	0.934	0.919	0.913
S.D	0.075	0.085	0.082	0.098	0.085	0.080	0.098	0.113	0.073	0.057	0.071	0.056
Q1	0.946	0.962	0.929	0.848	0.846	0.891	0.800	0.794	0.864	0.927	0.896	0.912
Q3	1.000	1.000	1.000	0.989	1.000	1.000	1.000	0.972	0.905	0.962	0.958	0.934
Median	0.983	1.000	1.000	0.901	0.935	0.991	0.850	0.897	0.879	0.943	0.948	0.922
Pvt.												
Mean	0.931	0.911	0.919	0.918	0.929	0.937	0.905	0.914	0.907	0.908	0.919	0.911
S.D	0.086	0.079	0.092	0.077	0.081	0.095	0.108	0.099	0.075	0.080	0.068	0.063
Q1	0.899	0.852	0.877	0.855	0.850	0.931	0.816	0.888	0.857	0.865	0.892	0.886
Q3	1.000	0.995	1.000	1.000	1.000	1.000	1.000	0.995	0.970	0.970	0.967	0.961
Median	0.962	0.922	0.951	0.919	0.975	0.979	0.939	0.946	0.910	0.920	0.931	0.921

*Note** : S.D. denotes stanadard deviation, Q1 denotes first-quartile, Q3 denotes third quartile.

TABLE 4.4

Inter-Bank Average Scale Efficiency Scores Over the Different Time Periods

Banks/Years	*1985*	*1986*	*1987*	*1988-89*	*1989-90*	*1990-91*	*1991-92*	*1992-93*	*1993-94*	*1994-95*	*1995-96*	*1996-97*	*1997-98*
(1)	*(2)*	*(3)*	*(4)*	*(5)*	*(6)*	*(7)*	*(8)*	*(9)*	*(10)*	*(11)*	*(12)*	*(13)*	*(14)*
Allahabad Bank	0.976	0.943	0.911	0.891	0.829	0.802	0.817	0.918	0.895	0.8	0.812	0.782	0.888
Andhra Bank	0.973	0.988	0.986	0.958	0.956	0.979	0.777	0.838	0.872	0.916	0.894	0.878	0.954
Bank of Baroda	0.915	0.985	0.997	0.986	0.958	1	0.994	0.971	1	0.99	0.96	0.994	0.993
Bank of India	0.938	0.983	0.998	0.987	0.966	0.952	0.99	0.946	0.998	0.997	0.99	0.985	0.999
Bank of Maharashtra	0.973	0.97	0.93	0.968	0.944	0.923	0.845	0.882	0.825	0.877	0.938	0.903	0.952
Canara Bank	0.913	0.971	1	1	1	0.86	0.964	0.941	0.969	0.982	0.962	0.997	0.998
Central Bank of India	0.942	0.994	0.963	0.941	0.914	0.972	0.823	0.979	0.804	0.876	0.912	0.895	0.949
Corporation Bank	0.894	0.943	1	0.967	0.976	0.974	1	0.991	0.959	0.995	0.961	0.981	1
Dena Bank	0.972	0.978	0.966	0.949	0.963	0.946	0.858	0.979	0.986	0.939	0.938	0.932	0.966
Indian Bank	0.957	0.995	0.996	0.984	0.981	0.951	0.995	0.964	0.942	0.981	0.88	0.851	0.741
Indian Overseas Bank	0.911	0.983	0.998	0.984	0.967	0.945	0.995	0.882	0.94	0.979	0.936	0.909	0.961
OBC	0.949	0.989	0.999	0.973	0.973	1	0.995	0.948	0.999	0.997	0.956	0.985	0.996
Punjab and Sind Bank	0.949	1	0.987	0.972	0.956	0.94	0.772	0.797	0.965	0.977	0.869	0.87	0.957
Punjab National Bank	0.933	0.995	0.985	0.972	0.963	0.997	0.874	0.972	0.994	0.951	0.961	0.93	0.967
Syndicate Bank	0.92	0.959	1	0.909	0.863	0.714	0.983	0.99	0.997	0.957	0.98	0.943	0.972

UCO	0.909	0.993	0.971	0.929	0.912	0.874	0.854	0.961	0.705	0.864	0.832	0.729	0.808
Union Bank of India	0.975	0.989	0.999	0.975	0.968	0.965	0.907	0.984	0.994	0.989	0.972	0.911	0.97
United Bank of India	0.94	0.999	0.984	0.963	0.994	0.991	0.784	0.526	0.613	0.62	0.719	0.61	0.943
Vijaya Bank	0.916	0.967	0.999	0.992	0.997	0.989	0.932	0.964	0.985	0.977	0.899	0.902	0.944
State Bank of India	0.959	0.971	0.965	0.978	0.865	0.854	0.986	0.899	0.918	0.978	0.983	0.844	0.863
State Bank of B&J	0.897	0.867	0.955	0.944	0.997	0.953	0.99	0.998	0.997	0.966	0.952	0.946	1
State Bank of Hyderabad	0.911	0.872	0.908	0.977	0.973	0.989	0.981	1	1	0.998	0.988	0.981	0.999
State Bank of Indore	0.909	0.884	0.971	0.993	0.994	0.977	0.992	0.998	1	1	1	0.97	1
State Bank of Mysore	0.933	0.892	0.934	0.94	0.964	0.909	0.96	0.998	0.997	0.978	0.965	0.974	1
State Bank of Patiala	0.989	0.994	0.952	0.95	0.972	0.905	1	1	0.992	0.999	0.984	0.989	1
State Bank of Saurashtra	0.902	0.91	0.876	0.829	0.821	0.868	0.996	0.991	0.996	1	1	0.992	0.981
State Bank of Travancore	0.958	0.971	1	0.944	0.993	0.993	0.952	0.998	0.951	0.999	0.973	0.938	0.986
Bharat Overseas Bank	1	1	1	1	1	1	1	1	1	1	0.941	0.997	0.965
City Union Bank	0.978	0.999	1	0.897	0.924	0.935	0.855	0.99	0.963	0.951	0.936	0.904	0.876
Ing Vysya Bank	0.986	0.976	0.979	0.966	0.993	0.983	0.936	0.873	0.99	1	1	1	0.812
Karnataka Bank	0.973	0.972	0.973	0.93	0.931	0.848	0.784	0.956	0.975	0.946	0.911	0.949	0.94
Lord Krishna Bank	0.976	1	1	1	0.972	0.966	0.676	0.98	0.97	0.944	0.957	0.883	0.719
Nainital Bank	0.983	0.927	0.948	0.906	0.91	0.906	0.758	0.918	0.951	0.757	0.873	0.864	0.931
Tamilnad Mercantile Bank	1	1	1	1	1	1	1	1	1	1	1	1	1
Bank of Rajasthan	0.991	0.995	0.992	0.961	0.96	0.975	0.881	0.989	0.993	0.995	0.935	0.835	0.902
Catholic Syrian Bank	0.991	1	0.948	0.998	0.995	0.938	0.818	0.925	0.979	0.826	0.801	0.749	0.74

(Contd.)

Table 4.4 (*Contd.*)

(1)	(2)	(3)	(4)	(5)	(6)	(7)	(8)	(9)	(10)	(11)	(12)	(13)	(14)
Dhanalakshmi Bank	1	1	0.993	0.97	1	0.972	0.7	0.924	0.868	0.85	0.726	0.663	0.71
Federal Bank	1	0.99	0.93	0.961	0.993	0.935	0.791	0.901	0.99	0.996	0.994	0.927	0.891
Jammu & Kashmir Bank	1	0.886	0.859	0.867	0.811	0.874	1	1	1	1	0.991	0.977	0.996
Karur Vysya Bank	1	0.99	0.975	0.932	0.944	1	0.923	0.979	0.989	0.991	1	0.937	1
Lakshmi Vilas Bank	1	1	0.974	0.861	0.873	0.991	0.869	0.92	1	1	0.998	0.838	0.804
Ratnakar Bank	0.954	0.994	0.911	0.882	0.805	0.745	0.646	0.784	1	0.703	0.758	0.735	0.831
Sangli Bank	0.988	0.99	0.981	0.939	0.947	0.905	0.865	0.981	0.998	0.86	0.877	0.689	0.858
South Indian Bank	1	0.992	0.982	0.991	0.976	0.969	0.863	0.99	1	0.889	0.901	0.694	0.776
United Western Bank	0.949	0.968	0.959	0.999	0.994	0.991	0.835	0.996	0.992	0.99	1	0.972	0.928
All CBs													
Mean	0.957	0.970	0.970	0.954	0.949	0.937	0.894	0.943	0.955	0.940	0.929	0.894	0.921
S.D	0.034	0.038	0.035	0.041	0.055	0.067	0.099	0.083	0.080	0.087	0.074	0.102	0.087
Q1	0.933	0.968	0.955	0.939	0.931	0.906	0.823	0.920	0.951	0.916	0.899	0.851	0.876
Q3	0.988	0.995	0.998	0.984	0.993	0.989	0.990	0.991	0.998	0.997	0.984	0.977	0.996
Median	0.959	0.988	0.981	0.966	0.966	0.953	0.907	0.972	0.990	0.978	0.956	0.927	0.954
PSBs													
Mean	0.938	0.962	0.971	0.958	0.950	0.934	0.927	0.938	0.937	0.947	0.934	0.912	0.955
S.D	0.028	0.041	0.034	0.036	0.050	0.068	0.081	0.098	0.097	0.083	0.065	0.090	0.063

Q1	0.912	0.951	0.959	0.944	0.950	0.907	0.856	0.930	0.929	0.945	0.906	0.887	0.951
Q3	0.959	0.991	0.999	0.981	0.979	0.984	0.993	0.991	0.997	0.996	0.977	0.981	0.999
Median	0.938	0.978	0.985	0.968	0.966	0.952	0.964	0.971	0.985	0.978	0.960	0.932	0.970
NBs													
Mean	0.940	0.980	0.983	0.963	0.952	0.935	0.903	0.918	0.918	0.930	0.914	0.894	0.945
S.D	0.026	0.017	0.025	0.028	0.044	0.075	0.085	0.109	0.110	0.093	0.069	0.098	0.067
Q1	0.916	0.971	0.978	0.954	0.950	0.932	0.834	0.900	0.884	0.897	0.887	0.874	0.947
Q3	0.965	0.994	0.999	0.984	0.975	0.984	0.992	0.976	0.994	0.986	0.961	0.962	0.983
Median	0.940	0.985	0.996	0.972	0.963	0.952	0.907	0.961	0.965	0.977	0.938	0.909	0.961
SBI													
Mean	0.932	0.920	0.945	0.944	0.947	0.931	0.982	0.985	0.981	0.990	0.981	0.954	0.979
S.D	0.033	0.051	0.039	0.051	0.067	0.055	0.017	0.035	0.030	0.014	0.017	0.049	0.047
Q1	0.907	0.881	0.928	0.943	0.939	0.896	0.976	0.996	0.982	0.978	0.971	0.944	0.985
Q3	0.958	0.971	0.967	0.977	0.993	0.980	0.993	0.999	0.998	0.999	0.991	0.983	1.000
Median	0.922	0.901	0.954	0.947	0.973	0.931	0.988	0.998	0.997	0.999	0.984	0.972	1.000
Pvt.													
Mean	0.987	0.982	0.967	0.948	0.946	0.941	0.844	0.950	0.981	0.928	0.922	0.867	0.871
S.D	0.016	0.030	0.037	0.048	0.062	0.066	0.107	0.057	0.032	0.093	0.086	0.116	0.096
Q1	0.979	0.980	0.951	0.912	0.926	0.913	0.786	0.921	0.976	0.867	0.883	0.771	0.806
Q3	1.000	1.000	0.993	0.996	0.994	0.989	0.913	0.990	1.000	0.999	0.997	0.966	0.938
Median	0.991	0.993	0.977	0.961	0.966	0.968	0.859	0.980	0.991	0.971	0.939	0.894	0.884

(Contd.)

TABLE 4.4 (*Contd.*)

Banks/Years	*1998-99*	*1999-2000*	*2000-01*	*2001-02*	*2002-03*	*2003-04*	*2004-05*	*2005-06*	*1986-92*	*1993-99*	*2000-06*	*1985-06*
(1)	*(15)*	*(16)*	*(17)*	*(18)*	*(19)*	*(20)*	*(21)*	*(22)*	*(23)*	*(24)*	*(25)*	*(26)*
Allahabad Bank	0.822	0.864	0.811	0.84	0.894	0.858	0.832	0.805	0.881	0.845	0.843	0.857
Andhra Bank	0.893	0.953	0.854	0.911	0.979	0.952	1	0.894	0.945	0.892	0.935	0.924
Bank of Baroda	0.969	0.991	0.984	0.974	0.961	0.971	0.982	0.955	0.976	0.982	0.974	0.978
Bank of India	0.995	0.997	0.999	0.997	0.992	0.984	0.945	0.974	0.973	0.987	0.984	0.982
Bank of Maharashtra	0.918	0.899	0.88	0.881	0.883	0.829	0.819	0.901	0.936	0.899	0.870	0.902
Canara Bank	0.896	0.968	0.97	0.995	0.999	0.978	0.994	0.996	0.958	0.964	0.986	0.969
Central Bank of India	0.921	0.895	0.864	0.851	0.967	0.945	0.911	0.981	0.936	0.905	0.916	0.919
Corporation Bank	1	0.974	1	0.997	1	0.979	1	1	0.965	0.984	0.993	0.981
Dena Bank	0.907	0.925	0.793	0.882	0.906	1	0.793	1	0.947	0.950	0.900	0.932
Indian Bank	0.819	0.883	0.928	0.988	0.951	0.975	0.962	0.971	0.980	0.883	0.951	0.938
Indian Overseas Bank	0.938	0.941	0.954	0.988	0.976	0.994	0.995	0.999	0.969	0.935	0.978	0.961
OBC	1	0.99	1	1	1	1	0.981	0.985	0.983	0.983	0.994	0.986
Punjab and Sind Bank	0.907	0.942	0.932	0.924	0.926	0.943	0.92	0.982	0.939	0.906	0.938	0.928
Punjab National Bank	0.981	0.94	0.949	0.938	0.991	0.979	0.959	0.989	0.960	0.965	0.964	0.963
Syndicate Bank	0.943	0.942	0.927	0.942	0.986	0.96	0.94	0.93	0.907	0.969	0.947	0.941
UCO	0.782	0.861	0.862	0.978	0.927	0.925	0.883	0.89	0.920	0.812	0.904	0.879

Union Bank of India	0.906	0.921	0.932	0.933	0.95	0.916	0.894	0.929	0.968	0.961	0.925	0.951
United Bank of India	0.835	0.835	0.808	0.958	0.937	0.913	0.895	0.941	0.951	0.695	0.898	0.848
Vijaya Bank	0.929	0.939	0.935	0.898	0.967	0.975	0.927	0.937	0.970	0.943	0.940	0.951
State Bank of India	0.868	0.827	0.821	0.928	0.927	0.781	0.84	0.967	0.940	0.908	0.870	0.906
State Bank of B&J	0.981	1	1	0.998	0.995	0.984	1	0.986	0.943	0.977	0.995	0.972
State Bank of Hyderabad	1	1	1	1	0.979	0.995	0.948	0.982	0.944	0.995	0.986	0.975
State Bank of Indore	1	0.984	0.992	0.993	1	1	0.944	0.983	0.960	0.995	0.985	0.980
State Bank of Mysore	0.975	0.998	0.985	0.997	1	0.944	1	1	0.933	0.984	0.989	0.969
State Bank of Patiala	1	1	1	1	1	0.94	0.982	0.974	0.966	0.995	0.985	0.982
State Bank of Saurashtra	0.944	0.991	0.999	0.991	0.991	0.993	0.985	0.994	0.886	0.986	0.992	0.955
State Bank of Travancore	0.978	0.999	0.998	0.986	0.983	0.995	0.971	0.999	0.973	0.975	0.990	0.979
Bharat Overseas Bank	0.938	0.923	0.916	0.992	0.905	0.861	0.942	0.903	1.000	0.977	0.920	0.966
City Union Bank	1	0.998	0.963	0.991	0.942	0.93	0.831	0.927	0.941	0.946	0.940	0.942
Ing Vysya Bank	0.989	0.994	0.995	0.999	1	1	0.846	0.971	0.974	0.952	0.972	0.966
Karnataka Bank	0.807	0.801	0.857	0.991	0.942	0.976	0.938	0.827	0.916	0.926	0.905	0.916
Lord Krishna Bank	0.953	0.807	0.949	1	1	0.976	0.714	0.789	0.941	0.915	0.891	0.916
Nainital Bank	0.943	0.897	0.787	0.916	0.975	0.913	0.831	0.975	0.905	0.891	0.899	0.899
Tamilnad Mercantile Bank	1	0.981	0.999	1	0.987	1	1	1	1.000	1.000	0.995	0.998
Bank of Rajasthan	0.871	0.899	0.886	0.961	0.936	0.917	0.704	0.684	0.965	0.931	0.855	0.917
Catholic Syrian Bank	0.666	0.846	0.846	0.967	0.987	0.921	0.791	0.769	0.955	0.812	0.875	0.881

(Contd.)

TABLE 4.4 (*Contd.*)

(1)	(15)	(16)	(17)	(18)	(19)	(20)	(21)	(22)	(23)	(24)	(25)	(26)
Dhanalakshmi Bank	0.664	0.8	0.805	0.957	1	0.812	0.652	0.721	0.948	0.772	0.821	0.847
Federal Bank	0.995	0.991	0.992	0.997	0.986	0.988	0.948	0.97	0.943	0.956	0.982	0.960
Jammu & Kashmir Bank	1	0.996	0.958	1	0.926	0.816	0.948	0.96	0.900	0.995	0.943	0.946
Karur Vysya Bank	0.939	1	1	1	0.987	1	0.952	1	0.966	0.976	0.991	0.978
Lakshmi Vilas Bank	1	1	1	0.98	0.935	0.841	0.69	0.634	0.938	0.937	0.869	0.915
Ratnakar Bank	0.737	0.796	0.813	1	0.873	0.68	0.72	0.729	0.848	0.793	0.802	0.814
Sangli Bank	0.669	0.762	0.668	0.673	0.598	0.654	0.545	0.53	0.945	0.847	0.633	0.808
South Indian Bank	0.764	0.895	0.873	0.908	0.868	0.937	0.694	0.778	0.968	0.859	0.850	0.892
United Western Bank	0.997	1	0.845	0.98	0.997	0.96	0.8	0.851	0.956	0.982	0.919	0.953
All CBs												
Mean	0.912	0.930	0.918	0.957	0.953	0.931	0.886	0.910	0.947	0.928	0.926	0.934
S.D	0.097	0.071	0.081	0.062	0.066	0.081	0.113	0.113	0.030	0.069	0.070	0.047
Q1	0.871	0.895	0.857	0.933	0.935	0.916	0.831	0.890	0.938	0.899	0.898	0.915
Q3	0.995	0.994	0.995	0.997	0.992	0.984	0.971	0.985	0.968	0.982	0.985	0.969
Median	0.939	0.942	0.935	0.986	0.976	0.960	0.938	0.967	0.948	0.950	0.940	0.946
PSBs												
Mean	0.930	0.943	0.932	0.954	0.965	0.952	0.937	0.961	0.949	0.936	0.949	0.945
S.D	0.063	0.054	0.070	0.050	0.035	0.054	0.061	0.046	0.026	0.068	0.045	0.039

Q1	0.901	0.910	0.872	0.926	0.944	0.942	0.903	0.939	0.938	0.906	0.921	0.926
Q3	0.981	0.991	0.999	0.996	0.994	0.989	0.984	0.992	0.969	0.983	0.986	0.976
Median	0.938	0.942	0.949	0.978	0.979	0.975	0.948	0.981	0.951	0.964	0.964	0.955
NBs												
Mean	0.914	0.929	0.915	0.941	0.957	0.951	0.928	0.950	0.951	0.919	0.939	0.936
S.D	0.064	0.047	0.067	0.052	0.037	0.046	0.063	0.051	0.027	0.073	0.043	0.041
Q1	0.895	0.897	0.863	0.905	0.932	0.934	0.895	0.930	0.938	0.896	0.910	0.922
Q3	0.956	0.961	0.962	0.988	0.989	0.979	0.982	0.987	0.970	0.967	0.976	0.966
Median	0.918	0.940	0.932	0.942	0.967	0.971	0.940	0.971	0.958	0.943	0.940	0.941
SBI												
Mean	0.968	0.975	0.974	0.987	0.984	0.954	0.959	0.986	0.943	0.977	0.974	0.965
S.D	0.045	0.060	0.062	0.024	0.025	0.074	0.052	0.012	0.027	0.029	0.042	0.025
Q1	0.967	0.989	0.990	0.990	0.982	0.943	0.947	0.980	0.938	0.977	0.985	0.965
Q3	1.000	1.000	1.000	0.999	1.000	0.995	0.989	0.995	0.962	0.995	0.991	0.980
Median	0.980	0.999	0.999	0.995	0.993	0.989	0.977	0.985	0.944	0.985	0.988	0.974
Pvt.												
Mean	0.885	0.910	0.897	0.962	0.936	0.899	0.808	0.834	0.945	0.915	0.892	0.917
S.D	0.130	0.088	0.094	0.077	0.094	0.104	0.129	0.139	0.036	0.071	0.086	0.054
Q1	0.775	0.817	0.845	0.963	0.928	0.846	0.707	0.739	0.939	0.867	0.859	0.894
Q3	0.997	0.996	0.985	1.000	0.987	0.976	0.941	0.968	0.966	0.971	0.943	0.958
Median	0.941	0.911	0.901	0.991	0.959	0.926	0.816	0.839	0.946	0.934	0.902	0.917

*Note** : S.D denotes stanadard deviation, Q1 denotes first-quartile, Q3 denotes third quartile.

TABLE 4.5

Inter-Bank Average Allocative Efficiency Scores Over the Different Time Periods

Banks/Years	*1985*	*1986*	*1987*	*1988-89*	*1989-90*	*1990-91*	*1991-92*	*1992-93*	*1993-94*	*1994-95*	*1995-96*	*1996-97*	*1997-98*
(1)	*(2)*	*(3)*	*(4)*	*(5)*	*(6)*	*(7)*	*(8)*	*(9)*	*(10)*	*(11)*	*(12)*	*(13)*	*(14)*
Allahabad Bank	0.888	0.845	0.767	0.673	0.719	0.798	0.917	0.958	0.967	0.991	0.93	0.95	0.986
Andhra Bank	0.835	0.827	0.87	0.855	0.842	0.823	0.985	0.949	0.951	0.937	0.905	0.933	0.983
Bank of Baroda	0.752	0.684	0.643	0.6	0.65	0.808	0.691	0.831	0.953	0.982	0.998	0.92	1
Bank of India	0.733	0.652	0.625	0.589	0.634	0.727	0.756	0.979	0.971	0.987	0.959	0.996	0.998
Bank of Maharashtra	0.899	0.897	0.86	0.878	0.863	0.89	0.945	0.896	0.889	0.935	0.858	0.896	0.959
Canara Bank	0.841	0.819	0.825	0.803	0.785	0.745	0.959	0.991	0.966	0.987	0.951	0.98	0.987
Central Bank of India	0.802	0.793	0.805	0.785	0.816	0.767	0.99	0.961	0.909	0.977	0.887	0.917	0.97
Corporation Bank	0.969	0.954	0.923	0.893	0.883	0.858	0.988	0.999	1	0.905	0.999	0.89	0.997
Dena Bank	0.922	0.927	0.879	0.857	0.888	0.905	0.95	0.959	0.92	0.975	0.92	0.943	0.987
Indian Bank	0.741	0.676	0.673	0.596	0.636	0.69	0.747	0.757	0.997	0.995	0.939	0.966	0.909
Indian Overseas Bank	0.811	0.776	0.783	0.707	0.769	0.877	0.954	0.981	0.997	0.992	0.963	0.974	0.994
OBC	0.859	0.884	0.854	0.803	0.799	0.701	0.823	0.975	0.995	0.991	0.94	0.879	0.995
Punjab and Sind Bank	0.892	0.935	0.886	0.85	0.855	0.893	0.989	0.945	0.919	0.995	0.942	0.955	0.985
Punjab National Bank	0.81	0.805	0.793	0.769	0.809	0.747	0.905	0.991	0.932	0.994	0.909	0.923	0.975
Syndicate Bank	0.863	0.876	0.916	0.89	0.896	0.947	0.933	0.907	0.888	0.922	0.861	0.877	0.952

UCO	0.972	0.951	0.875	0.762	0.757	0.864	0.954	0.963	0.921	0.957	0.852	0.867	0.92
Union Bank of India	0.916	0.902	0.898	0.872	0.867	0.888	0.993	0.984	0.951	0.997	0.971	0.985	0.997
United Bank of India	0.829	0.86	0.874	0.838	0.894	0.813	0.977	0.991	0.999	0.899	0.874	0.926	0.982
Vijaya Bank	0.983	0.974	0.91	0.771	0.829	0.886	0.942	0.915	0.927	0.975	0.921	0.927	0.976
State Bank of India	0.889	0.836	0.79	0.722	0.768	0.873	0.915	0.997	0.95	0.967	0.9	0.937	0.973
State Bank of B&J	0.989	0.979	0.994	0.889	0.907	0.987	0.905	0.898	0.895	0.888	0.829	0.866	0.953
State Bank of Hyderabad	0.977	0.994	0.998	0.88	0.903	0.955	0.981	0.979	0.955	0.987	0.924	0.953	0.983
State Bank of Indore	0.959	0.988	0.883	0.836	0.874	0.941	0.939	0.936	0.926	0.97	0.885	0.895	0.963
State Bank of Mysore	0.977	0.977	0.961	0.958	0.966	0.987	0.907	0.927	0.895	0.964	0.867	0.897	0.955
State Bank of Patiala	0.93	0.612	0.977	0.909	0.888	0.92	1	1	0.956	0.967	0.944	0.957	0.989
State Bank of Saurashtra	0.982	0.997	0.982	0.985	0.962	0.993	0.928	0.92	0.895	0.979	0.888	0.934	0.959
State Bank of Travancore	0.997	0.979	0.925	0.93	0.896	0.929	0.976	0.964	0.986	0.992	0.925	0.952	0.986
Bharat Overseas Bank	0.945	0.899	1	1	1	0.983	0.767	0.977	1	0.99	0.992	0.838	0.812
City Union Bank	0.913	0.894	0.969	0.997	0.995	0.928	0.955	0.971	0.944	0.998	0.972	0.994	0.976
Ing Vysya Bank	0.987	0.977	0.994	0.999	0.994	0.999	0.909	0.751	0.781	0.701	1	0.733	0.988
Karnataka Bank	0.962	0.947	0.951	0.969	0.946	0.991	0.979	0.989	0.947	0.989	0.97	0.916	0.997
Lord Krishna Bank	0.782	0.852	0.78	0.833	0.731	0.501	0.758	0.889	0.934	0.994	0.886	0.717	0.939
Nainital Bank	0.983	0.999	0.984	0.988	0.966	0.975	0.976	0.971	0.903	0.877	0.869	0.912	0.986
Tamilnad Mercantile Bank	1	1	1	1	1	1	1	1	1	1	1	1	1
Bank of Rajasthan	0.954	0.995	0.994	0.997	0.997	0.993	0.992	0.982	0.942	0.994	0.984	0.968	0.988
Catholic Syrian Bank	0.947	0.919	0.992	0.989	0.963	0.916	0.938	0.97	0.937	0.985	0.941	0.958	0.988

(*Contd.*)

TABLE 4.5 (*Contd.*)

(1)	(2)	(3)	(4)	(5)	(6)	(7)	(8)	(9)	(10)	(11)	(12)	(13)	(14)
Dhanalakshmi Bank	0.773	0.779	0.771	0.822	0.826	0.674	0.83	0.889	0.904	0.99	0.998	0.747	0.997
Federal Bank	0.936	0.915	0.962	0.986	0.961	0.993	0.932	0.997	0.983	0.998	0.993	0.83	0:814
Jammu & Kashmir Bank	0.963	0.891	0.938	0.983	0.996	0.909	0.957	0.985	1	1	0.965	0.974	0.996
Karur Vysya Bank	0.919	0.926	0.998	1	0.983	1	0.949	0.98	0.973	0.945	0.993	0.933	1
Lakshmi Vilas Bank	1	1	0.951	0.98	0.988	0.895	0.933	0.905	0.968	1	0.959	0.984	0.978
Ratnakar Bank	0.883	0.863	0.842	0.962	0.978	0.967	0.965	0.953	0.916	0.927	0.9	0.914	0.99
Sangli Bank	0.89	0.931	0.974	0.983	0.986	0.997	0.962	0.946	0.89	0.936	0.86	0.889	0.913
South Indian Bank	0.923	0.927	0.966	0.942	0.912	0.836	0.916	0.951	1	0.994	0.938	0.974	0.999
United Western Bank	0.93	0.941	0.96	0.97	0.956	0.955	0.965	0.968	0.944	0.992	0.955	0.995	0.976
All CBs													
Mean	0.905	0.89	0.893	0.873	0.879	0.883	0.925	0.947	0.944	0.965	0.931	0.919	0.97
S.D	0.076	0.098	0.099	0.118	0.103	0.110	0.076	0.056	0.044	0.052	0.048	0.066	0.041
Q1	0.859	0.845	0.842	0.803	0.816	0.823	0.915	0.927	0.919	0.957	0.888	0.895	0.963
Q3	0.922	0.915	0.916	0.889	0.894	0.905	0.949	0.964	0.947	0.987	0.939	0.933	0.985
Median	0.969	0:974	0.974	0.983	0.966	0.975	0.976	0.982	0.973	0.994	0.970	0.966	0.994
PSBs													
Mean	0.890	0.867	0.858	0.811	0.828	0.860	0.924	0.946	0.945	0.967	0.916	0.929	0.975
S.D	0.081	0.112	0.100	0.107	0.090	0.089	0.080	0.055	0.037	0.032	0.044	0.037	0.023

Q1	0.832	0.812	0.799	0.766	0.777	0.803	0.911	0.924	0.920	0.961	0.886	0.897	0.961
Q3	0.971	0.964	0.920	0.885	0.891	0.925	0.979	0.983	0.969	0.991	0.943	0.954	0.988
Median													
NBs													
Mean	0.859	0.844	0.824	0.778	0.800	0.822	0.916	0.944	0.950	0.968	0.925	0.932	0.976
S.D	0.075	0.096	0.091	0.101	0.086	0.076	0.092	0.062	0.037	0.032	0.044	0.039	0.025
Q1	0.811	0.799	0.788	0.735	0.763	0.757	0.911	0.930	0.921	0.947	0.896	0.907	0.973
Q3	0.908	0.915	0.883	0.856	0.865	0.887	0.981	0.983	0.983	0.992	0.955	0.961	0.995
Median	0.859	0.860	0.860	0.803	0.816	0.823	0.950	0.961	0.951	0.982	0.930	0.927	0.985
SBI													
Mean	0.963	0.920	0.939	0.889	0.896	0.948	0.944	0.953	0.932	0.964	0.895	0.924	0.970
S.D	0.036	0.135	0.072	0.082	0.061	0.041	0.037	0.038	0.035	0.032	0.037	0.034	0.015
Q1	0.952	0.942	0.915	0.869	0.885	0.927	0.913	0.925	0.895	0.966	0.881	0.897	0.958
Q3	0.984	0.990	0.985	0.937	0.921	0.987	0.977	0.984	0.955	0.981	0.924	0.952	0.984
Median	0.977	0.979	0.969	0.899	0.900	0.948	0.934	0.950	0.938	0.969	0.894	0.936	0.968
Pvt.													
Mean	0.927	0.925	0.946	0.967	0.954	0.917	0.927	0.949	0.943	0.962	0.954	0.904	0.963
S.D	0.064	0.059	0.072	0.053	0.070	0.132	0.071	0.060	0.054	0.073	0.046	0.094	0.059
Q1	0.915	0.895	0.951	0.969	0.957	0.911	0.920	0.947	0.921	0.955	0.939	0.851	0.976
Q3	0.963	0.970	0.994	0.997	0.995	0.993	0.965	0.982	0.981	0.997	0.993	0.974	0.997
Median	0.941	0.927	0.968	0.985	0.981	0.971	0.952	0.971	0.944	0.991	0.968	0.925	0.988

(*Contd.*)

TABLE 4.5 (*Contd.*)

Banks/Years	*1998-99*	*1999-2000*	*2000-01*	*2001-02*	*2002-03*	*2003-04*	*2004-05*	*2005-06*	*1986-92*	*1993-99*	*2000-06*	*1985-06*
(1)	*(15)*	*(16)*	*(17)*	*(18)*	*(19)*	*(20)*	*(21)*	*(22)*	*(23)*	*(24)*	*(25)*	*(26)*
Allahabad Bank	0.96	0.976	0.996	0.993	0.982	0.986	1	0.957	0.801	0.963	0.984	0.916
Andhra Bank	0.949	0.994	0.914	0.938	0.961	0.984	1	0.986	0.862	0.944	0.968	0.925
Bank of Baroda	0.889	0.999	0.964	0.925	0.999	0.991	0.992	0.983	0.690	0.939	0.979	0.869
Bank of India	0.898	0.991	0.987	0.951	0.98	0.978	0.998	0.994	0.674	0.970	0.983	0.875
Bank of Maharashtra	0.99	0.989	0.977	0.956	0.999	0.987	0.998	0.97	0.890	0.918	0.982	0.930
Canara Bank	0.923	0.991	0.977	0.954	1	0.983	0.999	0.993	0.825	0.969	0.985	0.927
Central Bank of India	0.994	0.982	0.987	0.999	0.951	0.926	0.949	0.941	0.823	0.945	0.962	0.910
Corporation Bank	0.806	0.899	0.876	0.867	0.934	0.962	0.998	0.965	0.924	0.942	0.929	0.932
Dena Bank	0.939	0.993	0.968	0.942	0.991	0.999	0.998	1	0.904	0.949	0.984	0.946
Indian Bank	0.947	0.972	0.997	0.988	0.976	0.929	0.979	0.969	0.680	0.930	0.973	0.861
Indian Overseas Bank	0.918	0.994	0.987	0.974	0.99	0.976	0.978	0.984	0.811	0.974	0.983	0.923
OBC	0.82	0.781	0.724	0.818	0.985	0.94	0.778	0.772	0.818	0.942	0.828	0.863
Punjab and Sind Bank	0.911	0.99	0.985	0.979	0.988	0.902	0.908	0.928	0.900	0.950	0.954	0.935
Punjab National Bank	0.995	0.967	0.996	0.985	0.954	0.943	0.981	0.988	0.805	0.960	0.973	0.913
Syndicate Bank	0.983	0.963	0.949	0.98	0.896	0.954	0.975	0.988	0.903	0.913	0.958	0.925
UCO	0.963	0.938	0.978	0.977	0.976	0.954	0.993	0.999	0.876	0.920	0.974	0.923
Union Bank of India	0.919	0.998	0.874	0.91	0.996	0.988	0.999	0.833	0.905	0.972	0.943	0.940

United Bank of India	0.983	0.999	0.999	0.98	0.967	0.918	0.976	0.939	0.869	0.951	0.968	0.929
Vijaya Bank	0.981	1	0.998	0.982	0.982	0.993	0.999	0.994	0.899	0.946	0.993	0.946
State Bank of India	0.984	0.99	0.983	0.965	0.995	0.98	0.995	0.975	0.828	0.958	0.983	0.923
State Bank of B&J	0.954	0.966	1	0.935	0.942	0.925	0.986	0.949	0.950	0.898	0.958	0.935
State Bank of Hyderabad	0.962	0.995	0.98	0.971	0.998	0.944	0.999	0.995	0.955	0.963	0.983	0.967
State Bank of Indore	1	0.968	0.996	0.979	1	1	1	0.996	0.917	0.939	0.991	0.949
State Bank of Mysore	0.952	0.944	0.992	0.931	0.95	0.901	0.928	0.995	0.962	0.922	0.949	0.944
State Bank of Patiala	0.98	1	1	1	1	0.94	0.996	0.842	0.891	0.970	0.968	0.943
State Bank of Saurashtra	0.996	0.973	0.992	0.976	0.986	0.978	0.975	0.976	0.976	0.939	0.979	0.965
State Bank of Travancore	0.987	0.991	0.984	0.989	0.988	0.991	0.999	0.999	0.947	0.970	0.992	0.970
Bharat Overseas Bank	0.737	0.859	0.88	0.82	0.949	0.929	0.885	0.842	0.942	0.907	0.881	0.910
City Union Bank	0.953	0.998	0.931	0.919	0.951	0.923	0.986	0.998	0.950	0.973	0.958	0.960
Ing Vysya Bank	0.813	0.974	0.845	0.807	0.992	1	0.903	0.935	0.980	0.824	0.922	0.909
Karnataka Bank	0.784	0.943	0.89	0.829	0.965	0.992	0.894	0.959	0.964	0.942	0.925	0.943
Lord Krishna Bank	0.94	0.977	0.824	1	1	1	0.982	0.995	0.748	0.900	0.968	0.872
Nainital Bank	0.994	0.989	0.968	0.947	0.91	0.869	0.908	0.924	0.982	0.930	0.931	0.948
Tamilnad Mercantile Bank	0.951	0.973	0.886	0.882	0.99	1	1	1	1.000	0.993	0.962	0.985
Bank of Rajasthan	0.986	0.985	0.997	0.955	0.978	0.992	0.993	0.993	0.989	0.978	0.985	0.984
Catholic Syrian Bank	0.985	0.989	0.991	0.987	0.96	0.933	0.919	0.893	0.952	0.966	0.953	0.957
Dhanalakshmi Bank	0.849	0.999	0.971	0.934	1	0.99	0.96	0.955	0.782	0.911	0.973	0.888
Federal Bank	0.801	0.999	0.921	0.923	0.969	0.929	0.998	0.894	0.955	0.917	0.948	0.940

(Contd.)

TABLE 4.5 (*Contd.*)

(1)	(15)	(16)	(17)	(18)	(19)	(20)	(21)	(22)	(23)	(24)	(25)	(26)
Jammu & Kashmir Bank	0.928	0.816	0.687	0.852	0.965	0.931	0.783	0.75	0.948	0.978	0.826	0.918
Karur Vysya Bank	0.808	1	0.884	0.914	0.921	1	0.992	1	0.968	0.947	0.959	0.958
Lakshmi Vilas Bank	1	1	1	0.929	0.999	0.989	0.991	0.995	0.964	0.971	0.986	0.974
Ratnakar Bank	0.992	0.989	0.971	1	0.977	0.939	0.923	0.927	0.923	0.942	0.961	0.942
Sangli Bank	0.967	0.957	0.929	0.907	0.907	0.836	0.839	0.827	0.960	0.914	0.886	0.920
South Indian Bank	0.888	0.997	0.941	0.887	0.93	0.958	0.998	0.927	0.917	0.963	0.948	0.943
United Western Bank	0.918	0.982	0.835	0.905	0.986	0.999	0.993	0.985	0.954	0.964	0.955	0.958
All CBs												
Mean	0.931	0.97	0.942	0.939	0.971	0.959	0.963	0.949	0.893	0.944	0.956	0.931
S.D	0.069	0.047	0.072	0.053	0.028	0.038	0.056	0.063	0.084	0.030	0.038	0.030
Q1	0.911	0.968	0.914	0.914	0.954	0.931	0.949	0.928	0.828	0.930	0.949	0.918
Q3	0.952	0.989	0.977	0.951	0.980	0.976	0.991	0.975	0.917	0.946	0.968	0.935
Median	0.984	0.995	0.992	0.980	0.992	0.991	0.998	0.994	0.955	0.966	0.983	0.948
PSBs												
Mean	0.948	0.972	0.965	0.957	0.977	0.961	0.977	0.960	0.862	0.947	0.967	0.925
S.D	0.050	0.045	0.059	0.041	0.025	0.030	0.046	0.057	0.083	0.020	0.032	0.029
Q1	0.921	0.968	0.973	0.940	0.964	0.940	0.977	0.953	0.820	0.939	0.960	0.919
Q3	0.984	0.994	0.996	0.981	0.996	0.987	0.999	0.994	0.911	0.963	0.983	0.944

Median												
NBs												
Mean	0.935	0.969	0.954	0.953	0.974	0.963	0.974	0.957	0.835	0.947	0.963	0.915
S.D	0.054	0.052	0.068	0.046	0.026	0.029	0.053	0.059	0.079	0.018	0.036	0.027
Q1	0.915	0.970	0.957	0.940	0.964	0.942	0.977	0.949	0.808	0.941	0.960	0.911
Q3	0.982	0.994	0.992	0.981	0.991	0.987	0.999	0.991	0.900	0.962	0.983	0.931
Median	0.947	0.990	0.978	0.974	0.982	0.976	0.993	0.983	0.862	0.946	0.973	0.925
SBI												
Mean	0.977	0.978	0.991	0.968	0.982	0.957	0.985	0.966	0.928	0.945	0.975	0.950
S.D	0.019	0.019	0.008	0.024	0.023	0.035	0.024	0.053	0.049	0.026	0.016	0.017
Q1	0.960	0.968	0.984	0.958	0.977	0.936	0.983	0.969	0.911	0.935	0.966	0.941
Q3	0.989	0.992	0.997	0.982	0.999	0.983	0.999	0.995	0.957	0.965	0.985	0.965
Median	0.982	0.982	0.992	0.974	0.992	0.961	0.996	0.986	0.949	0.949	0.981	0.947
Pvt.												
Mean	0.905	0.968	0.908	0.911	0.964	0.956	0.942	0.933	0.938	0.940	0.940	0.939
S.D	0.085	0.051	0.078	0.058	0.030	0.049	0.064	0.071	0.066	0.041	0.041	0.031
Q1	0.822	0.973	0.881	0.883	0.950	0.930	0.904	0.902	0.944	0.915	0.926	0.918
Q3	0.981	0.998	0.970	0.944	0.989	0.997	0.993	0.995	0.967	0.970	0.961	0.958
Median	0.934	0.987	0.925	0.917	0.967	0.974	0.971	0.945	0.954	0.945	0.954	0.943

*Note** : S.D denotes stanadard deviation, Q1 denotes first-quartile, Q3 denotes third quartile.

Table 4.6
Inter-Bank Average Cost X-Efficiency Scores Over the Different Time Periods

Banks/Years	*1985*	*1986*	*1987*	*1988-89*	*1989-90*	*1990-91*	*1991-92*	*1992-93*	*1993-94*	*1994-95*	*1995-96*	*1996-97*	*1997-98*
(1)	*(2)*	*(3)*	*(4)*	*(5)*	*(6)*	*(7)*	*(8)*	*(9)*	*(10)*	*(11)*	*(12)*	*(13)*	*(14)*
Allahabad Bank	0.681	0.677	0.59	0.524	0.503	0.589	0.643	0.598	0.504	0.548	0.584	0.608	0.707
Andhra Bank	0.689	0.704	0.763	0.698	0.705	0.58	0.463	0.372	0.467	0.676	0.614	0.588	0.824
Bank of Baroda	0.685	0.667	0.616	0.55	0.554	0.808	0.614	0.728	0.953	0.972	0.884	0.706	0.797
Bank of India	0.572	0.554	0.518	0.448	0.457	0.503	0.66	0.507	0.582	0.678	0.634	0.629	0.727
Bank of Maharashtra	0.762	0.731	0.649	0.702	0.724	0.582	0.509	0.359	0.446	0.638	0.75	0.713	0.845
Canara Bank	0.768	0.795	0.825	0.803	0.785	0.641	0.821	0.872	0.698	0.888	0.74	0.646	0.638
Central Bank of India	0.708	0.769	0.66	0.602	0.662	0.522	0.5	0.463	0.377	0.59	0.63	0.612	0.757
Corporation Bank	0.817	0.85	0.857	0.815	0.8	0.599	0.659	0.699	0.807	0.845	0.881	0.873	0.997
Dena Bank	0.842	0.814	0.768	0.746	0.829	0.639	0.554	0.569	0.663	0.795	0.777	0.821	0.929
Indian Bank	0.611	0.57	0.598	0.507	0.624	0.586	0.648	0.507	0.55	0.545	0.437	0.496	0.385
Indian Overseas Bank	0.677	0.684	0.633	0.538	0.566	0.743	0.684	0.697	0.937	0.517	0.478	0.473	0.567
OBC	0.788	0.793	0.817	0.769	0.764	0.701	0.663	0.673	0.819	0.986	0.899	0.845	0.906
Punjab and Sind Bank	0.824	0.935	0.805	0.716	0.673	0.564	0.448	0.342	0.465	0.651	0.474	0.54	0.684
Punjab National Bank	0.668	0.646	0.65	0.621	0.686	0.508	0.512	0.674	0.661	0.673	0.684	0.668	0.779
Syndicate Bank	0.794	0.79	0.916	0.809	0.771	0.65	0.563	0.395	0.576	0.618	0.642	0.601	0.668
UCO	0.786	0.803	0.669	0.559	0.468	0.468	0.455	0.5	0.324	0.566	0.463	0.399	0.486

Union Bank of India	0.709	0.818	0.81	0.718	0.736	0.585	0.623	0.614	0.701	0.77	0.742	0.706	0.812
United Bank of India	0.74	0.784	0.74	0.704	0.882	0.579	0.438	0.201	0.289	0.316	0.373	0.319	0.705
Vijaya Bank	0.886	0.89	0.848	0.689	0.817	0.633	0.554	0.638	0.653	0.669	0.517	0.58	0.671
State Bank of India	0.853	0.812	0.762	0.706	0.664	0.746	0.903	0.896	0.832	0.945	0.884	0.791	0.84
State Bank of B&J	0.803	0.824	0.794	0.767	0.673	0.721	0.873	0.808	0.777	0.778	0.775	0.792	0.953
State Bank of Hyderabad	0.781	0.865	0.829	0.741	0.725	0.712	0.882	0.918	0.859	0.936	0.871	0.834	0.961
State Bank of Indore	0.872	0.802	0.745	0.696	0.754	0.704	0.837	0.774	0.926	0.97	0.885	0.868	0.963
State Bank of Mysore	0.805	0.858	0.793	0.767	0.931	0.698	0.711	0.77	0.824	0.8	0.786	0.821	0.955
State Bank of Patiala	0.567	0.485	0.716	0.624	0.862	0.799	1	1	0.91	0.863	0.835	0.773	0.989
State Bank of Saurashtra	0.886	0.907	0.861	0.817	0.79	0.751	0.823	0.895	0.852	0.979	0.817	0.786	0.941
State Bank of Travancore	0.747	0.757	0.727	0.81	0.688	0.579	0.602	0.771	0.836	0.771	0.76	0.665	0.783
Bharat Overseas Bank	0.945	0.899	1	1	1	0.983	0.767	0.977	1	0.99	0.933	0.69	0.724
City Union Bank	0.866	0.893	0.969	0.824	0.872	0.752	0.738	0.821	0.763	0.808	0.801	0.777	0.66
Ing Vysya Bank	0.806	0.851	0.823	0.786	0.899	0.772	0.631	0.656	0.764	0.701	1	0.733	0.802
Karnataka Bank	0.822	0.821	0.808	0.793	0.837	0.687	0.615	0.794	0.702	0.823	0.75	0.869	0.937
Lord Krishna Bank	0.763	0.852	0.78	0.833	0.711	0.484	0.512	0.872	0.906	0.938	0.847	0.633	0.626
Nainital Bank	0.831	0.835	0.887	0.836	0.82	0.78	0.615	0.74	0.631	0.613	0.731	0.747	0.918
Tamilnad Mercantile Bank	1	1	1	1	1	1	1	1	1	1	1	1	1
Bank of Rajasthan	0.736	0.785	0.773	0.787	0.77	0.732	0.651	0.72	0.757	0.929	0.677	0.597	0.637
Catholic Syrian Bank	0.884	0.919	0.939	0.926	0.926	0.64	0.563	0.584	0.744	0.641	0.606	0.564	0.593
Dhanalakshmi Bank	0.773	0.779	0.741	0.795	0.826	0.613	0.527	0.713	0.785	0.842	0.713	0.495	0.707

(Contd.)

TABLE 4.6 (Contd.)

(1)	(2)	(3)	(4)	(5)	(6)	(7)	(8)	(9)	(10)	(11)	(12)	(13)	(14)
Federal Bank	0.88	0.808	0.874	0.679	0.954	0.677	0.525	0.551	0.666	0.861	0.812	0.536	0.541
Jammu & Kashmir Bank	0.963	0.765	0.805	0.798	0.728	0.547	0.957	0.985	1	1	0.934	0.746	0.972
Karur Vysya Bank	0.901	0.901	0.965	0.908	0.905	1	0.719	0.776	0.745	0.872	0.993	0.853	1
Lakshmi Vilas Bank	1	1	0.927	0.843	0.863	0.887	0.753	0.795	0.968	1	0.957	0.825	0.786
Ratnakar Bank	0.737	0.733	0.689	0.714	0.737	0.721	0.623	0.562	0.916	0.651	0.682	0.672	0.822
Sangli Bank	0.731	0.775	0.75	0.703	0.793	0.662	0.635	0.68	0.846	0.702	0.69	0.542	0.784
South Indian Bank	0.923	0.899	0.878	0.856	0.891	0.636	0.578	0.61	1	0.734	0.775	0.541	0.639
United Western Bank	0.807	0.814	0.764	0.766	0.758	0.596	0.5	0.735	0.759	0.773	0.834	0.966	0.906
All CBs													
Mean	0.793	0.798	0.785	0.740	0.764	0.675	0.657	0.685	0.739	0.775	0.746	0.688	0.780
S.D	0.101	0.106	0.113	0.121	0.129	0.127	0.149	0.188	0.187	0.162	0.158	0.148	0.152
Q1	0.736	0.765	0.727	0.696	0.688	0.585	0.554	0.569	0.653	0.651	0.642	0.588	0.671
Q3	0.866	0.858	0.857	0.810	0.862	0.743	0.738	0.795	0.859	0.929	0.871	0.792	0.929
Median	0.794	0.808	0.793	0.766	0.770	0.650	0.631	0.699	0.763	0.778	0.760	0.690	0.786
PSBs													
Mean	0.753	0.762	0.739	0.683	0.707	0.637	0.653	0.639	0.677	0.740	0.697	0.672	0.788
S.D	0.089	0.109	0.099	0.106	0.121	0.092	0.157	0.203	0.198	0.172	0.160	0.146	0.158
Q1	0.687	0.694	0.655	0.612	0.663	0.580	0.533	0.504	0.527	0.628	0.599	0.595	0.695

Q3	0.811	0.821	0.814	0.767	0.788	0.708	0.766	0.773	0.834	0.876	0.826	0.792	0.935
Median	0.768	0.793	0.762	0.704	0.724	0.633	0.643	0.673	0.698	0.770	0.742	0.668	0.797
NBs													
Mean	0.737	0.751	0.723	0.659	0.685	0.604	0.580	0.548	0.604	0.681	0.642	0.622	0.731
S.D	0.081	0.101	0.111	0.112	0.126	0.083	0.101	0.166	0.191	0.166	0.159	0.143	0.150
Q1	0.683	0.681	0.641	0.555	0.595	0.572	0.505	0.429	0.466	0.578	0.498	0.560	0.670
Q3	0.791	0.809	0.814	0.732	0.778	0.640	0.654	0.674	0.700	0.783	0.746	0.706	0.818
Median	0.740	0.784	0.740	0.698	0.705	0.586	0.563	0.569	0.582	0.669	0.634	0.612	0.727
SBI													
Mean	0.789	0.789	0.778	0.741	0.761	0.714	0.829	0.854	0.852	0.880	0.827	0.791	0.923
S.D	0.101	0.131	0.050	0.064	0.095	0.064	0.122	0.086	0.048	0.088	0.050	0.060	0.072
Q1	0.787	0.805	0.749	0.699	0.686	0.706	0.846	0.783	0.826	0.816	0.798	0.791	0.954
Q3	0.858	0.860	0.803	0.778	0.808	0.747	0.887	0.902	0.872	0.951	0.874	0.824	0.962
Median	0.804	0.818	0.778	0.754	0.740	0.717	0.855	0.852	0.844	0.900	0.826	0.792	0.954
Pvt.													
Mean	0.854	0.852	0.854	0.825	0.849	0.732	0.662	0.754	0.831	0.827	0.819	0.710	0.781
S.D	0.089	0.076	0.097	0.090	0.089	0.152	0.141	0.140	0.125	0.132	0.126	0.152	0.148
Q1	0.781	0.791	0.775	0.786	0.776	0.637	0.567	0.662	0.748	0.710	0.718	0.572	0.644
Q3	0.918	0.899	0.936	0.853	0.904	0.778	0.733	0.815	0.955	0.936	0.934	0.813	0.915
Median	0.849	0.843	0.849	0.811	0.850	0.704	0.627	0.738	0.775	0.833	0.807	0.712	0.785

(*Contd.*)

TABLE 4.6 (*Contd.*)

Banks/Years	*1998-99*	*1999-2000*	*2000-01*	*2001-02*	*2002-03*	*2003-04*	*2004-05*	*2005-06*	*1986-92*	*1993-99*	*2000-06*	*1985-06*
(1)	*(15)*	*(16)*	*(17)*	*(18)*	*(19)*	*(20)*	*(21)*	*(22)*	*(23)*	*(24)*	*(25)*	*(26)*
Allahabad Bank	0.686	0.727	0.697	0.722	0.834	0.787	0.778	0.737	0.601	0.605	0.755	0.654
Andhra Bank	0.696	0.735	0.649	0.725	0.912	0.922	1	0.8	0.657	0.605	0.820	0.694
Bank of Baroda	0.826	0.768	0.775	0.734	0.781	0.818	0.817	0.75	0.642	0.838	0.778	0.753
Bank of India	0.689	0.688	0.807	0.717	0.786	0.724	0.624	0.659	0.530	0.635	0.715	0.627
Bank of Maharashtra	0.785	0.76	0.746	0.702	0.725	0.655	0.68	0.637	0.666	0.648	0.701	0.671
Canara Bank	0.789	0.745	0.792	0.721	0.779	0.756	0.761	0.711	0.777	0.753	0.752	0.761
Central Bank of India	0.724	0.729	0.677	0.697	0.821	0.752	0.796	0.712	0.632	0.593	0.741	0.655
Corporation Bank	0.806	0.876	0.876	0.782	0.934	0.921	0.998	0.965	0.771	0.844	0.907	0.841
Dena Bank	0.806	0.751	0.756	0.753	0.885	0.999	0.765	1	0.742	0.766	0.844	0.784
Indian Bank	0.46	0.528	0.604	0.571	0.704	0.78	0.785	0.741	0.592	0.483	0.673	0.583
Indian Overseas Bank	0.568	0.622	0.669	0.71	0.761	0.796	0.861	0.858	0.646	0.605	0.754	0.669
OBC	0.82	0.773	0.724	0.818	0.985	0.94	0.736	0.725	0.756	0.850	0.814	0.807
Punjab and Sind Bank	0.585	0.644	0.705	0.63	0.735	0.714	0.805	0.735	0.709	0.534	0.710	0.651
Punjab National Bank	0.855	0.748	0.765	0.759	0.91	0.84	0.811	0.775	0.613	0.713	0.801	0.709
Syndicate Bank	0.664	0.733	0.785	0.814	0.823	0.704	0.751	0.732	0.756	0.595	0.763	0.705
UCO	0.542	0.626	0.64	0.66	0.667	0.632	0.608	0.594	0.601	0.469	0.632	0.567

Union Bank of India	0.681	0.712	0.709	0.765	0.821	0.741	0.728	0.687	0.714	0.718	0.738	0.723
United Bank of India	0.509	0.534	0.546	0.713	0.784	0.721	0.788	0.79	0.695	0.387	0.697	0.593
Vijaya Bank	0.701	0.737	0.73	0.713	0.87	0.902	0.833	0.79	0.760	0.633	0.796	0.730
State Bank of India	0.855	0.819	0.807	0.732	0.784	0.765	0.835	0.943	0.778	0.863	0.812	0.818
State Bank of B&J	0.903	0.966	1	0.92	0.909	0.9	0.986	0.901	0.779	0.827	0.940	0.849
State Bank of Hyderabad	0.962	0.995	0.98	0.87	0.879	0.846	0.752	0.916	0.791	0.906	0.891	0.863
State Bank of Indore	1	0.953	0.988	0.972	1	1	0.757	0.838	0.773	0.912	0.930	0.872
State Bank of Mysore	0.88	0.914	0.939	0.84	0.95	0.845	0.928	0.995	0.795	0.834	0.916	0.848
State Bank of Patiala	0.92	1	1	1	1	0.884	0.805	0.653	0.722	0.899	0.906	0.842
State Bank of Saurashtra	0.941	0.907	0.824	0.83	0.813	0.834	0.763	0.675	0.834	0.887	0.807	0.842
State Bank of Travancore	0.753	0.747	0.793	0.707	0.771	0.786	0.848	0.784	0.701	0.763	0.777	0.747
Bharat Overseas Bank	0.666	0.673	0.796	0.757	0.716	0.754	0.833	0.727	0.942	0.854	0.751	0.849
City Union Bank	0.953	0.975	0.814	0.741	0.747	0.8	0.75	0.826	0.845	0.798	0.808	0.817
Ing Vysya Bank	0.722	0.852	0.622	0.727	0.992	1	0.62	0.819	0.795	0.768	0.805	0.789
Karnataka Bank	0.61	0.61	0.669	0.779	0.768	0.878	0.784	0.719	0.769	0.784	0.744	0.765
Lord Krishna Bank	0.861	0.737	0.683	1	1	0.908	0.538	0.619	0.705	0.812	0.784	0.767
Nainital Bank	0.937	0.887	0.762	0.868	0.887	0.794	0.754	0.901	0.801	0.760	0.836	0.799
Tamilnad Mercantile Bank	0.951	0.884	0.886	0.882	0.978	1	1	1	1.000	0.993	0.947	0.980
Bank of Rajasthan	0.629	0.705	0.794	0.764	0.819	0.697	0.532	0.527	0.748	0.707	0.691	0.715
Catholic Syrian Bank	0.496	0.668	0.737	0.727	0.909	0.86	0.703	0.65	0.828	0.604	0.751	0.728

(*Contd.*)

TABLE 4.6 (Contd.)

(1)	(15)	(16)	(17)	(18)	(19)	(20)	(21)	(22)	(23)	(24)	(25)	(26)
Dhanalakshmi Bank	0.535	0.76	0.748	0.811	1	0.804	0.626	0.665	0.722	0.684	0.773	0.727
Federal Bank	0.686	0.774	0.74	0.783	0.791	0.761	0.76	0.753	0.771	0.665	0.766	0.734
Jammu & Kashmir Bank	0.928	0.743	0.658	0.852	0.894	0.76	0.613	0.638	0.795	0.938	0.737	0.823
Karur Vysya Bank	0.759	1	0.884	0.914	0.839	1	0.891	1	0.900	0.857	0.933	0.896
Lakshmi Vilas Bank	1	1	1	0.787	0.809	0.78	0.635	0.595	0.896	0.904	0.801	0.867
Ratnakar Bank	0.731	0.787	0.79	1	0.853	0.639	0.665	0.676	0.708	0.719	0.773	0.733
Sangli Bank	0.612	0.628	0.599	0.595	0.537	0.523	0.45	0.438	0.721	0.694	0.539	0.651
South Indian Bank	0.612	0.817	0.776	0.72	0.8	0.897	0.693	0.708	0.809	0.702	0.773	0.761
United Western Bank	0.75	0.982	0.497	0.744	0.754	0.633	0.515	0.531	0.715	0.818	0.665	0.733
All CBs												
Mean	0.752	0.783	0.765	0.778	0.838	0.810	0.755	0.753	0.745	0.738	0.783	0.755
S.D	0.147	0.127	0.120	0.100	0.101	0.111	0.127	0.134	0.094	0.136	0.086	0.090
Q1	0.664	0.712	0.683	0.720	0.779	0.752	0.680	0.665	0.701	0.635	0.741	0.705
Q3	0.861	0.884	0.807	0.830	0.909	0.897	0.817	0.826	0.795	0.844	0.814	0.823
Median	0.750	0.751	0.762	0.757	0.821	0.796	0.761	0.735	0.756	0.760	0.773	0.753
PSBs												
Mean	0.756	0.768	0.777	0.762	0.838	0.813	0.800	0.782	0.705	0.710	0.791	0.735
S.D	0.142	0.127	0.122	0.097	0.091	0.097	0.096	0.112	0.078	0.149	0.083	0.093

Q1	0.684	0.720	0.701	0.712	0.780	0.747	0.755	0.712	0.644	0.605	0.739	0.662
Q3	0.855	0.848	0.816	0.816	0.910	0.892	0.834	0.848	0.772	0.841	0.832	0.829
Median	0.785	0.747	0.765	0.732	0.821	0.796	0.788	0.750	0.714	0.718	0.778	0.730
NBs												
Mean	0.694	0.707	0.719	0.721	0.817	0.795	0.786	0.758	0.677	0.646	0.757	0.693
S.D	0.116	0.084	0.078	0.059	0.084	0.102	0.099	0.100	0.072	0.129	0.065	0.075
Q1	0.625	0.666	0.673	0.706	0.770	0.723	0.744	0.712	0.622	0.594	0.712	0.652
Q3	0.798	0.750	0.770	0.756	0.878	0.871	0.814	0.790	0.749	0.736	0.799	0.741
Median	0.696	0.733	0.724	0.721	0.821	0.780	0.785	0.737	0.666	0.633	0.754	0.694
SBI												
Mean	0.902	0.913	0.916	0.859	0.888	0.858	0.834	0.838	0.772	0.861	0.872	0.835
S.D	0.076	0.089	0.092	0.105	0.092	0.073	0.085	0.125	0.042	0.051	0.064	0.039
Q1	0.886	0.924	0.949	0.848	0.887	0.845	0.769	0.854	0.774	0.841	0.895	0.844
Q3	0.946	0.973	0.991	0.933	0.963	0.888	0.868	0.923	0.792	0.900	0.919	0.852
Median	0.912	0.934	0.960	0.855	0.894	0.846	0.820	0.870	0.779	0.875	0.899	0.845
Pvt.												
Mean	0.747	0.805	0.748	0.803	0.839	0.805	0.687	0.711	0.804	0.781	0.771	0.785
S.D	0.157	0.128	0.117	0.102	0.118	0.132	0.140	0.154	0.085	0.102	0.091	0.078
Q1	0.616	0.713	0.673	0.742	0.774	0.756	0.615	0.624	0.728	0.703	0.746	0.733
Q3	0.911	0.886	0.796	0.864	0.905	0.892	0.759	0.803	0.841	0.845	0.804	0.822
Median	0.727	0.781	0.755	0.781	0.829	0.797	0.679	0.692	0.795	0.776	0.773	0.766

*Note** : S.D denotes stanadard deviation, Q1 denotes first-quartile, Q3 denotes third quartile.

TABLE 4.7

Inter-Temporal and Inter-Bank Pattern of Returns to Scale

Banks/Years	*1985*	*1986*	*1987*	*1988-89*	*1989-90*	*1990-91*	*1991-92*	*1992-93*	*1993-94*	*1994-95*
(1)	*(2)*	*(3)*	*(4)*	*(5)*	*(6)*	*(7)*	*(8)*	*(9)*	*(10)*	*(11)*
Allahabad Bank	irs	irs	irs	irs	irs	irs	irs	irs	irs	irs
Andhra Bank	drs	irs	irs	irs	irs	irs	irs	irs	irs	irs
Bank of Baroda	drs	drs	irs	irs	irs	—	drs	irs	—	drs
Bank of India	drs	drs	irs	irs	irs	irs	drs	irs	irs	irs
Bank of Maharashtra	drs	irs	irs	irs	irs	irs	irs	irs	irs	irs
Canara Bank	drs	drs	—	—	—	drs	drs	drs	drs	drs
Central Bank of India	drs	drs	irs	irs	irs	irs	irs	irs	irs	irs
Corporation Bank	drs	drs	—	drs	drs	drs	—	irs	drs	drs
Dena Bank	drs	irs	irs	irs	irs	irs	irs	irs	irs	irs
Indian Bank	drs	drs	irs	irs	irs	irs	drs	irs	irs	irs
Indian Overseas Bank	drs	drs	irs	irs	irs	drs	drs	drs	drs	irs
OBC	drs	drs	irs	irs	irs	—	irs	irs	irs	irs
Punjab and Sind Bank	drs	—	irs	irs	irs	irs	irs	irs	irs	irs
Punjab National Bank	drs	drs	irs	irs	irs	irs	irs	irs	irs	irs
Syndicate Bank	drs	drs	—	drs	drs	drs	irs	irs	drs	irs
UCO	drs	drs	irs	irs	irs	irs	irs	irs	irs	irs
Union Bank of India	drs	drs	irs	irs	irs	irs	irs	irs	irs	irs
United Bank of India	drs	drs	irs	irs	irs	irs	irs	irs	irs	irs
Vijaya Bank	drs	drs	irs	irs	drs	irs	irs	irs	irs	irs
State Bank of India	drs	drs	drs	drs	drs	drs	drs	drs	drs	drs

State Bank of B&J	drs	drs	drs	drs	irs	drs	irs	irs	drs	irs
State Bank of Hyderabad	drs	drs	drs	drs	irs	irs	drs	—	—	drs
State Bank of Indore	drs	drs	drs	irs	irs	irs	irs	irs	—	—
State Bank of Mysore	drs	drs	drs	drs	drs	drs	irs	irs	drs	irs
State Bank of Patiala	irs	irs	irs	irs	drs	drs	—	—	drs	irs
State Bank of Saurashtra	drs	drs	drs	drs	drs	drs	drs	drs	drs	—
State Bank of Travancore	drs	drs	—	drs	irs	irs	irs	irs	drs	drs
Bharat Overseas Bank	—	—	—	—	—	—	—	—	—	—
City Union Bank	irs	drs	—	irs	irs	irs	irs	irs	irs	irs
Ing Vysya Bank	irs	irs	irs	irs	irs	irs	irs	drs	irs	—
Karnataka Bank	irs	irs	irs	irs	irs	irs	irs	irs	irs	irs
Lord Krishna Bank	irs	—	—	—	irs	irs	irs	irs	irs	irs
Nainital Bank	irs	irs	irs	irs	irs	irs	irs	irs	irs	irs
Tamilnad Mercantile Bank	—	—	—	—	—	—	—	—	—	—
Bank of Rajasthan	drs	irs	irs	irs	irs	irs	irs	irs	irs	irs
Catholic Syrian Bank	irs	—	drs	irs	drs	irs	irs	irs	irs	irs
Dhanalakshmi Bank	—	—	irs	drs	—	irs	irs	irs	irs	irs
Federal Bank	—	drs	drs	irs	drs	irs	irs	irs	irs	irs
Jammu & Kashmir Bank	—	irs	irs	irs	irs	irs	—	—	—	—
Karur Vysya Bank	—	drs	drs	irs	irs	—	irs	irs	irs	drs
Lakshmi Vilas Bank	—	—	irs	irs	irs	irs	irs	irs	—	—
Ratnakar Bank	irs	drs	irs	irs	irs	irs	irs	irs	—	irs
Sangli Bank	drs	drs	drs	irs	irs	irs	irs	irs	drs	irs
South Indian Bank	—	drs	drs	drs	drs	irs	irs	irs	—	irs
United Western Bank	drs	drs	drs	drs	drs	irs	irs	irs	irs	irs

(Contd.)

TABLE 4.7 (*Contd.*)

Banks/Years	*1995-96*	*1996-97*	*1997-98*	*1998-99*	*1999-2000*	*2000-01*	*2001-02*	*2002-03*	*2003-04*	*2004-05*	*2005-06*
(1)	*(12)*	*(13)*	*(14)*	*(15)*	*(16)*	*(17)*	*(18)*	*(19)*	*(20)*	*(21)*	*(22)*
Allahabad Bank	irs	irs	irs	irs	irs	irs	irs	irs	irs	irs	irs
Andhra Bank	irs	irs	irs	irs	irs	irs	irs	irs	irs	—	irs
Bank of Baroda	drs	irs	irs	drs	irs	irs	irs	irs	irs	irs	irs
Bank of India	irs	irs	drs	drs	drs	drs	irs	irs	irs	irs	irs
Bank of Maharashtra	irs	irs	irs	irs	irs	irs	irs	irs	irs	irs	irs
Canara Bank	drs	drs	irs	drs	drs	drs	drs	irs	drs	drs	drs
Central Bank of India	irs	irs	irs	irs	irs	irs	irs	irs	irs	irs	irs
Corporation Bank	drs	drs	—	—	drs	—	irs	—	drs	—	—
Dena Bank	irs	irs	irs	irs	irs	irs	irs	irs	—	irs	—
Indian Bank	irs	irs	irs	irs	irs	irs	irs	irs	irs	irs	irs
Indian Overseas Bank	irs	irs	irs	irs	irs	irs	irs	irs	irs	irs	irs
OBC	drs	drs	irs	—	drs	—	—	—	—	irs	irs
Punjab and Sind Bank	irs	irs	irs	irs	irs	irs	irs	irs	irs	irs	irs
Punjab National Bank	irs	irs	irs	irs	irs	irs	irs	irs	irs	irs	irs
Syndicate Bank	irs	irs	irs	irs	irs	irs	irs	irs	irs	irs	irs
UCO	irs	irs	irs	irs	irs	irs	irs	irs	irs	irs	irs
Union Bank of India	irs	irs	irs	irs	irs	irs	irs	irs	irs	irs	irs
United Bank of India	irs	irs	irs	irs	irs	irs	irs	irs	irs	irs	irs
Vijaya Bank	irs	irs	irs	irs	irs	irs	irs	irs	irs	irs	irs
State Bank of India	drs	drs	drs	drs	drs	drs	drs	drs	drs	drs	drs

State Bank of B&J	irs	irs	—	irs	—	—	drs	irs	irs	—	irs
State Bank of Hyderabad	irs	irs	irs	—	—	—	—	irs	irs	irs	drs
State Bank of Indore	—	irs	—	—	drs	drs	drs	—	—	irs	drs
State Bank of Mysore	irs	irs	—	irs	irs	irs	drs	—	irs	—	—
State Bank of Patiala	drs	irs	—	—	—	—	—	—	drs	irs	irs
State Bank of Saurashtra	—	irs	drs	drs	drs	irs	drs	irs	irs	irs	irs
State Bank of Travancore	irs	irs	irs	drs	drs	irs	irs	irs	irs	drs	drs
Bharat Overseas Bank	drs	drs	irs	irs	irs	irs	irs	irs	irs	irs	irs
City Union Bank	irs	irs	irs	—	drs	irs	irs	irs	irs	irs	irs
Ing Vysya Bank	—	—	drs	drs	irs	drs	irs	—	—	irs	irs
Karnataka Bank	irs	irs	irs	irs	irs	irs	irs	irs	irs	irs	irs
Lord Krishna Bank	irs	irs	irs	irs	irs	irs	—	—	irs	irs	irs
Nainital Bank	irs	irs	irs	irs	irs	irs	irs	irs	irs	irs	irs
Tamilnad Mercantile Bank	—	—	—	—	irs	irs	—	irs	—	—	—
Bank of Rajasthan	irs	irs	irs	irs	irs	irs	irs	irs	irs	irs	irs
Catholic Syrian Bank	irs	irs	irs	irs	irs	irs	irs	irs	irs	irs	irs
Dhanalakshmi Bank	irs	irs	irs	irs	irs	irs	irs	—	irs	irs	irs
Federal Bank	irs	irs	irs	drs	drs	irs	drs	irs	irs	irs	irs
Jammu & Kashmir Bank	drs	irs	drs	—	drs	drs	—	drs	drs	irs	irs
Karur Vysya Bank	—	irs	—	irs	—	—	—	irs	—	irs	—
Lakshmi Vilas Bank	irs	irs	irs	—	—	—	irs	irs	irs	irs	irs
Ratnakar Bank	irs	irs	irs	irs	irs	irs	—	irs	irs	irs	irs
Sangli Bank	irs	irs	irs	irs	irs	irs	irs	irs	irs	irs	irs
South Indian Bank	irs	irs	irs	irs	irs	irs	irs	irs	irs	irs	irs
United Western Bank	—	drs	drs	irs	—	irs	drs	irs	irs	irs	irs

TABLE 4.8

Inter-Bank Average Super Efficiency Scores Over the Different Time Periods

Banks/Years	*1985*	*1986*	*1987*	*1988-89*	*1989-90*	*1990-91*	*1991-92*	*1992-93*	*1993-94*	*1994-95*	*1995-96*	*1996-97*	*1997-98*
(1)	*(2)*	*(3)*	*(4)*	*(5)*	*(6)*	*(7)*	*(8)*	*(9)*	*(10)*	*(11)*	*(12)*	*(13)*	*(14)*
Allahabad Bank	0.769	0.803	0.771	0.778	0.701	0.735	0.697	0.627	0.520	0.552	0.629	0.640	0.716
Andhra Bank	0.827	0.853	0.879	0.816	0.836	0.706	0.470	0.394	0.491	0.721	0.679	0.631	0.837
Bank of Baroda	0.911	0.974	0.957	0.915	0.853	1.172	0.888	0.875	1.044	0.989	0.887	0.768	0.797
Bank of India	0.781	0.851	0.828	0.760	0.722	0.694	0.871	0.519	0.599	0.686	0.660	0.632	0.729
Bank of Maharashtra	0.846	0.815	0.754	0.801	0.839	0.656	0.541	0.401	0.503	0.683	0.875	0.796	0.882
Canara Bank	0.914	0.970	1.101	1.055	1.065	0.862	0.856	0.879	0.723	0.899	0.779	0.660	0.647
Central Bank of India	0.882	0.971	0.820	0.768	0.812	0.681	0.504	0.481	0.416	0.603	0.711	0.668	0.781
Corporation Bank	0.846	0.892	0.927	0.914	0.905	0.698	0.664	0.701	0.807	0.934	0.882	0.982	1.142
Dena Bank	0.916	0.877	0.876	0.871	0.936	0.708	0.586	0.593	0.721	0.815	0.846	0.870	0.942
Indian Bank	0.827	0.844	0.890	0.852	0.981	0.849	0.868	0.670	0.553	0.548	0.464	0.513	0.425
Indian Overseas Bank	0.834	0.879	0.808	0.762	0.736	0.846	0.716	0.711	0.941	0.520	0.496	0.485	0.571
OBC	0.916	0.898	0.959	0.959	0.958	1.030	0.805	0.691	0.824	0.995	0.956	0.962	0.911
Punjab and Sind Bank	0.924	1.088	0.906	0.843	0.787	0.633	0.451	0.364	0.507	0.655	0.503	0.565	0.695
Punjab National Bank	0.824	0.803	0.820	0.808	0.849	0.682	0.567	0.680	0.709	0.678	0.753	0.723	0.798
Syndicate Bank	0.921	0.903	1.019	0.909	0.860	0.689	0.604	0.436	0.649	0.671	0.746	0.685	0.702

UCO	0.809	0.845	0.764	0.734	0.617	0.544	0.477	0.518	0.351	0.592	0.544	0.460	0.530
Union Bank of India	0.775	0.906	0.902	0.824	0.852	0.660	0.626	0.625	0.738	0.771	0.764	0.717	0.814
United Bank of India	0.893	0.911	0.846	0.840	0.987	0.712	0.449	0.204	0.287	0.351	0.425	0.344	0.717
Vijaya Bank	0.903	0.913	0.932	0.894	0.987	0.716	0.587	0.698	0.704	0.686	0.563	0.625	0.688
State Bank of India	0.958	0.972	0.964	0.978	0.865	0.853	0.985	0.899	0.876	0.977	0.983	0.844	0.864
State Bank of B&J	0.816	0.843	0.801	0.862	0.740	0.729	0.962	0.899	0.869	0.874	0.936	0.915	1.063
State Bank of Hyderabad	0.802	0.872	0.834	0.841	0.803	0.747	0.898	0.938	0.900	0.947	0.942	0.876	0.977
State Bank of Indore	0.906	0.811	0.844	0.834	0.864	0.748	0.890	0.827	1.038	1.020	1.037	0.969	1.001
State Bank of Mysore	0.825	0.877	0.824	0.802	0.963	0.708	0.784	0.831	0.919	0.828	0.907	0.914	1.003
State Bank of Patiala	0.613	0.793	0.733	0.686	0.969	0.865	1.191	1.129	0.953	0.893	0.885	0.808	1.009
State Bank of Saurashtra	0.899	0.907	0.876	0.829	0.820	0.758	0.887	0.974	0.952	1.007	0.918	0.842	0.980
State Bank of Travancore	0.748	0.772	0.785	0.870	0.768	0.625	0.616	0.800	0.848	0.777	0.821	0.698	0.795
Bharat Overseas Bank	1.126	1.084	1.352	1.346	1.211	1.139	1.020	1.085	1.160	1.037	0.941	0.824	0.891
City Union Bank	0.946	0.995	1.064	0.823	0.875	0.810	0.773	0.844	0.807	0.810	0.823	0.782	0.677
Ing Vysya Bank	0.819	0.869	0.827	0.787	0.903	0.773	0.695	0.874	0.981	1.180	1.296	1.011	0.812
Karnataka Bank	0.851	0.866	0.849	0.818	0.887	0.695	0.628	0.805	0.741	0.832	0.773	0.950	0.940
Lord Krishna Bank	0.973	1.045	1.042	1.050	0.973	0.961	0.666	0.980	0.968	0.943	0.956	0.881	0.667
Nainital Bank	0.847	0.834	0.902	0.846	0.848	0.800	0.631	0.762	0.697	0.701	0.841	0.818	0.930
Tamilnad Mercantile Bank	1.167	1.134	1.095	1.245	1.189	1.117	1.143	1.403	1.090	1.043	1.207	1.289	1.053
Bank of Rajasthan	0.773	0.789	0.777	0.788	0.772	0.740	0.655	0.733	0.802	0.934	0.689	0.617	0.646

(Contd.)

TABLE 4.8 (*Contd.*)

(1)	(2)	(3)	(4)	(5)	(6)	(7)	(8)	(9)	(10)	(11)	(12)	(13)	(14)
Catholic Syrian Bank	0.935	1.006	0.945	0.936	0.959	0.699	0.600	0.602	0.795	0.650	0.645	0.589	0.600
Dhanalakshmi Bank	1.109	1.012	0.961	0.964	1.129	0.907	0.637	0.800	0.865	0.850	0.716	0.664	0.710
Federal Bank	0.944	0.878	0.906	0.689	0.994	0.685	0.564	0.553	0.679	0.861	0.816	0.645	0.665
Jammu & Kashmir Bank	1.077	0.855	0.856	0.812	0.731	0.601	1.200	1.021	1.061	1.109	0.967	0.766	0.977
Karur Vysya Bank	0.982	0.975	0.963	0.909	0.921	1.396	0.755	0.793	0.764	0.921	1.017	0.914	1.317
Lakshmi Vilas Bank	1.441	1.308	0.968	0.865	0.874	0.991	0.807	0.875	1.017	1.301	0.996	0.838	0.803
Ratnakar Bank	0.839	0.849	0.814	0.741	0.754	0.748	0.648	0.589	1.014	0.705	0.756	0.735	0.831
Sangli Bank	0.824	0.832	0.771	0.716	0.805	0.669	0.660	0.718	0.950	0.751	0.802	0.611	0.858
South Indian Bank	1.033	0.969	0.907	0.906	0.978	0.761	0.633	0.642	1.043	0.737	0.828	0.555	0.639
United Western Bank	0.867	0.865	0.794	0.791	0.792	0.627	0.516	0.760	0.806	0.778	0.872	0.971	0.930
All CBs													
Mean	0.899	0.911	0.894	0.863	0.882	0.787	0.726	0.738	0.793	0.818	0.812	0.757	0.821
S.D	0.135	0.105	0.115	0.127	0.124	0.169	0.192	0.225	0.209	0.190	0.184	0.175	0.174
Q1	0.824	0.845	0.820	0.797	0.805	0.693	0.603	0.600	0.692	0.685	0.706	0.632	0.694
Q3	0.935	0.971	0.957	0.909	0.963	0.849	0.868	0.875	0.952	0.943	0.936	0.876	0.940
Median	0.882	0.878	0.876	0.840	0.864	0.735	0.664	0.733	0.807	0.815	0.823	0.766	0.812
PSBs													
Mean	0.847	0.883	0.867	0.845	0.855	0.752	0.720	0.680	0.720	0.766	0.763	0.726	0.815
S.D	0.074	0.070	0.086	0.079	0.104	0.128	0.195	0.218	0.212	0.177	0.176	0.167	0.170

Q1	0.812	0.844	0.814	0.801	0.795	0.685	0.576	0.519	0.537	0.663	0.645	0.631	0.709
Q3	0.909	0.909	0.917	0.883	0.947	0.802	0.879	0.853	0.888	0.917	0.897	0.857	0.960
Median	0.846	0.877	0.846	0.840	0.852	0.712	0.697	0.691	0.723	0.771	0.779	0.717	0.798
NBs													
Mean	0.859	0.894	0.882	0.848	0.857	0.751	0.643	0.582	0.636	0.703	0.693	0.670	0.754
S.D	0.054	0.070	0.089	0.080	0.114	0.147	0.153	0.175	0.195	0.168	0.160	0.163	0.160
Q1	0.825	0.848	0.820	0.789	0.800	0.682	0.522	0.458	0.505	0.598	0.553	0.595	0.692
Q3	0.912	0.912	0.930	0.901	0.947	0.790	0.761	0.695	0.730	0.793	0.812	0.745	0.826
Median	0.846	0.892	0.879	0.840	0.852	0.706	0.604	0.625	0.649	0.683	0.711	0.660	0.729
SBI													
Mean	0.821	0.856	0.832	0.838	0.849	0.754	0.902	0.912	0.919	0.915	0.929	0.858	0.961
S.D	0.108	0.065	0.068	0.081	0.084	0.077	0.165	0.106	0.061	0.087	0.064	0.082	0.088
Q1	0.789	0.807	0.797	0.822	0.794	0.724	0.861	0.830	0.874	0.863	0.901	0.833	0.949
Q3	0.901	0.884	0.852	0.864	0.889	0.782	0.968	0.947	0.952	0.984	0.953	0.914	1.005
Median	0.820	0.858	0.829	0.837	0.842	0.747	0.894	0.899	0.909	0.920	0.927	0.860	0.991
Pvt.													
Mean	0.975	0.954	0.933	0.891	0.922	0.840	0.735	0.824	0.902	0.897	0.886	0.803	0.830
S.D	0.165	0.132	0.142	0.173	0.141	0.209	0.193	0.205	0.146	0.179	0.170	0.185	0.182
Q1	0.848	0.858	0.833	0.789	0.816	0.696	0.631	0.722	0.797	0.758	0.780	0.650	0.669
Q3	1.066	1.010	0.967	0.930	0.977	0.947	0.769	0.875	1.016	1.014	0.964	0.906	0.930
Median	0.945	0.924	0.907	0.834	0.895	0.767	0.657	0.796	0.907	0.856	0.835	0.800	0.821

(*Contd.*)

TABLE 4.8 (*Contd.*)

Banks/Years	*1998-99*	*1999-2000*	*2000-01*	*2001-02*	*2002-03*	*2003-04*	*2004-05*	*2005-06*	*1986-92*	*1993-99*	*2000-06*	*1985-06*
(1)	*(15)*	*(16)*	*(17)*	*(18)*	*(19)*	*(20)*	*(21)*	*(22)*	*(23)*	*(24)*	*(25)*	*(26)*
Allahabad Bank	0.713	0.744	0.699	0.728	0.850	0.798	0.778	0.770	0.751	0.628	0.767	0.715
Andhra Bank	0.733	0.739	0.711	0.774	0.949	0.938	1.186	0.812	0.769	0.641	0.872	0.761
Bank of Baroda	0.928	0.768	0.804	0.793	0.782	0.826	0.824	0.763	0.953	0.898	0.794	0.882
Bank of India	0.768	0.694	0.819	0.754	0.802	0.740	0.625	0.663	0.787	0.656	0.728	0.724
Bank of Maharashtra	0.794	0.767	0.765	0.734	0.726	0.664	0.681	0.657	0.750	0.705	0.713	0.723
Canara Bank	0.856	0.752	0.810	0.756	0.779	0.768	0.761	0.716	0.974	0.778	0.763	0.838
Central Bank of India	0.728	0.742	0.685	0.697	0.862	0.812	0.840	0.757	0.777	0.627	0.771	0.725
Corporation Bank	1.061	0.974	1.122	0.901	1.005	0.957	1.194	1.145	0.835	0.930	1.043	0.936
Dena Bank	0.859	0.756	0.781	0.800	0.893	1.009	0.767	1.024	0.824	0.806	0.861	0.831
Indian Bank	0.485	0.544	0.607	0.578	0.721	0.839	0.802	0.766	0.873	0.523	0.694	0.696
Indian Overseas Bank	0.619	0.625	0.679	0.729	0.768	0.815	0.880	0.873	0.797	0.620	0.767	0.728
OBC	1.010	0.990	1.032	1.061	1.188	1.170	0.945	0.940	0.932	0.907	1.047	0.962
Punjab and Sind Bank	0.642	0.651	0.717	0.644	0.744	0.792	0.886	0.792	0.805	0.562	0.746	0.704
Punjab National Bank	0.860	0.773	0.769	0.772	0.953	0.890	0.827	0.785	0.765	0.743	0.824	0.777
Syndicate Bank	0.675	0.761	0.828	0.832	0.918	0.738	0.770	0.740	0.844	0.652	0.798	0.765
UCO	0.563	0.667	0.653	0.675	0.683	0.662	0.612	0.595	0.684	0.508	0.650	0.614

Union Bank of India	0.741	0.713	0.811	0.840	0.824	0.749	0.729	0.826	0.792	0.738	0.785	0.772
United Bank of India	0.517	0.534	0.547	0.729	0.810	0.785	0.808	0.841	0.805	0.406	0.722	0.644
Vijaya Bank	0.715	0.737	0.731	0.726	0.885	0.908	0.834	0.796	0.847	0.668	0.802	0.773
State Bank of India	0.869	0.826	0.821	0.759	0.788	0.780	0.840	0.967	0.939	0.902	0.826	0.889
State Bank of B&J	0.948	1.036	1.071	0.984	0.964	0.974	1.054	0.950	0.822	0.929	1.005	0.919
State Bank of Hyderabad	1.007	1.010	1.012	0.897	0.881	0.896	0.753	0.922	0.828	0.941	0.910	0.893
State Bank of Indore	1.119	0.985	0.993	0.994	1.092	1.112	0.757	0.842	0.842	1.001	0.968	0.937
State Bank of Mysore	0.925	0.967	0.946	0.902	1.056	0.937	1.052	1.081	0.826	0.904	0.992	0.907
State Bank of Patiala	0.939	1.105	1.225	1.161	1.053	0.940	0.809	0.776	0.836	0.945	1.010	0.930
State Bank of Saurashtra	0.944	0.932	0.829	0.850	0.824	0.853	0.783	0.692	0.854	0.945	0.823	0.874
State Bank of Travancore	0.764	0.754	0.806	0.715	0.781	0.794	0.849	0.785	0.740	0.786	0.783	0.770
Bharat Overseas Bank	0.902	0.783	0.905	0.923	0.755	0.812	0.942	0.865	1.183	0.977	0.855	1.005
City Union Bank	1.027	0.978	0.876	0.807	0.785	0.865	0.760	0.828	0.898	0.824	0.843	0.855
Ing Vysya Bank	0.888	0.875	0.737	0.900	1.175	1.145	0.687	0.877	0.811	1.006	0.914	0.910
Karnataka Bank	0.779	0.647	0.752	0.940	0.796	0.886	0.877	0.750	0.799	0.831	0.807	0.812
Lord Krishna Bank	0.916	0.756	0.830	1.404	1.107	0.910	0.548	0.622	0.959	0.901	0.882	0.914
Nainital Bank	0.942	0.896	0.787	0.918	0.976	0.912	0.830	0.975	0.815	0.813	0.899	0.843
Tamilnad Mercantile Bank	1.084	0.909	0.999	1.005	0.987	1.017	1.154	1.147	1.156	1.167	1.031	1.118
Bank of Rajasthan	0.638	0.716	0.795	0.801	0.838	0.703	0.537	0.530	0.756	0.723	0.703	0.727
Catholic Syrian Bank	0.505	0.676	0.743	0.737	0.947	0.921	0.765	0.728	0.869	0.627	0.788	0.761

(Contd.)

TABLE 4.8 (*Contd.*)

(1)	(15)	(16)	(17)	(18)	(19)	(20)	(21)	(22)	(23)	(24)	(25)	(26)
Dhanalakshmi Bank	0.631	0.760	0.769	0.868	1.035	0.811	0.652	0.696	0.960	0.748	0.799	0.835
Federal Bank	0.855	0.774	0.803	0.849	0.817	0.819	0.761	0.843	0.809	0.725	0.809	0.781
Jammu & Kashmir Bank	1.099	0.911	0.958	1.030	0.926	0.817	0.783	0.852	0.876	1.000	0.897	0.924
Karur Vysya Bank	0.940	1.185	1.010	1.007	0.911	1.045	0.898	1.043	0.986	0.952	1.014	0.984
Lakshmi Vilas Bank	1.063	1.066	1.183	0.846	0.810	0.790	0.640	0.599	1.036	0.985	0.848	0.956
Ratnakar Bank	0.738	0.797	0.813	1.158	0.873	0.680	0.721	0.729	0.770	0.767	0.824	0.787
Sangli Bank	0.631	0.655	0.644	0.658	0.593	0.626	0.538	0.530	0.754	0.760	0.606	0.707
South Indian Bank	0.689	0.819	0.825	0.812	0.859	0.938	0.694	0.764	0.884	0.733	0.816	0.811
United Western Bank	0.816	1.150	0.595	0.823	0.765	0.634	0.519	0.540	0.750	0.848	0.718	0.772
All CBs												
Mean	0.821	0.820	0.829	0.850	0.878	0.855	0.799	0.804	0.852	0.794	0.834	0.826
S.D	0.170	0.148	0.149	0.156	0.130	0.124	0.153	0.146	0.103	0.161	0.107	0.106
Q1	0.707	0.731	0.741	0.737	0.787	0.789	0.727	0.728	0.791	0.665	0.770	0.753
Q3	0.940	0.932	0.905	0.918	0.953	0.937	0.849	0.873	0.884	0.929	0.897	0.910
Median	0.855	0.768	0.806	0.823	0.859	0.826	0.783	0.785	0.826	0.786	0.816	0.812
PSBs												
Mean	0.807	0.798	0.825	0.807	0.873	0.857	0.839	0.825	0.824	0.754	0.832	0.803
S.D	0.164	0.151	0.162	0.131	0.126	0.122	0.142	0.129	0.068	0.163	0.112	0.098
Q1	0.714	0.725	0.714	0.728	0.782	0.783	0.764	0.760	0.782	0.634	0.765	0.724

Q3	0.934	0.949	0.887	0.873	0.951	0.937	0.865	0.897	0.845	0.905	0.891	0.891
Median	0.794	0.756	0.806	0.772	0.850	0.826	0.809	0.792	0.824	0.743	0.798	0.773
NBs												
Mean	0.751	0.733	0.767	0.764	0.850	0.835	0.829	0.803	0.819	0.684	0.797	0.767
S.D	0.155	0.113	0.134	0.102	0.120	0.123	0.152	0.128	0.073	0.139	0.103	0.090
Q1	0.658	0.681	0.692	0.727	0.774	0.759	0.764	0.749	0.773	0.624	0.737	0.719
Q3	0.858	0.764	0.810	0.797	0.906	0.899	0.860	0.834	0.845	0.760	0.813	0.804
Median	0.733	0.742	0.765	0.754	0.824	0.812	0.808	0.785	0.805	0.656	0.771	0.761
SBI												
Mean	0.939	0.952	0.963	0.908	0.930	0.911	0.862	0.877	0.836	0.919	0.915	0.890
S.D	0.102	0.114	0.145	0.142	0.128	0.107	0.123	0.126	0.054	0.062	0.092	0.053
Q1	0.911	0.905	0.827	0.827	0.815	0.838	0.776	0.783	0.825	0.903	0.825	0.885
Q3	0.963	1.017	1.027	0.986	1.053	0.949	0.900	0.955	0.845	0.945	0.995	0.921
Median	0.942	0.976	0.969	0.899	0.922	0.916	0.824	0.882	0.832	0.935	0.939	0.900
Pvt.												
Mean	0.841	0.853	0.835	0.916	0.886	0.852	0.739	0.773	0.893	0.855	0.836	0.861
S.D	0.175	0.160	0.139	0.168	0.139	0.139	0.164	0.175	0.131	0.137	0.102	0.108
Q1	0.702	0.757	0.756	0.815	0.799	0.795	0.643	0.641	0.802	0.751	0.801	0.783
Q3	0.941	0.910	0.898	0.989	0.968	0.919	0.819	0.861	0.959	0.971	0.893	0.922
Median	0.871	0.808	0.808	0.884	0.866	0.842	0.740	0.757	0.872	0.828	0.833	0.839

*Note** : S.D denotes stanadard deviation, Q1 denotes first-quartile, Q3 denotes third quartile.

Table 5.1

Inter-Bank Average Effciency Change Index Over the Different Time Periods

Banks/Years	*1986*	*1987*	*1988-89*	*1989-90*	*1990-91*	*1991-92*	*1992-93*	*1993-94*	*1994-95*	*1995-96*	*1996-97*	*1997-98*	*1998 99*
(1)	*(2)*	*(3)*	*(4)*	*(5)*	*(6)*	*(7)*	*(8)*	*(9)*	*(10)*	*(11)*	*(12)*	*(13)*	*(14)*
Allahabad Bank	1.044	0.961	1.012	0.899	1.053	0.951	0.89	0.835	1.06	1.136	1.019	1.12	0.996
Andhra Bank	1.031	1.032	0.931	1.024	0.842	0.667	0.834	1.253	1.467	0.94	0.929	1.331	0.874
Bank of Baroda	1.071	0.982	0.956	0.931	1.172	0.889	0.985	1.142	0.99	0.895	0.866	1.039	1.165
Bank of India	1.089	0.976	0.917	0.949	0.959	1.26	0.594	1.157	1.146	0.961	0.956	1.154	1.052
Bank of Maharashtra	0.963	0.925	1.059	1.051	0.779	0.825	0.742	1.253	1.361	1.281	0.91	1.107	0.901
Canara Bank	1.063	1.03	1	1	0.86	0.994	1.028	0.821	1.245	0.865	0.848	0.98	1.324
Central Bank of India	1.099	0.846	0.935	1.057	0.839	0.743	0.953	0.86	1.457	1.175	0.941	1.169	0.933
Corporation Bank	1.056	1.042	0.984	0.991	0.771	0.956	1.05	1.153	1.157	0.944	1.113	1.02	1
Dena Bank	0.961	0.996	0.995	1.073	0.756	0.826	1.016	1.215	1.132	1.037	1.029	1.081	0.913
Indian Bank	1.022	1.054	0.958	1.152	0.865	1.023	0.771	0.824	0.992	0.851	1.103	0.824	1.146
Indian Overseas Bank	1.056	0.917	0.942	0.968	1.151	0.846	0.991	1.324	0.554	0.953	0.979	1.176	1.085
OBC	0.979	1.067	1	0.998	1.046	0.805	0.858	1.191	1.21	0.96	1.006	0.947	1.098
Punjab and Sind Bank	1.082	0.908	0.927	0.936	0.802	0.717	0.8	1.396	1.294	0.768	1.124	1.229	0.923
Punjab National Bank	0.973	1.021	0.987	1.049	0.802	0.833	1.202	1.042	0.955	1.112	0.961	1.104	1.075
Syndicate Bank	0.981	1.108	0.909	0.947	0.798	0.879	0.722	1.488	1.033	1.112	0.918	1.024	0.963

UCO	1.043	0.906	0.961	0.841	0.878	0.879	1.09	0.677	1.683	0.918	0.847	1.149	1.064
Union Bank of India	1.172	0.995	0.912	1.032	0.776	0.952	0.994	1.182	1.047	0.989	0.939	1.135	0.91
United Bank of India	1.021	0.93	0.991	1.174	0.722	0.63	0.453	1.426	1.215	1.211	0.807	2.087	0.721
Vijaya Bank	1.014	1.019	0.959	1.103	0.725	0.823	1.184	1.01	0.974	0.818	1.116	1.098	1.039
State Bank of India	1.012	0.994	1.014	0.884	0.988	1.155	0.911	0.975	1.116	1.005	0.858	1.023	1.006
State Bank of B&J	1.038	0.949	1.079	0.859	0.985	1.32	0.932	0.965	1.01	1.068	0.978	1.093	0.947
State Bank of Hyderabad	1.089	0.954	1.013	0.953	0.93	1.205	1.044	0.959	1.054	0.994	0.929	1.116	1.023
State Bank of Indore	0.893	1.039	0.986	1.037	0.866	1.193	0.928	1.209	1	1	0.97	1.031	1
State Bank of Mysore	1.066	0.94	0.969	1.204	0.733	1.109	1.06	1.107	0.901	1.094	1.009	1.093	0.925
State Bank of Patiala	1.301	0.925	0.936	1.415	0.894	1.151	1	0.952	0.937	0.992	0.913	1.238	0.939
State Bank of Saurashtra	1.009	0.963	0.946	0.991	0.921	1.173	1.097	0.978	1.051	0.919	0.915	1.166	0.963
State Bank of Travancore	1.032	1.016	1.109	0.881	0.812	0.99	1.298	1.061	0.916	1.058	0.85	1.137	0.961
Bharat Overseas Bank	1	1	1	1	1	1	1	1	1	0.941	0.875	1.082	1.014
City Union Bank	1.053	1.001	0.826	1.061	0.925	0.954	1.094	0.956	1.001	1.019	0.948	0.865	1.479
Ing Vysya Bank	1.067	0.95	0.951	1.15	0.854	0.899	1.256	1.121	1.022	1	1	0.812	1.094
Karnataka Bank	1.014	0.98	0.964	1.081	0.784	0.906	1.277	0.923	1.122	0.929	1.228	0.99	0.828
Lord Krishna Bank	1.024	1	1	0.972	0.994	0.7	1.451	0.989	0.973	1.014	0.923	0.755	1.374
Nainital Bank	0.988	1.078	0.939	1.003	0.942	0.788	1.209	0.917	1.001	1.203	0.973	1.138	1.013
Tamilnad Mercantile Bank	1	1	1	1	1	1	1	1	1	1	1	1	1
Bank of Rajasthan	1.022	0.987	1.013	0.979	0.954	0.891	1.116	1.095	1.164	0.736	0.897	1.045	0.99

(*Contd.*)

TABLE 5.1 (*Contd.*)

(1)	(2)	(3)	(4)	(5)	(6)	(7)	(8)	(9)	(10)	(11)	(12)	(13)	(14)
Catholic Syrian Bank	1.072	0.947	0.989	1.026	0.727	0.86	1.002	1.318	0.82	0.989	0.915	1.019	0.84
Dhanalakshmi Bank	1	0.961	1.006	1.035	0.91	0.697	1.264	1.082	0.98	0.84	0.928	1.07	0.888
Federal Bank	0.939	1.029	0.758	1.443	0.686	0.827	0.981	1.227	1.272	0.948	0.791	1.028	1.288
Jammu & Kashmir Bank	0.859	1	0.946	0.9	0.823	1.663	1	1	1	0.967	0.792	1.274	1.025
Karur Vysya Bank	0.992	0.994	0.939	1.014	1.087	0.758	1.044	0.967	1.206	1.084	0.915	1.093	0.939
Lakshmi Vilas Bank	1	0.974	0.883	1.015	1.135	0.814	1.089	1.138	1	0.998	0.84	0.959	1.244
Ratnakar Bank	1.018	0.964	0.907	1.015	0.989	0.867	0.913	1.696	0.703	1.079	0.97	1.13	0.888
Sangli Bank	1.014	0.925	0.929	1.125	0.825	0.993	1.091	1.322	0.789	1.069	0.761	1.407	0.738
South Indian Bank	0.97	0.938	0.999	1.074	0.778	0.83	1.017	1.559	0.739	1.118	0.673	1.152	1.078
United Western Bank	0.997	0.921	0.992	1.004	0.787	0.829	1.467	1.059	0.968	1.121	1.112	0.956	0.879
All CBs													
Mean	1.024	0.980	0.963	1.023	0.879	0.917	0.995	1.089	1.041	0.996	0.936	1.085	1.002
S.D	0.068	0.052	0.059	0.119	0.123	0.196	0.196	0.207	0.202	0.114	0.106	0.196	0.152
Q1	0.997	0.947	0.936	0.968	0.787	0.825	0.928	0.967	0.974	0.941	0.875	1.020	0.923
Q3	1.056	1.016	1.000	1.061	0.985	1.000	1.094	1.215	1.157	1.079	1.000	1.149	1.075
Median	1.021	0.982	0.964	1.014	0.865	0.889	1.002	1.082	1.010	0.998	0.929	1.093	1.00
PSBs													
Mean	1.040	0.980	0.976	1.008	0.871	0.938	0.922	1.073	1.088	0.995	0.953	1.121	0.992
S.D	0.075	0.060	0.050	0.122	0.123	0.187	0.184	0.201	0.219	0.121	0.088	0.214	0.113

Q1	1.011	0.935	0.939	0.942	0.789	0.826	0.846	0.962	0.991	0.930	0.912	1.035	0.929
Q3	1.069	1.026	1.000	1.054	0.945	1.130	1.047	1.212	1.213	1.081	1.008	1.160	1.058
Median	1.038	0.982	0.969	0.998	0.860	0.951	0.985	1.107	1.054	0.992	0.941	1.107	0.996
NBs													
Mean	1.037	0.983	0.964	1.006	0.864	0.858	0.880	1.094	1.129	0.987	0.964	1.126	1.001
S.D	0.054	0.067	0.040	0.084	0.138	0.142	0.193	0.229	0.244	0.141	0.097	0.253	0.132
Q1	0.998	0.928	0.933	0.948	0.778	0.814	0.786	0.935	1.013	0.907	0.914	1.032	0.918
Q3	1.067	1.031	0.993	1.054	0.919	0.952	1.022	1.253	1.270	1.112	1.024	1.162	1.080
Median	1.043	0.995	0.959	1.000	0.839	0.846	0.953	1.157	1.146	0.960	0.956	1.107	1.000
SBI													
Mean	1.050	0.972	1.005	1.014	0.887	1.159	1.027	1.022	0.996	1.015	0.926	1.110	0.970
S.D	0.115	0.040	0.061	0.192	0.087	0.093	0.127	0.092	0.075	0.055	0.056	0.070	0.035
Q1	1.011	0.947	0.963	0.883	0.853	1.141	0.931	0.964	0.932	0.994	0.899	1.078	0.945
Q3	1.072	1.000	1.030	1.079	0.944	1.196	1.069	1.073	1.052	1.061	0.972	1.144	1.002
Median	1.035	0.959	1.000	0.972	0.908	1.164	1.022	0.977	1.005	1.003	0.922	1.105	0.962
Pvt.													
Mean	1.000	0.980	0.944	1.045	0.892	0.887	1.116	1.114	0.975	0.997	0.911	1.032	1.016
S.D	0.048	0.039	0.068	0.114	0.124	0.210	0.161	0.218	0.152	0.107	0.128	0.155	0.199
Q1	0.993	0.953	0.932	1.001	0.796	0.817	1.001	0.992	0.969	0.953	0.849	0.967	0.888
Q3	1.021	1.000	1.000	1.071	0.993	0.942	1.244	1.205	1.017	1.077	0.972	1.121	1.090
Median	1.000	0.984	0.958	1.015	0.918	0.864	1.090	1.071	1.000	1.000	0.919	1.037	1.007

(Contd.)

TABLE 5.1 (*Contd.*)

Banks/Years	*1999-2000*	*2000-01*	*2001-02*	*2002-03*	*2003-04*	*2004-05*	*2005-06*	*1986-92*	*1993-99*	*2000-06*	*1986-06*	*1993-06*
(1)	(15)	(16)	(17)	(18)	(19)	(20)	(21)	(22)	(23)	(24)	(25)	(26)
Allahabad Bank	1.043	0.939	1.04	1.167	0.94	0.975	0.989	0.985	1.002	1.011	1.000	1.007
Andhra Bank	1.009	0.961	1.088	1.227	0.987	1.067	0.811	0.910	1.065	1.014	0.999	1.040
Bank of Baroda	0.828	1.046	0.987	0.987	1.056	0.997	0.927	0.996	1.006	0.973	0.991	0.989
Bank of India	0.905	1.179	0.921	1.064	0.924	0.844	1.06	1.019	0.982	0.979	0.992	0.981
Bank of Maharashtra	0.968	0.995	0.961	0.99	0.914	1.026	0.964	0.928	1.057	0.973	0.987	1.014
Canara Bank	0.879	1.077	0.932	1.032	0.986	0.99	0.941	0.989	1.000	0.975	0.988	0.987
Central Bank of India	1.019	0.923	1.018	1.237	0.942	1.034	0.901	0.911	1.053	1.006	0.992	1.029
Corporation Bank	0.974	1.027	0.902	1.109	0.957	1.045	1	0.962	1.060	1.000	1.009	1.029
Dena Bank	0.88	1.032	1.025	1.118	1.119	0.767	1.303	0.928	1.057	1.022	1.004	1.039
Indian Bank	1.12	1.116	0.954	1.248	1.163	0.956	0.953	1.008	0.920	1.067	0.996	0.991
Indian Overseas Bank	1.01	1.084	1.075	1.055	1.06	1.08	0.991	0.975	0.980	1.050	1.002	1.014
OBC	0.99	1.01	1	1	1	0.945	0.994	0.979	1.031	0.991	1.001	1.011
Punjab and Sind Bank	1.015	1.1	0.898	1.156	1.065	1.118	0.894	0.888	1.051	1.030	0.992	1.041
Punjab National Bank	0.9	0.994	1.004	1.237	0.934	0.928	0.949	0.939	1.061	0.987	0.998	1.024
Syndicate Bank	1.128	1.087	1.004	1.105	0.804	1.043	0.961	0.932	1.016	1.013	0.989	1.015
UCO	1.185	0.98	1.033	1.012	0.97	0.923	0.972	0.916	1.024	1.008	0.985	1.016

Union Bank of India	0.963	1.137	1.036	0.981	0.91	0.972	1.132	0.966	1.024	1.016	1.003	1.020
United Bank of India	1.031	1.024	1.331	1.114	0.968	1.029	1.042	0.892	1.021	1.072	0.997	1.046
Vijaya Bank	1.033	0.992	0.992	1.22	1.026	0.918	0.954	0.931	1.028	1.016	[illegible]	1.022
State Bank of India	0.952	0.993	0.924	1.038	0.991	1.075	1.152	1.005	0.982	1.015	1.000	0.998
State Bank of B&J	1.056	1	0.983	0.981	1.009	1.027	0.95	1.029	0.997	1.000	1.008	0.999
State Bank of Hyderabad	1	1	0.896	0.983	1.018	0.84	1.223	1.020	1.015	0.988	1.007	1.002
State Bank of Indore	0.984	1.007	1.001	1.007	1	0.757	1.112	0.997	1.017	0.976	0.996	0.996
State Bank of Mysore	1.047	0.978	0.953	1.108	0.937	1.067	1	0.992	1.024	1.011	1.010	1.018
State Bank of Patiala	1.065	1	1	1	0.94	0.86	0.96	1.086	0.991	0.973	1.012	0.982
State Bank of Saurashtra	0.987	0.891	1.024	0.97	1.034	0.918	0.883	0.997	1.009	0.956	0.987	0.982
State Bank of Travancore	0.987	1.07	0.886	1.093	1.016	1.07	0.924	0.968	1.031	1.004	1.002	1.017
Bharat Overseas Bank	0.867	1.156	1.02	0.818	1.076	1.16	0.917	1.000	0.986	0.994	0.993	0.990
City Union Bank	0.978	0.895	0.922	0.973	1.103	0.878	1.089	0.967	1.037	0.973	0.993	1.005
Ing Vysya Bank	0.986	0.841	1.224	1.11	1	0.687	1.275	0.973	1.036	0.998	1.004	1.017
Karnataka Bank	0.831	1.162	1.25	0.847	1.113	0.989	0.855	0.950	1.031	0.995	0.993	1.012
Lord Krishna Bank	0.824	1.098	1.207	1	0.909	0.603	1.135	0.941	1.044	0.946	0.978	0.994
Nainital Bank	0.952	0.877	1.165	1.064	0.937	0.91	1.174	0.952	1.059	1.005	1.007	1.032
Tamilnad Mercantile Bank	0.909	1.099	1.001	0.987	1.013	1	1	1.000	1.000	1.000	1.000	1.000
Bank of Rajasthan	1.121	1.113	1.005	1.047	0.839	0.764	0.988	0.973	0.996	0.974	0.981	0.985
Catholic Syrian Bank	1.341	1.1	0.991	1.285	0.972	0.831	0.952	0.929	0.975	1.054	0.988	1.014

(*Contd.*)

TABLE 5.1 (*Contd.*)

(1)	(15)	(16)	(17)	(18)	(19)	(20)	(21)	(22)	(23)	(24)	(25)	(26)
Dhanalakshmi Bank	1.208	1.011	1.127	1.152	0.812	0.803	1.068	0.927	0.999	1.014	0.982	1.007
Federal Bank	0.905	1.037	1.057	0.961	1.004	0.929	1.107	0.918	1.062	0.998	0.995	1.029
Jammu & Kashmir Bank	0.911	1.052	1.044	0.926	0.882	0.959	1.087	1.000	1.000	0.977	0.992	0.989
Karur Vysya Bank	1.065	1	1	0.911	1.098	0.898	1.114	0.958	1.031	1.009	1.001	1.020
Lakshmi Vilas Bank	1	1	0.846	0.957	0.974	0.813	0.933	0.965	1.031	0.929	0.975	0.979
Ratnakar Bank	1.08	1.021	1.23	0.873	0.779	1.058	1.012	0.958	1.019	0.998	0.993	1.009
Sangli Bank	1.037	0.982	1.019	0.902	1.057	0.858	0.986	0.964	0.994	0.975	0.978	0.985
South Indian Bank	1.188	1.006	0.986	1.058	1.09	0.741	1.1	0.926	1.013	1.015	0.987	1.014
United Western Bank	1.225	0.596	1.382	0.929	0.828	0.819	1.04	0.918	1.067	0.943	0.976	1.003
All CBs												
Mean	1.003	1.01	1.024	1.04	0.977	0.924	1.012	0.963	1.019	0.998	0.995	1.020
S.D	0.11	0.099	0.116	0.111	0.088	0.122	0.107	0.040	0.030	0.029	0.009	0.018
Q1	0.952	0.992	0.961	0.981	0.937	0.844	0.95	0.929	1.000	0.976	0.988	0.994
Q3	1.056	1.084	1.044	1.11	1.034	1.029	1.089	0.996	1.037	1.014	1.001	1.020
Median	1	1.01	1.004	1.032	0.987	0.945	0.991	0.965	1.021	1.000	0.994	1.011
PSBs												
Mean	0.995	1.022	0.992	1.079	0.985	0.968	0.993	0.967	1.018	1.004	0.998	1.011
S.D	0.079	0.066	0.087	0.092	0.072	0.096	0.107	0.047	0.032	0.028	0.008	0.019

Q1	0.966	0.993	0.943	1	0.94	0.921	0.945	0.930	1.001	0.983	0.992	0.997
Q3	1.038	1.074	1.025	1.137	1.022	1.044	1.021	0.997	1.041	1.015	1.003	1.023
Median	1	1.007	1	1.064	0.987	0.99	0.964	0.975	1.021	1.006	0.998	1.014
NBs												
Mean	0.99	1.035	1.007	1.105	0.982	0.978	0.982	0.949	1.022	1.010	0.996	1.016
S.D	0.091	0.069	0.094	0.095	0.083	0.084	0.102	0.040	0.037	0.029	0.007	0.019
Q1	0.934	0.993	0.958	1.022	0.937	0.937	0.945	0.922	1.004	0.989	0.992	1.009
Q3	1.032	1.086	1.035	1.194	1.041	1.039	0.997	0.982	1.055	1.019	1.001	1.02
Median	1.009	1.027	1.004	1.109	0.97	0.99	0.964	0.939	1.024	1.011	0.996	1.016
SBI												
Mean	1.009	0.991	0.957	1.021	0.993	0.944	1.019	1.011	1.008	0.990	1.003	0.999
S.D	0.041	0.049	0.052	0.053	0.036	0.124	0.122	0.035	0.017	0.021	0.008	0.013
Q1	0.986	0.989	0.917	0.983	0.978	0.855	0.944	0.995	0.996	0.975	0.999	0.992
Q3	1.049	1.002	1	1.052	1.017	1.068	1.122	1.022	1.018	1.006	1.008	1.006
Median	0.994	1	0.968	1.004	1.005	0.973	0.98	1.001	1.012	0.994	1.005	0.999
Pvt.												
Mean	1.014	0.992	1.074	0.983	0.965	0.862	1.042	0.956	1.021	0.988	0.990	1.004
S.D	0.147	0.136	0.136	0.116	0.109	0.135	0.102	0.027	0.027	0.030	0.010	0.015
Q1	0.91	0.987	1	0.915	0.889	0.806	0.987	0.932	0.999	0.974	0.982	0.991
Q3	1.111	1.099	1.197	1.055	1.071	0.952	1.105	0.972	1.037	1.004	0.994	1.014
Median	0.993	1.016	1.032	0.967	0.987	0.868	1.054	0.958	1.025	0.996	0.992	1.006

*Note** : S.D denotes stanadard deviation, Q1 denotes first-quartile, Q3 denotes third quartile.

TABLE 5.2

Inter-Bank Average Technological Change Index Over the Different Time Periods

Banks/Years	*1986*	*1987*	*1988-89*	*1989-90*	*1990-91*	*1991-92*	*1992-93*	*1993-94*	*1994-95*	*1995-96*	*1996-97*	*1997-98*
(1)	(2)	(3)	(4)	(5)	(6)	(7)	(8)	(9)	(10)	(11)	(12)	(13)
Allahabad Bank	1.041	1.069	1.408	1	1.029	1.319	1.158	0.97	1.059	1.107	1.087	0.844
Andhra Bank	1.06	1.059	1.345	0.907	1.167	1.607	0.934	0.945	1.06	1.049	1.076	0.858
Bank of Baroda	1.039	1.069	1.428	1.024	1.061	1.367	1.013	1.115	1.041	1.091	1.078	0.991
Bank of India	1.048	1.064	1.427	1.018	1.028	1.302	1.31	0.985	1.048	1.119	1.098	0.91
Bank of Maharashtra	1.043	1.054	1.338	0.9	1.217	1.511	0.885	0.957	1.1	1.049	1.072	0.863
Canara Bank	1.062	1.101	1.335	0.929	1.115	1.707	0.879	0.965	1.055	1.108	1.094	0.906
Central Bank of India	1.046	1.101	1.366	0.947	1.117	1.615	0.836	0.966	1.088	1.063	1.076	0.863
Corporation Bank	1.019	1.001	1.348	0.901	1.21	1.615	0.916	1.003	1.041	1.119	1.075	1.061
Dena Bank	1.032	1.038	1.339	0.9	1.224	1.481	0.759	0.946	1.104	1.051	1.085	0.876
Indian Bank	1.045	1.055	1.435	1.003	1.089	1.327	1.368	1.056	1.083	0.957	1.063	1.059
Indian Overseas Bank	1.039	1.099	1.378	0.985	1.054	1.309	1.268	0.94	1.104	1.109	1.096	0.874
OBC	1.056	1.06	1.344	0.925	1.115	1.866	0.89	0.982	1.049	1.034	1.072	1.041
Punjab and Sind Bank	1.062	1.017	1.331	0.912	1.159	1.597	0.921	0.972	1.066	1.111	1.092	0.845
Punjab National Bank	1.054	1.091	1.37	0.934	1.135	1.814	0.786	0.945	1.107	1.056	1.076	0.861
Syndicate Bank	1.055	1.026	1.336	0.901	1.251	1.423	0.929	0.944	1.096	1.049	1.069	0.875
UCO	1.021	1.038	1.345	0.963	1.05	1.414	1.07	0.953	1.08	1.063	1.076	0.899

Union Bank of India	1.031	1.036	1.356	0.91	1.172	1.616	0.788	0.946	1.077	1.055	1.089	0.903
United Bank of India	1.071	1.042	1.328	0.849	1.111	1.612	1.046	0.956	1.132	0.991	1.099	0.858
Vijaya Bank	1	1.008	1.381	0.931	1.173	1.5	0.927	0.973	1.07	1.098	1.084	0.852
State Bank of India	1.058	1.052	1.427	0.997	1.049	1.474	0.996	0.967	1.055	1.098	1.095	0.849
State Bank of B&J	1.055	1.086	1.383	0.934	1.037	1.345	0.855	0.956	1.06	1.049	1.09	0.878
State Bank of Hyderabad	1.073	1.059	1.391	0.956	1.044	1.483	0.837	0.96	1.056	1.13	1.093	0.842
State Bank of Indore	1.041	1.03	1.41	0.94	1.151	1.443	0.844	0.973	1.103	1.067	1.07	0.869
State Bank of Mysore	1.03	1.022	1.394	0.892	1.241	1.341	0.816	0.963	1.071	1.081	1.084	0.88
State Bank of Patiala	1.074	1.188	1.386	0.804	1.047	1.525	0.698	0.906	1.093	1.036	1.088	0.847
State Bank of Saurashtra	0.998	1.016	1.382	0.887	1.117	1.367	0.872	0.966	1.096	1.075	1.096	0.857
State Bank of Travancore	1.005	0.996	1.368	0.899	1.223	1.492	0.803	0.963	1.064	1.063	1.104	0.869
Bharat Overseas Bank	1.063	1.132	1.396	0.908	1.032	1.519	0.975	1.045	1.038	1.064	1.072	1.081
City Union Bank	0.982	1.054	1.364	0.884	1.106	1.388	0.756	0.953	1.075	1.118	1.086	1.132
Ing Vysya Bank	1.026	1.038	1.369	0.908	1.168	1.6	1.133	1.09	1.271	0.959	0.877	1.542
Karnataka Bank	0.982	1	1.369	0.899	1.271	1.446	0.759	0.933	1.086	1.09	1.084	1.007
Lord Krishna Bank	0.96	1.003	1.357	0.825	0.98	1.324	1	0.961	1.067	1.06	1.039	1.381
Nainital Bank	1.049	1.002	1.334	0.901	1.242	1.693	0.666	0.903	1.082	1.019	1.073	0.864
Tamilnad Mercantile Bank	1.032	1.035	1.41	0.854	0.988	1.435	1.074	1.004	1.024	1.159	1.092	0.946
Bank of Rajasthan	1.026	1.009	1.391	0.912	1.127	1.516	0.738	0.932	1.076	1.121	1.085	0.88
Catholic Syrian Bank	0.971	1.02	1.361	0.862	1.206	1.398	0.726	0.929	1.104	1.064	1.086	0.901
Dhanalakshmi Bank	0.921	1.027	1.365	0.877	1.047	1.367	0.754	0.947	1.076	1.1	1.072	1.09

(Contd.)

TABLE 5.2 (*Contd.*)

(1)	(2)	(3)	(4)	(5)	(6)	(7)	(8)	(9)	(10)	(11)	(12)	(13)
Federal Bank	0.969	1.022	1.365	0.875	1.264	1.54	0.936	0.971	1.047	1.057	0.988	1.283
Jammu & Kashmir Bank	1.057	1.089	1.347	0.941	1.119	1.939	0.77	0.984	1.09	0.993	1.082	0.961
Karur Vysya Bank	1.003	1.032	1.379	0.919	1.139	1.381	0.835	0.965	1.099	1.033	1.067	1.176
Lakshmi Vilas Bank	1.065	0.962	1.395	0.875	0.969	1.34	0.934	0.947	1.165	0.952	1.066	1.173
Ratnakar Bank	0.939	1.015	1.343	0.875	1.241	1.628	0.672	0.905	1.079	1.019	1.072	0.868
Sangli Bank	1.016	1.03	1.37	0.901	1.222	1.463	0.73	0.926	1.094	1.053	1.075	0.922
South Indian Bank	0.969	1.016	1.362	0.861	1.17	1.349	0.801	0.977	1.086	1.075	1.087	0.898
United Western Bank	0.975	1.008	1.377	0.881	1.241	1.453	0.735	0.958	1.055	1.087	1.07	1.196
All CBs												
Mean	1.025	1.043	1.372	0.912	1.128	1.487	0.884	0.966	1.081	1.064	1.074	0.954
S.D	0.038	0.041	0.028	0.048	0.084	0.150	0.165	0.042	0.039	0.046	0.035	0.158
Q1	1.003	1.016	1.347	0.884	1.050	1.367	0.770	0.946	1.059	1.049	1.072	0.863
Q3	1.055	1.060	1.391	0.934	1.210	1.600	0.975	0.973	1.096	1.098	1.089	1.041
Median	1.039	1.036	1.369	0.907	1.127	1.474	0.872	0.961	1.077	1.063	1.082	0.898
PSBs												
Mean	1.043	1.054	1.373	0.930	1.123	1.492	0.928	0.969	1.076	1.069	1.084	0.892
S.D	0.021	0.040	0.033	0.051	0.072	0.151	0.168	0.039	0.024	0.040	0.011	0.065
Q1	1.032	1.028	1.345	0.901	1.052	1.367	0.837	0.950	1.058	1.049	1.076	0.858

Q3	1.057	1.069	1.393	0.960	1.173	1.610	1.005	0.973	1.096	1.103	1.094	0.901
Median	1.045	1.054	1.370	0.929	1.117	1.483	0.890	0.963	1.071	1.063	1.085	0.869
NBs												
Mean	1.043	1.054	1.365	0.938	1.128	1.518	0.969	0.974	1.077	1.066	1.082	0.905
S.D	0.017	0.030	0.035	0.048	0.068	0.168	0.179	0.044	0.026	0.044	0.011	0.073
Q1	1.036	1.037	1.339	0.904	1.075	1.391	0.882	0.946	1.057	1.049	1.076	0.860
Q3	1.056	1.069	1.380	0.974	1.173	1.615	1.058	0.978	1.098	1.108	1.091	0.908
Median	1.045	1.055	1.348	0.929	1.117	1.511	0.927	0.965	1.077	1.063	1.078	0.875
SBI												
Mean	1.041	1.055	1.393	0.912	1.111	1.432	0.837	0.957	1.075	1.075	1.090	0.861
S.D	0.029	0.060	0.018	0.058	0.084	0.072	0.083	0.021	0.020	0.029	0.010	0.015
Q1	1.024	1.021	1.383	0.891	1.046	1.362	0.813	0.959	1.059	1.060	1.087	0.849
Q3	1.062	1.066	1.398	0.944	1.169	1.485	0.859	0.966	1.094	1.085	1.095	0.871
Median	1.048	1.041	1.389	0.917	1.083	1.459	0.841	0.963	1.068	1.071	1.092	0.863
Pvt.												
Mean	0.999	1.027	1.370	0.886	1.136	1.481	0.823	0.962	1.088	1.055	1.058	1.057
S.D	0.043	0.037	0.019	0.027	0.102	0.154	0.140	0.047	0.054	0.055	0.051	0.194
Q1	0.970	1.008	1.361	0.875	1.062	1.383	0.736	0.932	1.069	1.023	1.068	0.906
Q3	1.031	1.034	1.379	0.906	1.236	1.535	0.936	0.976	1.093	1.089	1.085	1.175
Median	0.993	1.021	1.367	0.883	1.154	1.450	0.765	0.956	1.081	1.062	1.073	1.044

(*Contd.*)

TABLE 5.2 (*Contd.*)

Banks/Years	*1998-99*	*1999-2000*	*2000-01*	*2001-02*	*2002-03*	*2003-04*	*2004-05*	*2005-06*	*1986-92*	*1993-99*	*2000-06*	*1986-06*
(1)	*(14)*	*(15)*	*(16)*	*(17)*	*(18)*	*(19)*	*(20)*	*(21)*	*(22)*	*(23)*	*(24)*	*(25)*
Allahabad Bank	1.003	1.001	1.094	1.036	0.982	1.071	0.95	0.989	1.134	1.028	1.016	1.054
Andhra Bank	1.012	1.04	1.044	1.073	1.065	1.076	0.958	0.888	1.170	0.988	1.018	1.050
Bank of Baroda	0.907	1.139	1.039	1.055	1.084	1.089	0.962	1.004	1.153	1.032	1.052	1.074
Bank of India	0.92	1.098	0.993	1.129	1.069	1.076	0.912	0.924	1.138	1.048	1.026	1.066
Bank of Maharashtra	1.034	1.026	1.047	1.075	1.051	1.091	0.971	0.968	1.160	0.990	1.032	1.053
Canara Bank	0.917	1.054	1.003	1.156	1.066	1.083	0.939	0.975	1.184	0.985	1.037	1.060
Central Bank of India	1.039	0.991	1.108	0.985	0.935	1.116	0.974	0.968	1.179	0.985	1.009	1.048
Corporation Bank	0.903	1.16	1.102	1.149	1.112	1.069	1.037	1.007	1.159	1.014	1.090	1.082
Dena Bank	0.974	1.062	1.028	1.155	1.081	1.04	0.895	0.886	1.152	0.964	1.017	1.036
Indian Bank	0.789	1.186	0.969	1.267	0.972	1.058	0.953	0.956	1.148	1.042	1.045	1.074
Indian Overseas Bank	0.962	1.05	1.092	1.055	1.026	1.096	0.973	1.005	1.135	1.043	1.042	1.069
OBC	0.946	1.13	1.122	1.13	1.181	1.104	1.047	1.092	1.194	1.000	1.114	1.095
Punjab and Sind Bank	0.967	1.049	1.006	1.151	1.033	1.066	0.978	0.943	1.159	0.992	1.030	1.053
Punjab National Bank	1.01	0.975	1.07	1.024	0.938	1.091	0.974	0.987	1.203	0.971	1.007	1.049
Syndicate Bank	1.03	0.951	1.112	0.915	0.921	1.092	0.975	1.025	1.151	0.996	0.996	1.040
UCO	0.946	0.922	1.06	1.123	1.005	1.068	0.981	1.029	1.126	1.010	1.025	1.049
Union Bank of India	0.97	1.081	1.093	1.02	1.082	1.099	1.001	1.048	1.165	0.970	1.060	1.057

United Bank of India	1.034	1.01	1.125	1.041	0.987	1.051	0.96	0.880	1.145	1.013	1.005	1.048
Vijaya Bank	1.028	1.018	1.133	0.994	0.995	1.086	0.982	1.032	1.147	1.001	1.033	1.054
State Bank of India	0.922	1.033	1.016	1.082	1.023	1.076	0.943	0.909	1.161	0.994	1.010	1.047
State Bank of B&J	0.931	1.012	1.022	1.054	0.987	1.049	0.953	0.902	1.128	0.970	0.996	1.024
State Bank of Hyderabad	1.004	1.026	1.025	1.11	1.042	1.071	0.941	0.941	1.152	0.983	1.021	1.045
State Bank of Indore	1.037	1.012	0.961	1.28	1.029	1.065	0.919	0.981	1.154	0.990	1.030	1.051
State Bank of Mysore	0.988	1.004	1.016	1.123	1.025	1.025	0.897	0.798	1.139	0.978	0.979	1.024
State Bank of Patiala	1.026	1.014	1.135	0.974	0.99	1.078	0.974	1.050	1.146	0.946	1.029	1.032
State Bank of Saurashtra	1.012	0.96	1.06	1.076	0.998	1.063	0.918	0.992	1.113	0.992	1.008	1.032
State Bank of Travancore	0.874	1.089	0.995	1.09	0.987	1.074	0.947	0.988	1.144	0.957	1.023	1.033
Bharat Overseas Bank	0.902	1.167	1.117	1.279	1.107	1.081	1.061	1.067	1.156	1.023	1.123	1.097
City Union Bank	0.765	1.228	0.979	1.22	1.07	1.069	1.001	1.036	1.114	0.971	1.082	1.051
Ing Vysya Bank	0.707	1.543	0.919	1.522	1.116	0.931	0.927	1.066	1.163	1.053	1.120	1.109
Karnataka Bank	0.916	1.213	1.041	1.45	1.067	0.941	0.906	0.955	1.142	0.975	1.069	1.056
Lord Krishna Bank	0.727	1.432	0.85	1.907	0.882	0.838	0.893	0.949	1.058	1.018	1.055	1.043
Nainital Bank	1.039	0.987	1.151	0.893	0.92	1.131	0.97	0.986	1.177	0.938	1.001	1.027
Tamilnad Mercantile Bank	0.867	1.13	1.032	1.053	1.112	1.172	0.99	1.032	1.105	1.020	1.073	1.063
Bank of Rajasthan	0.865	1.058	1.053	1.101	1.015	1.05	0.912	1.026	1.144	0.947	1.029	1.032
Catholic Syrian Bank	0.898	1.04	0.996	1.357	0.866	0.924	0.902	0.989	1.119	0.950	1.000	1.016
Dhanalakshmi Bank	0.893	1.112	0.979	1.375	0.955	0.962	0.896	0.991	1.084	0.982	1.029	1.028
Federal Bank	0.748	1.359	0.977	1.188	1.086	1.075	1.002	1.020	1.149	0.993	1.095	1.074

(Contd.)

Table 5.2 (*Contd.*)

(1)	(14)	(15)	(16)	(17)	(18)	(19)	(20)	(21)	(22)	(23)	(24)	(25)
Jammu & Kashmir Bank	0.975	1.105	1.111	1.167	1.118	1.107	1.049	1.087	1.212	0.974	1.106	1.087
Karur Vysya Bank	0.784	1.193	1.025	1.082	1.088	1.127	0.987	0.950	1.128	0.985	1.062	1.053
Lakshmi Vilas Bank	0.779	1.29	0.908	1.427	0.957	0.94	0.895	0.973	1.084	0.994	1.039	1.036
Ratnakar Bank	1.036	1.007	1.03	1.383	0.897	1.021	0.974	0.986	1.146	0.939	1.034	1.031
Sangli Bank	0.927	0.955	1.091	1.072	1.008	1.046	0.97	0.986	1.150	0.953	1.017	1.032
South Indian Bank	0.957	1.104	0.988	1.236	1.085	0.996	0.932	1.023	1.105	0.978	1.048	1.039
United Western Bank	0.798	1.371	0.96	1.336	1.003	0.977	0.902	0.984	1.136	0.973	1.063	1.051
All CBs												
Mean	0.923	1.09	1.035	1.152	1.02	1.052	0.956	0.982	1.144	0.990	1.039	1.052
S.D	0.094	0.133	0.066	0.182	0.07	0.063	0.043	0.058	0.030	0.029	0.035	0.021
Q1	0.893	1.012	0.995	1.055	0.987	1.046	0.919	0.955	1.134	0.971	1.017	1.036
Q3	1.01	1.139	1.093	1.236	1.081	1.089	0.978	1.025	1.159	1.010	1.060	1.060
Median	0.946	1.054	1.032	1.123	1.025	1.071	0.96	0.987	1.147	0.988	1.030	1.050
PSBs												
Mean	0.968	1.039	1.053	1.083	1.023	1.075	0.959	0.967	1.153	0.995	1.027	1.052
S.D	0.061	0.063	0.052	0.081	0.058	0.02	0.036	0.064	0.020	0.026	0.028	0.017
Q1	0.927	1.007	1.016	1.039	0.987	1.066	0.942	0.933	1.141	0.981	1.009	1.042
Q3	1.019	1.072	1.098	1.13	1.066	1.09	0.975	1.006	1.160	1.011	1.035	1.059

Median	0.974	1.026	1.047	1.076	1.025	1.076	0.96	0.981	1.152	0.992	1.025	1.050
NBs												
Mean	0.966	1.047	1.064	1.078	1.029	1.08	0.969	0.978	1.158	1.003	1.034	1.059
S.D	0.063	0.07	0.049	0.081	0.067	0.019	0.036	0.057	0.021	0.026	0.029	0.015
Q1	0.933	1.006	1.034	1.03	0.985	1.069	0.956	0.950	1.146	0.986	1.017	1.049
Q3	1.02	1.09	1.105	1.14	1.075	1.092	0.98	1.016	1.167	1.021	1.043	1.068
Median	0.97	1.049	1.07	1.073	1.033	1.083	0.973	0.987	1.153	1.000	1.030	1.054
SBI												
Mean	0.973	1.018	1.028	1.096	1.01	1.062	0.936	0.942	1.142	0.976	1.012	1.036
S.D	0.058	0.036	0.051	0.086	0.022	0.018	0.024	0.077	0.016	0.017	0.018	0.010
Q1	0.929	1.01	1.011	1.071	0.989	1.06	0.919	0.907	1.136	0.967	1.005	1.030
Q3	1.016	1.028	1.034	1.113	1.026	1.075	0.949	0.989	1.153	0.990	1.024	1.045
Median	0.996	1.013	1.019	1.086	1.011	1.068	0.942	0.961	1.145	0.981	1.015	1.033
Pvt.												
Mean	0.86	1.173	1.009	1.263	1.016	1.018	0.952	1.005	1.131	0.981	1.057	1.051
S.D	0.102	0.163	0.078	0.227	0.087	0.089	0.054	0.041	0.037	0.032	0.037	0.026
Q1	0.78	1.07	0.978	1.118	0.956	0.946	0.903	0.985	1.108	0.958	1.030	1.032
Q3	0.924	1.275	1.05	1.381	1.088	1.08	0.989	1.031	1.150	0.993	1.080	1.061
Median	0.88	1.149	1.011	1.258	1.041	1.034	0.951	0.990	1.139	0.976	1.058	1.047

*Note** : S.D denotes stanadard deviation, Q1 denotes first-quartile, Q3 denotes third quartile.

TABLE 5.3

Inter-Bank Average Total Factor Productivity Change Index Over the Different Time Periods

Banks/Years	*1986*	*1987*	*1988-89*	*1989-90*	*1990-91*	*1991-92*	*1992-93*	*1993-94*	*1994-95*	*1995-96*	*1996-97*	*1997-98*
(1)	*(2)*	*(3)*	*(4)*	*(5)*	*(6)*	*(7)*	*(8)*	*(9)*	*(10)*	*(11)*	*(12)*	*(13)*
Allahabad Bank	1.087	1.027	1.424	0.899	1.083	1.255	1.031	0.81	1.122	1.258	1.108	0.946
Andhra Bank	1.093	1.093	1.252	0.929	0.982	1.072	0.78	1.184	1.556	0.986	1	1.142
Bank of Baroda	1.112	1.05	1.366	0.954	1.244	1.215	0.998	1.272	1.031	0.976	0.934	1.029
Bank of India	1.142	1.038	1.308	0.966	0.985	1.641	0.779	1.14	1.201	1.076	1.05	1.05
Bank of Maharashtra	1.004	0.976	1.417	0.946	0.948	1.246	0.656	1.199	1.497	1.345	0.976	0.955
Canara Bank	1.129	1.135	1.335	0.929	0.959	1.697	0.904	0.793	1.313	0.958	0.928	0.888
Central Bank of India	1.149	0.931	1.278	1.002	0.937	1.2	0.797	0.831	1.586	1.249	1.013	1.009
Corporation Bank	1.076	1.043	1.326	0.894	0.932	1.544	0.962	1.156	1.205	1.057	1.196	1.082
Dena Bank	0.992	1.034	1.333	0.966	0.926	1.223	0.771	1.149	1.249	1.09	1.116	0.947
Indian Bank	1.069	1.111	1.375	1.156	0.943	1.358	1.055	0.87	1.074	0.815	1.172	0.873
Indian Overseas Bank	1.096	1.007	1.298	0.953	1.212	1.107	1.256	1.245	0.611	1.056	1.072	1.028
OBC	1.033	1.131	1.344	0.923	1.166	1.503	0.764	1.169	1.269	0.993	1.078	0.986
Punjab and Sind Bank	1.149	0.923	1.235	0.853	0.929	1.145	0.736	1.357	1.379	0.854	1.227	1.038
Punjab National Bank	1.025	1.114	1.352	0.979	0.911	1.51	0.945	0.984	1.057	1.175	1.034	0.951
Syndicate Bank	1.035	1.137	1.214	0.853	0.998	1.251	0.671	1.405	1.132	1.167	0.981	0.896
UCO	1.065	0.94	1.292	0.81	0.921	1.243	1.167	0.645	1.818	0.976	0.911	1.033

Union Bank of India	1.207	1.031	1.238	0.94	0.909	1.538	0.784	1.118	1.128	1.044	1.023	1.025
United Bank of India	1.093	0.969	1.316	0.996	0.802	1.016	0.473	1.364	1.375	1.2	0.887	1.79
Vijaya Bank	1.014	1.028	1.325	1.028	0.85	1.234	1.098	0.983	1.043	0.898	1.209	0.936
State Bank of India	1.071	1.045	1.446	0.881	1.036	1.703	0.908	0.943	1.178	1.103	0.94	0.868
State Bank of B&J	1.095	1.031	1.493	0.803	1.021	1.775	0.797	0.922	1.071	1.12	1.066	0.959
State Bank of Hyderabad	1.168	1.011	1.41	0.912	0.971	1.787	0.873	0.92	1.114	1.122	1.015	0.94
State Bank of Indore	0.93	1.071	1.39	0.975	0.996	1.721	0.783	1.177	1.103	1.067	1.038	0.896
State Bank of Mysore	1.098	0.96	1.352	1.074	0.91	1.488	0.865	1.067	0.965	1.182	1.094	0.962
State Bank of Patiala	1.396	1.099	1.297	1.138	0.936	1.755	0.698	0.863	1.024	1.027	0.994	1.048
State Bank of Saurashtra	1.006	0.978	1.308	0.879	1.029	1.604	0.956	0.944	1.152	0.988	1.003	0.999
State Bank of Travancore	1.037	1.012	1.517	0.792	0.993	1.477	1.042	1.021	0.975	1.125	0.938	0.987
Bharat Overseas Bank	1.063	1.132	1.396	0.908	1.032	1.519	0.975	1.045	1.038	1.002	0.938	1.17
City Union Bank	1.035	1.055	1.126	0.938	1.023	1.324	0.826	0.911	1.077	1.139	1.029	0.979
Ing Vysya Bank	1.095	0.986	1.302	1.044	0.998	1.438	1.423	1.222	1.298	0.959	0.877	1.252
Karnataka Bank	0.996	0.979	1.32	0.973	0.996	1.31	0.97	0.862	1.219	1.012	1.331	0.997
Lord Krishna Bank	0.983	1.003	1.357	0.802	0.974	0.926	1.451	0.951	1.039	1.074	0.959	1.043
Nainital Bank	1.036	1.08	1.253	0.903	1.17	1.334	0.805	0.828	1.083	1.226	1.043	0.984
Tamilnad Mercantile Bank	1.032	1.035	1.41	0.854	0.988	1.435	1.074	1.004	1.024	1.159	1.092	0.946
Bank of Rajasthan	1.048	0.997	1.409	0.893	1.075	1.351	0.824	1.021	1.252	0.825	0.974	0.92
Catholic Syrian Bank	1.04	0.966	1.346	0.885	0.876	1.202	0.728	1.224	0.906	1.052	0.994	0.918
Dhanalakshmi Bank	0.921	0.986	1.373	0.908	0.953	0.953	0.953	1.024	1.054	0.925	0.995	1.167

(*Contd.*)

TABLE 5.3 (*Contd.*)

(1)	(2)	(3)	(4)	(5)	(6)	(7)	(8)	(9)	(10)	(11)	(12)	(13)
Federal Bank	0.91	1.051	1.035	1.262	0.867	1.274	0.918	1.191	1.333	1.002	0.781	1.32
Jammu & Kashmir Bank	0.907	1.089	1.274	0.847	0.921	3.223	0.77	0.984	1.09	0.961	0.857	1.224
Karur Vysya Bank	0.996	1.026	1.295	0.932	1.238	1.047	0.872	0.933	1.325	1.12	0.976	1.286
Lakshmi Vilas Bank	1.065	0.938	1.232	0.888	1.099	1.092	1.017	1.078	1.165	0.95	0.896	1.124
Ratnakar Bank	0.956	0.979	1.218	0.888	1.227	1.411	0.614	1.535	0.758	1.099	1.039	0.98
Sangli Bank	1.03	0.952	1.273	1.013	1.009	1.452	0.796	1.224	0.863	1.126	0.818	1.297
South Indian Bank	0.94	0.953	1.361	0.925	0.91	1.12	0.814	1.523	0.802	1.202	0.731	1.034
United Western Bank	0.972	0.929	1.366	0.885	0.977	1.205	1.078	1.015	1.022	1.218	1.191	1.142
All CBs												
Mean	1.050	1.022	1.321	0.933	0.992	1.364	0.880	1.052	1.126	1.059	1.005	1.035
S.D	0.087	0.061	0.087	0.093	0.103	0.360	0.192	0.195	0.219	0.118	0.118	0.162
Q1	1.004	0.978	1.278	0.885	0.929	1.205	0.780	0.933	1.038	0.986	0.938	0.947
Q3	1.095	1.055	1.373	0.973	1.029	1.519	0.998	1.191	1.252	1.139	1.072	1.082
Median	1.040	1.027	1.326	0.925	0.982	1.334	0.872	1.024	1.114	1.067	1.003	0.999
PSBs												
Mean	1.085	1.032	1.340	0.938	0.978	1.399	0.855	1.039	1.171	1.064	1.033	1.000
S.D	0.087	0.063	0.075	0.089	0.100	0.240	0.172	0.194	0.236	0.124	0.092	0.170
Q1	1.034	0.993	1.298	0.888	0.928	1.229	0.775	0.921	1.064	0.987	0.979	0.943

Q3	1.121	1.082	1.383	0.977	1.010	1.623	0.980	1.181	1.291	1.146	1.086	1.031
Median	1.087	1.031	1.333	0.940	0.959	1.477	0.865	1.067	1.132	1.067	1.023	0.986
NBs												
Mean	1.081	1.036	1.316	0.943	0.975	1.302	0.853	1.066	1.216	1.053	1.043	1.019
S.D	0.057	0.069	0.058	0.075	0.116	0.198	0.196	0.216	0.263	0.142	0.103	0.196
Q1	1.043	0.984	1.282	0.905	0.927	1.204	0.766	0.899	1.124	0.979	0.977	0.948
Q3	1.121	1.102	1.348	0.973	0.992	1.507	1.015	1.222	1.377	1.171	1.112	1.036
Median	1.087	1.031	1.333	0.940	0.959	1.477	0.865	1.067	1.132	1.067	1.023	0.986
SBI												
Mean	1.093	1.025	1.400	0.925	0.986	1.659	0.859	0.978	1.070	1.090	1.010	0.956
S.D	0.139	0.046	0.081	0.123	0.045	0.125	0.107	0.101	0.079	0.062	0.055	0.057
Q1	1.029	1.003	1.341	0.860	0.962	1.575	0.794	0.922	1.012	1.057	0.981	0.929
Q3	1.116	1.052	1.458	1.000	1.023	1.760	0.920	1.033	1.124	1.123	1.045	0.990
Median	1.083	1.022	1.400	0.897	0.995	1.712	0.869	0.944	1.087	1.112	1.009	0.961
Pvt.												
Mean	1.000	1.006	1.293	0.926	1.013	1.313	0.918	1.072	1.062	1.053	0.964	1.091
S.D	0.057	0.056	0.099	0.101	0.108	0.495	0.218	0.200	0.171	0.112	0.144	0.138
Q1	0.960	0.969	1.258	0.886	0.958	1.141	0.807	0.959	1.023	0.971	0.882	0.981
Q3	1.039	1.047	1.365	0.937	1.064	1.429	1.007	1.214	1.206	1.136	1.037	1.211
Median	1.013	0.992	1.311	0.906	0.997	1.317	0.895	1.023	1.066	1.063	0.975	1.084

(Contd.)

TABLE 5.3 (*Contd.*)

Banks/Years	*1998-99*	*1999-2000*	*2000-01*	*2001-02*	*2002-03*	*2003-04*	*2004-05*	*2005-06*	*1986-92*	*1993-99*	*2000-06*	*1986-06*
(1)	*(14)*	*(15)*	*(16)*	*(17)*	*(18)*	*(19)*	*(20)*	*(21)*	*(22)*	*(23)*	*(24)*	*(25)*
Allahabad Bank	0.999	1.044	1.027	1.078	1.146	1.007	0.926	0.977	1.117	1.031	1.027	1.055
Andhra Bank	0.885	1.05	1.003	1.168	1.307	1.063	1.023	0.72	1.065	1.053	1.033	1.050
Bank of Baroda	1.056	0.942	1.087	1.041	1.069	1.15	0.959	0.93	1.149	1.038	1.023	1.064
Bank of India	0.968	0.994	1.17	1.04	1.137	0.994	0.77	0.98	1.159	1.029	1.004	1.057
Bank of Maharashtra	0.932	0.992	1.041	1.033	1.04	0.997	0.996	0.933	1.076	1.047	1.004	1.040
Canara Bank	1.213	0.927	1.08	1.078	1.1	1.068	0.93	0.917	1.172	0.985	1.011	1.047
Central Bank of India	0.969	1.009	1.023	1.002	1.157	1.051	1.007	0.872	1.075	1.038	1.014	1.040
Corporation Bank	0.903	1.13	1.131	1.036	1.234	1.023	1.083	1.007	1.114	1.075	1.090	1.092
Dena Bank	0.889	0.935	1.061	1.183	1.208	1.163	0.687	1.155	1.069	1.018	1.039	1.041
Indian Bank	0.904	1.328	1.081	1.208	1.213	1.23	0.911	0.912	1.158	0.958	1.116	1.070
Indian Overseas Bank	1.044	1.061	1.184	1.134	1.083	1.162	1.051	0.996	1.106	1.022	1.094	1.072
OBC	1.039	1.119	1.134	1.13	1.181	1.104	0.99	1.085	1.168	1.032	1.105	1.097
Punjab and Sind Bank	0.893	1.064	1.107	1.034	1.195	1.136	1.094	0.843	1.029	1.042	1.062	1.045
Punjab National Bank	1.085	0.877	1.064	1.028	1.159	1.019	0.904	0.936	1.130	1.030	0.994	1.046
Syndicate Bank	0.992	1.072	1.208	0.919	1.018	0.878	1.017	0.985	1.072	1.012	1.009	1.029
UCO	1.007	1.092	1.039	1.16	1.017	1.035	0.906	1	1.031	1.034	1.033	1.033

Union Bank of India	0.882	1.041	1.243	1.057	1.061	0.999	0.973	1.187	1.125	0.993	1.076	1.060
United Bank of India	0.746	1.042	1.152	1.385	1.099	1.017	0.988	0.917	1.021	1.034	1.077	1.045
Vijaya Bank	1.068	1.051	1.123	0.986	1.213	1.114	0.902	0.984	1.069	1.029	1.049	1.048
State Bank of India	0.927	0.984	1.008	1	1.061	1.067	1.014	1.047	1.166	0.976	1.025	1.047
State Bank of B&J	0.882	1.069	1.022	1.036	0.968	1.058	0.979	0.857	1.161	0.968	0.996	1.033
State Bank of Hyderabad	1.027	1.026	1.025	0.995	1.024	1.09	0.791	1.151	1.175	0.998	1.009	1.052
State Bank of Indore	1.038	0.996	0.968	1.281	1.037	1.065	0.695	1.091	1.150	1.007	1.005	1.047
State Bank of Mysore	0.914	1.051	0.994	1.07	1.135	0.961	0.957	0.798	1.129	1.002	0.990	1.034
State Bank of Patiala	0.963	1.081	1.135	0.974	0.99	1.014	0.838	1.008	1.245	0.937	1.002	1.045
State Bank of Saurashtra	0.974	0.947	0.944	1.101	0.968	1.099	0.842	0.876	1.110	1.000	0.964	1.019
State Bank of Travancore	0.841	1.076	1.065	0.966	1.079	1.092	1.013	0.913	1.108	0.986	1.027	1.036
Bharat Overseas Bank	0.915	1.011	1.29	1.305	0.905	1.163	1.231	0.979	1.156	1.009	1.116	1.089
City Union Bank	1.132	1.2	0.876	1.125	1.041	1.18	0.879	1.128	1.077	1.007	1.054	1.044
Ing Vysya Bank	0.773	1.521	0.773	1.863	1.239	0.931	0.637	1.36	1.132	1.091	1.118	1.113
Karnataka Bank	0.758	1.008	1.21	1.812	0.904	1.048	0.897	0.816	1.085	1.005	1.063	1.049
Lord Krishna Bank	0.999	1.18	0.934	2.302	0.882	0.762	0.538	1.077	0.995	1.063	0.998	1.019
Nainital Bank	1.053	0.939	1.01	1.04	0.978	1.06	0.882	1.158	1.120	0.994	1.006	1.035
Tamilnad Mercantile Bank	0.867	1.028	1.134	1.054	1.098	1.187	0.99	1.032	1.105	1.020	1.073	1.063
Bank of Rajasthan	0.856	1.186	1.172	1.107	1.063	0.881	0.697	1.014	1.114	0.944	1.003	1.013
Catholic Syrian Bank	0.754	1.395	1.095	1.346	1.113	0.898	0.749	0.942	1.039	0.926	1.055	1.003

(Contd.)

TABLE 5.3 (*Contd.*)

Geometric Means

(1)	(14)	(15)	(16)	(17)	(18)	(19)	(20)	(21)	(22)	(23)	(24)	(25)
Dhanalakshmi Bank	0.793	1.344	0.99	1.55	1.1	0.781	0.719	1.058	1.005	0.981	1.044	1.010
Federal Bank	0.964	1.23	1.013	1.256	1.044	1.079	0.931	1.129	1.055	1.055	1.092	1.068
Jammu & Kashmir Bank	0.999	1.006	1.168	1.218	1.035	0.975	1.007	1.181	1.212	0.974	1.080	1.078
Karur Vysya Bank	0.736	1.271	1.025	1.082	0.991	1.238	0.886	1.058	1.081	1.016	1.071	1.055
Lakshmi Vilas Bank	0.97	1.29	0.908	1.208	0.915	0.916	0.727	0.908	1.046	1.025	0.966	1.010
Ratnakar Bank	0.919	1.087	1.052	1.7	0.784	0.795	1.031	0.998	1.098	0.957	1.032	1.024
Sangli Bank	0.684	0.989	1.071	1.093	0.909	1.105	0.832	0.972	1.108	0.948	0.991	1.009
South Indian Bank	1.031	1.311	0.994	1.219	1.148	1.086	0.69	1.126	1.023	0.990	1.063	1.025
United Western Bank	0.702	1.679	0.572	1.846	0.933	0.809	0.738	1.023	1.043	1.038	1.001	1.027
All CBs												
Mean	0.925	1.093	1.045	1.179	1.061	1.028	0.884	0.994	1.102	1.009	1.037	1.046
S.D	0.117	0.163	0.123	0.286	0.11	0.116	0.141	0.12	0.056	0.037	0.041	0.024
Q1	0.882	1.006	1.008	1.036	0.991	0.994	0.791	0.917	1.069	0.986	1.004	1.033
Q3	1.007	1.18	1.134	1.219	1.146	1.104	0.996	1.077	1.149	1.034	1.071	1.057
Median	0.932	1.051	1.061	1.101	1.063	1.058	0.911	0.996	1.108	1.012	1.032	1.045
PSBs												
Mean	0.96	1.034	1.076	1.074	1.104	1.059	0.929	0.96	1.115	1.013	1.032	1.050
S.D	0.093	0.084	0.074	0.103	0.088	0.073	0.107	0.109	0.053	0.031	0.039	0.018

Q1	0.898	0.993	1.024	1.015	1.039	1.016	0.903	0.913	1.074	0.996	1.005	1.040
Q3	1.033	1.071	1.133	1.132	1.17	1.102	1.01	1.008	1.159	1.034	1.055	1.056
Median	0.968	1.044	1.065	1.041	1.099	1.063	0.959	0.977	1.117	1.022	1.025	1.047
NBs												
Mean	0.967	1.036	1.101	1.085	1.136	1.061	0.948	0.96	1.099	1.026	1.045	1.054
S.D	0.103	0.096	0.067	0.103	0.08	0.082	0.099	0.105	0.048	0.026	0.038	0.018
Q1	0.896	0.993	1.046	1.035	1.073	1.01	0.915	0.917	1.070	1.019	1.012	1.042
Q3	1.042	1.068	1.143	1.147	1.202	1.125	1.012	0.998	1.139	1.038	1.077	1.062
Median	0.968	1.044	1.065	1.041	1.099	1.063	0.959	0.977	1.117	1.022	1.025	1.047
SBI												
Mean	0.944	1.028	1.019	1.049	1.031	1.055	0.884	0.961	1.155	0.984	1.002	1.039
S.D	0.068	0.049	0.059	0.103	0.058	0.047	0.117	0.125	0.044	0.023	0.020	0.011
Q1	0.906	0.993	0.988	0.99	0.985	1.047	0.826	0.871	1.124	0.974	0.994	1.034
Q3	0.987	1.071	1.035	1.078	1.066	1.091	0.988	1.058	1.168	1.001	1.013	1.047
Median	0.945	1.039	1.015	1.018	1.031	1.066	0.9	0.961	1.156	0.992	1.003	1.040
Pvt.												
Mean	0.874	1.189	1.001	1.356	0.998	0.983	0.821	1.047	1.082	1.001	1.045	1.040
S.D	0.134	0.2	0.168	0.364	0.114	0.154	0.168	0.12	0.055	0.044	0.044	0.031
Q1	0.762	1.015	0.948	1.112	0.911	0.885	0.721	0.984	1.044	0.976	1.004	1.015
Q3	0.992	1.306	1.124	1.663	1.089	1.1	0.923	1.128	1.112	1.023	1.073	1.061
Median	0.891	1.193	1.019	1.238	1.013	1.012	0.856	1.045	1.083	1.006	1.054	1.031

TABLE 5.4

Inter-Bank Average Pure Efficiency Change Index Over the Different Time Periods

Banks/Years	*1986*	*1987*	*1988-89*	*1989-90*	*1990-91*	*1991-92*	*1992-93*	*1993-94*	*1994-95*	*1995-96*	*1996-97*	*1997-98*
(1)	(2)	(3)	(4)	(5)	(6)	(7)	(8)	(9)	(10)	(11)	(12)	(13)
Allahabad Bank	1.08	0.995	1.035	0.966	1.088	0.934	0.793	0.856	1.186	1.119	1.058	0.987
Andhra Bank	1.015	1.033	0.959	1.025	0.822	0.84	0.774	1.205	1.397	0.962	0.946	1.226
Bank of Baroda	0.995	0.97	0.967	0.959	1.124	0.894	1.009	1.108	1	0.923	0.836	1.04
Bank of India	1.039	0.962	0.927	0.969	0.972	1.212	0.622	1.097	1.147	0.967	0.961	1.139
Bank of Maharashtra	0.966	0.964	1.018	1.077	0.797	0.901	0.71	1.339	1.28	1.199	0.946	1.049
Canara Bank	1	1	1	1	1	0.887	1.053	0.798	1.228	0.883	0.818	0.979
Central Bank of India	1.041	0.873	0.957	1.089	0.789	0.877	0.801	1.047	1.339	1.128	0.959	1.102
Corporation Bank	1.001	0.983	1.017	0.982	0.772	0.932	1.059	1.192	1.115	0.977	1.09	1
Dena Bank	0.956	1.008	1.013	1.057	0.77	0.911	0.89	1.205	1.189	1.038	1.036	1.043
Indian Bank	0.983	1.053	0.97	1.155	0.893	0.978	0.796	0.843	0.953	0.949	1.14	0.946
Indian Overseas Bank	0.978	0.903	0.956	0.985	1.178	0.803	1.118	1.242	0.532	0.996	1.008	1.113
OBC	0.938	1.057	1.027	0.998	1.018	0.809	0.901	1.129	1.213	1.002	0.977	0.936
Punjab and Sind Bank	1.027	0.919	0.942	0.952	0.816	0.872	0.775	1.153	1.278	0.864	1.123	1.118
Punjab National Bank	0.912	1.032	1	1.059	0.775	0.95	1.081	1.019	0.998	1.101	0.993	1.062
Syndicate Bank	0.941	1.062	1	0.996	0.965	0.639	0.717	1.477	1.077	1.086	0.954	0.994

UCO	0.955	0.927	1.004	0.857	0.916	0.9	0.968	0.923	1.374	0.953	0.966	1.037
Union Bank of India	1.155	0.985	0.935	1.039	0.778	1.012	0.916	1.171	1.052	1.007	1.002	1.065
United Bank of India	0.961	0.944	1.013	1.137	0.724	0.797	0.674	1.224	1.201	1.045	0.951	1.351
Vijaya Bank	0.96	0.987	0.966	1.098	0.731	0.873	1.145	0.989	0.982	0.888	1.113	1.048
State Bank of India	1	1	1	1	1	1	1	0.954	1.049	1	1	1
State Bank of B&J	1.075	0.861	1.092	0.814	1.031	1.271	0.925	0.965	1.043	1.084	0.984	1.033
State Bank of Hyderabad	1.137	0.916	0.942	0.957	0.914	1.214	1.024	0.959	1.056	1.004	0.936	1.096
State Bank of Indore	0.919	0.947	0.964	1.036	0.881	1.175	0.922	1.207	1	1	1	1
State Bank of Mysore	1.116	0.898	0.962	1.175	0.778	1.05	1.021	1.108	0.919	1.108	1	1.065
State Bank of Patiala	1.294	0.967	0.938	1.383	0.96	1.041	1	0.96	0.931	1.007	0.908	1.225
State Bank of Saurashtra	1	1	1	1	0.872	1.022	1.103	0.973	1.047	0.92	0.923	1.178
State Bank of Travancore	1.017	0.987	1.174	0.837	0.812	1.033	1.237	1.114	0.872	1.087	0.881	1.081
Bharat Overseas Bank	1	1	1	1	1	1	1	1	1	1	0.826	1.117
City Union Bank	1.03	1	0.92	1.03	0.914	1.044	0.945	0.982	1.014	1.035	0.981	0.893
Ing Vysya Bank	1.079	0.947	0.963	1.119	0.863	0.945	1.347	0.989	1.012	1	1	1
Karnataka Bank	1.015	0.979	1.008	1.081	0.86	0.98	1.047	0.906	1.156	0.965	1.178	1
Lord Krishna Bank	1	1	1	1	1	1	1	1	1	1	1	0.927
Nainital Bank	1.048	1.054	0.983	0.997	0.947	0.941	0.999	0.885	1.257	1.044	0.982	1.057
Tamilnad Mercantile Bank	1	1	1	1	1	1	1	1	1	1	1	1
Bank of Rajasthan	1.018	0.99	1.047	0.98	0.94	0.986	0.994	1.09	1.162	0.783	1.004	0.967

(Contd.)

TABLE 5.4 (*Contd.*)

(1)	(2)	(3)	(4)	(5)	(6)	(7)	(8)	(9)	(10)	(11)	(12)	(13)
Catholic Syrian Bank	1.062	1	0.939	1.03	0.771	0.986	0.887	1.246	0.972	1.019	0.978	1.031
Dhanalakshmi Bank	1	0.968	1.03	1.004	0.936	0.968	0.957	1.152	1	0.983	1.017	1
Federal Bank	0.948	1.096	0.733	1.396	0.728	0.977	0.861	1.116	1.266	0.949	0.848	1.069
Jammu & Kashmir Bank	0.969	1.032	0.936	0.964	0.763	1.453	1	1	1	0.976	0.803	1.251
Karur Vysya Bank	1.002	1.009	0.982	1.001	1.025	0.821	0.985	0.957	1.204	1.074	0.976	1.025
Lakshmi Vilas Bank	1	1	1	1	1	0.928	1.029	1.047	1	1	1	1
Ratnakar Bank	0.977	1.052	0.936	1.112	1.068	1	0.752	1.33	1	1	1	1
Sangli Bank	1.012	0.933	0.972	1.114	0.864	1.038	0.962	1.298	0.916	1.048	0.968	1.13
South Indian Bank	0.978	0.947	0.99	1.09	0.784	0.932	0.887	1.543	0.831	1.103	0.873	1.031
United Western Bank	0.977	0.93	0.953	1.009	0.789	0.984	1.23	1.064	0.97	1.11	1.145	1
All CBs												
Mean	1.011	0.980	0.980	1.029	0.891	0.965	0.942	1.075	1.059	1.006	0.976	1.050
S.D	0.068	0.051	0.059	0.107	0.116	0.136	0.150	0.160	0.159	0.078	0.084	0.089
Q1	0.977	0.947	0.956	0.985	0.789	0.900	0.887	0.973	1.000	0.967	0.946	1.000
Q3	1.030	1.000	1.004	1.081	1.000	1.012	1.024	1.192	1.189	1.048	1.002	1.096
Median	1.000	0.987	0.983	1.001	0.893	0.977	0.985	1.064	1.043	1.000	0.982	1.037
PSBs												
Mean	1.014	0.970	0.991	1.017	0.887	0.946	0.914	1.073	1.074	1.008	0.979	1.067
S.D	0.084	0.054	0.052	0.113	0.126	0.143	0.159	0.157	0.181	0.083	0.078	0.093

Q1	0.961	0.936	0.958	0.968	0.784	0.875	0.795	0.963	0.999	0.958	0.946	1.000
Q3	1.040	1.000	1.013	1.068	0.986	1.028	1.039	1.199	1.207	1.085	1.005	1.108
Median	1.000	0.983	1.000	1.000	0.881	0.932	0.925	1.108	1.056	1.002	0.977	1.049
NBs												
Mean	0.993	0.981	0.984	1.019	0.881	0.889	0.870	1.093	1.113	1.001	0.990	1.061
S.D	0.057	0.053	0.033	0.072	0.140	0.111	0.160	0.174	0.197	0.091	0.087	0.099
Q1	0.958	0.953	0.958	0.976	0.777	0.856	0.775	1.004	1.026	0.951	0.953	0.997
Q3	1.021	1.020	1.013	1.068	0.986	0.933	1.031	1.205	1.253	1.066	1.047	1.108
Median	0.983	0.985	1.000	1.000	0.822	0.894	0.890	1.129	1.186	0.996	0.977	1.048
SBI												
Mean	1.065	0.946	1.006	1.012	0.902	1.097	1.025	1.026	0.987	1.025	0.953	1.082
S.D	0.115	0.051	0.083	0.184	0.088	0.103	0.102	0.098	0.072	0.062	0.048	0.081
Q1	1.000	0.912	0.957	0.927	0.857	1.030	0.981	0.960	0.928	1.000	0.919	1.025
Q3	1.121	0.990	1.023	1.071	0.970	1.185	1.044	1.110	1.048	1.085	1.000	1.117
Median	1.046	0.957	0.982	1.000	0.898	1.046	1.011	0.969	1.022	1.006	0.960	1.073
Pvt.												
Mean	1.006	0.996	0.964	1.048	0.897	0.993	0.986	1.078	1.036	1.002	0.972	1.025
S.D	0.033	0.044	0.067	0.099	0.104	0.124	0.130	0.169	0.117	0.071	0.095	0.080
Q1	0.984	0.971	0.943	1.000	0.807	0.951	0.948	0.992	1.000	0.987	0.970	1.000
Q3	1.017	1.007	1.000	1.088	1.000	1.000	1.000	1.143	1.121	1.042	1.000	1.051
Median	1.000	1.000	0.983	1.007	0.925	0.985	0.997	1.024	1.000	1.000	0.991	1.000

(Contd.)

TABLE 5.4 (*Contd.*)

Banks/Years	*1998-99*	*1999-2000*	*2000-01*	*2001-02*	*2002-03*	*2003-04*	*2004-05*	*2005-06*	*1986-92*	*1993-99*	*2000-06*	*1986-06*
(1)	*(14)*	*(15)*	*(16)*	*(17)*	*(18)*	*(19)*	*(20)*	*(21)*	*(22)*	*(23)*	*(24)*	*(25)*
Allahabad Bank	1.076	0.993	1	1.005	1.097	0.979	1.006	1.023	1.015	1.002	1.014	1.010
Andhra Bank	0.934	0.945	1.073	1.02	1.142	1.015	1.017	0.908	0.945	1.045	1.015	1.003
Bank of Baroda	1.194	0.81	1.053	0.997	1	1.045	0.985	0.953	0.982	1.010	0.974	0.989
Bank of India	1.056	0.904	1.177	0.923	1.068	0.931	0.879	1.028	1.009	0.981	0.982	0.990
Bank of Maharashtra	0.934	0.988	1.016	0.96	0.987	0.974	1.038	0.877	0.950	1.044	0.976	0.991
Canara Bank	1.474	0.814	1.075	0.909	1.028	1.007	0.975	0.939	0.980	1.010	0.960	0.984
Central Bank of India	0.962	1.047	0.956	1.034	1.089	0.963	1.072	0.837	0.932	1.037	0.996	0.990
Corporation Bank	1	1	1	0.904	1.106	0.978	1.023	1	0.944	1.060	1.000	1.003
Dena Bank	0.973	0.862	1.204	0.921	1.089	1.013	0.967	1.034	0.948	1.048	1.008	1.003
Indian Bank	1.037	1.038	1.063	0.895	1.296	1.135	0.968	0.945	1.002	0.946	1.041	0.995
Indian Overseas Bank	1.111	1.007	1.069	1.039	1.069	1.041	1.078	0.988	0.961	0.988	1.041	0.998
OBC	1.093	1	1	1	1	1	0.964	0.99	0.971	1.031	0.993	0.999
Punjab and Sind Bank	0.975	0.977	1.112	0.906	1.153	1.046	1.147	0.837	0.919	1.027	1.019	0.991
Punjab National Bank	1.059	0.939	0.985	1.016	1.17	0.945	0.948	0.92	0.950	1.044	0.986	0.995
Syndicate Bank	0.993	1.129	1.104	0.987	1.057	0.826	1.065	0.972	0.922	1.022	1.015	0.989
UCO	1.1	1.077	0.979	0.911	1.067	0.972	0.968	0.965	0.925	1.037	0.990	0.986

Union Bank of India	0.975	0.948	1.122	1.035	0.963	0.943	0.996	1.091	0.977	1.024	1.012	1.006
United Bank of India	0.814	1.032	1.058	1.122	1.138	0.994	1.05	0.991	0.919	1.011	1.054	0.997
Vijaya Bank	1.057	1.021	0.996	1.033	1.132	1.018	0.965	0.943	0.929	1.029	1.014	0.992
State Bank of India	1	1	1	0.817	1.04	1.177	1	1	1.000	1.000	1.000	1.000
State Bank of B&J	0.965	1.036	1	0.985	0.984	1.021	1.011	0.963	1.013	0.999	1.000	1.003
State Bank of Hyderabad	1.022	1	1	0.896	1.004	1.001	0.882	1.18	1.007	1.013	0.991	1.003
State Bank of Indore	1	1	1	1	1	1	0.801	1.068	0.983	1.015	0.978	0.992
State Bank of Mysore	0.948	1.023	0.992	0.941	1.105	0.993	1.007	1	0.987	1.022	1.008	1.006
State Bank of Patiala	0.939	1.065	1	1	1	1	0.824	0.967	1.084	0.991	0.977	1.013
State Bank of Saurashtra	1	0.941	0.884	1.032	0.97	1.032	0.925	0.875	0.981	1.017	0.949	0.982
State Bank of Travancore	0.969	0.967	1.071	0.897	1.097	1.004	1.097	0.898	0.969	1.027	1.001	1.000
Bharat Overseas Bank	1.044	0.881	1.165	0.941	0.897	1.131	1.06	0.956	1.000	0.995	0.999	0.998
City Union Bank	1.296	0.98	0.927	0.896	1.024	1.117	0.983	0.976	0.988	1.014	0.984	0.996
Ing Vysya Bank	0.898	0.981	0.84	1.219	1.109	1	0.812	1.111	0.982	1.028	1.001	1.004
Karnataka Bank	0.964	0.838	1.086	1.081	0.891	1.074	1.03	0.969	0.985	1.027	0.991	1.001
Lord Krishna Bank	1.037	0.973	0.934	1.146	1	0.931	0.824	1.027	1.000	0.994	0.972	0.988
Nainital Bank	1	1	1	1	1	1	1	1	0.994	1.027	1.000	1.008
Tamilnad Mercantile Bank	1	0.927	1.078	1	1	1	1	1	1.000	1.000	1.000	1.000
Bank of Rajasthan	1.026	1.085	1.13	0.926	1.076	0.855	0.994	1.017	0.993	0.997	1.008	1.000
Catholic Syrian Bank	0.933	1.055	1.099	0.868	1.259	1.042	0.967	0.98	0.960	1.004	1.033	1.000

(*Contd.*)

TABLE 5.4 (*Contd.*)

(1)	(14)	(15)	(16)	(17)	(18)	(19)	(20)	(21)	(22)	(23)	(24)	(25)
Dhanalakshmi Bank	0.95	1.002	1.006	0.948	1.102	1	1	0.966	0.984	1.007	1.002	0.998
Federal Bank	1.154	0.908	1.036	1.052	0.972	1.001	0.969	1.081	0.954	1.027	1.001	0.996
Jammu & Kashmir Bank	1.02	0.915	1.093	1	1	1	0.826	1.073	1.000	1.000	0.983	0.994
Karur Vysya Bank	1	1	1	1	0.923	1.083	0.943	1.061	0.971	1.029	1.000	1.001
Lakshmi Vilas Bank	1	1	1	0.864	1.003	1.083	0.989	1.017	0.988	1.011	0.992	0.997
Ratnakar Bank	1	1	1	1	1	1	1	1	1.022	1.000	1.000	1.007
Sangli Bank	0.947	0.91	1.119	1.012	1.016	0.966	1.03	1.015	0.986	1.031	1.008	1.009
South Indian Bank	1.095	1.014	1.031	0.948	1.107	1.01	1	0.981	0.949	1.031	1.012	0.999
United Western Bank	0.819	1.221	0.705	1.191	0.913	0.86	0.982	0.978	0.937	1.041	0.964	0.982
All CBs												
Mean	1.013	0.98	1.024	0.981	1.044	1.002	0.976	0.984	0.975	1.016	0.998	0.998
S.D	0.11	0.078	0.088	0.083	0.085	0.067	0.076	0.068	0.033	0.021	0.021	0.007
Q1	0.964	0.941	1	0.921	1	0.978	0.965	0.956	0.950	1.000	0.986	0.992
Q3	1.056	1.021	1.078	1.02	1.102	1.032	1.017	1.017	1.000	1.029	1.008	1.003
Median	1	1	1.006	1	1.028	1	0.994	0.988	0.982	1.017	1.000	0.998
PSBs												
Mean	1.019	0.981	1.034	0.968	1.066	1	0.984	0.967	0.970	1.017	1.000	0.997
S.D	0.116	0.073	0.069	0.066	0.076	0.063	0.079	0.076	0.038	0.024	0.024	0.008

Q1	0.967	0.947	1	0.91	1	0.976	0.965	0.93	0.944	1.006	0.984	0.990
Q3	1.058	1.028	1.072	1.018	1.106	1.02	1.031	1	0.994	1.034	1.014	1.003
Median	1	1	1	0.987	1.068	1	0.996	0.967	0.971	1.022	1.000	0.997
NBs												
Mean	1.036	0.972	1.053	0.978	1.084	0.989	1.004	0.958	0.956	1.020	1.005	0.995
S.D	0.134	0.083	0.068	0.063	0.078	0.062	0.06	0.066	0.031	0.027	0.024	0.007
Q1	0.974	0.942	1	0.916	1.043	0.968	0.968	0.93	0.930	1.010	0.988	0.990
Q3	1.085	1.027	1.09	1.027	1.135	1.017	1.044	0.996	0.979	1.040	1.015	1.001
Median	1.037	0.993	1.058	0.997	1.089	0.994	0.996	0.965	0.950	1.027	1.008	0.995
SBI												
Mean	0.98	1.003	0.992	0.944	1.024	1.027	0.938	0.99	1.002	1.010	0.988	1.000
S.D	0.029	0.039	0.051	0.072	0.051	0.061	0.103	0.097	0.036	0.012	0.019	0.009
Q1	0.961	0.992	0.998	0.897	0.996	1	0.868	0.947	0.982	1.000	0.978	0.998
Q3	1	1.026	1	1	1.054	1.024	1.008	1.017	1.008	1.018	1.000	1.004
Median	0.985	1	1	0.963	1.002	1.003	0.963	0.984	0.994	1.014	0.995	1.002
Pvt.												
Mean	1.006	0.979	1.007	1	1.013	1.006	0.964	1.011	0.983	1.014	0.997	0.999
S.D	0.102	0.086	0.112	0.102	0.091	0.076	0.072	0.044	0.021	0.015	0.015	0.007
Q1	0.954	0.918	1	0.943	0.979	1	0.968	0.979	0.974	1.000	0.991	0.996
Q3	1.034	1.002	1.091	1.042	1.063	1.066	1	1.025	0.999	1.028	1.002	1.001
Median	1	0.991	1.019	1	1	1	0.992	1	0.987	1.013	1.000	0.999

*Note** : S.D denotes stanadard deviation, Q1 denotes first-quartile, Q3 denotes third quartile.

TABLE 5.5

Inter-Bank Average Scale Efficiency Change Index for the Different Time Periods

Banks/Years	*1986*	*1987*	*1988-89*	*1989-90*	*1990-91*	*1991-92*	*1992-93*	*1993-94*	*1994-95*	*1995-96*	*1996-97*	*1997-98*
(1)	(2)	(3)	(4)	(5)	(6)	(7)	(8)	(9)	(10)	(11)	(12)	(13)
Allahabad Bank	0.967	0.966	0.977	0.931	0.968	1.018	1.123	0.975	0.894	1.016	0.963	1.135
Andhra Bank	1.015	0.999	0.971	0.999	1.024	0.794	1.078	1.04	1.051	0.977	0.982	1.085
Bank of Baroda	1.076	1.012	0.989	0.972	1.043	0.994	0.977	1.03	0.99	0.97	1.036	0.999
Bank of India	1.048	1.015	0.989	0.979	0.986	1.04	0.955	1.054	0.999	0.994	0.995	1.013
Bank of Maharashtra	0.996	0.96	1.041	0.975	0.977	0.915	1.044	0.936	1.063	1.069	0.963	1.055
Canara Bank	1.063	1.03	1	1	0.86	1.121	0.976	1.03	1.014	0.979	1.036	1.002
Central Bank of India	1.056	0.969	0.978	0.971	1.063	0.847	1.19	0.822	1.088	1.042	0.981	1.061
Corporation Bank	1.055	1.06	0.968	1.009	0.998	1.026	0.992	0.967	1.037	0.967	1.02	1.02
Dena Bank	1.005	0.988	0.983	1.015	0.982	0.907	1.141	1.008	0.952	0.999	0.993	1.037
Indian Bank	1.04	1.001	0.988	0.997	0.969	1.046	0.969	0.977	1.041	0.897	0.967	0.871
Indian Overseas Bank	1.079	1.015	0.986	0.983	0.977	1.054	0.886	1.066	1.041	0.956	0.972	1.056
OBC	1.043	1.01	0.974	1	1.028	0.995	0.953	1.054	0.998	0.959	1.03	1.011
Punjab and Sind Bank	1.053	0.987	0.985	0.983	0.983	0.822	1.032	1.211	1.012	0.89	1.001	1.1
Punjab National Bank	1.067	0.99	0.987	0.991	1.035	0.877	1.112	1.023	0.957	1.01	0.968	1.04
Syndicate Bank	1.042	1.043	0.909	0.95	0.827	1.377	1.007	1.008	0.959	1.024	0.962	1.031
UCO	1.092	0.977	0.957	0.982	0.958	0.977	1.126	0.733	1.225	0.963	0.877	1.109

Union Bank of India	1.014	1.01	0.976	0.993	0.996	0.94	1.085	1.01	0.995	0.983	0.937	1.065
United Bank of India	1.062	0.985	0.979	1.032	0.997	0.791	0.671	1.165	1.012	1.159	0.849	1.545
Vijaya Bank	1.056	1.033	0.993	1.005	0.992	0.943	1.034	1.021	0.992	0.92	1.003	1.047
State Bank of India	1.012	0.994	1.014	0.884	0.988	1.155	0.911	1.022	1.065	1.005	0.858	1.023
State Bank of B&J	0.966	1.102	0.989	1.056	0.956	1.039	1.008	1	0.969	0.985	0.993	1.058
State Bank of Hyderabad	0.958	1.042	1.075	0.996	1.016	0.992	1.019	1	0.999	0.989	0.993	1.019
State Bank of Indore	0.973	1.098	1.023	1.002	0.983	1.015	1.006	1.002	1	1	0.97	1.031
State Bank of Mysore	0.956	1.046	1.007	1.025	0.943	1.056	1.039	1	0.981	0.987	1.009	1.026
State Bank of Patiala	1.005	0.957	0.998	1.023	0.931	1.105	1	0.992	1.007	0.985	1.005	1.011
State Bank of Saurashtra	1.009	0.963	0.946	0.991	1.057	1.148	0.994	1.005	1.004	1	0.992	0.989
State Bank of Travancore	1.014	1.029	0.944	1.052	1	0.958	1.049	0.952	1.05	0.974	0.965	1.052
Bharat Overseas Bank	1	1	1	1	1	1	1	1	1	0.941	1.059	0.968
City Union Bank	1.022	1.001	0.897	1.03	1.012	0.914	1.157	0.973	0.987	0.984	0.966	0.969
Ing Vysya Bank	0.989	1.003	0.987	1.028	0.99	0.952	0.933	1.134	1.01	1	1	0.812
Karnataka Bank	0.999	1.001	0.956	1	0.911	0.924	1.22	1.02	0.971	0.963	1.042	0.99
Lord Krishna Bank	1.024	1	1	0.972	0.994	0.7	1.451	0.989	0.973	1.014	0.923	0.815
Nainital Bank	0.943	1.022	0.956	1.005	0.995	0.837	1.211	1.036	0.796	1.153	0.99	1.077
Tamilnad Mercantile Bank	1	1	1	1	1	1	1	1	1	1	1	1
Bank of Rajasthan	1.004	0.998	0.968	1	1.015	0.904	1.123	1.005	1.002	0.94	0.893	1.081
Catholic Syrian Bank	1.009	0.948	1.054	0.996	0.943	0.873	1.13	1.058	0.844	0.97	0.935	0.988
Dhanalakshmi Bank	1	0.993	0.977	1.031	0.972	0.72	1.32	0.94	0.98	0.854	0.913	1.07

(Contd.)

TABLE 5.5 (*Contd.*)

(1)	(2)	(3)	(4)	(5)	(6)	(7)	(8)	(9)	(10)	(11)	(12)	(13)
Federal Bank	0.991	0.939	1.034	1.033	0.941	0.846	1.138	1.099	1.005	0.998	0.933	0.962
Jammu & Kashmir Bank	0.886	0.969	1.01	0.935	1.078	1.144	1	1	1	0.991	0.986	1.019
Karur Vysya Bank	0.99	0.985	0.956	1.012	1.06	0.923	1.061	1.01	1.002	1.009	0.937	1.067
Lakshmi Vilas Bank	1	0.974	0.883	1.015	1.135	0.877	1.059	1.087	1	0.998	0.84	0.959
Ratnakar Bank	1.042	0.917	0.968	0.913	0.926	0.867	1.214	1.275	0.703	1.079	0.97	1.13
Sangli Bank	1.002	0.991	0.957	1.009	0.955	0.956	1.134	1.018	0.861	1.02	0.786	1.245
South Indian Bank	0.992	0.99	1.009	0.985	0.993	0.89	1.147	1.011	0.889	1.013	0.77	1.117
United Western Bank	1.021	0.991	1.041	0.995	0.997	0.843	1.193	0.996	0.998	1.01	0.972	0.956
All CBs												
Mean	1.013	0.999	0.983	0.994	0.986	0.951	1.056	1.013	0.984	0.990	0.959	1.033
S.D	0.040	0.036	0.037	0.033	0.053	0.125	0.125	0.084	0.079	0.054	0.063	0.108
Q1	0.996	0.985	0.968	0.983	0.968	0.877	1.000	0.996	0.973	0.970	0.937	0.999
Q3	1.043	1.015	1.000	1.012	1.012	1.026	1.134	1.036	1.012	1.010	1.000	1.067
Median	1.009	0.999	0.986	1.000	0.992	0.952	1.044	1.008	1.000	0.991	0.972	1.031
PSBs												
Mean	1.026	1.010	0.986	0.992	0.981	0.991	1.009	1.000	1.013	0.988	0.974	1.051
S.D	0.040	0.038	0.031	0.035	0.052	0.125	0.098	0.087	0.059	0.051	0.048	0.109
Q1	1.005	0.986	0.975	0.981	0.969	0.928	0.977	0.985	0.991	0.969	0.964	1.016

Q3	1.056	1.032	0.996	1.007	1.008	1.050	1.064	1.030	1.041	1.003	1.002	1.060
Median	1.040	1.010	0.986	0.996	0.986	0.995	1.008	1.008	1.004	0.985	0.982	1.037
NBs												
Mean	1.043	1.002	0.980	0.987	0.981	0.965	1.011	1.001	1.015	0.986	0.974	1.061
S.D	0.031	0.027	0.024	0.023	0.057	0.135	0.115	0.104	0.068	0.061	0.048	0.128
Q1	1.028	0.986	0.975	0.977	0.973	0.892	0.973	0.976	0.991	0.961	0.963	1.017
Q3	1.063	1.015	0.989	1.000	1.011	1.033	1.099	1.047	1.041	1.013	1.002	1.075
Median	1.053	1.001	0.983	0.991	0.986	0.977	1.032	1.021	1.012	0.979	0.981	1.047
SBI												
Mean	0.986	1.028	0.999	1.002	0.984	1.056	1.002	0.996	1.009	0.991	0.972	1.026
S.D	0.026	0.055	0.042	0.054	0.041	0.072	0.042	0.020	0.033	0.010	0.049	0.022
Q1	0.964	0.986	0.978	0.995	0.953	1.009	0.999	0.998	0.995	0.985	0.969	1.017
Q3	1.010	1.059	1.016	1.032	1.004	1.116	1.024	1.003	1.018	1.000	0.996	1.036
Median	0.989	1.036	1.003	1.013	0.986	1.048	1.007	1.000	1.002	0.988	0.993	1.025
Pvt.												
Mean	0.995	0.984	0.980	0.997	0.994	0.893	1.132	1.034	0.941	0.995	0.936	1.007
S.D	0.034	0.026	0.045	0.032	0.055	0.100	0.125	0.076	0.089	0.060	0.079	0.105
Q1	0.991	0.977	0.956	0.995	0.959	0.851	1.060	1.000	0.910	0.974	0.916	0.964
Q3	1.008	1.000	1.007	1.014	1.009	0.945	1.207	1.053	1.000	1.012	0.989	1.075
Median	1.000	0.992	0.982	1.000	0.995	0.897	1.136	1.011	0.993	0.999	0.952	0.995

(Contd.)

TABLE 5.5 (*Contd.*)

Banks/Years	*1998-99*	*1999-2000*	*2000-01*	*2001-02*	*2002-03*	*2003-04*	*2004-05*	*2005-06*	*1986-92*	*1993-99*	*2000-06*	*1986-06*
(1)	*(14)*	*(15)*	*(16)*	*(17)*	*(18)*	*(19)*	*(20)*	*(21)*	*(22)*	*(23)*	*(24)*	*(25)*
Allahabad Bank	0.926	1.051	0.939	1.035	1.064	0.961	0.97	0.967	0.971	1.001	0.997	0.990
Andhra Bank	0.937	1.067	0.896	1.067	1.075	0.973	1.05	0.894	0.963	1.020	1.000	0.996
Bank of Baroda	0.976	1.022	0.993	0.99	0.987	1.01	1.012	0.972	1.014	0.997	0.998	1.002
Bank of India	0.997	1.002	1.002	0.998	0.996	0.992	0.96	1.031	1.009	1.001	0.997	1.002
Bank of Maharashtra	0.964	0.979	0.979	1.001	1.002	0.939	0.989	1.100	0.977	1.012	0.997	0.996
Canara Bank	0.898	1.08	1.002	1.026	1.004	0.98	1.016	1.002	1.009	0.990	1.015	1.004
Central Bank of India	0.97	0.973	0.965	0.984	1.136	0.978	0.964	1.077	0.978	1.016	1.009	1.002
Corporation Bank	1	0.974	1.027	0.997	1.003	0.979	1.022	1.000	1.019	1.000	1.000	1.006
Dena Bank	0.938	1.02	0.857	1.112	1.027	1.104	0.793	1.260	0.979	1.008	1.014	1.001
Indian Bank	1.105	1.079	1.05	1.065	0.963	1.025	0.987	1.009	1.006	0.973	1.025	1.001
Indian Overseas Bank	0.977	1.003	1.014	1.035	0.988	1.018	1.002	1.003	1.015	0.992	1.009	1.005
OBC	1.004	0.99	1.01	1	1	1	0.981	1.004	1.008	1.001	0.998	1.002
Punjab and Sind Bank	0.947	1.039	0.989	0.991	1.003	1.018	0.975	1.068	0.966	1.023	1.011	1.002
Punjab National Bank	1.014	0.958	1.01	0.988	1.057	0.988	0.979	1.031	0.989	1.017	1.001	1.003
Syndicate Bank	0.97	0.998	0.984	1.017	1.046	0.974	0.979	0.990	1.011	0.994	0.998	1.001
UCO	0.968	1.1	1.002	1.134	0.948	0.998	0.954	1.008	0.989	0.988	1.019	0.999
Union Bank of India	0.934	1.016	1.013	1.001	1.018	0.964	0.976	1.038	0.988	1.000	1.003	0.997

United Bank of India	0.886	0.999	0.968	1.186	0.978	0.975	0.98	1.051	0.970	1.009	1.017	1.000
Vijaya Bank	0.983	1.011	0.996	0.96	1.077	1.007	0.951	1.011	1.003	0.999	1.001	1.001
State Bank of India	1.006	0.952	0.993	1.131	0.999	0.842	1.075	1.152	1.005	0.982	1.016	1.000
State Bank of B&J	0.981	1.019	1	0.998	0.997	0.989	1.016	0.986	1.017	0.999	1.001	1.005
State Bank of Hyderabad	1.001	1	1	1	0.979	1.016	0.952	1.036	1.012	1.003	0.997	1.004
State Bank of Indore	1	0.984	1.007	1.001	1.007	1	0.944	1.041	1.015	1.001	0.997	1.004
State Bank of Mysore	0.975	1.023	0.986	1.013	1.003	0.944	1.059	1.000	1.005	1.002	1.003	1.003
State Bank of Patiala	1	1	1	1	1	0.94	1.044	0.992	1.002	1.000	0.996	0.999
State Bank of Saurashtra	0.963	1.049	1.008	0.992	1.001	1.002	0.992	1.009	1.017	0.992	1.007	1.005
State Bank of Travancore	0.992	1.022	0.999	0.988	0.996	1.013	0.975	1.029	0.999	1.004	1.003	1.002
Bharat Overseas Bank	0.972	0.984	0.992	1.083	0.912	0.952	1.094	0.959		0.991	0.995	0.995
City Union Bank	1.142	0.998	0.966	1.029	0.95	0.988	0.893	1.115	0.978	1.023	0.989	0.997
Ing Vysya Bank	1.218	1.005	1.001	1.004	1.001	1	0.846	1.148	0.991	1.008	0.997	0.999
Karnataka Bank	0.859	0.992	1.07	1.156	0.95	1.036	0.961	0.882	0.964	1.004	1.003	0.992
Lord Krishna Bank	1.325	0.847	1.176	1.054	1	0.976	0.732	1.104	0.941	1.050	0.973	0.989
Nainital Bank	1.013	0.952	0.877	1.165	1.064	0.937	0.91	1.174	0.958	1.032	1.005	1.000
Tamilnad Mercantile Bank	1	0.981	1.019	1.001	0.987	1.013	1	1	1.000	1.000	1.000	1.000
Bank of Rajasthan	0.965	1.033	0.985	1.085	0.974	0.98	0.768	0.972	0.981	0.999	0.966	0.982
Catholic Syrian Bank	0.9	1.271	1	1.143	1.021	0.933	0.859	0.971	0.969	0.971	1.021	0.987
Dhanalakshmi Bank	0.935	1.206	1.006	1.189	1.045	0.812	0.803	1.105	0.942	0.992	1.012	0.984
Federal Bank	1.116	0.996	1.001	1.005	0.989	1.002	0.959	1.024	0.962	1.033	0.996	0.998

(*Contd.*)

TABLE 5.5 (*Contd.*)

(1)	(14)	(15)	(16)	(17)	(18)	(19)	(20)	(21)	(22)	(23)	(24)	(25)
Jammu & Kashmir Bank	1.005	0.996	0.962	1.044	0.926	0.882	1.161	1.013		1.000	0.994	0.998
Karur Vysya Bank	0.939	1.065	1	1	0.987	1.013	0.952	1.05	0.987	1.002	1.009	1.000
Lakshmi Vilas Bank	1.244	1	1	0.98	0.954	0.899	0.821	0.918	0.977	1.02	0.937	0.977
Ratnakar Bank	0.888	1.08	1.021	1.23	0.873	0.779	1.058	1.012	0.937	1.019	0.998	0.987
Sangli Bank	0.779	1.14	0.877	1.007	0.888	1.094	0.833	0.972	0.978	0.964	0.967	0.969
South Indian Bank	0.984	1.172	0.975	1.04	0.956	1.08	0.741	1.122	0.976	0.983	1.003	0.988
United Western Bank	1.074	1.003	0.845	1.16	1.017	0.963	0.834	1.064	0.979	1.026	0.978	0.995
All CBs												
Mean	0.988	1.023	0.987	1.044	0.995	0.975	0.947	1.028	0.987	1.003	0.999	0.997
S.D	0.097	0.07	0.054	0.069	0.049	0.062	0.095	0.072	0.022	0.017	0.016	0.008
Q1	0.939	0.992	0.979	1	0.978	0.961	0.91	0.992	0.976	0.994	0.997	0.995
Q3	1.004	1.049	1.007	1.083	1.017	1.01	1.002	1.064	1.006	1.012	1.009	1.002
Median	0.977	1.003	1	1.013	1	0.988	0.975	1.012	0.989	1.001	1.000	1.000
PSBs												
Mean	0.974	1.015	0.988	1.025	1.012	0.985	0.984	1.026	0.997	1.001	1.005	1.001
S.D	0.042	0.037	0.039	0.055	0.04	0.044	0.052	0.066	0.018	0.011	0.008	0.003
Q1	0.955	0.994	0.985	0.995	0.996	0.974	0.967	1	0.984	0.995	0.998	1.000
Q3	1	1.031	1.008	1.035	1.023	1.009	1.014	1.04	1.012	1.006	1.010	1.004

Median	0.976	1.011	1	1.001	1.002	0.989	0.98	1.009	1.005	1.001	1.001	1.002
NBs												
Mean	0.967	1.018	0.983	1.029	1.019	0.993	0.974	1.025	0.993	1.002	1.006	1.001
S.D	0.048	0.04	0.045	0.058	0.046	0.035	0.051	0.072	0.019	0.013	0.009	0.004
Q1	0.938	0.994	0.974	0.994	0.992	0.975	0.967	1.001	0.977	0.995	0.998	0.999
Q3	0.99	1.045	1.01	1.05	1.052	1.009	0.996	1.045	1.009	1.011	1.013	1.002
Median	0.97	1.011	0.996	1.001	1.003	0.988	0.979	1.009	0.989	1.001	1.001	1.001
SBI												
Mean	0.99	1.006	0.999	1.014	0.998	0.967	1.006	1.029	1.009	0.998	1.003	1.003
S.D	0.015	0.029	0.007	0.047	0.008	0.059	0.049	0.053	0.007	0.007	0.006	0.002
Q1	0.98	0.996	0.998	0.997	0.997	0.943	0.969	0.998	1.004	0.997	0.997	1.002
Q3	1	1.022	1.002	1.004	1.002	1.005	1.048	1.037	1.015	1.002	1.004	1.004
Median	0.996	1.01	1	1	1	0.995	1.004	1.019	1.009	1.001	1.002	1.004
Pvt.												
Mean	1.011	1.036	0.985	1.074	0.971	0.96	0.894	1.031	0.973	1.006	0.991	0.991
S.D	0.143	0.101	0.073	0.078	0.051	0.082	0.121	0.082	0.020	0.022	0.020	0.009
Q1	0.936	0.993	0.968	1.006	0.95	0.934	0.824	0.972	0.962	0.994	0.981	0.987
Q3	1.106	1.076	1.005	1.153	1.001	1.01	0.961	1.105	0.985	1.022	1.003	0.998
Median	0.992	1.002	1	1.049	0.981	0.978	0.876	1.019	0.977	1.003	0.997	0.993

*Note** : S.D denotes stanadard deviation, Q1 denotes first-quartile, Q3 denotes third quartile.

TABLE 5.6
Classification of Banks on the Basis of TFP Growth and its Indices—1986-92

	1986-1992/Bank's Name
TFP	*Best Performers*: Bank of Baroda, Bank of India, Canara Bank, Indian Bank, Oriental Bank of Commerce, State Bank of India, State Bank of B&J, State Bank of Hyderabad, State Bank of Indore, State Bank of Patiala, Bharat Overseas Bank and Jammu & Kashmir Bank.
	Worst Performers: Andhra Bank, Punjab & Sind Bank, United Commercial Bank, United Bank of India, Lord Krishna Bank, Catholic Syrian Bank, Dhanalakshmi Bank, Federal Bank, Lakshmi Vilas Bank, South Indian Bank and United Western Bank.
	Middle Robust Banks: Allahabad Bank, Corporation Bank, Punjab National Bank, Union Bank of India, State Bank of Mysore, State Bank of Saurashtra, State Bank of Travancore, Ing Vysya Bank, Nainital Bank, Bank of Rajasthan and Sangli Bank.
	Low Robust Banks: Bank of Maharashtra, Central Bank of India, Dena Bank, Indian Overseas Bank, Syndicate Bank, Vijaya Bank, City Union Bank, Karnataka Bank, Tamilnad Mercantile Bank, Karur Vysya Bank and Ratnakar Bank.
TCH	*Best Performers*: Allahabad Bank, Andhra Bank, Bank of Baroda, Bank of India, Bank of Maharashtra, Canara Bank, Central Bank of India, Corporation Bank, Dena Bank, Indian Bank, Indian Overseas Bank, Oriental Bank of Commerce, Punjab & Sind Bank, Punjab National Bank, Syndicate Bank, United Commercial Bank, Union Bank of India, United Bank of India, Vijaya Bank, State Bank of India, State Bank of B&J, State Bank of Hyderabad, State Bank of Indore, State Bank of Mysore, State Bank of Patiala, State Bank of Saurashtra, State Bank of Travancore, Bharat Overseas Bank, City Union Bank, Ing Vysya Bank, Karnataka Bank, Lord Krishna Bank, Nainital Bank, Tamilnad Mercantile Bank, Bank of Rajasthan, Catholic Syrian Bank, Dhanalakshmi Bank, Federal Bank, Jammu & Kashmir Bank, Karur Vysya Bank, Lakshmi Vilas Bank, Ratnakar Bank, Sangli Bank, South Indian Bank and United Western Bank. *Worst Performer* : No bank *Middle Robust Banks* : No Bank *Low Robust Banks* : No Bank

EFFCH	*Best Performers*: Bank of Baroda, Bank of India, Indian Bank, State Bank of India, State Bank of B&J, State Bank of Hyderabad, State Bank of Indore, State Bank of Patiala, State Bank of Saurashtra, Bharat Overseas Bank, Tamilnad Mercantile Bank and Jammu & Kashmir Bank.
	Worst Performers: Andhra Bank, Bank of Maharashtra, Central Bank of India, Dena Bank, Punjab & Sind Bank, United Commercial Bank, United Bank of India, Dhanalakshmi Bank, Federal Bank, South Indian Bank and United Western Bank.
	Middle Robust Banks: Allahabad Bank, Canara Bank, Indian Overseas Bank, Oriental Bank of Commerce, Union Bank of India, State Bank of Mysore, State Bank of Travancore, City Union Bank, Ing Vysya Bank, Bank of Rajasthan and Lakshmi Vilas Bank.
	Low Robust Banks: Corporation Bank, Punjab National Bank, Syndicate Bank, Vijaya Bank, Karnataka Bank, Lord Krishna Bank, Nainital Bank, Catholic Syrian Bank, Karur Vysya Bank, Ratnakar Bank and Sangli Bank.

TABLE 5.7
Classification of Banks on the Basis of TFP Growth and its Indices—1993-99

	1993/99 Bank's Name
TFP	*Best Performers*: Andhra Bank, Bank of Baroda, Bank of Maharashtra, Central Bank of India, Corporation Bank, Punjab & Sind Bank, United Commercial Bank, United Bank of India, Ing Vysya Bank, Lord Krishna Bank, Federal Bank and United Western Bank.
	Worst Performers: Canara Bank, Indian Bank, State Bank of India, State Bank of B&J, State Bank of Patiala, Bank of Rajasthan, Catholic Syrian Bank, Dhanalakshmi Bank, Jammu & Kashmir Bank, Ratnakar Bank and Sangli Bank.
	Middle Robust Banks: Allahabad Bank, Bank of India, Dena Bank, Indian Overseas Bank, Oriental Bank of Commerce, Punjab National Bank, Syndicate Bank, Vijaya Bank, Tamilnad Mercantile Bank, Karur Vysya Bank and Lakshmi Vilas Bank.
	Low Robust Banks: Union Bank of India, State Bank of Hyderabad, State Bank of Indore, State Bank of Mysore, State Bank of Saurashtra, State Bank of Travancore, Bharat Overseas Bank, City Union Bank, Karnataka Bank, Nainital Bank and South Indian Bank.
TCH	*Best Performers*: Bank of India, Indian Bank, Indian Overseas Bank and Ing Vysya Bank.
	Worst Performers: Andhra Bank, Bank of Maharashtra, Canara Bank, Central Bank of India, Dena Bank, Oriental Bank of Commerce, Punjab & Sind Bank, Punjab National Bank, Syndicate Bank, Union Bank of India, Vijaya Bank, State Bank of India, State Bank of B&J, State Bank of Hyderabad, State Bank of Indore, State Bank of Mysore, State Bank of Patiala, State Bank of Saurashtra, State Bank of Travancore, City Union Bank, Karnataka Bank, Nainital Bank, Bank of Rajasthan, Catholic Syrian Bank, Dhanalakshmi Bank, Federal Bank, Jammu & Kashmir Bank, Karur Vysya Bank, Lakshmi Vilas Bank, Ratnakar Bank, Sangli Bank, South Indian Bank and United Western Bank.
	Middle Robust Banks: Allahabad Bank, Bank of Baroda, Bharat Overseas Bank, Lord Krishna Bank and Tamilnad Mercantile Bank.
	Low Robust Banks: Corporation Bank, United Commercial Bank and United Bank of India

EFFCH	*Best Performers*: Andhra Bank, Bank of Maharashtra, Central Bank of India, Corporation Bank, Dena Bank, Punjab & Sind Bank, Punjab National Bank, City Union Bank, Lord Krishna Bank, Nainital Bank, Federal Bank and United Western Bank. *Worst Performers*: Bank of India, Indian Bank, Indian Overseas Bank, State Bank of India, State Bank of B&J, State Bank of Patiala, Bharat Overseas Bank, Bank of Rajasthan, Catholic Syrian Bank, Dhanalakshmi Bank and Sangli Bank. *Middle Robust Banks*: Oriental Bank of Commerce, United Commercial Bank, Union Bank of India, United Bank of India, Vijaya Bank, State Bank of Mysore, State Bank of Travancore, Ing Vysya Bank, Karnataka Bank, Karur Vysya Bank and Lakshmi Vilas Bank. *Low Robust Banks*: Allahabad Bank, Bank of Baroda, Canara Bank, Syndicate Bank, State Bank of Hyderabad, State Bank of Indore, State Bank of Saurashtra, Tamilnad Mercantile Bank, Jammu & Kashmir Bank, Ratnakar Bank and South Indian Bank.

TABLE 5.8
Classification of Banks on the Basis of TFP Growth and its Indices—2000-06

	2000/06 Bank's Name
TFP	*Best Performers*: Corporation Bank, Indian Bank, Indian Overseas Bank, Oriental Bank of Commerce, Union Bank of India, United Bank of India, Bharat Overseas Bank, Ing Vysya Bank, Tamilnad Mercantile Bank, Federal Bank, Jammu & Kashmir and Karur Vysya Bank.
	Worst Performers: Punjab National Bank, State Bank of B&J, State Bank of Mysore, State Bank of Patiala, State Bank of Saurashtra, Lord Krishna Bank, Bank of Rajasthan, Lakshmi Vilas Bank, Sangli Bank and United Western Bank.
	Middle Robust Banks: Andhra Bank, Dena Bank, Punjab & Sind Bank, United Commercial Bank, Vijaya Bank, City Union Bank, Karnataka Bank, Catholic Syrian Bank, Dhanalakshmi Bank, Ratnakar Bank and South Indian Bank.
	Low Robust Banks: Allahabad Bank, Bank of Baroda, Bank of India, Bank of Maharashtra, Canara Bank, Central Bank of India, Syndicate Bank, State Bank of India, State Bank of Hyderabad, State Bank of Indore, State Bank of Travancore and Nainital Bank.
TCH	*Best Performers*: Corporation Bank, Oriental Bank of Commerce, Bharat Overseas Bank, City Union Bank, Ing Vysya Bank, Karnataka Bank, Tamilnad Mercantile Bank, Federal Bank, Jammu & Kashmir Bank and United Western Bank.
	Worst Performers: Allahabad Bank, Andhra Bank, Bank of India, Bank of Maharashtra, Canara Bank, Central Bank of India, Dena Bank, Punjab & Sind Bank, Punjab National Bank, Syndicate Bank, United Commercial Bank, United Bank of India, Vijaya Bank, State Bank of India, State Bank of B&J, State Bank of Hyderabad, State Bank of Indore, State Bank of Mysore, State Bank of Patiala, State Bank of Saurashtra, State Bank of Travancore, Nainital Bank, Bank of Rajasthan, Catholic Syrian Bank, Dhanalakshmi Bank, Lakshmi Vilas Bank, Ratnakar Bank and Sangli Bank.
	Middle Robust Banks: Bank of Baroda, Union Bank of India, Lord Krishna Bank and Karur Vysya Bank.
	Low Robust Banks: Indian Bank, Indian Overseas Bank, South Indian Bank.

EFFCH	*Best Performers*: Andhra Bank, Dena Bank, Indian Bank, Indian Overseas Bank, Punjab & Sind Bank, Union Bank of India, United Bank of India, Vijaya Bank, State Bank of India, Catholic Syrian Bank, Dhanalakshmi Bank and South Indian Bank
	Worst Performers: Bank of Baroda, Bank of Maharashtra, Canara Bank, State Bank of Patiala, State Bank of Saurashtra, City Union Bank, Lord Krishna Bank, Bank of Rajasthan, Lakshmi Vilas Bank, Sangli Bank and United Western Bank.
	Middle Robust Banks: Allahabad Bank, Central Bank of India, Corporation Bank, Syndicate Bank, United Commercial Bank, State Bank of B&J, State Bank of Mysore, State Bank of Travancore, Nainital Bank, Tamilnad Mercantile Bank and Karur Vysya Bank.
	Low Robust Banks: Bank of India, Oriental Bank of Commerce, Punjab National Bank, State Bank of Hyderabad, State Bank of Indore, Bharat Overseas Bank, Ing Vysya Bank, Karnataka Bank, Federal Bank, Jammu & Kashmir Bank and Ratnakar Bank.

Table 5.9

Classification of Banks on the Basis of TFP Growth and its Indices—1986-06

	1985/06 Bank's Name
TFP	*Best Performers*: Bank of Baroda, Bank of India, Corporation Bank, Indian Bank, Indian Overseas Bank, Oriental Bank of Commerce, Union Bank of India, Bharat Overseas Bank, Ing Vyasa Bank, Tamilnad Mercantile Bank, Federal Bank and Jammu & Kashmir Bank.
	Worst Performers: Syndicate Bank, State Bank of Saurashtra, Lord Krishna Bank, Bank of Rajasthan, Catholic Syrian Bank, Dhanalakshmi Bank, Lakshmi Vilas Bank, Ratnakar Bank, Sangli Bank, South Indian Bank and United Western Bank.
	Middle Robust Banks: Allahabad Bank, Andhra Bank, Canara Bank, Punjab National Bank, Punjab & Sind Bank, United Bank of India, Vijaya Bank, State Bank of India, State Bank of Hyderabad, State Bank of Indore, State Bank of Patiala, Karnataka Bank and Karur Vysya Bank.
	Low Robust Banks: Bank of Maharashtra, Central Bank of India, Dena Bank, United Commercial Bank, State Bank of B&J, State Bank of Mysore, State Bank of Travancore, City Union Bank and Nainital Bank.
TCH	*Best Performers*: Bank of Baroda, Bank of India, Canara Bank, Corporation Bank, Indian Bank, Indian Overseas Bank, Oriental Bank of Commerce, Union Bank of India, Bharat Overseas Bank, Ing Vysya Bank, Tamilnad Mercantile Bank, Federal Bank and Jammu & Kashmir Bank.
	Worst Performers: Dena Bank, State Bank of B&J, State Bank of Mysore, State Bank of Patiala, State Bank of Saurashtra, State Bank of Travancore, Nainital Bank, Bank of Rajasthan, Catholic Syrian Bank, Dhanalakshmi Bank, Lakshmi Vilas Bank, Ratnakar Bank and Sangli Bank.
	Middle Robust Banks: Allahabad Bank, Andhra Bank, Bank of Maharashtra, Central Bank of India, Punjab & Sind Bank, Punjab National Bank, United Commercial Bank, United Bank of India, Vijaya Bank, State Bank of Indore, City Union Bank, Karnataka Bank, Karur Vysya Bank and United Western Bank.
	Low Robust Banks: Syndicate Bank, State Bank of India, State Bank of Hyderabad, Lord Krishna Bank and South Indian Bank.

EFFCH	*Best Performers*: Corporation Bank, Dena Bank, Indian Overseas Bank, Oriental Bank of Commerce, Union Bank of India, State Bank of B&J, State Bank of Hyderabad, State Bank of Mysore, State Bank of Patiala, State Bank of Travancore, Ing Vysya Bank, Nainital Bank and Karur Vysya Bank. *Worst Performers*: Bank of Maharashtra, United Commercial Bank, State Bank of Saurashtra, Lord Krishna Bank, Bank of Rajasthan, Dhanalakshmi Bank, Lakshmi Vilas Bank, Sangli Bank, South Indian Bank and United Western Bank. *Middle Robust Banks*: Allahabad Bank, Andhra Bank, Indian Bank, Punjab National Bank, United Bank of India, Vijaya Bank, State Bank of India, State Bank of Indore, Tamilnad Mercantile Bank and Federal Bank. *Low Robust Banks*: Bank of Baroda, Bank of India, Canara Bank, Central Bank of India, Punjab & Sind Bank, Syndicate Bank, Bharat Overseas Bank, City Union Bank, Karnataka Bank, Catholic Syrian Bank, Jammu & Kashmir and Ratnakar Bank.

Bibliography

Abrol, P.N. (1987), *Commercial Banking*, Anmol Publications, Delhi (India).

Ahluwalia, I.J. (1991), *Productivity Growth in Indian Manufacturing*, Oxford University Press, New Delhi.

Ahluwalia, I.J. and Q.F.R Shankar (edited) (1985), *Low Productivity and High Cost—The Managerial Challenge*, Tata Mcgraw-Hill, New Delhi, pp. 56-61.

Altanbus, Y., J. Goddard and P. Molyneux (1999), "Technical Change in Banking", *Economic Letters*, Vol. 64, pp. 215-29.

Altanbus, Y., S. Carbo and P. Molyneux (2003), *Ownership and Performance in European and U.S Banking—A Comparison of Commercial, Co-Operative and Savings Banks, DOCUMENTO DE TRABAJO*, No. 180/2003 and ISBN: 84-89116-07-5.

Altunbas, Y., E.P.M Gardner, P. Molyneux and B. Moore (2001), "Efficiency in European Banking", *European Economic Review*, Vol. 25, pp 1931-55.

Altunbas, Y. and S.P. Chakravarty (1998), "Efficiency measures and the banking structure in Europe", *Economic Letters*, Vol. 60, pp. 205-08.

Andersen, P. and N.C. Petersen (1993), "A Procedure for Ranking Efficient Units in Data Envelopment Analysis", *Management Science*, Vol. 39, No. 10, pp. 1261-64.

Ashton, J. and P. Hardwick (2000), "Estimating Inefficiencies in Banking: A Survey", *The Journal of Interdisciplinary Economics*, Vol. 11, pp. 1-33.

Aslan, H. (2002), *Deregulation, Crisis and Efficiency: The Case of Turkish Banks,* Paper presented at annual 2002 METU Conference and 2002 American Economic Association annual meetings.

Ataullah, A. and H. Le (2006), "Economic reforms and bank efficiency in developing countries: the case of the Indian banking industry", *Applied Financial Economics,* Vol. 16, No. 9, pp. 653-63.

Avkiran, N.K. (1999), *Productivity Analysis in the Services Sector with Data Envelopment Analysis,* University of Queensland, Camira, Australia.

Avkiran, N.K. (2006), *Productivity Analysis in the Services Sector with Data Envelopment Analysis (Third Edition),* University of Queensland Business School, The University of Queensland, Australia.

Baltagi, B.H. (2001), *Econometric Analysis of Panel Data,* John Wiley and Sons Ltd., West Sussex, England.

Banker, R.D. and R. Morey (1986a), "Efficiency Analysis for Exogenously Fixed Inputs and Outputs", *Journal of Operations Research,* Vol. 34, No. 4, pp. 513-21.

Banker, R.D. and R. Morey (1986b), "The Use of Categorical Variables in Data Envelopment Analysis", *Journal of Management Science,* Vol. 32, No. 12, pp. 1613-27.

Banker, R.D. and R.M. Thrall (1992), "Estimation of Returns to Scale Using Data Envelopment Analysis", *European Journal of Operational Research,* Vol. 62, No. 1, pp. 35-44.

Banker, R.D., A. Charnes and W.W. Cooper (1984), "Some Models for Estimating Technical and Scale Inefficiencies in Data Envelopment Analysis", *Management Science,* Vol. 30, No. 9, pp. 1078-92.

Barr, R.S., L.M. Seiford and T.F. Siems (1994), "Forecasting Bank Failure: A Non-parametric Frontier Estimation Approach", *Recherches Economiques de Louvain,* Vol. 60, pp. 417-29.

Bayda, V.V. (2003), *Evaluation of North Dakota Farm Production Efficiency and Financial Performance over Time,* Thesis submitted to North Dakota State University of Agricultural and Applied Science, Fargo, North Dakota.

Benston, G.J. (1965), "Branch Banking and Economies of Scale", *The Journal of Finance,* Vol. 20, pp. 312-31.

Benston, G.J., G.A. Hanweck and D.B. Humphrey (1982), "Scale Economies in Banking: A Restructuring and Reassessment", *Journal of Money and Banking,* Vol. 14, No. 4, pp. 435-56.

Berg, S.A., F.R. Forsund and E.S. Jansen (1991), "Technical efficiency of Norwegian banks: A non-parametric approach to efficiency measurement", *Journal of Productivity Analysis,* Vol. 2, pp. 127-42.

Berg, S.A., F.R. Forsund and E.S. Jansen (1992), "Malmquist Indices of Productivity Growth during the Deregulation of Norwegian Banking, 1980-89", *Scandinavian Journal of Economics,* Vol. 94, pp. 211-28.

Berger, A.N. and D.B. Humphrey (1991), "The Dominance of inefficiencies over scale and product mix economies in banking", *Journal of Monetary Economics,* Vol. 28, pp 117-48.

Berger, A.N. and D.B. Humphrey (1992), "Measurement and Efficiency Issues in Commercial Banking", In: Z. Grilliches (Edited), *Measurement Issues in the Service Sectors,* National Bureau of Economic Research, University of Chicago Press, Chicago IL, pp. 245-79.

Berger, A.N. and D.B. Humphrey (1997), "Efficiency of Financial Institutions: International Survey and Directions for Future Research", *European Journal of Operational Research,* Vol. 98, No. 2, pp. 175-212.

Berger, A.N., G.A. Hanweck and D.B. Humphrey (1987), "Competitive Viability in Banking: Scale, Scope and Product Mix Economies", *Journal of Monetary Economics,* Vol. 20, pp. 501-23.

Berger, A.N., W.C. Hunter and S.G. Timme (1993), "The Efficiency of Financial Institutions: A Review and Preview of Research, Past, Present and Future", *Journal of Banking and Finance,* Vol. 17, pp. 221-49.

Bhasin, N. (2007), *Banking and Financial Markets in India 1947 to 2007,* New Century Publications, New Delhi, India.

Bhattacharyya, A., A. Bhattacharyya and S.C. Kumbhakar (1997), "Changes in Economic Regime and Productivity Growth: A Study of Indian Public Sector Banks", *Journal of Comparative Economics,* Vol. 25, pp. 196-219.

Bhattacharyya, A., C.A.K. Lovell and P. Sahay (1997), "The impact of liberalization on the productive efficiency of Indian commercial banks", *European Journal of Operational Research*, Vol. 98, pp. 332-45.

Bhaumik, S.K. and R. Dimova (2004), "How Important is Ownership in a Market with Level Playing Field? The Indian Banking Sector Revisited, *Journal of Comparative Economics*, Vol. 32, pp. 165-80.

Bhide, M.G., A. Prasad and S. Ghosh (2001), *Emerging Challenges in Indian Banking*, Working Paper No. 103, Stanford University, Standford.

Bjurek, H. (1996), "The Malmquist Total Factor Productivity Index", *Scandinavian Journal of Economics*, Vol. 98, No. 2, pp. 303-13.

Bos, J.W.B. and C.J.M. Kool (2004), *Bank Efficiency: The Role of Bank Strategy and Local Market Conditions*, DNB Working Paper 002, Central Bank Research Department, Netherlands.

Boulding, K.E. (1961), "Some difficulties in the concept of economic input", *National Bureau of Economic Research*, Vol. 25, pp. 331-34.

Boussofiane, A., R.G. Dyson and E. Thanassoulis (1991), "Applied Data Envelopment Analysis", *European Journal of Operational Research*, Vol. 52, pp. 1-15.

Carbo, S., E.P.M. Gardenar and J. Williams (2003), "A note on technical change in banking: the case of European savings Banks", *Applied Economics*, Vol. 35, pp. 705-09.

Casu, B. and C. Girardone (2004), "Large Banks' Efficiency in the Single European Market", *The Service Industries Journal*, Vol. 24, No. 6, pp. 129-42.

Caves, D.W., L.R. Christensen and W.E. Diewert (1982), "The economic theory of index numbers and the measurement of input, output and productivity, *Econometrica*, Vol. 50, No. 6, pp. 1393-1414.

Chaffai, M.E. (1997), "Estimating input-specific technical inefficiency: the case of the Tunisian banking industry", *European Journal of Operational Research*, Vol. 98, pp. 314-31.

Charnes, A. and W.W. Cooper (1990), "Data Envelopment Analysis", In H.E Bradley (edited) *Operational Research*, Pergamon Press, Oxford.

Charnes, A., W.W. Cooper and E. Rhodes (1981), "Evaluating Program and Managerial Efficiency: An Application of Data Envelopment Analysis to Program Follow Through", *Journal of Management Science,* Vol. 27, No. 6, pp. 668-97.

Charnes, A.; W.W. Cooper and E. Rhodes (1978), "Measuring the efficiency of decision-making units", *European Journal of Operational Research,* Vol. 2, pp. 429-44.

Chatterjee, G. (1997), "Scale Economies in Banking—Indian Experience in Deregulated Era", *Reserve Bank of India Occasional Papers,* Vol. 18, No. 1, pp. 37-59.

Chaudhary, S. and A. Tripathy (2003-04), "Measuring Bank Performance: An Application of Data Envelopment Analysis", *Prajnan,* Vol. XXXII, No. 4, pp. 287-331.

Chen, T-Y. (2001), "An Estimation of X-inefficiency in Taiwan's Banks", *Applied Financial Economics,* Vol. 11, pp. 237-42.

Coelli, T. and S. Perelman (1996b), *A Comparison of Parametric and Non-parametric Distance Functions: With Application to European Railways,* CREPP Discussion Paper No. 96/11, University of Liege, Liege.

Coelli, T., D.S.P. Rao and G. Battese (1998), *An Introduction to Efficiency and Productivity Analysis,* Kluwer Academic Publishers, Boston.

Coelli, T.J. (1995), "Recent Developments in Frontier Modeling and Efficiency Measurement", *Australian Journal of Agricultural Economics,* Vol. 39, No. 3, pp. 219-45.

Coelli, T.J. (1996), *A Guide to DEAP Version 2.1: A Data Envelopment Analysis (Computer) Program,* Center for Efficiency and Productivity Analysis (CEPA) Working Paper 96/08.

Collins, S. (2002), International financial integration and growth in developing countries: Issues and implications for Africa, in: *African Economic Research Consortium: Plenary Session,* Vol. 13, Supplement 2, Oxford University Press, London.

Colwell, R.J. and E.P. Davis (1994), "Output and Productivity in Banking", *Scandinavian Journal of Economics,* Vol. 94, pp. 111-29.

Cooper, W.W., L.M. Seiford and J. Zhu (2004) (edited), "Data Envelopment Analysis: History, Models and Interpretations", In *Handbook on Data Envelopment*

Analysis, Chapter 1, pp. 1-39, Kluwer Academic Publishers, Boston (with W.W. Cooper and Joe Zhu).

Cooper, W.W., L.M. Seiford and K. Tone (2000), *Data Envelopment Analysis—Comprehensive Text with Models, Applications, References and DEA-Solver Software*, Kluwer Academic Publisher, Boston.

Cornwell, C., P. Schmidt and R.C. Sickles (1990), "Production Frontier with Cross-Sectional and Time-Series Variations in Efficiency Levels", *Journal of Econometrics*, Vol. 46, No. (1/2), pp. 18-200.

Das, A. (1997), "Technical, Allocative and Scale Efficiency of Public Sector Banks in India", *Reserve Bank of India Occasional Papers*, Vol. 18, No. 2 & 3, pp. 279-301.

Das, A. (1999-00), "Efficiency of Public Sector Banks: An Application of Data Envelopment Analysis", *Prajnan*, Vol. XXVIII, No. 2, pp. 119-31.

Das, A. (2002), "Risk and Productivity Change of Public Sector Banks", *Economic and Political Weekly*, pp. 437-48 (February 2, 2002).

Das, A. and S. Ghosh (2003), "Size, Non-Performing Loan, Capital and Productivity Change: Evidence from State Owned Banks", *Journal of Quantitative Economics*, old series, Vol. 19, No. 2, pp. 47-66.

Das, A. and S. Ghosh (2006), "Financial deregulation and efficiency: An empirical analysis of Indian banks during the post-reform period", *Review of Financial Economics*, Vol. 15, pp. 193-221.

Das, A., A. Nag and S.C. Ray (2005), "Liberalization, Ownership and Efficiency in Indian Banking: A Non-parametric Analysis", *Economic and Political Weekly*, pp. 1190-97.

De Young, R. (1997), "A diagnostic test for the distribution-free efficiency estimator: an example using U.S. commercial bank data", *European Journal of Operational Research*, Vol. 98, pp. 243-49.

De, Prithwis Kumar (2004), "Technical Efficiency, Ownership, and Reforms: An Econometric Study of Indian Banking Industry", *Indian Economic Review*, Vol. XXXIX, No. 1, pp. 261-94.

Denison, E.F. (1967), *Why Growth Rates Differ: Post-war Experience in Nine Western Countries*, The Brookings institution, Washington D.C.

Dogan, E. and D.K. Fausten (2002), *Productivity and Technical change in Malaysian Banking*, Discussion papers ISSN 1441-5429, No. 05/02.

Doshit, Y., R. Dhokai and N. Lodhia (2003), *Productive Efficiency of Indian Banks: An Analysis*, Paper presented at International Conference on 'Business and Finance' held during December 15-16, 2003 at ICFAI, Hyderabad.

Drake, L. (2001), "Efficiency and productivity change in UK banking", *Applied Financial Economics*, Vol. 11, pp. 557-71.

Drake, L., M.J.B. Hall and R. Simper (2006), "The Impact of Macroeconomic and Regulatory Factors on Bank Efficiency: A Non-parametric Analysis of Hong Kong's Banking System", *Journal of Banking and Finance*, Vol. 30, No. 5, pp. 1443-66.

Economic Intelligence Services (2006), *National Income Statistics: 2006*, Center for Monitoring Indian Economy, Mumbai.

Economic Intelligence Services (2007), *National Income Statistics: 2007*, Center for Monitoring Indian Economy, Mumbai.

Elyasiani, E. and S. Mehdian (1990), "Efficiency in the Commercial Banking Industry, A Production Frontier Approach" *Applied Economics*, Vol. 22, pp. 539-51.

English, M., S. Grosskopf, K. Hayes and S. Yaisawarng (1993), "Output Allocative and Technical Efficiency of Banks", *Journal of Banking and Finance*, Vol. 17, No. 2-3, pp. 349-66.

Estrada, D. and P. Osorio (2004), *Effects of Financial Capital on Columbian Banking Efficiency*, Paper presented at APPC 2004, hosted by Center for Efficiency and Productivity Analysis, University of Queensland, Brisbane, Australia.

Fare, R., S. Grosskopf and C.A.K. Lovell (1983), "The Structure of Technical Efficiency", *Scandinavian Journal of Economics*, Vol. 85, pp. 181-90.

Fare, R., S. Grosskopf and C.A.K. Lovell (1985), *The Measurement of Efficiency of Production*, Kluwer Academic Publishers, Boston.

Fare, R., S. Grosskopf and C.A.K. Lovell (1994a), *Production Frontiers*, Cambridge, MA: Cambridge University Press.

Fare, R., S. Grosskopf., B. Lindgren, and P. Roos (1989), "Productivity Developments in Swedish Hospitals: A Malmquist Output Index Approach" In: Charnes, A., W.W. Cooper., A.Y. Lewin and L.M. Seiford (Edited), *Data Envelopment Analysis: Theory, Methodology and Applications*: 23-272, Kluwer Academic Publishers, Boston.

Fare, R., S. Grosskopf., M. Norris and Z. Zhang (1994), "Productivity Growth, Technical Progress and Efficiency Change in Industrialized Countries: The Structure of Technical Efficiency", *The American Economic Review*, Vol. 84, No. 1, pp. 66-83.

Farrell, M.J. (1957), 'The Measurement of Productive Efficiency", *Journal of the Royal Statistical Society*, Vol. 120, Series A (General), Part III.

Fat, C.S. and L.G. Hua (1998), "Share Performance and Profit efficiency of Banks in an Oligopolistic Market: Evidence from Singapore", IDEAS: *Journal of Multinational Financial Management*, Vol. 8, issue 2-3 month, pp. 155-68.

Favero, C.A. and L. Papi (1995), "Technical efficiency and scale efficiency in the Italian banking sector: a non-parametric approach", *Applied Economics*, Vol. 27, pp. 385-95.

Ferrier, G.D. and C.A.K Lovell (1990), "Measuring Cost Efficiency in Banking: Econometric and Linear Programming Evidence, *Journal of Econometrics*, Vol. 46, pp. 229-45.

Fisher (1922), *The making of index numbers* (Houghton-Mifflin, Boston, MA).

Fixler, D. and K. Zieschang (1991), "Measuring the Nominal Value of Financial Services in the National Income Accounts", *Journal of Economic Inquiry*, Vol. 29, pp. 53-68

Fixler, D. and K. Zieschang (1999), "The productivity of the banking sector: integrating financial and production approaches to measuring financial service output", *Canadian Journal of Economics*, Vol. 32, No. 2, pp. 546-69.

Forsund, F.R. and L. Hjalmarsson (1979), "Frontier Production Functions and Technical Progress: A Study of General Milk Production in Swedish Dairy Plants", *Economic Journal*, Vol. 89, pp. 294-315.

Fries, S. and A. Taci (2005), "Cost efficiency of banks in transition: Evidence from 289 banks in 15 post-communist countries", *Journal of Banking and Finance,* Vol. 29, pp. 55-81.

Fukuyama, H. (1993), "Technical and scale efficiency of Japanese commercial banks: a non-parametric approach", *Applied Economics,* Vol. 25, pp. 1101-12.

Fukuyama, H. (1995), "Measuring efficiency and productivity growth in Japanese banking: a non-parametric frontier approach", *Applied Financial Economics,* Vol. 5, pp. 95-107.

Fung, M.K. (2006), "Scale Economies, X-Efficiency, and Convergence of Productivity among Bank Holding Companies", *Journal of Banking and Finance,* Vol. 30, pp. 2857-74.

Galagedera, Don U.A. and P. Edirisuriya (2005), "Performance of Indian commercial banks (1995-2002): an application of data envelopment analysis and Malmquist productivity index", *South Journal of Management,* Vol. 12, pp. 52-74.

Gilligan, T; M. Smirlock and W. Marshall (1989), "Scale and Scope Economies in the Multi-Product Banking Firm", *Journal of Monetary Economics,* Vol. 13, pp. 303-405.

Glass, J.C. and D.G. Mckillop (1991), "Efficiency in Irish Banking: Theory and Evidence", *Applied Financial Economics,* Vol. 1, pp. 235-40.

Government of India (2007), *Brochure on Group and Sub-Group CPI Number*: Central Statistical Organization, Ministry of Statistics and Programme Implementation, New Delhi.

Greene, W.H. (2003), *Econometric Analysis,* Fifth Edition, Pearson Education.

Grifell-Tatje, E. and C.A.K. Lovell (1995), "A note on the Malmquist productivity index", *Economic Letters,* Vol. 47, pp. 169-75.

Grifell-Tatje, E. and C.A.K. Lovell (1996), "Deregulation and Productivity Decline: The Case of Spanish Savings Banks", *European Economic Review,* Vol. 40, pp. 1281-1303.

Grifell-Tatje, E. and C.A.K. Lovell (1997), "The sources of productivity change in Spanish banking", *European Journal of Operational Research,* Vol. 98, pp. 364-80.

Grigorian, D.A. and V. Manole (2002), *Determinants of Commercial Bank Performance in Transition—An Application of Data Envelopment Analysis*, Working Paper 2850, World Bank Policy Research, June 2002.

Gropper, D.M. (1991), "An Empirical Investigation of Changes in Scale Economies for the Commercial Banking Firm: 1979-86", *Journal of Money and Banking*, Vol. 23, No. 4, pp. 718-27.

Grosskopf, S. (1993), "Production frontiers and productive efficiency" in: Harold O. Fried; C.A. Knox Lovell and S.S. Schmidt (edited), *The Measurement of Productive Efficiency: Techniques and Applications*: 3-67, Oxford University Press, New York.

Gujrati, D.N. (2003), *Basic Econometrics*, International Edition (Fourth Edition), Mcgraw Hill, Boston.

Hanson, J.A. and S. Kathuria (1999), *India: A Financial Sector for the Twenty-first Century*, Oxford University Press, New Delhi, India.

Hasan, I. and K. Marton (2003), "Development and Efficiency of the Banking Sector in a Transitional Economy: Hungarian Experience", *Journal of Banking and Finance*, Vol. 27, pp. 2249-71.

Hauner, D. (2004), "Explaining Efficiency Differences among Large German and Austrian Banks", *IMF Working Paper*, WP/2004/140.

Howcraft, B. and A. Ataullah (2006), "Total Factor Productivity Change: An Examination of the Commercial Banking Industry in India and Pakistan", *The Services Industries Journal*, Vol. 26, No. 2, pp. 189-202.

Hunter, W.C. and S.G. Timme (1991), "Technological Change in Large U.S Commercial Banks", *Journal of Business*, Vol. 64, No. 3, pp. 339-62.

Indian Banks Association (2004), *IBA Bulletin* (special issue): IBA, January 2004, Mumbai.

Indian Banks Association, *Annual Accounts of Banks* (various issues): IBA, Mumbai.

Indian Banks Association, *Financial Analysis of Banks* (various issues), Volume I and II: IBA, Mumbai.

Indian Banks Association, *IBA Bulletins* (various issues): IBA, Mumbai.

Indian Banks Association, *Performance Highlights of Banks* (various issues): IBA, Mumbai.

Indian Banks Association, *Profile of Bank* (various issues): IBA, Mumbai.

Isik, I. and M. Kabir Hassan (2003), "Efficiency, Ownership and Market Structure, Corporate Control and Governance in the Turkish Banking Industry", *Journal of Business, Finance and Accounting*, Vol. 30, No. 9-10, pp. 1363-1421, November/December 2003.

Isik, I. and M.K. Hassan (2002), "Technical, scale and allocative efficiencies of Turkish banking industry", *Journal of Banking & Finance*, Vol. 26, pp. 719-66.

Isik, I. and M.K. Hassan (2003), "Financial Disruption and Bank Productivity: The 1994 Experience of Turkish Banks", *The Quarterly Review of Economics and Finance*, Vol. 43, pp. 291-320.

Isik, I., U. Meleke and E. Isik (2002), *Liberalization, Ownership and Productivity in Turkish Banking*, Paper submitted to the 9th Annual Conference of the Economic Research Forum, October 2002, Assessed from the site: http://www.erf.org.eg/ems/.

Jackson, P.M. and M.D. Fethi (2000), *Evaluating the Technical Efficiency of Turkish Commercial Banks: An Application of DEA and Tobit Analysis*, Paper presented at International DEA Symposium, University of Queensland, Brisbane, Australia, 2-4 July, 2000.

Jalan, B. (2002), *Indian Banking and Finance—Managing New Challenges*, Banking Economists Conference, Kolkata, 14 January 2002.

Joshi, V. and I.M.D. Little (1996), *India's Economic Reforms: 1991-2001*, Oxford, Clarendon Press.

Kalirajan, K.P. and R.T. Shand (1997), "A Generalised Measure of Technical Efficiency", *Applied Economics*, Vol. 24, pp. 225-34.

Ketkar, K., A. Noulas and M. Aggarwal (2003), "An Analysis of Efficiency and Productivity Growth of the Indian Banking Sector", *Finance India*, Vol. XVII, No. 2, pp. 511-21.

Ketkar, K.W. and S.L. Ketkar (2008), *Performance and Profitability of Indian Banks in the Post Liberalization Period*, Paper presented at the 2008 World Congress on National Accounts and Economic Performance Measures for Nations, May 13-17, 2008, Washington DC.

Khamliche, R. (1998), *Ranking Methodologies versus Data Envelopment Analysis: A Comment on the Andersen and Petersen's Procedure for Ranking Efficient Units in DEA*, IS-MG 98/13, I.S.R.O, December 98, Brussels Free University.

Khamliche, R. and B. Mareschal (1999), *The performance assessment of European airlines "Data Envelopment Analysis" versus "Multicriteria Decision Aid"*, Technical Report TR/SMG/1999-010, SMG, Université Libre de Bruxelles, 1999.

Khan, M.Y. (1980), *Indian Financial System: Theory and Practice*, Vikas Publishing House Pvt. Ltd., Delhi (India).

Koski, H.J. and S.K. Majumdar (2000), "Convergence in telecommunications infrastructure development in OECD countries", *Information Economics and Policy*, Vol. 12, pp. 111-31.

Kovea, P. (2003), "The Performance of Indian Banks during Financial Liberalization", *IMF Working Paper*, WP/03/150.

Kumar, P. (2006), *Banking Sector Efficiency in Globalised Economy*, Deep & Deep Publications Pvt. Ltd, New Delhi, India.

Kumar, S. (2001), *Productivity and Factor Substitution, Theory and Analysis*, Deep and Deep Publications Pvt. Ltd, New Delhi, India.

Kumar, S. (2008), "An Analysis of Efficiency Profitability Relationship in Indian Public Sector Banks", *Global Business Review*, Vol. 9, No. 1, pp. 115-29.

Kumar, S. and N. Arora (2008), "An Evaluation of Technical Efficiency of Indian Capital Goods Industries: A Non-Parametric Frontier Approach, *Productivity*, Vol. 48, No. 2, pp. 182-97.

Kumar, S. and N. Arora (2008), "Technical and Scale Efficiency in Indian Manufacturing Sector: A Cross-sectional Analysis Using Deterministic Frontier Approach", *Asian Economic Review*, Vol. 49, No. 3, pp. 433-58.

Kumar, S. and R. Gulati (2009), "Did efficiency of Indian public sector banks converge with banking reforms", *International Review Economics*, Vol. 56, pp. 47-84.

Kumar, S. and S. Verma (2002-03), "Technical Efficiency, Benchmarks and Targets: A Case Study of Indian Public Sector Banks", *Prajnan*, Vol. XXXI, No. 4, pp. 275-99.

Kumbhakar, S., A. L-Vivas., C.A. Knox Lovell and I. Hasan (2001), "The Effects of Deregulation on the performance of Financial Institutions: The Case of Spanish Saving Banks", *Journal of Money, Credit and Banking,* Vol. 33, No. 1, pp. 101-20.

Kumbhakar, S.C. (1990), "Production Frontiers, Panel Data and Time-Varying Technical Inefficiency", *Journal of Econometrics,* Vol. 46, No. (1/2), pp. 201-11.

Kumbhakar, S.C. and S. Sarkar (2003), "Deregulation, Ownership, and Productivity Growth in the Banking Industry: Evidence from India", *Journal of Money, Credit and Banking,* Vol. 35, (June 2003), No. 3, pp. 403-24.

Kwan, Simon H. (2006), "The X-efficiency of commercial banks in Hong Kong", *Journal of Banking & Finance,* Vol. 30, pp. 1127-47.

Lee, K., H.M. Pearson and R. Smith (1996), *Growth and Convergence; A Multi-Country Empirical Analysis of Solow Growth Model,* ESRC Development Economics Study Group Annual Conference, University of Leicester.

Leibenstein, H. and S. Maital (1992), "Empirical Estimation and Partitioning of X-Inefficiency: A Data-Envelopment Approach", *AEA Papers and Proceedings,* Vol. 82, No. 2, pp. 428-38.

Li, Y., J-L Hu and Y-H Chiu (2003), "Ownership and Production Efficiency: Evidence from Taiwanese Banks", *The Services Industries Journal,* Vol. 24, No. 4.

Lovell, C.A.K. (1993), "Productive Frontiers and Productive Efficiency", In Fried, H.O., C.A.K. Lovell and S.S. Schmidt (Edited), *The Measurement of Productive Efficiency: Techniques and Applications,* Oxford University Press, New York.

Lozono-Vivas, A. (1998), "Efficiency and Technical change for Spanish Banks", *Applied Financial Economics,* Vol. 8, pp. 289-300.

Maghyereh, A. (2004), *The Effect of Financial Liberalization on the Efficiency of Financial Institutions: The Case of Jordanian Commercial Banks,* Hashemite University.

Malmquist, S. (1953), "Index Numbers and Indifference Surfaces", *Trabajos de Estatistica,* Vol. 4, pp. 209-42.

Mansor, S.A. and A. Radam (2000), "Productivity and Efficiency Performance of The Malaysian Life Insurance Industry", *Jurnal Ekonomi Malaysia,* Vol. 34, pp. 93-105.

Margano, H. and S.C. Sharma (2004), *Cost efficiency, Economies of Scale, Technological progress and Productivity in Indonesian Banks,* Discussion paper 2004-18, Faculty and Graduate Student Research, Central Bureau of Statistics, Jakarta.

Matousek, R. (2004), *Efficiency and Scale Economies in Banking: Empirical Evidence from Eight Accession Countries,* Paper presented at XIV Conference, A.I.S.S.E.C, Discussion Paper No. 04-6, Center for International Capital Markets, London Metropolitan University, London.

Mendes, V. and J. Rebelo (1999), "Productive efficiency, technological change and productivity in Portuguese banking", *Applied Financial Economics,* Vol. 9, pp. 513-21.

Mester, L.J. (1987), "A Multiproduct Cost Study of Savings and Loans", *Journal of Finance,* Vol. 42, pp. 423-45.

Mester, L.J. (1987), "Efficient Production of Financial Services; Scale and Scope Economics", *Business Review of Federal Reserve Bank of Philadelphia,* January/February, 1987, pp. 15-25.

Milma, A.P. and L. Hjalmarsson (2002), "Measurement of Inputs and Outputs in the Banking Industry", *Tranzanet Journal,* Vol. 3, No. 1, pp. 12-22.

Misra, A.K. and A.K. Das (2005), "Bank Scale Economies, Size and Efficiency: The Indian Experience", *IBA Bulletin,* Issue-January, pp. 145-49.

Mohan, R. (2004), "Financial Sector Reforms in India: Policies and Performance Analysis", *RBI Bulletin,* (Oct. 2004), pp. 851-77.

Mokhtarul Wadud; I.K.M. and S. Paul (2006), "Productivity Growth, Efficiency Change and Technical Progress: A Case Study of Australian Private Sector Industries", *The Indian Economic Journal,* Vol. 54, No. 2, pp. 145-65.

Mukherjee, A.; P. Nath and M.N. Pal (2002), "Performance benchmarking and strategic homogeneity of Indian banks", *International Journal of Bank Marketing,* Vol. 20, No. 3, pp. 122-39.

Narasimham, M. (1991), *"Report of the Committee on the Financial System"*, Nabhi Publication, New Delhi.

Narasimham, M. (1998), *The Banking Sector Reforms,* Nabhi Publication, New Delhi.

Neal, P. (2004), "X-Efficiency and Productivity Change in Australian Banking", *Australian Economic Papers*, Vol. 43, pp. 174-91.

Noulas, A.G. (1997), "Productivity Growth in the Hellenic banking industry: state *versus* private banks", *Applied Financial Economics*, Vol. 7, pp. 223-28.

Noulas, A.G. and K.W. Ketkar (1996), "Technical and Scale Efficiency in the Indian Banking Sector", *International Journal of Development Banking*, Vol. 14, No. 1, pp. 19-27.

Pai, D.T. (2001), "Indian Banking—Changing Scenario", *IBA Bulletin*, pp. 20-23.

Pastor, J.M. (2002), "Credit risk and efficiency in the European banking system: a three-stage analysis", *Applied Financial Economics*, Vol. 12, pp. 895-911.

Pathak, B.V. (2003), *Indian Financial System*, Pearson Education (Singapore) Pvt. Ltd.

Pedraja-Chaparro, F., J. Salinas-Jimenez and P. Smith (1997), "On the Role of Weight Restrictions in Data Envelopment Analysis", *Journal of Productivity Analysis*", Vol. 8, pp. 215-30.

Ram Mohan, K. (2002), "Financial Sector Reform: Narasimham Committee—Finished and Unfinished Agenda", In Rao. P.M. (edited), *Financial System and Economic Reforms*: 133-146. Deep & Deep Publications Pvt. Ltd, New Delhi.

Ram Mohan, T.T. (2002), "Deregulation and Performance of Public Sector Banks", *Economic and Political Weekly*, Vol. 37, No. 5, pp. 393-97.

Ram Mohan, T.T. and S. Ray (2004), *Productivity Growth and Efficiency in Indian Banking: A Comparison of Public, Private and Foreign Banks*, Working Paper 2004-27, Department of Economics Working Paper Series, University of Connecticut, Connecticut.

Ramachandran, B. (2003), *Economic Reforms Need Radical Changes*, Kalpaz Publications, New Delhi.

Ramanathan, R. (2003), *An Introduction to Data Envelopment Analysis: A Tool for Performance Measurement*, Sage Publications, New Delhi.

Rao, D.S.P and T.J. Coelli (2004), "Catch-up and Convergence in Global Agricultural Productivity", *Indian Economic Review*, Vol. XXXIX, No. 1, pp. 123-48.

Ray, I. and S. Sanyal (1994-95), "Scale Efficiency in Indian Commercial Banking: An Econometric Investigation", *Prajnan*, Vol. XXIII, No. 4 pp. 459-86.

Ray, I. and S. Sanyal (2002), "X-Efficiency Revisited: Its Concepts and Measurement in Commercial Banking Institutions", *Artha Vijnana*, Vol. XLIV, No. 2, pp. 155-68.

Reddy, Y.V. (1999), "Financial Sector Reform: Review and Prospects", *RBI Bulletin*, January 1999, pp. 33-93.

Reserve Bank of India (2008), "Efficiency, Productivity and Soundness of the Banking Sector", *Report on Currency and Finance*, pp. 393-446.

Reserve Bank of India, *RBI Bulletins* (various issues): RBI, Mumbai.

Reserve Bank of India, *Report on Currency and Finance* (various issues): RBI, Mumbai.

Reserve Bank of India, *Report on Trend and Progress in Banking* (various issues): RBI, Mumbai.

Reserve Bank of India, *Statistical Tables Relating to Banks in India* (various issues): RBI, Mumbai.

Rezvanian, R., N. Rao and S.M. Mehdian (2008), "Efficiency change, technological progress and productivity growth of private, public and foreign banks in India: evidence from the post-liberalization era", *Applied Financial Economics*, Vol. 18, pp. 1-13.

Rezvanian, R., R.T. Ariss and S.M. Mehdian (2007), *Cost Efficiency, Technological Progress and Productivity Growth of Public, Private, and Foreign Banks in People's Republic of China: Evidence from Pre and Post-WTO Accession*, Paper presented at Midwest finance association, Marriott, Feb. 27-March 1, 2008.

Rogers, K.E. (1998), "Nontraditional activities and the efficiency of US commercial banks", *Journal of Banking and Finance*, Vol. 22, pp. 467-82.

Saha, A. and T.S. Ravisankar (2000), "Rating of Indian Commercial Banks: A DEA Approach", *European Journal of Operational Research*, Vol. 124, pp. 187-203.

Sahoo, B.K. (1999), "A comparative application of data envelopment analysis and frontier translog production function for estimating returns to scale and efficiencies", *International Journal of Systems Science*, Vol. 30, No. 4, pp. 379-94.

Sala-i-Martin, X. (1994), "Economic Growth, Cross-Sectional Regressions and the Empirics of Economic Growth", *European Economic Review*, Vol. 38, pp. 739-47.

Sala-i-Martin, X. (1996), "Regional cohesion: evidence and theories of regional growth and convergence", *European Economic Review*, Vol. 40, pp. 1325-52.

Samal, B. (2001), "Indian banking System: Phases of Transition", *IBA Bulletin*, pp. 15-19.

Sanjeev G.M. (2006), "Data Envelopment Analysis (DEA) For Measuring Technical Efficiency of Banks", *VISION—The Journal of Business Perspective*, Vol. 10, No. 1, pp. 13-27.

Sathye, M. (2001), "X-efficiency in Australian banking: An empirical investigation", *Journal of Banking and Finance*, Vol. 25, pp. 613-30.

Sathye, M. (2003), "Efficiency of Banks in a Developing Economy: The Case of India", *European Journal of Operational Research*, Vol. 148, No. 3, pp. 662-71.

Scheel, H. (2000), *EMS: Efficiency Measurement System, User's Manual, Version 1.3*, Working Paper 2000-08-15, Assessed from the link: http://www.wiso.uni-dortmund.de/lsfg/or/scheel/ems/

Schmidt, P. and R.C. Sickles (1984), "Production Frontiers and Panel Data", *Journal of Business and Economic Statistics*, Vol. 2, pp. 299-326.

Schumpeter, J.A. (1934), *The Theory of Economic Development*, Oxford University Press, London.

Sealey, C.W. and J.T. Lindley (1977), "Inputs, outputs and a theory of production and cost at depository financial institutions", *Journal of Finance*, Vol. 32, pp. 1251-66.

Seelanatha, S.L. (2007), *Efficiency, Productivity Change and Market Structure of the banking industry in Sri Lanka*, Thesis Submitted to the Faculty of Business, University of Southern Queensland, Australia, 2007.

Sen, K. and R.R. Vaidya (1997), *The Process of Financial Liberalization in India*, Oxford University Press, New Delhi.

Sengupta, J. and B. Sahoo (2006), *Efficiency Models in Data Envelopment Analysis: Techniques of Evaluation of Productivity of Firms in a growing Economy*, Palgrave Macmillan Publications.

Sengupta, J.T. (1990a), "A Dynamic Efficiency Model Using Data Envelopment Analysis", *International Journal of Production Economics*, Vol. 62, No. 3, pp. 209-18.

Sensarma, R. (2005), "Cost and Profit Efficiency of Indian Banks during 1986-2003—A Stochastic Frontier Analysis," *Economic and Political Weekly*, pp. 1198-1209.

Shah, Vipan (1987), *Cost and Efficiency in Banking*, Printwell Publishers, Jaipur (India).

Shanmugam, K.R. and A. Das (2004), "Efficiency of Indian commercial banks during the reform period", *Applied Financial Economics*, Vol. 14, No. 9, pp. 681-86.

Sherman, H.D. and F. Gold (1985), "Bank Branch Operating Efficiency: Evaluation with Data Envelopment Analysis", *Journal of Banking and Finance*, Vol. 9, No. 2, pp. 297-305.

Shirai, S. (2001), "Assessment of India's Banking Sector Reforms from the Perspective of the Governance of the Banking System", Paper presented at the ESCAP-ADB Joint Workshop on *Mobilizing Domestic Finance for Development: Reassessment of Bank Finance and Debt Markets in Asia and the Pacific*, Bangkok, 22-23 November, 2001. Bangkong

Shirai, S. (2002), "Is India's Banking Sector Reform Successful", *KEIO SFC Journal*, Vol. 1, No. 1, pp. 150-63.

Shirai, Sayuri (2002), *Road from State to Market—Assessing the Gradual Approach to Banking Sector Reforms in India*, ADB Institute Research Paper Series No. 32, Asian Development Institute, Tokyo.

Singh, R.K. (2004), "Economic Reforms in India", In : Sharma, P.N., T.K. Shandilya and A. Kumari (edited), *Banking Sector Reforms in India: A Critical Appraisal*: 105-31, Abhijeet Publications, Delhi, Vol. One.

Singh, S., S.P. Yadav and S.P. Singh (2006), "A Data Envelopment Analysis Based Efficiency Assessment of Public Transport Sector of Uttar Pradesh State in India", *Indian Journal of Transport Management*, Jan-March, 2006.

Singh, I. and P. Kumar (2005), "Efficiency Analysis: The Case of Indian Banking Industry", *The Indian Economic Journal*, Vol. 52, No 3-4, pp. 133-38.

Singh, R.K. (2004), *Economic Reforms in India*, Abhijeet Publications, New Delhi, Volume One.

Singh, S. (2007), *Banking Sector Reforms in India*, Kanishka Publishers, Distributors, New Delhi.

Singh, S.K. (2002), "A Note on Economies of Scale in Selected STUs", *Indian Journal of Transport Management*, Vol. 26, No. 2, pp. 207-24.

Singh, S.P. and S. Aggarwal (2006), "Total Factor Productivity Growth, Technical Progress and Efficiency Change in Sugar Industry of Uttar Pradesh" *The Indian Economic Journal*, Vol. 54, No. 2, pp. 59-82.

Sinha, R.P. and B. Chatterjee (2005-06), "Intermediation Cost Efficiency of Indian Commercial Banks: A Data Envelopment. Analysis", *Prajnan*, Vol. XXXIV, No. 4, pp. 345-58.

Stulz, R. (2001), "Does financial structure matter for economic growth? A corporate finance perspective" In : Demigürç-Kurt, A. and R. Levine, (Edited), *Financial Structure and Economic Growth: A Cross-Country Comparison of Banks, Markets and Development*, Massachusetts: MIT Press.

Sturm, J-E. and B. Williams (2002), *Deregulation, Entry of Foreign Banks and Bank Efficiency in Australia*, CES_{IFO} Working Paper No. 816, Category 9: Industrial Organization, December 2002.

Subrahmanya, K.N. (1982) (edited), *Modern Banking in India*, Deep and Deep Publications, New Delhi.

Subrahmanyam, G. (1993), "Productivity Growth in Indian Public Sector Banks: 1970-89", *Journal of Quantitative Economics*, Vol. 9, No. 2, pp. 209-23.

Sufian, F. and Abdul Majid, M-Z (2007), "Deregulation, Consolidation and Banks Efficiency in Singapore: Evidence from Event Study Window Approach and Tobit Analysis", *International Review Economics*, Vol. 54, pp. 261-83.

Swamy, M.R. and S.V. Vasudevan (1980), *A Text Book of Banking (Law, Practice and Theory of Banking)*, S. Chand and Co. Ltd., Delhi (India).

Thorn, R.S. (1976), *Introduction to Money and Banking*, Harper International edition, Harper and Row Publishers, New York.

Todaro, M.P. and S.C. Smith (2006), *Economic Development*, Eighth edition, Pearson Education.

Tone, K. (2001), "A Slack Based Measure of Efficiency in Data Envelopment Analysis", *European Journal of Operation Research*, Vol. 130, pp. 498-509.

Tone, K. and B.K. Sahoo (2005), "Evaluating cost efficiency and returns to scale in the Life Insurance Corporation of India using data envelopment analysis", *Socio-Economic Planning Sciences*, Vol. 39, pp. 261-85.

Tornquist, L. (1936), "The Bank of Finland's Consumption Price Index", *Bank of Finland Monthly Bulletin*, Vol. 10, pp. 1-8.

Tortosa-Ausina, E. (2002a), "Exploring Efficiency Differences Over Time in the Spanish Banking Industry", *European Journal of Operation Research*, Vol. 139, No. 3, pp. 643-64.

Triplett, J.E. (1992), "Comments (Comments on the Papers of Berger and Humphrey (1992) and Fixler and Zischang (1992), cited in the reference) In: Griliches, Z. (Edited), *Output Measurement in the Service Sector*: 287-96, University of Chicago Press, Chicago.

Uppal, R.K. and R. Kaur (edited) (2007), *Banking in the New Millennium: Issues, Challenges and Strategies*, Mahamaya Publishing House, New Delhi (India).

Vasudevan, A. (2003), *Money and Banking*, Selected Research Papers of Reserve Bank of India, Academic Foundation, New Delhi.

Verma, M.S. (1999), *Report of the Working Group on Restructuring of Weak Public Sector Banks*, Reserve Bank of India, Mumbai.

Wheelock, D.C. and P.W. Wilson (2001), "New Evidence on returns to scale and product mix among U.S. Commercial Banks", *Journal of Monetary Economics*, Vol. 47, pp. 653-74.

Wu, S. (2005), Productivity and Efficiency Analysis of Australia Banking Sector under Deregulation, School of Accounting, Economics and Finance, Deakin University. Assessed from the link https://editorialexpress.com.

Yeh, Q-J. (1996), "The application of data envelopment analysis in conjunction with financial ratios for bank performance evaluation", *Journal of the Operational Research Society*, Vol. 47, pp. 980-88.

Yildrim, C. (2002), "Evolution of banking efficiency within an unstable macroeconomic environment: the case of Turkish commercial banks", *Applied Economics*, Vol. 34, pp. 2289-2301.

Yue, P. (1992), "Data Envelopment Analysis and Commercial Bank Performance: A primer with Applications to Missouri Banks", *Federal Reserve Bank of A. St. Louis*, January/February, pp. 31-45.

Zaim, O. (1995), "The effects of financial liberalization on the efficiency of Turkish Commercial Banks", *Applied Financial Economics*, Vol. 5, pp. 257-64.

Zhao, T., B. Casu and F. Alrssandra (2008), "Deregulation and productivity growth: a study of Indian commercial banking", *International Journal of Business Performance Management*, Vol. 10, No. 4, pp. 318-43.

Index